Hey, where's the color?

You're right, this is all in black and white.

It may seem a bit odd to have a book on web design in black and white, but the truth of the matter is that we didn't need to do this whole book in color— that just means we'd have to charge you more, and who wants that? But obviously this becomes a problem when we do have to talk about color, and Chapter 5 of this book is all about color. So we're providing that chapter in color for FREE online. Scan the QR code to the left to download it now, or head on over to **www.headfirstlabs.com/books/hfwd** to download it from there.

"Building websites has definitely become more than just writing code. *Head First Web Design* shows you what you need to know to give your users an appealing and satisfying experience. Another great Head First book!"

— Sarah Collings, User Experience Software Engineer

"Simplified, but far from dumbed-down. Practical and intuitive. I wish I had access to a book like this when I was getting started."

— Matt DiGangi, real life Web Designer

"*Head First Web Design* really demystifies the web design process and makes it possible for any web programmer to give it a try. For a web developer who has not taken web design classes, *Head First Web Design* confirmed and clarified a lot of theory and best practices that seem to be just assumed in this industry."

— Ashley Doughty, Senior Web Developer

"Finally a developer can fully understand the whole process of creating a GREAT website. Web Design 101, you finally got the book you needed/wanted."

—Johannes de Jong, Web Programmer

"The Head First series learning technique works well. You feel as though you are working through an actual design process instead of just reading a how-to manual. It's a much more holistic approach to learning. The books work with your mind, rather than against it."

—Jonathan Moore, owner of Forerunner Design

Other related books from O'Reilly

Learning Web Design

Web 2.0: A Strategy Guide

Ajax: The Definitive Guide

Website Optimization

Other books in O'Reilly's *Head First* series

Head First Java™

Head First Object-Oriented Analysis and Design (OOA&D)

Head First HTML with CSS and XHTML

Head First Design Patterns

Head First Servlets and JSP

Head First EJB

Head First PMP

Head First SQL

Head First Software Development

Head First JavaScript

Head First Ajax

Head First Physics

Head First Statistics

Head First Rails

Head First PHP & MySQL

Head First Algebra

Head First Web Design

Wouldn't it be dreamy if there was a web design book that went beyond code and really helped me make my websites work and look better? It's probably just a fantasy...

Ethan Watrall

Jeff Siarto

O'REILLY®

Beijing · Cambridge · Köln · Sebastopol · Tokyo

Head First Web Design

by Ethan Watrall and Jeff Siarto

Printed in the United States of America.

Published by O'Reilly Media, Inc., 1005 Gravenstein Highway North, Sebastopol, CA 95472.

O'Reilly Media books may be purchased for educational, business, or sales promotional use. Online editions are also available for most titles (*safari.oreilly.com*). For more information, contact our corporate/institutional sales department: (800) 998-9938 or *corporate@oreilly.com*.

Series Creators:	Kathy Sierra, Bert Bates
Series Editor:	Brett D. McLaughlin
Editors:	Brett D. McLaughlin, Louise Barr
Design Editor:	Louise Barr
Cover Designers:	Louise Barr, Steve Fehler
Production Editor:	Brittany Smith
Indexer:	Julie Hawks
Page Viewers:	Taylor and Sam

Jeff's Parents

Printing History:

December 2008: First Edition.

Ethan's daughter Taylor

Ethan's son Sam

ISBN: 978-0-596-52030-4

Love and thanks to my family—Jenn, Taylor, Sam (and Oscar and Persia).

— Ethan

To my Mom—for helping me realize my dreams and inspiring me to follow them. This book would not have been possible without you.

— Jeff

Authors of Head First Web Design

Jeff Siarto

Ethan Watrall is an Assistant Professor at Matrix: The Center for Humane Arts, Letters & Social Sciences Online, an Assistant Professor in the Department of Telecommunication, Information Studies, and Media, and an Adjunct Assistant Professor in the Department of History at Michigan State University. In addition, Ethan is a Principal Investigator in the Games for Entertainment & Learning Lab, and co- founder of both the undergraduate Specialization and Game Design Development and the MA in Serious Game Design at Michigan State University. Ethan teaches in a wide variety of areas including cultural heritage informatics, user centered & user experience design, game design, serious game design, game studies, and ancient Egyptian social history & archaeology. In addition to a wide variety of academic papers and conference presentations, Ethan has written a number of books on interactive design & web design.

When he's not being professorial, he's a world class comic book nerd (Killowog is so his favorite Green Lantern), a sci-fi dork (he'll argue to the grave that Tom Baker is the best Doctor ever), and an avid player of all sorts of games (digital, board, and tabletop). Ethan's digital alterego can be found at **www.captainprimate.com** or **www.twitter.com/captain_primate**.

Jeff Siarto is a user experience and web designer fresh out of grad school at Michigan State University. Jeff was a student of the standards-based web design movement—aspiring to the likes of Cederholm, Zeldman and Meyer—and worked as a web developer throughout his college years before signing on to co-author Head First Web Design in his second year of grad school. In addition to building websites, he also works to improve online courses and open education through simple, usable design. Jeff currently calls Chicago home and works as a freelance web developer and part time Iron Chef challenger. When he's not working, he likes to cook and eat (mostly eat) and make endless design changes to his blog at **www.siarto.com**.

You can see what Jeff is doing right now by checking out his Twitter feed at **www.twitter.com/jsiarto** or, if you're really bored, you can send him an email at **jeff@siarto.com**.

Table of Contents (Summary)

	Intro	xxi
1	Beauty is in the Eye of Your User: *Building Beautiful Web Pages*	1
2	Paper Covers Rock: *Pre-Production*	37
3	"So you take a left at the green water tower...": *Organizing Your Site*	69
4	Follow the Golden Rule: *Layout and Design*	109
5	Moving Beyond Monochrome: *Designing With Color*	159
6	"In 2 seconds, click 'Home'.": *Smart Navigation*	193
7	Yes, You Scan!: *Writing For the Web*	227
8	Inaccessibility Kills: *Accessibility*	275
9	The Pathway to Harmonious Design: *Listen to Your Users*	319
10	Keeping Your Site Fresh: *Evolutionary Design*	369
11	Mind Your Own Business: *The Business of Web Design*	403
i	Leftovers: The *Top Ten Things (We Didn't Cover)*	439

Table of Contents (the real thing)

Intro

Your brain on Web Design. Here *you* are trying to *learn* something, while here your *brain* is doing you a favor by making sure the learning doesn't *stick*. Your brain's thinking, "Better leave room for more important things, like which wild animals to avoid and whether naked snowboarding is a bad idea." So how *do* you trick your brain into thinking that your life depends on knowing web design?

Who is this book for?	xxii
We know what you're thinking	xxiii
Metacognition	xxv
Bend your brain into submission	xxvii
Read me	xxviii
The technical review team	xxx
Acknowledgments	xxxi

building beautiful web pages

Beauty is in the eye of your user

1

It's a great big (wide) world... but who's really out there?

So you've got your nice shiny XHTML and CSS diploma hanging on the wall, and the prospective clients are ringing your new business line off the hook. Cool, right? Yeah... until you get your first complaint about a bad layout, or a logo that's just so 1998. So how do you create **really beautiful websites** and still make sure they satisfy your users? It all begins with good planning. Then you've got to **write for the Web, know your audience**, and, above all else, make sure you're **designing for your users**, not yourself.

Your big chance with Red Lantern Design	2
Where do you start?	5
Draw up a blueprint first	7
Determine your top level navigation	13
Put it all in context	15
Show Jane some basic design sketches	16
Sketches keep the focus on functionality	17
Don't ruin a good design with bad copy	28
What makes text scannable?	29
Web design is all about communication, and your users	35

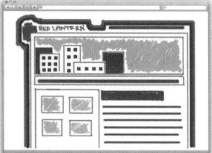

pre-production
Paper covers rock

2

Tired of butting heads with a picky client? Yeah, you know the type...
every time you show them their latest crazy design idea, they've already moved on to
another look... another color scheme... another entire website. So how do you deal
with **fickle clients** or those tricky **hard-to-get-right websites**? You start with paper,
pencil, and a big fat pink eraser. In this chapter, you'll learn how to work smart before
you dig into your HTML editor. Coming up with a **theme** and **visual metaphor** for your
site, mocking up sketches in **pencil**, and using **storyboards** will turn you into a nimble,
flexible web designer. So get out your sketch pad, and let's pre-produce!

Your first "international" gig...	38
Think before you code	40
A clear visual metaphor helps reinforce your site's theme	41
A theme represents your site's content	42
Brainstorming: The path to a visual metaphor	45
Develop a theme and visual metaphor for Mark	46
Your page elements shape your visual metaphor	49
Build a quick XHTML mock-up for Mark	56
And the CSS...	57
Use storyboards to develop ideas and save time without code	61
Don't design for yourself!	62
Let's create a storyboard for Mark	64

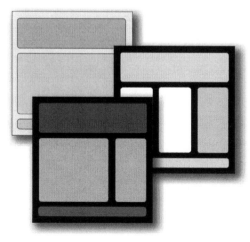

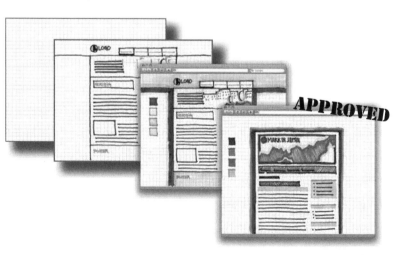

APPROVED

3

organizing your site

"So you take a left at the green water tower..."

A little shaky on your site navigation?

When it comes to the Web, **users are impatient**. They don't want to waste lots of time looking for the right button or wading through three levels of your JavaScript pull-down menus. That's why you've got to spend a lot of time getting your site's organization right... before you get into construction and design. Last chapter, you came up with a great theme and look for your site. In this chapter, you'll really amp things up with a **clear organization**. By the time you're done, you'll have a site that **tells your users where to go** and keeps them from ever getting lost again.

Fit your content into your layout	71
Organize your site's information	72
Keep your site organized with information architecture (IA)	79
IA–The card sorting way	80
Card Sorts Exposed	81
Sort your cards into related stacks	86
Give your stacks names that are short and descriptive	87
Which card sort is right?	92
Arrange your cards into a site hierarchy	93
IA diagrams are just card sorts on paper	95
IA diagrams are NOT just links between pages	96
Move from pre-production to production	100
Build Mark's site structure	101
Create index.html first...	102
...and then screen.css for style	103
Pre-production to production: the complete process	106

layout and design
Follow the Golden Rule

4

It pays to be a good listener... and to carry a pocket calculator.

We've been talking about **user-centered design** for a few chapters, but here's where you really put your listening skills to the test. In this chapter, you'll take your users' feedback and build a site that meets their needs. From **browsers** to **screen real estate**, it's all about giving your users what they really want. Not only that, you'll learn the secrets of the **rule of thirds**. Find out how a few easy presses of the *calculator*, a *ruler*, and some *gridlines* can turn your blase web page into a thing of **beauty**.

Name: **Ann**
Age: **28**
Internet Connectivity: **DSL**
Avg. time online/week for leisure: **15 hours**
Browser of choice: **Firefox**
Operating System: **Windows XP**
Screen Resolution: **800x600**
Occupation: **Student**
Details: **Ann considers herself very tech savvy. She actively participates in social networks and online communities. She also regularly shops online. Her laptop (which is a little old, but all she can really afford right now) is her primary computer—and where she does all of her web browsing.**

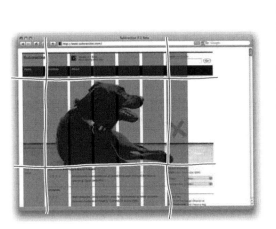

Design is about audience	110
Your newest gig: RPM Records	113
Pinpoint RPM's audience with personas	114
Let the personas be your guide...	120
Resolution impacts design and layout	122
Screen real estate determines how much of your site will display in your user's browser	124
Build an XHTML and CSS foundation optimized for 1024x768	128
Humans like things lined up and well-organized	132
How wide should my grid be? Use the Golden Ratio	133
The rule of thirds: A shortcut to the Golden Ratio	134
RPM and the Golden Ratio: An (anti) case study	135
Remember your personas and client?	139
Set up RPM 2.0 with the Blueprint Framework	141
Use Blueprint CSS rules to style RPM 2.0	144
Time to get your RPM groove on	145
Add some CSS to clean up the layout	149
Finish off the content and navigation markup	151
Add layout and typographic details with some more CSS	154

designing with color

Moving Beyond Monochrome

Color is the unsung hero of web design. A good color palette can draw your audience into your site, give them a powerful feeling of immersion, and keep them coming back for more. And when it comes to color and web design, it's not just about picking a **good color palette**, it's also about how you **apply** those colors. You can have a great color palette, but if you don't use those colors **thoughtfully**, people might avoid your site like the plague. By the end of this chapter, you'll not only be intimately familiar with the impact that color has on the web user, but you'll also be able to choose a great looking color palette that fits in—and even complements—your user-centered websites.

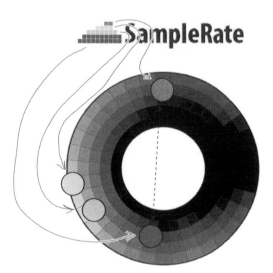

Help support your local music scene	160
9Rules: The blog network gold standard	161
Sometimes your choices are a bit... limited	162
Color has an emotional impact	163
The color wheel (where it all begins)	167
Use the color wheel to choose colors that "go together"	170
First, choose your base color	170
Use the triadic scheme to create usable color patterns	171
Get started on the SampleRate markup	173
Create the basic page layout with CSS	174
The opposite of heavy is... light	180
Create a richer color palette with the tetradic color scheme	182
Let's update the SampleRate CSS	186

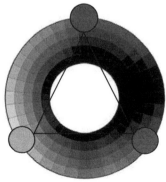
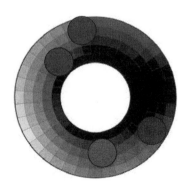

smart navigation

"In 2 seconds, click 'Home'."

6

What would the Web be without navigation?

Navigation is what makes the Web such a powerful information medium. But here's the thing: navigation is a lot more than just whipping up some cool-looking buttons and slapping them into your design. Building smart navigation starts with your information architecture and continues through your entire design process. But how does it work? How do you really make sure your users never get lost? In this chapter, we'll look at different styles of navigation, how IA guides your page links, and why icons (alone) aren't always iconic.

School's back in session	194
The first step to good navigation is good IA	197
What's really in a name, anyway?	198
Approach #1: Horizontally-tabbed navigation	204
Approach #2: Vertical navigation	206
Block elements are your friends	212
Let's float the block navigation on the CNM site	213
Icons don't SAY anything... they just look pretty	215
Add icons to your text, not the other way around	217
Update the CNM XHTML to use textual links	218
Now we can style our new block elements...	219
Primary navigation shouldn't change... but secondary navigation should	221
Each sub-page gets its own secondary navigation	222
Let's style the navigation with our CSS	223

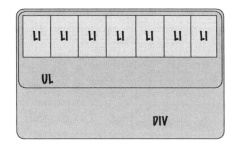

writing for the web

Yes, you scan!

Writing for the Web is just like any other kind of writing, right? Actually, writing for the Web is completely different than writing for print. People don't read text on the Web like they read text on a printed page. Instead of reading text from left to right, beginning to end, they **scan** it. All of the text on your site needs to be quickly **scannable** and **easily digestible** by the user. If not, users won't waste their time on your site, and they'll go somewhere else. In this chapter, you'll learn a bevy of tips and tricks for writing scannable text from scratch and making existing text easy to scan.

Build a better online newspaper	233
Hipster Intelligencer Online: project specs	234
The problem is TEXT	234
Improve your content with the Inverted Pyramid	241
Compress your copy	247
Add lists to your XHTML	257
Headings make your text even more scannable	259
Mix fonts to emphasize headings and other text	268
The level, not the size, of a heading conveys importance	269

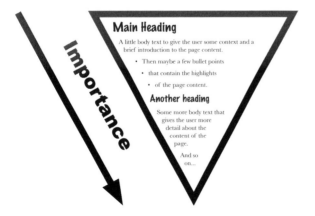

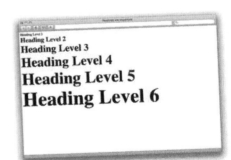

accessibility

Inaccessibility Kills

8

Who's missing out on experiencing your website right now?

You may have a beautiful, well-laid out, easily navigable site... but that doesn't mean everyone's enjoying it. Whether it's someone who's visually-impaired or just a user who has trouble distinguishing blues from greens, your site must be **accessible**. Otherwise, you're losing users and hurting your business. But don't worry: *accessibility isn't difficult!* By **planning the order of your markup**, using **ALT** attributes and **LONGDESC** tags, and **thinking about color**, you'll widen your audience immediately. Along the way, you may even get **WCAG certified**. What's that? Turn the page, and find out...

Audio-2-Go: inaccessible accessibility	276
Accessibility means making your site work for everyone	277
How does your site read?	278
A site's message should be clear...to everyone	280
Face it: computers are stupid!	281
A computer will read your image's ALT text	282
Convert your long ALT text to a LONGDESC	286
Your improvements are making a difference for some Audio-2-Go customers	288
Accessibility is not just about screen readers	289
Tabbing through a page should be orderly	291
Audio-2-Go is now a lot more accessible	294
WCAG Priority 1	298
Color shouldn't be your only form of communication	302
Life through web-safe eyes...	303
Life through color-blind eyes...	303
Audio-2-Go, via color-blind eyes	304
Those stars are a real problem	306
Background images are still your friend	307
There's more to ordering than just tabindexes	308

listen to your users

The Pathway to Harmonious Design

9

Good design is all about really listening to your users.

Your ***users can tell you what's wrong*** with your site, w***hat's right*** with your site, ***how you can fix things*** (if necessary) and *how you can improve your site*. There are lots of ways you can listen to your users. You can **listen to them in groups** (using tools like surveys), listen to them **individually** (with tools such as usability tests), and listen to their **collective actions on your site** (with tools such as site metrics and statistics). Whatever method you use, its all about "hearing" what your users are saying. If you do, your site will meet the needs of your audience and be that much better for it.

	PROS	CONS
Surveys	Require a relatively short time commitment from survey participants	Require a lot of advanced planning
	Can be administered to a huge amount of people	Written surveys may present problems for lower level readers
	Can be administered in lots of ways (paper, online, by phone, in person)	Survey questions might be misinterpreted
	Participants can often complete the survey at their own leisure	
Focus Groups	Allow participants to build on each other's ideas	Require larger time commitment from participants
	Collect information on a very specific topic from those who have a stake in the topic	Usually require compensation for the participants
	Benefits from a trained facilitator	Public environment may intimidate some participants
		Requires a trained facilitator

Problems over at RPM	320
Let your audience speak to you through focus groups and surveys	322
Surveys and focus groups aren't free	325
Surveys Exposed	327
Ask the right questions in your surveys	328
The final RPM Music user survey	338
The results are in!	340
Responses to the open-ended question:	341
Web browser usage	343
Fix RPM's CSS bug by moving the hover property	344
The building blocks of budget usability testing	351
Use a moderator script to organize the test	352
Friends and family can be a problem	359
The results of the usability test–what the users are telling you	360
A simple problem...	361
Site stats give your users (another) voice	363
Website analytics tools	364

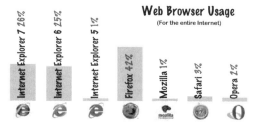

Web Browser Usage
(For the entire Internet)

Internet Explorer 7 26%
Internet Explorer 6 25%
Internet Explorer 5 1%
Firefox 42%
Mozilla 1%
Safari 3%
Opera 1%

evolutionary design

Keeping your site fresh

10

So you've built a bunch of awesome websites. Now it's time to kick back, relax, and watch the visitor numbers grow, right? Whoa, not so fast. *The Web never stops evolving*—and your site needs to keep up. You can **add new features**, **tweak the design**, or even **do a complete redesign**. An ever-changing site reflects your growing skills—which means *your site is always your best PR tool*.

Flash

JQuery JavaScript library

XHTML + CSS

Your portfolio so far...	370
Keeping your site and content fresh keeps your users coming back	372
Web design is about evolution, not revolution	375
Use CSS to evolve your site's design	376
Use JavaScript lightboxes to add interactivity to your site	388
Add Facebox to the Red Lantern home page	389
Edit your index file	390
Adding blog functionality with WordPress	395
Add a WordPress blog to the Red Lantern site	396
Blog Exposed	398
Change the look and feel of your blog with themes	400

the business of web design

Mind Your Own Business

Business in a web design book? Are you kidding me?

You've mastered pre-production, information architecture, navigation, color, and even accessibility. What's left in your path to web design mastery? Well, you're going to have to tackle the business issues of web design. You don't need a Harvard MBA, but you better know more than just where you deposit your check... or those checks may stop coming. Let's look at establishing good client relationships and understanding your intellectual property rights. The result? Increased profits and protection for your hard work.

11

The newest potential client: the Foo Bar	404
What Foo Bar wants in a bid	405
Let's build a quick mockup for the Foo Bar	406
Welcome to the world of design piracy	413
What kind of web worker are you?	416
Red Lantern's got a new prospective client	421
What really goes into designing a website?	424
Figure out a total bid...	425
Use a proposal letter to deliver a detailed quote to a client	431
The Trilobite podcast: a(nother) new challenge	433
Use Creative Commons to license your work	433
Creative Commons Licenses	434

leftovers

The Top Ten Things (we didn't cover)

We've really covered a lot of ground in this book. The thing is, there are some important topics and tidbits that didn't quite fit into any of the previous chapters. We feel pretty strongly about these and think that if we didn't at least cover them in passing, we'd be doing you a disservice. That is where this chapter comes into the picture. Well, it's not really a chapter; it's more like an appendix (ok, it *is* an appendix). But it's an awesome appendix of the top ten best bits that we couldn't let you go without.

#1: Cross-cultural & international design	440
#2: The future of web markup	442
#3: The future of CSS	444
#4: Designing for mobile devices	445
#5: Developing web applications	446
#6: Rhythm in your layout	447
#7: Text contrast	448
#8: Match link names with their destination page	449
#9: Contrast is a fundamental layout device	450
#10: More tools for design	451

However, the potential of the web to deliver full scale applications didn't hit the mainstream till Google introduced Gmail, quickly followed by Google Maps, web based applications with rich user interfaces and PC-equivalent interactivity. The collection of technologies used by Googl[e] christened AJAX, in a seminal essay by Jesse Garrett of web design firm Adaptive Path.

The bursting of the dot-com bubble in the fall of 2001 marked a turning point for the web. Many people concluded that the web was overhyped, when, in fact, bubbles and consequent shakeouts appear to be a common feature of all technological revolutions. Shakeouts typically mark the point at which an ascendant technology is ready to take its place at center stage.

The first of those principle[s] that was also a rallying cry [...] went down in flames after a heated battle with Microsoft. What's more, two of our initial Web 1.0 exemplars, DoubleClick and Akamai, were both pioneers in treating the web as a platform. People don't often think of it as "web services," but in fact, ad serving was the first widely deployed web service, and the first widely deployed "mashup" (to use another term that has gained currency of late).

how to use this book

Intro

In this section we answer the burning question:
"So why DID they put that in a Web Design book?"

Who is this book for?

If you can answer "yes" to all of these:

1 Are you **comfortable with XHTML & CSS** but don't have any experience with web design?

2 Do you consider yourself a web developer (working in a fun environment like PHP, Ruby on Rails, .NET) and **want to become a better web designer**?

3 Do you **need to understand web design for a course, your line of work,** or you simply want to impress people at parties with your vast knowledge of The Golden Ratio and the Web Content Accessibility Guidelines?

this book is for you.

Who should probably back away from this book?

If you can answer "yes" to any of these:

1 Are you someone who d**oesn't have any experience with HTML/XHTML & CSS**?

2 Are you an **accomplished web or graphic designer looking for a reference book**?

3 Are you someone who likes to build webpages with tools like **Frontpage and Dreamweaver**, so you don't ever have to look at code?

If this is the case, don't worry. Go pick up Head First HTML with CSS & XHTML by Elisabeth Freeman and Eric Freeman, and then come back to this book.

this book is not for you.

[Note from marketing: this book is for anyone with a credit card.]

We know what you're thinking

"How can *this* be a serious Web Design book?"

"What's with all the graphics?"

"Can I actually *learn* it this way?"

We know what your *brain* is thinking

Your brain craves novelty. It's always searching, scanning, *waiting* for something unusual. It was built that way, and it helps you stay alive.

So what does your brain do with all the routine, ordinary, normal things you encounter? Everything it *can* to stop them from interfering with the brain's *real* job—recording things that *matter*. It doesn't bother saving the boring things; they never make it past the "this is obviously not important" filter.

How does your brain *know* what's important? Suppose you're out for a day hike and a tiger jumps in front of you, what happens inside your head and body?

Neurons fire. Emotions crank up. *Chemicals surge.*

And that's how your brain knows...

This must be important! Don't forget it!

But imagine you're at home, or in a library. It's a safe, warm, tiger-free zone. You're studying. Getting ready for an exam. Or trying to learn some tough technical topic your boss thinks will take a week, ten days at the most.

Just one problem. Your brain's trying to do you a big favor. It's trying to make sure that this *obviously* non-important content doesn't clutter up scarce resources. Resources that are better spent storing the really *big* things. Like tigers. Like the danger of fire. Like the old school NES cheat code for Contra (↑ ↑ ↓ ↓←→ ←→BA). And there's no simple way to tell your brain, "Hey brain, thank you very much, but no matter how dull this book is, and how little I'm registering on the emotional Richter scale right now, I really *do* want you to keep this stuff around."

Your brain thinks THIS is important.

Great. Only 450 more dull, dry, boring pages.

Your brain thinks THIS isn't worth saving.

We think of a "Head First" reader as a <u>learner</u>.

So what does it take to *learn* something? First, you have to *get* it, then make sure you don't *forget* it. It's not about pushing facts into your head. Based on the latest research in cognitive science, neurobiology, and educational psychology, *learning* takes a lot more than text on a page. We know what turns your brain on.

Some of the Head First learning principles:

Make it visual. Images are far more memorable than words alone, and make learning much more effective (up to 89% improvement in recall and transfer studies). It also makes things more understandable. **Put the words within or near the graphics** they relate to, rather than on the bottom or on another page, and learners will be up to *twice* as likely to solve problems related to the content.

Use a conversational and personalized style. In recent studies, students performed up to 40% better on post-learning tests if the content spoke directly to the reader, using a first-person, conversational style rather than taking a formal tone. Tell stories instead of lecturing. Use casual language. Don't take yourself too seriously. Which would *you* pay more attention to: a stimulating dinner party companion, or a lecture?

Sidebars can hold everything from link lists to extra body content. They can also be useful for ancillary navigation and archive links for blogs.

Activities

Notes about the daily things Mark did in Japan.

Bars and Nightlife

A look at the bars and nightlife in and around Tokyo and Kyoto.

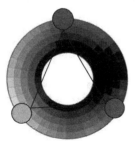

Get the learner to think more deeply. In other words, unless you actively flex your neurons, nothing much happens in your head. A reader has to be motivated, engaged, curious, and inspired to solve problems, draw conclusions, and generate new knowledge. And for that, you need challenges, exercises, and thought-provoking questions, and activities that involve both sides of the brain and multiple senses.

It sure seems like nobody considered I'd be using a screen reader for this site...

Get—and keep—the reader's attention. We've all had the "I really want to learn this but I can't stay awake past page one" experience. Your brain pays attention to things that are out of the ordinary, interesting, strange, eye-catching, unexpected. Learning a new, tough, technical topic doesn't have to be boring. Your brain will learn much more quickly if it's not.

Touch their emotions. We now know that your ability to remember something is largely dependent on its emotional content. You remember what you care about. You remember when you *feel* something. No, we're not talking heart-wrenching stories about a boy and his dog. We're talking emotions like surprise, curiosity, fun, "what the...?", and the feeling of "I Rule!" that comes when you solve a puzzle, learn something everybody else thinks is hard, or realize you know something that "I'm more technical than thou" Bob from engineering *doesn't*.

Metacognition: thinking about thinking

If you really want to learn, and you want to learn more quickly and more deeply, pay attention to how you pay attention. Think about how you think. Learn how you learn.

Most of us did not take courses on metacognition or learning theory when we were growing up. We were *expected* to learn, but rarely *taught* to learn.

But we assume that if you're holding this book, you really want to learn how to design user-friendly websites. And you probably don't want to spend a lot of time. If you want to use what you read in this book, you need to *remember* what you read. And for that, you've got to *understand* it. To get the most from this book, or *any* book or learning experience, take responsibility for your brain. Your brain on *this* content.

The trick is to get your brain to see the new material you're learning as Really Important. Crucial to your well-being. As important as a tiger. Otherwise, you're in for a constant battle, with your brain doing its best to keep the new content from sticking.

I wonder how I can trick my brain into remembering this stuff...

So just how *DO* you get your brain to treat Web Design like it was a hungry tiger?

There's the slow, tedious way, or the faster, more effective way. The slow way is about sheer repetition. You obviously know that you *are* able to learn and remember even the dullest of topics if you keep pounding the same thing into your brain. With enough repetition, your brain says, "This doesn't *feel* important to him, but he keeps looking at the same thing *over* and *over* and *over*, so I suppose it must be."

The faster way is to do **anything that increases brain activity,** especially different *types* of brain activity. The things on the previous page are a big part of the solution, and they're all things that have been proven to help your brain work in your favor. For example, studies show that putting words *within* the pictures they describe (as opposed to somewhere else in the page, like a caption or in the body text) causes your brain to try to makes sense of how the words and picture relate, and this causes more neurons to fire. More neurons firing = more chances for your brain to *get* that this is something worth paying attention to, and possibly recording.

A conversational style helps because people tend to pay more attention when they perceive that they're in a conversation, since they're expected to follow along and hold up their end. The amazing thing is, your brain doesn't necessarily *care* that the "conversation" is between you and a book! On the other hand, if the writing style is formal and dry, your brain perceives it the same way you experience being lectured to while sitting in a roomful of passive attendees. No need to stay awake.

But pictures and conversational style are just the beginning...

Here's what WE did:

We used ***pictures***, because your brain is tuned for visuals, not text. As far as your brain's concerned, a picture really *is* worth a thousand words. And when text and pictures work together, we embedded the text *in* the pictures because your brain works more effectively when the text is *within* the thing the text refers to, as opposed to in a caption or buried in the text somewhere.

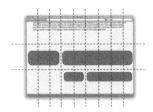

We used ***redundancy***, saying the same thing in *different* ways and with different media types, and *multiple senses*, to increase the chance that the content gets coded into more than one area of your brain.

We used concepts and pictures in ***unexpected*** ways because your brain is tuned for novelty, and we used pictures and ideas with at least *some* ***emotional*** *content*, because your brain is tuned to pay attention to the biochemistry of emotions. That which causes you to *feel* something is more likely to be remembered, even if that feeling is nothing more than a little ***humor***, ***surprise***, or ***interest.***

We used a personalized, ***conversational style***, because your brain is tuned to pay more attention when it believes you're in a conversation than if it thinks you're passively listening to a presentation. Your brain does this even when you're *reading*.

We included more than 80 ***activities***, because your brain is tuned to learn and remember more when you ***do*** things than when you *read* about things. And we made the exercises challenging-yet-do-able, because that's what most people prefer.

Test Drive

We used ***multiple learning styles***, because *you* might prefer step-by-step procedures, while someone else wants to understand the big picture first, and someone else just wants to see an example. But regardless of your own learning preference, *everyone* benefits from seeing the same content represented in multiple ways.

We include content for ***both sides of your brain***, because the more of your brain you engage, the more likely you are to learn and remember, and the longer you can stay focused. Since working one side of the brain often means giving the other side a chance to rest, you can be more productive at learning for a longer period of time.

Sharpen your pencil

And we included ***stories*** and exercises that present ***more than one point of view,*** because your brain is tuned to learn more deeply when it's forced to make evaluations and judgments.

We included ***challenges***, with exercises, and by asking ***questions*** that don't always have a straight answer, because your brain is tuned to learn and remember when it has to *work* at something. Think about it—you can't get your *body* in shape just by *watching* people at the gym. But we did our best to make sure that when you're working hard, it's on the *right* things. That ***you're not spending one extra dendrite*** processing a hard-to-understand example, or parsing difficult, jargon-laden, or overly terse text.

We used ***people***. In stories, examples, pictures, etc., because, well, because *you're* a person. And your brain pays more attention to *people* than it does to *things*.

Here's what YOU can do to bend your brain into submission

So, we did our part. The rest is up to you. These tips are a starting point; listen to your brain and figure out what works for you and what doesn't. Try new things.

Cut this out and stick it on your refrigerator.

1 **Slow down. The more you understand, the less you have to memorize.**

Don't just *read*. Stop and think. When the book asks you a question, don't just skip to the answer. Imagine that someone really *is* asking the question. The more deeply you force your brain to think, the better chance you have of learning and remembering.

2 **Do the exercises. Write your own notes.**

We put them in, but if we did them for you, that would be like having someone else do your workouts for you. And don't just *look* at the exercises. **Use a pencil.** There's plenty of evidence that physical activity *while* learning can increase the learning.

3 **Read the "There are No Dumb Questions"**

That means all of them. They're not optional sidebars, ***they're part of the core content!*** Don't skip them.

4 **Make this the last thing you read before bed. Or at least the last challenging thing.**

Part of the learning (especially the transfer to long-term memory) happens *after* you put the book down. Your brain needs time on its own, to do more processing. If you put in something new during that processing time, some of what you just learned will be lost.

5 **Talk about it. Out loud.**

Speaking activates a different part of the brain. If you're trying to understand something, or increase your chance of remembering it later, say it out loud. Better still, try to explain it out loud to someone else. You'll learn more quickly, and you might uncover ideas you hadn't known were there when you were reading about it.

6 **Drink water. Lots of it.**

Your brain works best in a nice bath of fluid. Dehydration (which can happen before you ever feel thirsty) decreases cognitive function.

7 **Listen to your brain.**

Pay attention to whether your brain is getting overloaded. If you find yourself starting to skim the surface or forget what you just read, it's time for a break. Once you go past a certain point, you won't learn faster by trying to shove more in, and you might even hurt the process.

8 **Feel something.**

Your brain needs to know that this *matters*. Get involved with the stories. Make up your own captions for the photos. Groaning over a bad joke is *still* better than feeling nothing at all.

9 **Design and Build Websites**

There's only one way to become an experienced web designer: design and build websites. Now, this might mean building layouts on paper, doing card sorts to develop your information architecture, or writing lots of CSS. The point is that you will never become a great web designer if you just read about it—you need to *do* it. We're going to give you a lot of practice: every chapter has exercises that pose problems for you to solve or asks questions that you need to think about. Don't just skip over them—a lot of the learning happens when you work on the exercises. We included a solution to each exercise, so don't be afraid to peek at the solution if you get stuck, but try to solve the problem before you look at the solution. And definitely get it working before you move on to the next part of the book.

Read Me

This is a learning experience, not a reference book. We deliberately stripped out everything that might get in the way of learning whatever it is we're working on at that point in the book. And the first time through, you need to begin at the beginning because the book makes assumptions about what you've already seen and learned.

We start off by teaching one of the most important concepts in web design—the design process—and then we move on to more specific design topics.

The design process is the foundation for developing a great-looking website. Each step gets you closer to better pages, and along the way, you create everything from a visual metaphor to a map of the site's content. Once you understand the overall design process, you can then dive into the details and begin building beautiful websites.

We advocate standards compliant XHTML & CSS.

All of the code that you write during the course of going through this book is standards compliant. This is really important to us, and we would (adamantly) argue that understanding how to think in and write standards compliant XHTML (XHTML 1.0 Strict) & CSS (CSS 2.1) is one of the hallmarks of a talented web designer. There will be no tables for layout, no style information in your markup, and all those <p> tags will be properly closed.

All of the code in this book is available on the Head First site.

Most of the projects in this book will require you to download the code for that particular chapter. Actually, you should just download all the code from the beginning so that you have it ready when the time comes. Sometimes we will ask you to make changes to code that already exists and will provide and "before" and "after" version of the markup and stylesheets.

Every bit of code is not fully explained

We assume that you have a working knowledge of XHTML and CSS and, therefore, don't make it a point to explain every nuance of the code. The important stuff is covered, and the downloadable examples are well documented. Remember, we're trying to make you a better designer not teach you the ins and outs of XHTML and CSS.

The terms "comps" and "storyboards" are used interchangeably.

We introduce storyboarding in this book as method for quickly mocking up design ideas without committing tons of time to code. Sometimes these are referred to as "storyboads," but other times we use the term "comp" (or composition) in reference to the same thing.

We assume that you are using modern browsers.

While we've taken every measure to make sure that our code is cross-browser compatible, you should use a modern browser (IE7+, Safari, Firefox) when putting together the sites in this book. While older browsers (notably IE6 and below) will work, you results may vary, as those browsers are buggy and incredibly finicky.

The activities are NOT optional.

The exercises and activities are not add-ons; they're part of the core content of the book. Some of them are to help with memory, some are for understanding, and some will help you apply what you've learned. Don't skip the exercises.

The redundancy is intentional and important.

One distinct difference in a Head First book is that we want you to really get it. And we want you to finish the book remembering what you've learned. Most reference books don't have retention and recall as a goal, but this book is about learning, so you'll see some of the same concepts come up more than once.

Our markup and CSS examples are as lean as possible.

Our readers tell us that it's frustrating to wade through 200 lines of markup or CSS looking for the two lines they need to understand. Most examples in this book are shown within the smallest possible context so that the part you're trying to learn is clear and simple. Don't expect all of the examples to be robust—or even complete. They are written specifically for learning and aren't always fully-functional.

We've placed files (markup, CSS, images, complete pages) on the Web so you can copy and paste them into your text/markup/code editor. You'll find them at **http://www.headfirstlabs.com/books/hfwd**

The technical review team

Sarah Collings

Johannes de Jong

Matt DiGangi

Ashley Doughty

Corey McGlone

Pauline McNamara

Jonathan Moore

Technical Reviewers:

Sarah Collings has worked in web design and development for over 7 years and is currently developing usable web applications as a User Experience Software Engineer at Digital River, Inc. She has a Bachelor of Fine Arts in Graphic Design and is working toward a Master's in Software Engineering. In her spare time, Sarah enjoys running and spending time outdoors with her fiancé.

Johannes de Jong is an old dinosaur mainframer that loves to go over to the wild side—building websites, from time to time. His latest experiment is a Google Maps site built with Apex from Oracle, and yes, he will use this book to redesign it.

Matt DiGangi is the creator, designer, and editor of the website Thieves Jargon (www.thievesjargon.com). He lives in Boston.

Ashley Doughty is a Senior Web Developer from Maine, living and working in the Greater Boston area. She is a hard core Christian, wife, daughter, reader and GEEK. She loves coding so much that she even does it in her free time.

Corey McGlone has been involved in web development for ten years and has spent the last seven years working primarily in web application development for Schnieder Logistics, Relion Corporation, and Mayo Clinic. He's an avid music lover, is married, and has one little boy at home.

Pauline McNamara has worked with university e-Learning projects in Switzerland for the past 6 years, most recently at the Swiss Federal Institute of Technology in Zurich. Her current learning passion involves raising an adorable puppy with her partner (who's also adorable).

Jonathan Moore is the owner of Forerunner Design, web design and development (www.forerunnerdesign.com).

Acknowledgments

Our editor:

A crazy big thanks to our editor, **Brett McLaughlin**. Even though he was overloaded with a ton of other books, he always had great feedback and suggestions for how to make our book sharper, smoother, and a far more effective learning tool.

Brett McLaughlin

Lou Barr

A huge thanks must go out to **Lou Barr**, who took chapters that we thought looked awesome to begin with, and made them look incredibly polished (and even awesomer)—and we are really grateful for this.

The O'Reilly team:

To **Sanders Kleinfeld**, **Caitrin McCullough**, **Karen Shaner**, who all kept various aspects of the production process running smoothly.

To **Brittany Smith**, the book's Production Editor, who made sure that when the book went to production, everything ran smoothly and efficiently.

Finally, to **Laurie Petrycki**, who had faith in our abilities and our vision enough to let us write this book in the first place.

Ethan's friends, family, and colleagues:

First off, to my wife **Jenn**, who damn near deserves sainthood for putting up with the sheer number of hours I've put into this book (and away from her) and the grumpy mood that I was almost constantly in as a result. To my son **Sam**, who one day (somewhere in the middle of me writing the book) asked, "Daddy, are you ever going to stop working so you can play with me?" The book is done, Sam. Let's do something fun! To my daughter **Taylor**, who, while she most likely won't admit it, probably thinks it's cool to see her name (and picture) in the book. To **my colleagues at MATRIX** (especially **Mark Kornbluh** and **Dean Rehberger**) for their support (particularly, when I was in the thick of finishing the book off). To my grad students **Joe**, **Pete**, and **Steen**, who made it their morning ritual (especially near the end) to stick their heads in my office to see how the book was doing. And to my big moose of a chocolate lab **Oscar**—just because.

Jeffs's friends, family, and colleagues:

To **Allie**, for putting up with months of me working until two in the morning. Also, your InDesign tips were essential to the production of this book; without them, all the images would be stretched and pixelated. To my **mom Jill, dad Jeff, and brother Jason.** You guys have been an inspiration to me, and I love you all very much. To **Rich, Brian and Rabbott (Ryan) and everyone else in the Communication Arts and Sciences Dean's Office at MSU.** You guys gave me an opportunity to work in one of the best IT offices in Michigan and allowed me the freedom to develop the skills I needed to write this book. I am forever grateful for the path you guys have lead me down, and this book wouldn't have been possible without your support.

Safari® Books Online

 When you see a Safari® icon on the cover of your favorite technology book that means the book is available online through the O'Reilly Network Safari Bookshelf.

Safari offers a solution that's better than e-books. It's a virtual library that lets you easily search thousands of top tech books, cut and paste code samples, download chapters, and find quick answers when you need the most accurate, current information. Try it for free at http://safari.oreilly.com.

1 building beautiful web pages

Beauty is in the eye of your user

> I know he said you're just another boring one-column waitress, Mom, but I think you're the best... you're *always* paying attention to your users. What else could anyone want?

It's a great big (wide) world... but who's really out there?

So you've got your nice shiny XHTML and CSS diploma hanging on the wall, and the prospective clients are ringing your new business line off the hook. Cool, right? Yeah... until you get your first complaint about a bad layout, or a logo that's just *so* 1998. So how do you create **really beautiful websites** and still make sure they **satisfy your users**? It all begins with good **planning**. Then you've got to **write for the Web**, **know your audience**, and, above all else, make sure you're **designing for your users**, not yourself.

Your big chance with Red Lantern Design

Jane's just bought a small web design studio. Red Lantern Design's been producing small sites for local businesses for several years, and now Jane wants to expand their client-base. But there's a problem...

The old Red Lantern webmaster used a WYSIWYG editor to create the company's own site, and now no one can edit the files. Jane's hired you to build a new site that will bring Red Lantern up to modern web standards and bag the company more lucrative clients.

I've bought a kiosk at an international business conference in a week. I don't know a thing about web design, but I know you do. So you need to design a *really* impressive new website as quickly and efficiently as possible. Think you can do that?

Jane, Entrepreneur and new owner of Red Lantern Design.

Well, sure you can. Where do you think you should start?

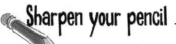

Sharpen your pencil

Here's the current Red Lantern site. Take a look at the screenshot and, using your web design expertise, annotate it. Note what you like. What do you dislike? Do you see any problems?

Jane loves Japanese culture. That's why she bought the company. She loved the name.

Sharpen your pencil
Solution

Here's what we thought about the site. Your answers may be a little different, so don't worry if you didn't catch all of these.

There's not much contrast between the menu and the background image, or the body text and the gray center column.

Shouldn't there be something to grab potential clients' interest on the front page? Like news or a featured project...

The logo's cool – but doesn't feel connected to the layout.

There's lots of wasted space at the top of the page before we get to the menu and content.

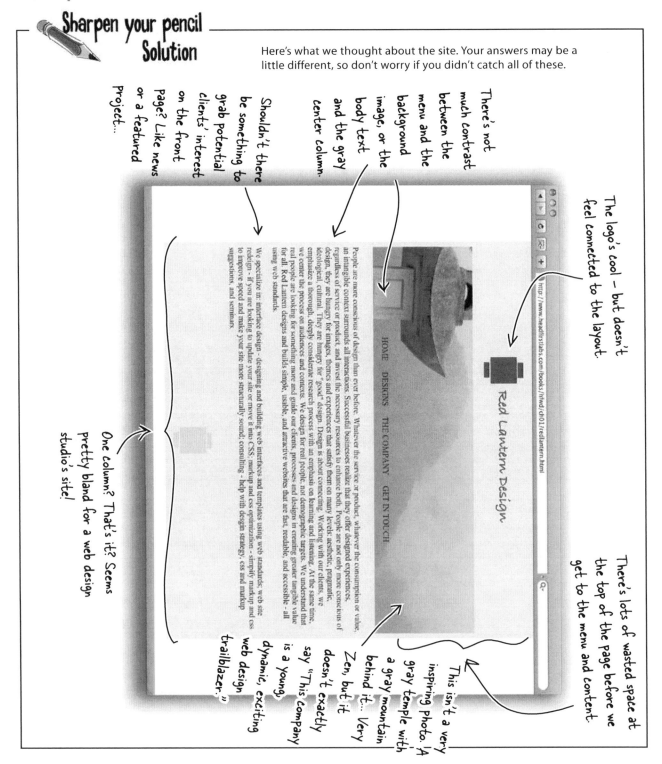

Red Lantern Design

HOME   DESIGNS   THE COMPANY   GET IN TOUCH

http://www.headfirstlabs.com/books/hfwd/ch01/redlantern.html

People are more conscious of design than ever before. Whatever the service or product, whatever the consumption or value, an intangible content surrounds all interactions. Successful businesses realize that they offer designed experiences, regardless of service or product, and invest the necessary resources to enhance them both. People are not only more conscious of design, they are hungry for images, themes and experiences that satisfy them on many levels: aesthetic, pragmatic, ideological, cultural. They are hungry for "good" design. Design is about connecting. Working with our clients, we emphasize a thorough, deeply considerate research process with an emphasis on learning and listening. At the same time, we center the process on audiences and contexts. We design for real people, not demographic targets. We understand that real people are looking for something more and guide our clients, processes and designs in creating greater tangible value for all. Red Lantern designs and builds simple, usable, and attractive websites that are fast, readable, and accessible – all using web standards.

We specialize in: interface design - designing and building web interfaces and templates using web standards; web site redesign - if you are looking to update your site or move it into CSS: markup and css optimization - simply markup and css to improve speed and make your site more structurally sound; consulting - help with design strategy, css and markup suggestions, and seminars.

One column? That's it? Seems pretty bland for a web design studio's site!

This isn't a very inspiring photo. A gray temple with a gray mountain behind it... Very Zen, but it doesn't exactly say "This company is a young, dynamic, exciting web design trailblazer."

Where do you start?

There's not a lot that's good about the existing Red Lantern site—the logo's nice, but that's a pretty damning comment on the rest of the design if that's all there is to like. But if there's so much wrong, how can we figure out what to work on next? Where would *you* start?

> Uh, yeah, so uh, I know where *I'd* start. I, uh, know HTML. So I'd start with the code. Get to it right away. Then I'd work up some, uh, CSS and uh, that's it! Okay?

Joe Blow thinks he's a fancy schmancy web designer. What do you think?

Sharpen your pencil

Is Joe right? Is there anything else to do? Where would *you* start?

....

....

....

....

....

Are you kidding me? How am I supposed to know where to start? I've got a whole bunch of stuff I need to do, so you tell me. What should I do first?

"Where should I start?" and "Where should I go from there?" are really good questions.

The fact you're still asking yourself those questions without opening a text editor is a good sign. The answer to both is, always follow a **design process**. A design process structures your project so that you stay on task and don't go off in every different direction all at once without accomplishing anything but stress, stress, and more stress.

A process is really just a *workflow* that determines the order you do things on a web design project. Imagine you're building a house for someone. It's their dream home, they've got a ton of ideas on their wishlist, and you also need to include the usual things you'd expect to find in a house: walls, floors roof, kitchen, bedroom, bathroom, living areas...

Now ask yourself where you'd start? Would you build the walls first? Would you pick out fabrics, or draw up a blueprint? Which one is going to pay off two weeks from now? Two months? Two years?

Draw up a blueprint <u>FIRST</u>

So building a website *is* a lot like building a house. If you start with a blueprint, you'll know exactly where you're headed at every step: foundations, load-bearing walls, and so on. For a website, you use **Information Architecture** (or **IA**). IA is the process by which you break your website's content into chunks and then organize those chunks hierarchically in relation to one another in a way that's logical.

Most of the time, each chunk of information is content (text, images, etc.) that lives on a single page. IA is also closely linked with building your site's navigation. So, if you've got bad IA, chances are, you'll have a bad navigation system as well. If your site doesn't have solid IA, it will feel disorganized and confusing to users. And that will make users go someplace else to get what they're looking for.

Architecture for your house starts with a blueprint.

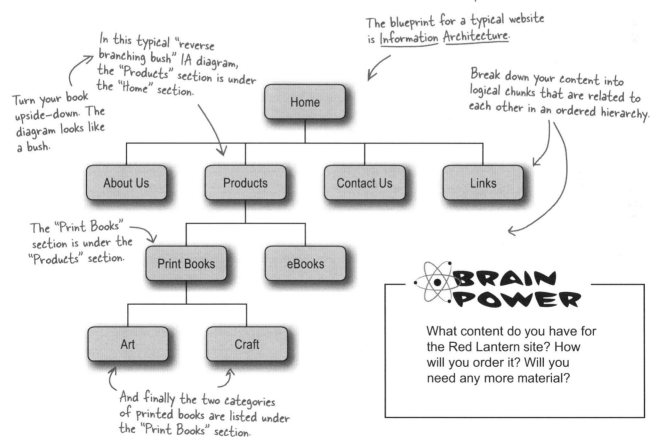

The blueprint for a typical website is <u>Information</u> <u>Architecture</u>.

In this typical "reverse branching bush" IA diagram, the "Products" section is under the "Home" section.

Break down your content into logical chunks that are related to each other in an ordered hierarchy.

Turn your book upside-down. The diagram looks like a bush.

The "Print Books" section is under the "Products" section.

And finally the two categories of printed books are listed under the "Print Books" section.

BRAIN POWER

What content do you have for the Red Lantern site? How will you order it? Will you need any more material?

 Sharpen your pencil

Start the Information Architecture process by asking Jane about the content she wants for the site.

Here's a memo from Jane telling you what sections she wants on the site. Write down a one or two word description for that "chunk" of content.

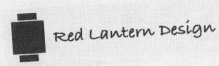 Red Lantern Design

MEMO

From: Jane

Subject: Site content

Let's have a section of the site where we put news items and updates about Red Lantern.

We definitely need a section of the site where we can show off all of the awesome work we're going to do.

The site needs a contact page. How would we ever get clients without a contact page?!

I think it would be good to have a section of the site about the company—what we do... that kind of thing.

We need to make sure they know we do consulting and web design!

....

....

....

....

....

Once you've worked out the sections of information for the Red Lantern Design site, you can start to build your Information Architecture diagram. Fill in the spaces provided with your individual sections from the facing page.

Your IA diagram will always start with your home or main page at the top of the hierarchy.

Home

Remember, each new row is a subsection of the section above.

What "chunks" of content might live in these two sections?

Sharpen your pencil
Solution

You started the Information Architecture process by asking Jane about the content she wants on the site.

Jane let you know what she thought the sections should be. Here are some possible one or two word descriptions for each "chunk" of content.

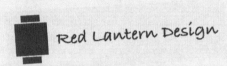 Red Lantern Design

MEMO

From: Jane

Subject: Site content

Let's have a section of the site where we put <u>news</u> items and <u>updates</u> about Red Lantern.

We definitely need a section of the site where we can <u>show off</u> all of the awesome <u>work</u> we're going to do.

The site needs a <u>contact</u> page. How would we ever get clients without a contact page?!

I think it would be good to have a section of the site <u>about the company</u>--what we do...that kind of thing.

We need to make sure they know we do <u>consulting</u> and <u>web design</u>!

News & Updates
....

Portfolio
....

Contact
....

About Us
....

Consulting, Design
....

Given these "chunks" of information, how does your IA diagram look?

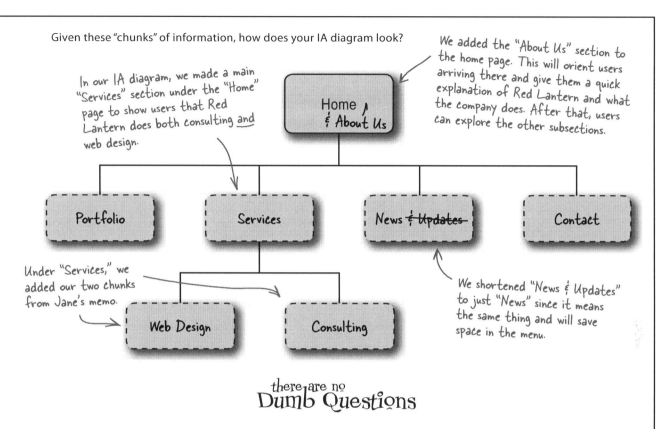

In our IA diagram, we made a main "Services" section under the "Home" page to show users that Red Lantern does both consulting _and_ web design.

We added the "About Us" section to the home page. This will orient users arriving there and give them a quick explanation of Red Lantern and what the company does. After that, users can explore the other subsections.

Home & About Us

Portfolio

Services

News & Updates

Contact

Under "Services," we added our two chunks from Jane's memo.

We shortened "News & Updates" to just "News" since it means the same thing and will save space in the menu.

Web Design

Consulting

there are no Dumb Questions

Q: Do IA diagrams always have to look like a reverse branching bush?

A: No, though the reverse branching bush is probably the most common way IA diagrams are done. Honestly, any kind of diagram that accurately and clearly represents the sections and subsections of content (and the hierarchical relationship between them) works just fine.

Q: Will the people I design sites for always be as clear as Jane about what sections they want?

A: Yes... and no. You'll be amazed at the extra details about sections and design ideas that come from just _talking_ to people. Just because they may not know the names that sections on a site are commonly called, doesn't mean they don't have a clear idea about what they want their site to contain. Then it's up to you to organize the sections logically and hierarchically.

Q: Couldn't I just skip this part of the process? This IA diagram and the one on page 7 look pretty similar...

A: No! Don't skip IA, as it can often determine parts of the design when you come to lay out the site. Besides, although there are some similarities of structure, every site is different, and some sites will have a lot of subsections. The more content you have and the deeper your IA diagram, the more complex your navigation system will be. You'll not only need top level navigation, but second tier navigation as well. But don't worry, we'll cover dealing with IA in a lot more detail in Chapter 3.

Q: Is an IA diagram just like a sitemap? The "chunks" just look like links...

A: An IA diagram shows a hierarchical relationship between sections and subsections of content in a site. It isn't meant to show links between sections, but you will use it when you put together the navigation for your site. In fact, let's take a look at that next...

C'mon, all we need for good navigation is some buttons that link to all the pages in our IA diagram, and we're good to go...

Will that be enough to help your users find their way around the site?

You need to think about navigation *twice* in the design process? First, you need to think about your navigational elements—yes, things like buttons and nav bars—while you work on the *overall layout* of the site.

Navigation will show up again when you begin writing the *code* and building the layout elements that have to do with users finding their way around the site, as well as linking your pages together. But don't jump the gun, you need to start by organizing your top level navigation.

Information Architecture isn't just important for organizing your site's information; it's a big deal for your navigation as well. So, when it comes to building your site's navigation, keep your IA diagram close at hand.

Determine your top level navigation

Top level navigation is usually the most prominent navigational element—the tabbed nav bar at the top of the page, the vertical nav menu in a secondary column, etc. More often that not, your top level navigation links to those sections one tier below the home page in your IA diagram.

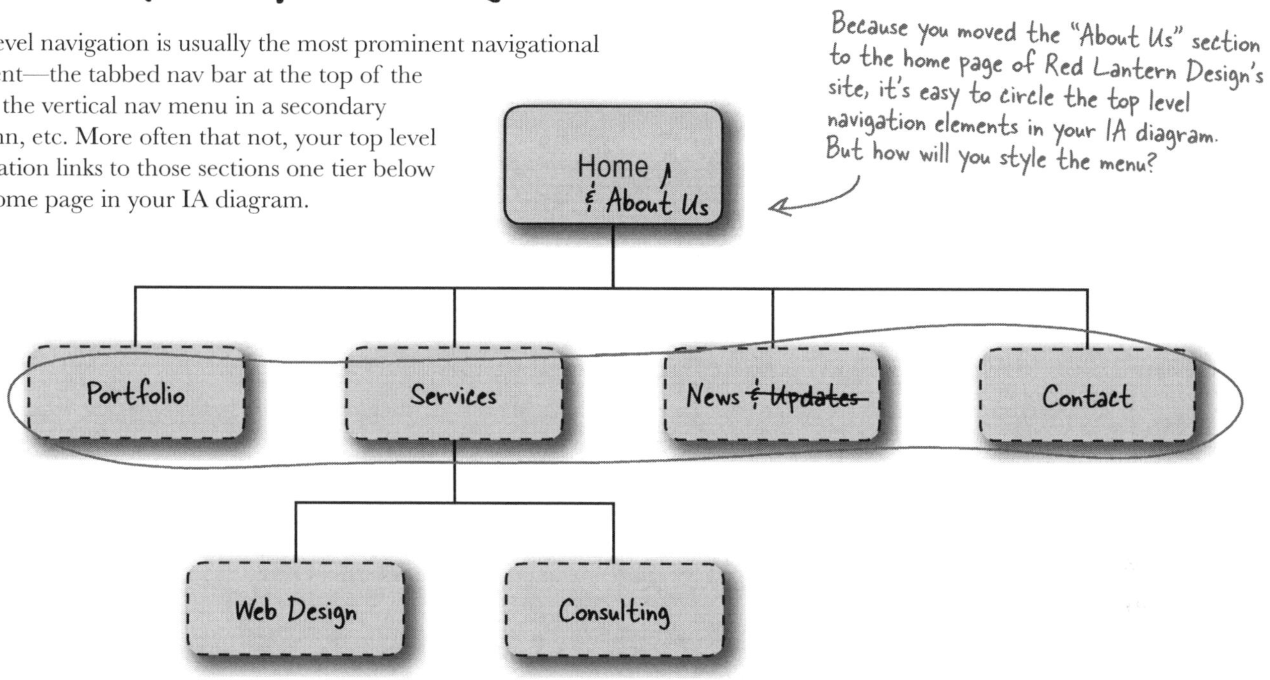

Because you moved the "About Us" section to the home page of Red Lantern Design's site, it's easy to circle the top level navigation elements in your IA diagram. But how will you style the menu?

Home & About Us

Portfolio   Services   News & Updates   Contact

Web Design   Consulting

Sharpen your pencil

Draw a few sketches of the kinds of menu you're already familiar with and start thinking about which menu type would suit the Red Lantern site.

Sharpen your pencil
Solution

Which top level navigation design do you think will work best for the Red Lantern Design site? If you don't know, how do you think you'll work it out?

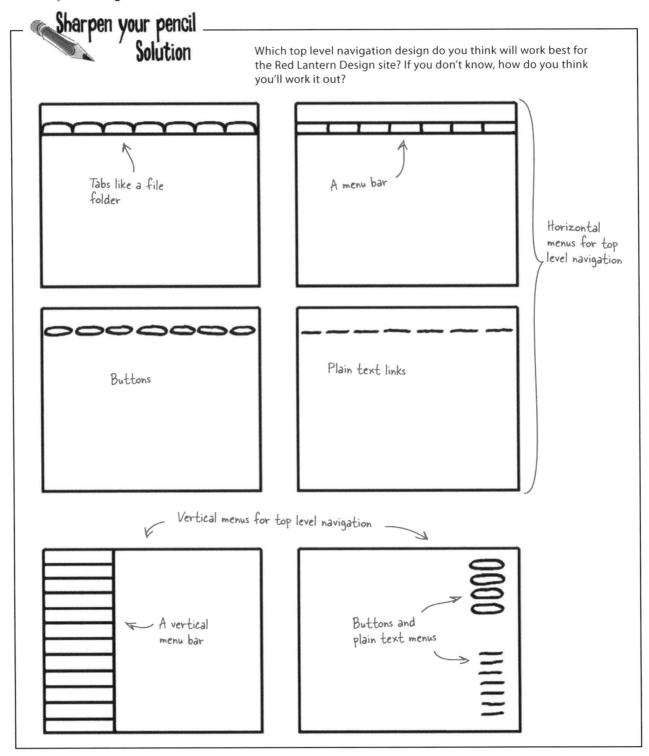

Tabs like a file folder

A menu bar

Horizontal menus for top level navigation

Buttons

Plain text links

Vertical menus for top level navigation

A vertical menu bar

Buttons and plain text menus

Put it all in context

The point of the top level navigation is to show your users where they are within your site's main structure. We'll come back to navigation in a lot more detail in Chapter 6, but for now, you need to ask yourself how you'll style the menu on the Red Lantern site. Time to start thinking about which menu type would suit the site and where it would fit on the page.

Horizontal tabs

Horizontal tabs are used for top level navigation on loads of sites because they save a lot of space.

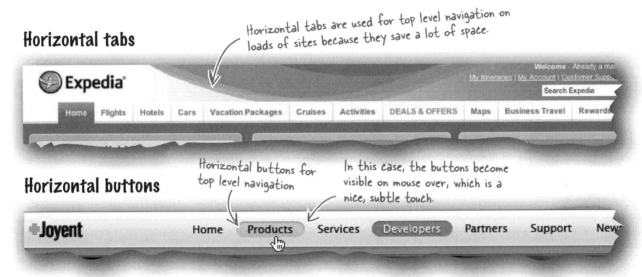

Horizontal buttons

Horizontal buttons for top level navigation

In this case, the buttons become visible on mouse over, which is a nice, subtle touch.

Vertical menu

Vertical menu for top level navigation.

Back when people first started adding menus to their sites, this was the most popular type of menu.

Vertical tabs

Vertical tabs for top level navigation styled with CSS and images add a real notebook feel to this site.

Notice this site's content is written in French. See appendix I for dealing with multi-language sites.

Show Jane some basic design sketches

So you've got the main content mapped out. What will you need to do next? At this stage, it's a good idea to show Jane some basic design sketches...

Hold it right there! IA diagrams, sketching designs on paper... What's with all the drawing? I thought this was a book on **WEB** design. I don't see much of that happening so far...

Having a clear idea of where you want to put the building blocks on screen saves valuable development time.

It's much quicker to sketch a few designs on paper and get Jane's reaction before you start than it is to waste time working up the code for a bunch of designs when she can only pick one...

Sketches keep the focus on <u>functionality</u>

Your first sketches should be black and white and drawn on paper. That way, Jane will be completely focused on the basic layout of the design (instead of what color the background of the page is or how great her logo looks placed over that image or... you get the picture).

Your designs should show Jane some basic layouts with the content she's requested in various configurations on the page. The sketches should make Jane ask herself questions like: "Do I want a large image at the top of the page?", "How many columns do I want?", "Where should the menu go?", and so on.

Sharpen your pencil

Here's the first sketch we showed Jane. She didn't like it because it looks almost exactly like the existing design, but with the main content section broken into two columns.

Now it's up to you to come up with a basic design Jane *does* like. Draw at least three more concepts on your own sheets of paper.

This design is too similar to the existing site design for Jane... time for you to go back to the drawing board.

Use horizontal lines instead of actual text. You don't need too much detail at this stage.

Use the sketches to get your ideas down on paper. You can work out the details later.

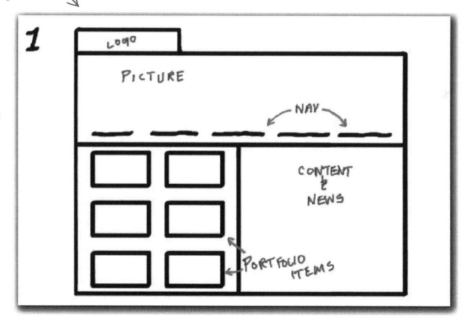

Sharpen your pencil
Solution

Basic black and white sketches keep the focus on the main layout. It's time to show the basic layout concepts to Jane. Which will she choose?

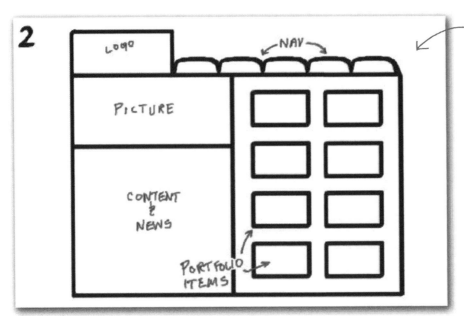

Design #2 has horizontal tabs for the menu. Under the logo and menu, there's space in the two-column design for a picture and the news section beneath that, while on the right are small thumbnail images of sites Red Lantern's designed.

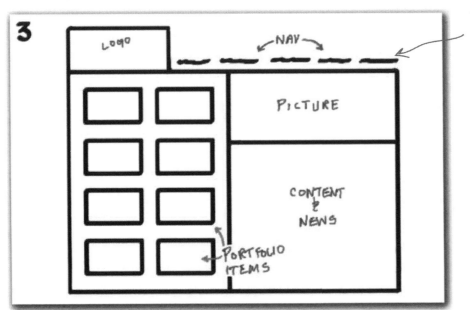

Design #3 has a plain textual menu in place of the tabs, and it's switched the position of the portfolio and content sections.

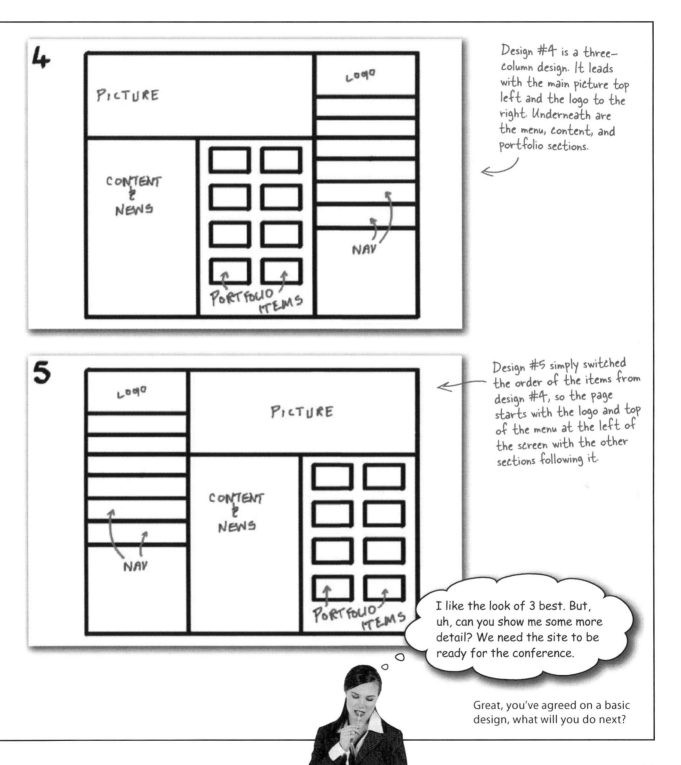

4

PICTURE

LOGO

CONTENT & NEWS

NAV

PORTFOLIO ITEMS

Design #4 is a three-column design. It leads with the main picture top left and the logo to the right. Underneath are the menu, content, and portfolio sections.

5

LOGO

PICTURE

CONTENT & NEWS

NAV

PORTFOLIO ITEMS

Design #5 simply switched the order of the items from design #4, so the page starts with the logo and top of the menu at the left of the screen with the other sections following it.

I like the look of 3 best. But, uh, can you show me some more detail? We need the site to be ready for the conference.

Great, you've agreed on a basic design, what will you do next?

> So we've agreed on a basic layout with Jane, but what should our next step be? Firing up the ol' text editor, grabbing some sample content from Jane, and working up an XHTML storm?

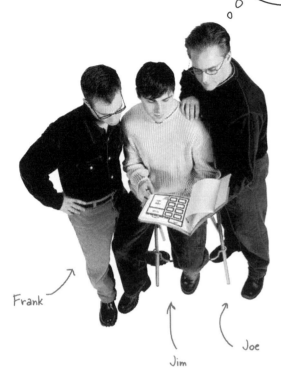

Frank

Jim

Joe

Frank: Nope. We're going to stick to pen and paper for now. What do you think about adding some color to those sketches?

Jim: Why would I do that? Can't I just get going with the code and test different colors using CSS stylesheets?

Frank: Well, this way, you get a chance to see how colors interact with one another, how interface and layout elements play off one another once they're in color, how your navigation system looks in relation to the rest of the layout, and generally whether content's represented in the best way possible.

Joe: Wow. That sounds like a tall order for one little sketch. Couldn't we just have shown Jane a few color versions instead of going with the black and white sketches?

Frank: Clients can get distracted by color too early in the process. It's best to show them something that gives them an idea of the functionality of the site—

Joe:—before we start on the look and feel part of the design process. I get it. The sketches provide us with a painless way to catch any potential design problems before we start coding our design, and they become major obstacles.

Frank: There you go. But we're not just doing one sketch here, Joe.

Joe: No?

Frank:—

Jim:—No. We're going to do a ton, all in different colors, and show them all to Jane like we did with the first sketches, right?

Frank: Kinda. What we're actually doing is creating *storyboards* to test a few variations. We'll show Jane the best one or two.

Jim: Wait. What?

Frank: Yeah, these are like the storyboards—you know, that sequence of little sketches that look like a comic strip—the film industry uses to test out shots before rolling the cameras. We're doing the same thing. Here, let me show you a neat trick for creating good storyboards.

Sharpen your pencil

Now that you know what kind of layout Jane wants for the Red Lantern Design site, it's time to storyboard it. Take a sheet of paper and a pencil and go to work. Be as detailed as possible in what you come up with. If you've got some handy, use pencil crayons to add color to your storyboards.

Browser Template

Here's a cool little trick to use when you're designing storyboards. Take a screenshot of a website—any will do. Open up your favorite image editing program, and erase the actual website content.

Now you have a browser template to draw your storyboards in.

Sharpen your pencil
Solution

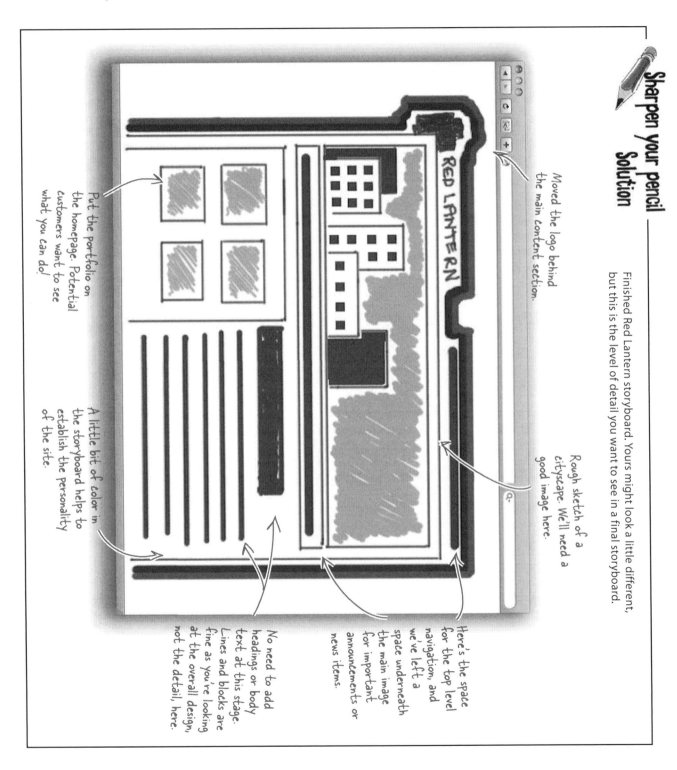

Finished Red Lantern storyboard. Yours might look a little different, but this is the level of detail you want to see in a final storyboard.

Rough sketch of a cityscape. We'll need a good image here.

Moved the logo behind the main content section.

Here's the space for the top level navigation, and we've left a space underneath the main image for important announcements or news items.

No need to add headings or body text at this stage. Lines and blocks are fine as you're looking at the overall design, not the detail, here.

A little bit of color in the storyboard helps to establish the personality of the site.

Put the portfolio on the homepage. Potential customers want to see what you can do!

Fireside Chats

Tonight's talk: **Pencil and Design Program discuss Storyboards**

Pencil:

Yo, Design Program, can you clear something up for me?

Well, I've gotten a little confused over here. Some people have started calling me "wireframe," but I thought that was a term that's used to describe code mockups...

Design Program:

Sure. What's up?

Yeah. It can be confusing, as people also use the term "wireframe" to refer to a code mockup that isn't totally fleshed out yet. But now isn't the time to get into code.

Code [eavesdropping]:

Hey! I heard that.

Pencil:

Sorry, buddy, but Design Program's right. You might think you're saving time by diving right into HTML, but it could end up costing you in the long run. See, if your client (or you) doesn't like the design you came up with and wants to go in a completely different direction, you've just invested tons of time in to HTML (and probably CSS) that you're not going to use. It's a lot easier to file a storyboard away and start with a fresh sheet of paper.

Design Program:

—or a new file. *I'd* go the formal route right from the start. It saves a ton of time as you can copy details right out of the storyboards into the final design if they work.

I'm not so sure. I prefer not to get all hung up on detail. The whole point of storyboards is that they're a quick and flexible way to brainstorm ideas and get some designs down. Besides, why waste a ton of time slaving over every pixel's placement in several designs when the client's only going to pick one?

I guess you might have kind of a point there, but are you really going to show your messy, smudged, coffee-stained, self to the client, Pencil?

I guess if you're preparing a pitch for a potential client, it *might* be a good idea to come up with something more polished and formal. But I still think detailed hand-drawn storyboards should be your first stop when you start to design a new site.

The storyboards look absolutely wonderful. The design and layout for the site look great. But the conference is in two days... Can I see it on screen?

<u>Now</u> it's time to prototype the site in code

Building a prototype in code has some great advantages. First, even though your design might look great on paper, it might not work (technically speaking) when you code it up. The prototype will give you an opportunity to quickly fix anything (code-wise) before you invest too much time in building a polished finished product.

Also, if you're working with clients, a code prototype gives you something to show them, and just like your storyboards, you can get useful feedback and make iterative changes.

What do you mean, iterative?

Iteration is a design methodology that lets you test, analyze, and refine prototypes of work in progress. At each stage, you go through each of the steps in the design process— it's cyclical—until you get something you (and your client) are happy with.

Ready Bake Code

Go ahead and grab the files for the first code prototype from:

www.headfirstlabs.com/books/hfwd/ch01

Then we'll give it a quick test drive to see how everything's looking.

```
/* Red Lantern redesign */

body {
  margin: 0;
  padding: 0;
  background: #7a212
  font-family: Helve
  font-size: 62.5%;
  color: #333;
}

h1, h2, p, ul, li
  margin: 0;
  padding: 0;
}

p {
  font-size: 1.4e
  line-height: 1
}

ul {
  list-style-ty
}
```

```
<!DOCTYPE html PUBLIC "-//W3C//DTD XHTML 1.0 Strict//EN"
        "http://www.w3.org/TR/xhtml1/DTD/xhtml1-strict.dtd">
<html xmlns="http://www.w3.org/1999/xhtml" xml:lang="en" lang="en">
<head>
    <title>Red Lantern Design</title>
        <meta http-equiv="Content-Type" content="text/html;
charset=utf-8"/>
        <link rel="stylesheet" href="stylesheets/screen.css" type="text/
css"
media="screen" />
</head>
<body>
    <div id="masthead">
        <h1><img alt="Red Lantern logo" src="images/rl_logo.png" /></h1>
        <ul id="nav">
            <li><a class="active" title="Red Lantern home"
href="index.html">Home</a></li>
            <li><a title="Design services"
href="services.html">Services</a></li>
            <li><a title="Our work" href="portfolio.html">Portfolio</a></
li>
            <a title="Contact Red Lantern"
ml">Contact</a></li>
```

Repeat yourself

Remember, you need HTML for every page in your IA diagram. Once you've downloaded it, duplicate the code and name the files accordingly. You'll link them together in the end.

```
">
header">
alt="tokyo buildings" src="images/tokyo.jpg" />
```

Test Drive

Time to check the site out in your browser. Once you've tested the site,
show it to Jane to get some fast feedback on this iteration.

Exercise

Here's the text Jane just sent over. Grab a stopwatch and set it for 15 seconds. Hit the Start button, and begin reading this text. When your time's up, write down what this text is about.

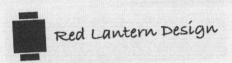

Red Lantern Design

MEMO

From: Jane

Subject: Site content

People are more conscious of design than ever before. Whatever the service or product, whatever the consumption or value, an intangible context surrounds all interactions. Successful businesses realize that they offer designed experiences, regardless of service or product, and invest the necessary resources to enhance both. People are not only more conscious of design, they are hungry for images, themes and experiences that satisfy them on many levels: aesthetic, pragmatic, ideological, cultural. They are hungry for "good" design. Design is about connecting. Working with our clients, we emphasize a thorough, deeply considerate research process with an emphasis on learning and listening. At the same time, we center the process on audiences and contexts. We design for real people, not demographic targets. We understand that real people are looking for something more and guide our clients, processes and designs in creating greater tangible value for all. Red Lantern designs and builds simple, usable, and attractive websites that are fast, readable, and accessible - all using web standards.

We specialize in: interface design - designing and building web interfaces and templates using web standards; web site redesign - if you are looking to update your site or move it into CSS; markup and css optimization - simplify markup and css to improve speed and make your site more structurally sound; consulting - help with design strategy, css and markup suggestions, and seminars.

....

....

....

Don't ruin a good design with bad copy

All the awesome design work, storyboarding, and prototyping in the world is not going to save your site if you don't have any content (or if the way you present your content stinks). So how will you ensure your content's interesting?

Writing for the web is different than writing for regular print.

Come on, writing is writing. There's no reason to re-write some text, especially for a website...

Instead of reading your content from left to right, beginning to end, like a book, users scan the text for keywords and concepts—to give them an idea about the contents of the page.

When you combine this with the fact that users generally don't spend that much time on individual pages, you know you are going to have to write differently. The word of the day is **scannability**!

What makes text scannable?

There are several techniques you can use to make your text scannable. Short paragraphs, headings, bullet points, and clear meaning will all help users scan your content more easily.

A brief introductory section provides an overview of the text. That way, the reader knows what they are getting into right off the bat.

Emphasis (bold and italic text) highlights important terms for the user.

Clearly written headers give the reader information about the whole article and its subsections.

Short paragraphs are easier to read than huge blocks of text (which are harder to read and comprehend on a computer screen).

Bullet points are a super-fast way to give facts to your users.

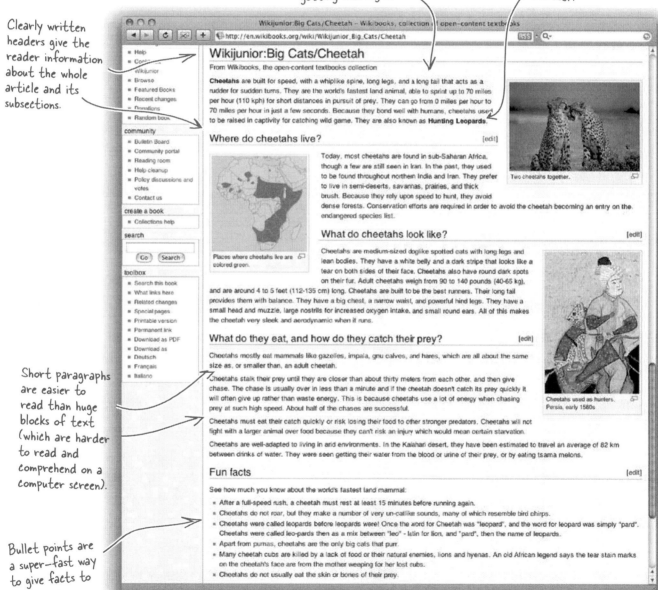

LONG EXERCISE

Here's the text Jane just sent over again. Rework the copy so that it follows the scannability checklist.

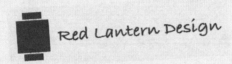
Red Lantern Design

MEMO

From: Jane

Subject: Site content

People are more conscious of design than ever before. Whatever the service or product, whatever the consumption or value, an intangible context surrounds all interactions. Successful businesses realize that they offer designed experiences, regardless of service or product, and invest the necessary resources to enhance both. People are not only more conscious of design, they are hungry for images, themes and experiences that satisfy them on many levels: aesthetic, pragmatic, ideological, cultural. They are hungry for "good" design. Design is about connecting. Working with our clients, we emphasize a thorough, deeply considerate research process with an emphasis on learning and listening. At the same time, we center the process on audiences and contexts. We design for real people, not demographic targets. We understand that real people are looking for something more and guide our clients, processes and designs in creating greater tangible value for all. Red Lantern designs and builds simple, usable, and attractive websites that are fast, readable, and accessible - all using web standards.

We specialize in: interface design - designing and building web interfaces and templates using web standards; web site redesign - if you are looking to update your site or move it into CSS; markup and css optimization - simplify markup and css to improve speed and make your site more structurally sound; consulting - help with design strategy, css and markup suggestions, and seminars.

You don't have to use them all, just the ones that work for your content.

Scannability Checklist

☐ **Clearly written headers**

☐ **Small(ish) paragraphs**

☐ **Use bold and italics to emphasize important words or phrases.**

☐ **Use lists (ordered or unordered) for appropriate content.**

Long Exercise Solution

You edited Jane's text, following the scannability checklist.

Scannability Checklist

- ☑ **Clearly written headers**
- ☑ **Small(ish) paragraphs**
- ☐ **Use bold and italics to emphasize important words or phrases.**
- ☑ **Use lists (ordered or unordered) for appropriate content.**

Red Lantern Design

MEMO

From: Jane

Subject: Site content

People are more conscious of design than ever before. Whatever the service or product, whatever the consumption or value, an intangible context surrounds all interactions. Successful businesses realize that they offer designed experiences, regardless of service or product, and invest the necessary resources to enhance both. People are not only more conscious of design, they are hungry for images, themes and experiences that satisfy them on many levels: aesthetic, pragmatic, ideological, cultural. They are hungry for "good" design. Design is about connecting. Working with our clients, we emphasize a thorough, deeply considerate research process with an emphasis on learning and listening. At the same time, we center the process on audiences and contexts. We design for real people, not demographic targets. We understand that real people are looking for something more and guide our clients, processes and designs in creating greater tangible value for all. Red Lantern designs and builds simple, usable, and attractive websites that are fast, readable, and accessible - all using web standards.

We specialize in: interface design - designing and building web interfaces and templates using web standards; web site redesign - if you are looking to update your site or move it into CSS; markup and css optimization - simplify markup and css to improve speed and make your site more structurally sound; consulting - help with design strategy, css and markup suggestions, and seminars.

Your text might look a little different, but as long as you've used the techniques to make the text more scannable, your users will thank you.

Headings orient the user within the text. Note, you won't need one at the top of the page, as the logo will serve as a header for the page.

Welcome to the New Red Lantern Design

Red Lantern is a small web design and consulting firm specializing in standards–based web design and development. Our goal is to build simple, beautiful webpages that make your information easy to find and your users happy.

If you or your company are interested in working with us, please check out our portfolio of design and branding work and contact us with your project details. We look forward to hearing from you and making your presence on the web a little simpler and easier to find.

View our full portfolio

Contact Red Lantern

These links will be a short unordered list with the bullet points removed by our CSS.

That's a serious rework right there. Mine wasn't anywhere near as, uh, comprehensive. Won't Jane be mad at you for cutting out all her carefully crafted words?

Sure, she could be. But this version is short, to the point, and a lot more compelling.

It tells users exactly what Red Lantern does, and what they can expect from working together. We edited out a ton of content—long words, sentences that you had to read three times to understand, and so on—that would have clouded this simple message.

Besides, worst case, we can compromise with Jane and put back in some of her text... carefully edited, of course!

Test Drive

Once you've edited your text so that it's more scannable, all you need to do is update the text in the code markup that you've already developed for Red Lantern, test it in your browser, and if you're happy with it, show it to Jane.

I love it! Yes, even the shorter text. You were right to cut most of mine. Your skills are going to help put Red Lantern on the map! I can't wait to start some new projects.

Web design is all about communication, and your USERS

So how do the two versions of Jane's site compare? Every site's ultimate aim is to communicate something to its users. If your website doesn't communicate what you want it to, your audience will go to another site looking for the experience or content that you couldn't give them.

This is known as **User-Centered Design**. When you build a website, you're building it for your users, not for you. You design for your user's strengths and weaknesses. You want to use every technique possible to bring users to your site, help them find what they're looking for, make sure they have a rewarding experience, and keep them coming back.

The process you followed in this chapter—

Pre-production using Information Architecture and storyboards to build a blueprint for your site so that you're as efficient and focused as possible when you go digital.

Navigation is based on your IA diagram. It's more than just linking pages together. Navigation helps your users find information.

Layout uses HTML and CSS to build the site's interface (which you already came up with on paper back in the pre-production phase).

Writing "fills" the design up with the scannable content that your visitors come to the site for.

—had just one aim: to produce a great-looking site that tells users all about Red Lantern Design.

The old design didn't communicate much at all to users...

The new site had users at the center of the design process from the get go. As a result, it grabs the user's interest and tells them a compelling story.

Your Web Design Toolbox

Wow... 36 pages in and you've already managed to totally rework a pretty crummy looking website. Next chapter: we dig deeper into pre-production.

BULLET POINTS

- When you design sites, you should practice user-centered design—creating sites that focus on meeting the needs of your users.

- A design process helps you structure a project so that you stay on task and get things done in an efficient manner.

- Most, if not all, web design projects have 4 components: pre-production, layout, navigation, and writing.

- Information Architecture is the process by which your website's content is broken into chunks and then organized hierarchically in relation to one another.

- Developing your site's IA is a two step process: organizing your site's information, and building an IA diagram.

- An IA diagram visually represents the hierarchical organization of sections and subsections of information in your site.

- Top level navigation usually links to those sections in your information architecture one tier below your home/main page.

- The design of your top level navigation depends on the overall design and layout.

- There are a handful of great models for designing top level navigation: horizontal tabs, horizontal buttons, vertical menu, vertical tabs.

- Storyboards are used to visualize your design and test basic layout concepts before you jump into code.

- Storyboards are a great way to catch potential design problems before you spend time coding your site.

- Writing for the web is different than writing for print.

- Web users scan webpages instead of reading them from beginning to end.

- Web content needs to be written so that it's scannable.

2 pre-production

Paper covers rock

> Wow, you really *can* erase things when you use a pencil instead of a text editor. Who would have thought?!

Tired of butting heads with a picky client? Yeah, you know the type... every time you show them their latest crazy design idea, they've already moved on to another look... another color scheme... another entire website. So how do you deal with *fickle clients* or those tricky *hard-to-get-right websites*? You start with paper, pencil, and a big fat pink eraser. In this chapter, you'll learn how to work smart before you dig into your HTML editor. Coming up with a **theme** and **visual metaphor** for your site, mocking up sketches in **pencil**, and using **storyboards** will turn you into a nimble, flexible web designer. So get out your sketch pad, and let's pre-produce!

Your first "international" gig...

Mark loves to travel. After college, he took a year off to backpack around Japan and experience everything the island nation had to offer–from sushi to samurai. Now that he's back, he wants to document his experience. It's up to you to build Mark a great, engaging website detailing his trip to Japan.

Mark

Tokyo metro map

Menu

Japan

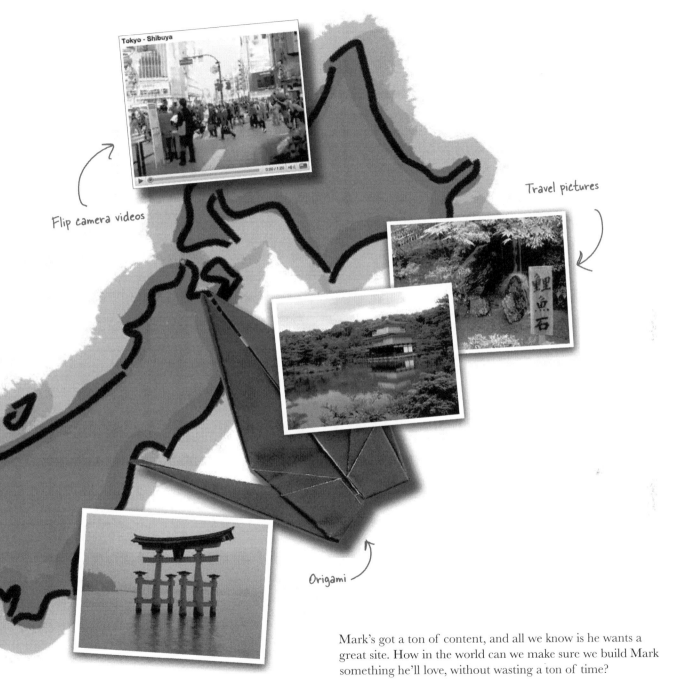

Tokyo - Shibuya

Flip camera videos

Travel pictures

Origami

Mark's got a ton of content, and all we know is he wants a great site. How in the world can we make sure we build Mark something he'll love, without wasting a ton of time?

How would you start building Mark's site?

Think before you code

Pre-production is all about getting things right *before* you dive into writing XHTML and CSS. Its all about getting your site's design right on paper. That way, when you get to the point where you go to code, you know *exactly* what you are building. For Mark's site, we can get our ideas down, before we spend a ton of time fitting text and pictures into a layout scheme Mark might totally hate.

Pre-production is also about letting your user approve what you're doing—on the front-end, when you can still make changes easily. There's nothing worse than investing days or even weeks into a design and *then* finding out the client hated it.

Start with a <u>visual</u> <u>metaphor</u>

One sure way to get your site looking right is to figure out what the site is about. In other words, what is the site's theme, and how can you express that visually? A **visual metaphor** takes advantage of familiar visual elements (likes images, interface elements, icons, colors, or fonts) and reinforce the site's theme.

Suppose you're building a job posting site. The postings could be made to look like an actual bulletin board using a good visual metaphor:

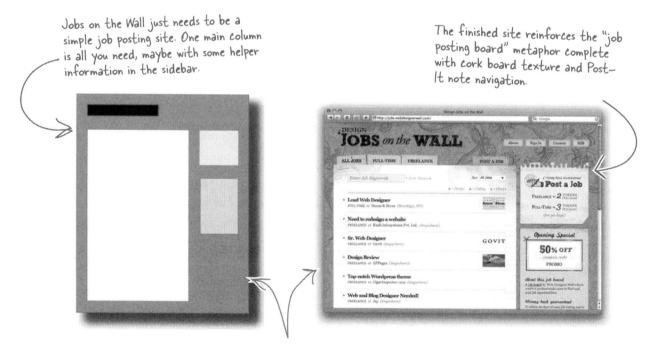

Jobs on the Wall just needs to be a simple job posting site. One main column is all you need, maybe with some helper information in the sidebar.

The finished site reinforces the "job posting board" metaphor complete with cork board texture and Post-It note navigation.

A clear visual metaphor helps reinforce your site's <u>theme</u>

Suppose you're creating a children's online community site geared for kids ages 7 to 10. Visually, you'd want to use bright and bold primary colors with cartoony interface elements and fonts. These design elements reinforce the subject matter of the site: kid oriented, fun, etc. The look of the site actually tells you what the site's about.

A visual metaphor can range from subtle (using colors that give the user an abstract feeling that the designer wants to associate with the site's theme) to direct (using graphics that tie right into the site's name or identity–like using graphics of rocket ships for a site called Rocket Ship Designs).

Bright bold colors and an arctic theme help set the visual metaphor for this site.

Cartoon penguins and comic-book style typography are definitely geared toward a younger audience.

Visual metaphors, themes, what's the difference? And I thought you said I should be designing on paper, anyway?

A <u>theme</u> represents your site's content

The word **theme** is used to refer to all kinds of different things in the world of web design—which can be kind of confusing. In this case, a theme is your site's purpose and content. So, the theme of amazon.com is an online merchant that focuses mostly on books. The visual metaphor uses design elements (color, graphics, typography, etc.) that reinforce the site's theme.

Here are a few more good examples of theme and visual metaphor working well together:

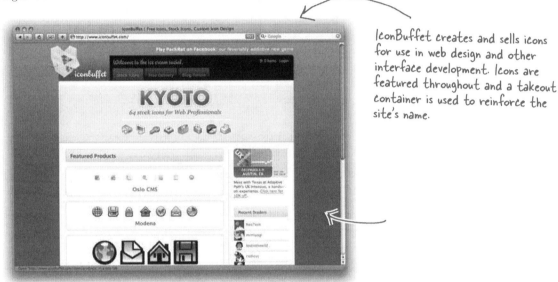

IconBuffet creates and sells icons for use in web design and other interface development. Icons are featured throughout and a takeout container is used to reinforce the site's name.

Silverback is an application for performing user testing on websites. Because a Silverback is also a type of animal, the jungle and gorilla theme is used throughout.

Unlike IconBuffet, Silverback's visual metaphor is more apparent. They make the page look like a gorilla's surroundings, complete with jungle color scheme, leaves at the top of the page and an amazing logo/icon of a gorilla with a clipboard. Hence, "Guerilla Usability Testing."

Sharpen your pencil

Take a look at the screenshots below. Write down the site's theme and circle (**yes, draw in the book**) some of the design elements that are used in the site's visual metaphor. Remember, a site's theme is its content/purpose, while the visual metaphors are the design elements that are used to reinforce the theme.

....

....

....

....

....

....

....

....

....

....

Sharpen your pencil
Solution

Your job was to write down the site's theme and circle some of the design elements that are used in the site's visual metaphor. What did you think the theme of each site was? Here's what we wrote down.

Bite marks used throughout the page remind you that this is a site about food.

Serious Eats is a food website and blog. The logo and bite marks on the navigation tabs help reinforce the food theme throughout the page.

The colors are bright and "appetizing." Green, orange, red, peach—colors you'd want to "eat."

The Morning News is a news-based web magazine. Its multi-column, newspaper-style layout and simple design reinforce the news theme.

A multi-column layout similar to that of a news paper. Also, the columns are staggered, with some spanning the width of two, others just one.

Generous use of whitespace and a grid-based layout help reinforce the newspaper theme.

Brainstorming: The path to a visual metaphor

Let's get back to Mark's site... we need to figure out the theme, and come up with a good visual metaphor. Not only that, but we want to figure this out without thinking too much about how many columns his site will need, or what sort of navigation Mark might like.

Mark may be your buddy, but when you're designing his site, he's your client... and the boss!

Developing a visual metaphor is really all about brainstorming–spending some time really thinking about your client's content, audience, and what visual elements they want to see on the page. And remember one thing: **don't discredit any ideas or concepts you come up with.** Just write them all down... you can refine things later..

The brainstorm list can include design ideas, content considerations, site sections and even color and imagery.

Write down everything that comes to your mind. Don't judge an idea until the end.

Map of Japan
Food: Sushi, sashimi, fish, Japanese pancakes
Hiroshima
The Golden Palace
Japanese flag
Travel journal/blog
Photo slideshow
Food page

⚛BRAIN POWER

Do a quick brainstorm for Mark's site and write down any design, content or visual element ideas you come up with. Remember, write down everything–you can filter out bad ideas later.

Develop a theme and visual metaphor for Mark

Coming up with a theme and a visual metaphor can be tricky. Once you know what content you have to work with and have a few brainstorming sessions under your belt, it's time to start thinking about the best way to convey and display that content to your client's users. Color, layout, and element placement are all important factors when deciding the best way to reinforce a site's theme.

So once you're clear on a theme, here's what you need to do:

1 **Choose some color palettes**

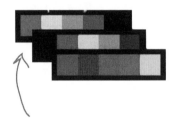

Make layout decisions based on content. The more columns you have, the more space you have to fill. Also remember that whitespace is important. You don't have to fill every available pixel.

2 **Design layouts based on content**

The use of imagery, iconography, and text can help reinforce the site's theme by making the site "look like the content."

This is where your brainstorming will help the most. Use your list of ideas to come up with display elements that help emphasize your site's main themes..

3 **Use visual elements to reinforce the theme**

A visual metaphor uses common visual elements (colors, fonts, icons, etc) to help reinforce a site's theme.

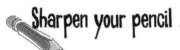

Sharpen your pencil

Write down two possible central themes for Mark's site. Then come up with several design elements (remember, these can be fonts, colors, logos, icons, interface elements, etc.) that will contribute to a cool visual metaphor for Mark's site and reinforce his site's theme.

Here's where time with a paper and pencil can pay off big-time when you get ready to dig into XHTML and CSS.

❶ Central Themes

....

❷ Interface Elements

....

....

....

Sharpen your pencil
Solution

Write down two possible central themes for Mark's site. Then come up with several design elements (remember, these can be fonts, colors, logos, icons, interface elements, etc.) that will contribute to a cool visual metaphor for Mark's site and reinforce his site's theme. Here's what we wrote down...

It's ok if you came up with something different. Just make sure your ideas are in the right ballpark for a site on Japanese culture.

1 **Central Themes**

Japan travel diary .... A traveler's guide to Japan ....

Let's emphasize the trip Mark took, and what Japan was really like. This could also turn out to be a great resource for others planning a trip or traveling to Japan.

2 **Interface Elements**

Header with large image .... Map of Japan ....

Mark took great pictures. We need to show them off!

Japan's geography is very unique. That's a place where we can use visuals a lot.

One main navigation .... Single sidebar ....

Simplicity is key, and Mark doesn't have tons of trips to record... just the one.

Again, simplicity. We really don't have enough content to fill multiple sidebars.

Your page elements shape your visual metaphor

Once you have a general site theme and have started to think about what you want on your site, you need to consider where all your client's content is going to go. How you lay out your site affects your overall visual metaphor a lot... it dictates what can and can't appear on a given page. For example, if you only have a single column, it may be difficult to make your site "feel" like a newspaper or magazine. But add a few more columns and you can make that page mimic the grid-like, multi-column layouts of your typical daily paper.

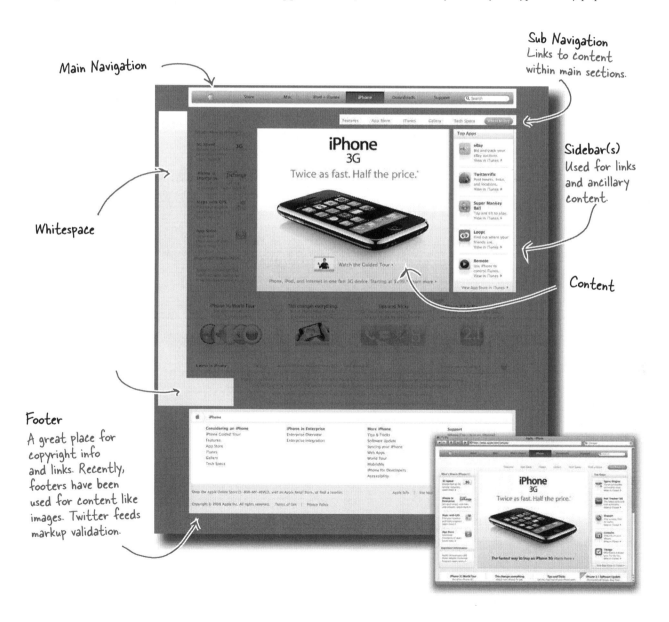

Main Navigation

Sub Navigation
Links to content within main sections.

Sidebar(s)
Used for links and ancillary content.

Whitespace

Content

Footer
A great place for copyright info and links. Recently, footers have been used for content like images. Twitter feeds markup validation.

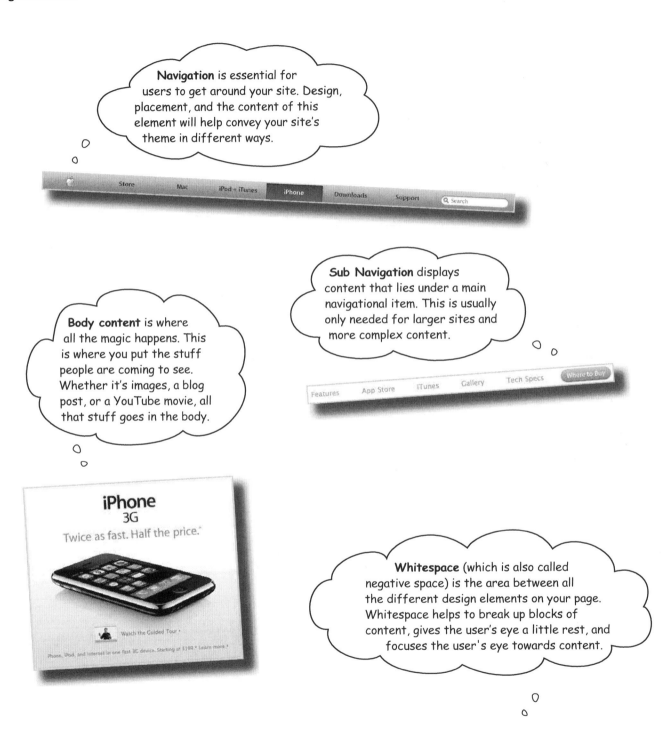

Navigation is essential for users to get around your site. Design, placement, and the content of this element will help convey your site's theme in different ways.

Sub Navigation displays content that lies under a main navigational item. This is usually only needed for larger sites and more complex content.

Body content is where all the magic happens. This is where you put the stuff people are coming to see. Whether it's images, a blog post, or a YouTube movie, all that stuff goes in the body.

Whitespace (which is also called negative space) is the area between all the different design elements on your page. Whitespace helps to break up blocks of content, gives the user's eye a little rest, and focuses the user's eye towards content.

The **footer** portion of your layout can hold anything from copyright information to duplicate navigation links. Users will often look to this section for links or content that can't be located anywhere else on the site.

Sidebars can hold everything from link lists to extra body content. They can also be useful for ancillary navigation and archive links for blogs.

there are no Dumb Questions

Q: Do I need to use all of these elements for every site?

A: Nope, these are just examples of the general page elements you might end up using. Remember, each website is different. In all cases, your client's content (and their theme) will determine what page elements you end up using in your final layout. In fact, if you try to use all of these page elements on every site, you're going to end up with a design that doesn't make any sense to you (or to your users).

Q: Does every site need a theme and visual metaphor?

A: Yes and no. Not every site needs a gorilla-themed metaphor or a snazzy newspaper layout to reinforce its content. But in most circumstances, your site is going to have some sort of theme, even if it is only expressed through the content and writing on the site. Remember, content is a design element and can be used just like whitespace and sidebars.

Q: What if I don't start with any content? Or I want to just start a blog or something really simple?

A: Even if you don't have any content (images, articles, videos, etc.) initially, you still need to make a conscious decision about the overall theme of the site. If you're starting a blog, what kind of topics are you going to write about? If it's more of a journal, well then there's your theme. All websites have a theme, even if it's just about you.

Exercise

To finalize the visual metaphor for Mark's site, we need to look at some different color and layout combinations and see how they will work with our content. Check out the following layout and color mockups and write down your thoughts on how well each of them represent Mark's content. *Remember to think about the themes and visual elements you identified in the previous exercise.*

Here are a few pictures and items Mark brought back from Japan.

....
....
....
....
....
....

Single-column layout with bright pastel colors.

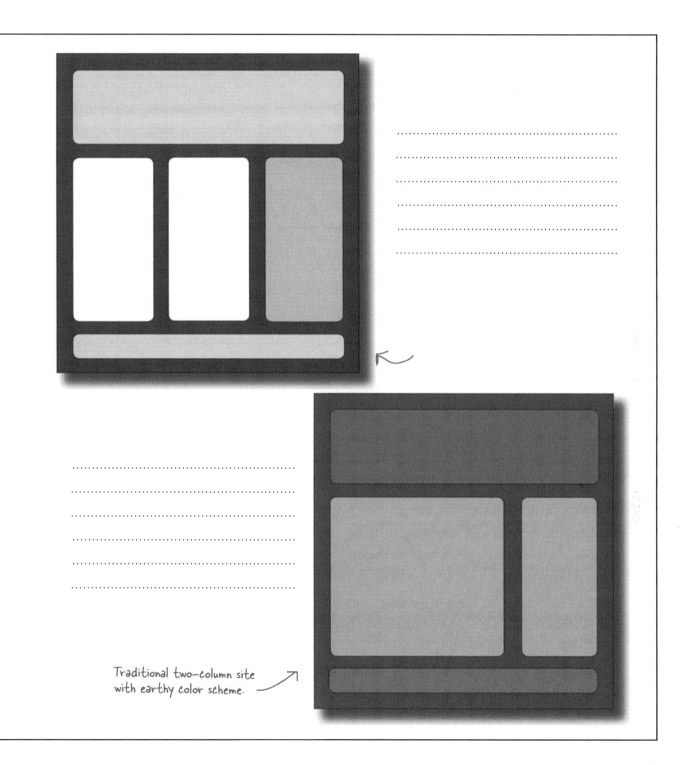

Traditional two-column site with earthy color scheme.

Exercise Solution

To finalize the visual metaphor for Mark's site, we need to look at some different color and layout combinations and see how they will work with our content. Check out the following layout and color mockups and write down your thoughts on how well each of them represent Mark's content. *Remember to think about the themes and visual elements you identified in the previous exercise.*

These colors don't really seem to fit the theme of a Japanese travel site. The light pastels just don't work.

Although single-column sites are simple, this isn't enough space to highlight all the content that Mark has brought back from his trip.

The two-column layout should give us enough room, but this color pattern still isn't working.

The earth tones are nice, but a little dark for the theme. Japan is an island, so shouldn't we see some blue in there?

A large map of Japan would look really good in the header. When a visitor comes to the site, there would be no doubt as to the theme and content of the page.

The blue works well with the theme. The other colors are more neutral and will allow us to be creative when placing visual elements.

This layout/color combination gives us all the room we need to display Mark's content. It uses a simple color palette that emphasizes blue; it's perfect since Japan is an island nation.

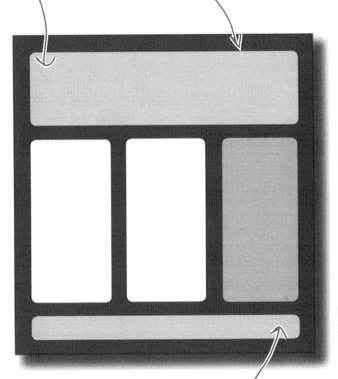

Three columns should work well for Mark. Not only is this an interesting look, it will allow him to present lots of information to his users.

Build a quick XHTML mock-up for Mark

Just because you're focusing on pencil and paper doesn't mean you have to abandon XHTML altogether. Now that we've got some well-thought out ideas, let's build a very simple mockup of Mark's site in XHTML with some simple CSS to add color and formatting.

Fire up your favorite text or HTML editor and create a new file:

XHTML Strict DOCTYPE

```
<!DOCTYPE html PUBLIC "-//W3C//DTD XHTML 1.0 Strict//EN"
        "http://www.w3.org/TR/xhtml1/DTD/xhtml1-strict.dtd">
<html xmlns="http://www.w3.org/1999/xhtml" xml:lang="en" lang="en">
<head>
  <title>Mark in Japan</title>
  <meta http-equiv="Content-Type" content="text/html; charset=utf-8" />
  <link rel="stylesheet" href="screen.css" type="text/css" media="screen" />
</head>
<body>
<div id="wrap">
  <div id="header">
    <h1>Mark in Japan</h1>
  </div>
  <div id="content-left">
    <p>Lorem ipsum dolor sit amet, consectetuer adipiscing elit. Pellentesque quis
        nisl eget est viverra placerat. ...</p>
  </div>
  <div id="content-center">
    <p>Nulla facilisi. Cras ac tellus fringilla tortor iaculis</p>
  </div>
  <div id="sidebar">
    <ul>
      <li>Fusce diam. Pellentesque bibendum. Nulla viverra vestibulum justo.
          Pellentesque pulvinar sapien.</li>
      <li>Cras vestibulum elit id nibh hendrerit eleifend. Pellentesque id ante.
          Sed volutpat blandit mi.</li>
      <li>Morbi at tellus facilisis augue tempor pharetra. Vestibulum porta
          condimentum dui.</li>
      <li>Class aptent taciti sociosqu ad litora torquent per conubia nostra, per
          inceptos himenaeos.</li>
    </ul>
  </div>
  <div id="footer">
    <p>Copyright &copy; Mark in Japan, all rights reserved.</p>
  </div>
</div>
</body>
</html>
```

Link to the CSS file (it just needs to be in the same folder as this file)

Dummy text (we'll fill in Mark's content later)

It's a good idea to throw in a list or two, just to get a look at different styles of content.

And the CSS...

We'll need `screen.css`, too, a simple CSS stylesheet for displaying
Mark's site:

```
/* screen.css */
body {
        margin: 0;
        background: #112b63;
        font-family: Georgia, serif;
        line-height: 1.2em;
}
h1, p, ul {
        margin: 0;                        All these elements
        padding: 10px;                    share the same rules.
}
ul {
        padding: 10px;
        list-style-type: none;
}
ul li {                                   Remove the bullets from the
        margin: 0 0 10px 0;               unordered list.
        padding: 0;
}
#wrap {                      "margin: 0 auto" centers the whole site in the browser.
        margin: 0 auto;
        padding: 10px 20px 20px 20px;
        width: 880px;
        background: #0b204c;
        border-top: 10px solid #091a3f;
}
#header {
        background: #ead9b8;
        height: 150px;
}
#content-left, #content-center {
        float: left;                      Both column <div>s and
        width: 280px;                     the sidebar use the "float:
        margin: 20px 20px 20px 0;         left" declaration to create a
        background: #fff;                 three-column look.
}
#sidebar {
        float: left;
        width: 280px;
        margin: 20px 0 20px 0;
        background: #ccc;
}
#footer {
        clear: both;                      Make sure the footer displays
        background: #ead9b8;              below the columns.
}
```

The end result when you join the XHTML and CSS from the previous two pages. Still bare-bones and basic, but it will give Mark a good idea of where we are headed.

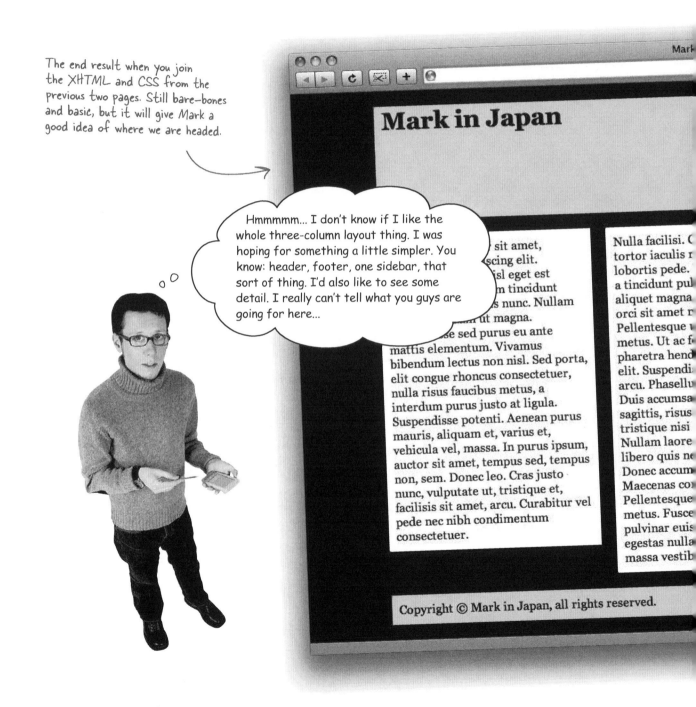

Hmmmmm... I don't know if I like the whole three-column layout thing. I was hoping for something a little simpler. You know: header, footer, one sidebar, that sort of thing. I'd also like to see some detail. I really can't tell what you guys are going for here...

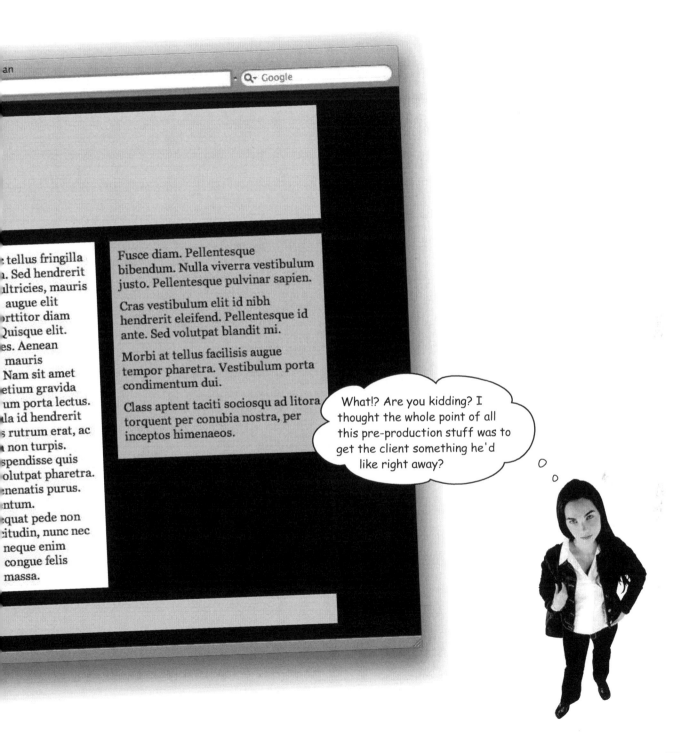

tellus fringilla
. Sed hendrerit
ltricies, mauris
augue elit
rttitor diam
Quisque elit.
es. Aenean
mauris
Nam sit amet
etium gravida
um porta lectus.
la id hendrerit
s rutrum erat, ac
non turpis.
spendisse quis
olutpat pharetra.
enenatis purus.
ntum.
quat pede non
itudin, nunc nec
neque enim
congue felis
massa.

Fusce diam. Pellentesque
bibendum. Nulla viverra vestibulum
justo. Pellentesque pulvinar sapien.

Cras vestibulum elit id nibh
hendrerit eleifend. Pellentesque id
ante. Sed volutpat blandit mi.

Morbi at tellus facilisis augue
tempor pharetra. Vestibulum porta
condimentum dui.

Class aptent taciti sociosqu ad litora
torquent per conubia nostra, per
inceptos himenaeos.

What!? Are you kidding? I
thought the whole point of all
this pre-production stuff was to
get the client something he'd
like right away?

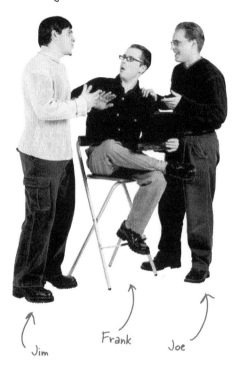

Ok, it's clear that Mark isn't really happy with our design, and we have to come up with something different. So now we have to throw everything away and start over. This sucks...

Jim

Frank

Joe

Joe: Can't we reuse some of the work we've already done?

Jim: What, built another XHTML page using our theme? Then we'll be right back where we started... and Mark still might not like what we come up with.

Frank: But it's like you just said... we still have a theme that should work. And I don't even think our visual metaphor has to be totally scrapped, right? We just need to show Mark some different variations.

Joe: What about Photoshop? We could build the sites there and show him PDF versions of the designs. If he likes them, we already have a leg up on the visuals and imagery needed for the final sites.

Jim: By the time we finish a handful of comps in Photoshop, we could have done them in XHTML and CSS, too. That's still a ton of work. And what if Mark doesn't like those, either?

Frank: What if we just draw some ideas out on paper? We can sketch our site ideas, add a little color, and send them to Mark to get his approval. If he doesn't like them, we can draw some more. That shouldn't take any time at all.

Jim: Hmmm... and because they're on paper, Mark could draw on them too, giving us a better idea of what he's looking for when he doesn't like something.

Joe: You know, this could work. So we can reuse our theme, but deliver two or three different designs on paper and give Mark some nice choices. I like that...

Jim: The drawings don't have to be really detailed, either, right? They just have to give Mark an idea of what his finished site is going to look like.

Use <u>storyboards</u> to develop ideas and save time without code

One of the most important things in pre-production is the **storyboard** (sometimes called **concept art**). Storyboards are used to visualize your design in its entirety. They give you a chance to see how colors interact with one another, how interface elements play off one another, how your navigational system looks, how your visual metaphor plays out, and whether content is represented in the best way possible... without getting into code.

In fact, storyboards are like another level of brainstorming. You already did some brainstorming on the theme... now it's time to brainstorm your visual metaphor and design element ideas.

Well, maybe getting into XHTML so early wasn't such a good idea after all... time to get back out the pencil and paper.

Don't be afraid to write on your boards. Marking them up is one of the advantages of testing designs on paper.

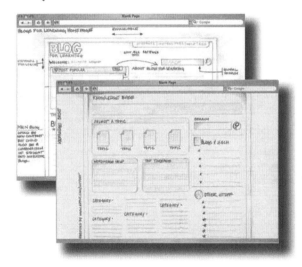

A basic hand-drawn storyboard can turn into a pretty detailed website.

Try creating your storyboards in a photocopy of an empty browser window. This is a great way to give your client a "web" context for your ideas.

> Okay, even if we used storyboards, Mark still wouldn't have liked our design. So how can we make sure he likes the next version we come up with?

Don't design for yourself!

Remember, when you're designing for a client, it isn't about you—it's about the **client's** needs. And taking the client's needs into account obviously starts as early as storyboarding. Getting your client (that's Mark, remember?) involved in your design process could be as simple as sitting down for a meeting, having them fill out a design survey, or sending them early storyboard designs throughout the pre-production process. Not only will this allow you to build designs that your clients really like, they will be appreciate being involved in the process.

We came up with things that *we* liked about Mark's content, but maybe we should have asked *Mark* what he wanted out of his website...

Somewhere I'd like to see a map of Japan. The geography is so cool, and I think it needs to be on the site somewhere.

I want to see as much of my content as possible in the final design.

I'd really like a simple, two-column layout, like a lot of these blogs that you see.

I have lots of images. I think one would look good as the main header image.

⚛ BRAIN POWER

What did we do wrong? Based on Mark's thoughts above, how would you change the ideas we came up with on page 54? What would you keep the same?

Let's create a storyboard for Mark

Let's build Mark a different version of his site, on paper. We know a lot more about what he wants, this time, too... a logo, two columns, and lots of space for content.

So get out some paper. Here's what you need to do:

❶ Find some paper and make a grid

Grab a piece of paper (8.5 x 11 is perfectly fine) and sketch out or fold the paper to create a grid. You might even want to use a piece of graph paper, which has the grid built right in. A nice grid provides a way to line up elements when you are creating your storyboard. Grids also provide a foundation that allow you to lay out your site so that things line up, appear ordered and well-organized, and make sense to users' eyes.

We'll talk a lot more about grids in Chapter 4.

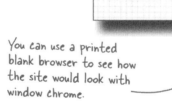

You can use a printed blank browser to see how the site would look with window chrome.

❷ Sketch out your design

Here's where you get let out your inner design geek. Layout your site, and sketch logos, images, and anything else that comes to mind. **All of the site's text can be replaced by lines or a box with the words "text appears here." The point of the storyboard is not to see the actual content–it's to play with and finalize the layout.**

Focus on the major elements, not slogans or text links. Just give your client a <u>basic</u> <u>idea</u> of their site.

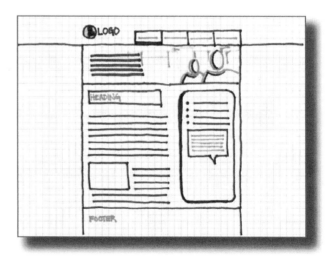

❸ Add color and finalize your storyboard

It's pretty important that you add color to your storyboards—color changes everything. So break out your pencil crayons and add color to your storyboard. Even though your favorite shade of crayola blue might not be web safe, your colors should be close enough to see how they play off of one another when your idea goes digital. When you are finished with the colors, fill in any missing details– and Voila! One supremely awesome storyboard!

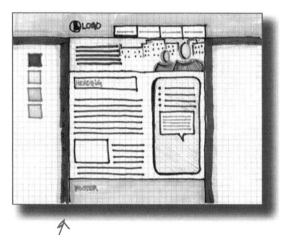
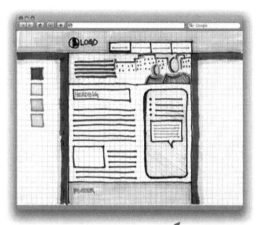

Here is what the storyboard looks like with browser chrome.

This is the point in the process where you need to show the client your work. Give them two, maybe three, options and tell them to give you as much feedback as possible (even drawing on them if need be).

Exercise

Sketch out two storyboards for Mark. Make sure that each meets his needs, but are different enough to give him a choice.

This is great! I like the simple layout, and the map of Japan in the header is perfect. Can't wait to see the finished design.

We put this storyboard in a browser, so Mark could get an idea of how the finished site would look on screen.

Here's another design we did, but Mark didn't like this one. Still, it only took about an hour to put together two full-color storyboards.

there are no Dumb Questions

Q: Can I use Photoshop or another image editing program to do my storyboards?

A: You can create your storyboards any way you want. The whole idea is to mock-up design ideas as quickly as possible, though. Photoshop will inevitably give you more control and detail, but might take you longer. However, having digital versions of your designs, whether you create them in a program or scan your sketches into the computer, will allow you to quickly email ideas to your client for review. In the end, do what you're most comfortable and efficient with.

Q: Why can't I add text to my storyboards?

A: Text (content) really isn't that important during the storyboarding stage. Your main focus should be on large layout elements and possibly color schemes. Your text will come later, after you design your navigation and information architecture. For now, just put dummy text–sometimes called Lorem Ipsum text–or thick lines that represent text.

Q: What is the best way to add color?

A: If you're hand-drawing your boards, colored pencils work the best. They are cleaner and more detailed than markers and won't bleed through your paper. If Photoshop is more your style, then the sky is the limit.

Either way, the point is to keep things simple, and represent how the site will look when it's online. We'll talk a lot more about color in Chapter 5, so don't get too hung up on color right now. Just do your best, and see what your client responds to.

Your Web Design Toolbox

You should have several storyboards in place and a nice array of design techniques: themes, visual metaphors, and storyboarding. Next up: going digital with an approved storyboard.

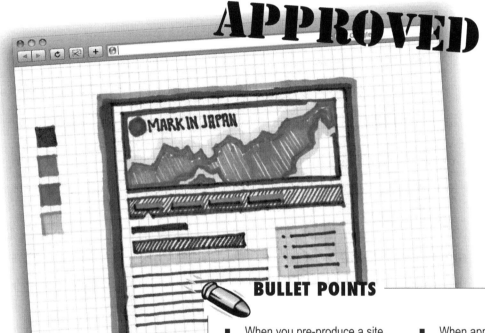

BULLET POINTS

- When you pre-produce a site, you are able to try out design ideas on paper–thereby avoiding potential mistakes in coding which could cost time, effort, and possibly money.

- A visual metaphor leverages visual elements (images, icons, colors, or fonts) in order to unconsciously reinforce the site's subject matter.

- When applying a visual metaphor to your site, be subtle and don't overdo it.

- Storyboards are hand drawn concept art storyboards that are used to visualize your design as a complete entity.

3 organizing your site

"So you take a left at the green water tower..."

Ted, honey, you don't have any idea how to get to Margie's loft, do you?

Look, how hard can it be? There are signs everywhere, and I know exactly what I'm looking for... *I think...*

A little shaky on your site navigation?

When it comes to the Web, **users are impatient**. They don't want to waste lots of time looking for the right button or wading through three levels of your JavaScript pull-down menus. That's why you've got to spend a lot of time getting your site's organization right... *before* you get into construction and design. Last chapter, you came up with a great theme and look for your site. In this chapter, you'll really amp things up with a **clear organization**. By the time you're done, you'll have a site that *tells your users where to go* and keeps them from ever getting lost again.

Mark really likes the simplicity of this storyboard we built for him in the last chapter.

Fit your content into your layout

On his voyages throughout Japan, Mark collected a lot of material. He took pictures, kept a daily journal, collected items (maps, travel booklets, trinkets, etc.), and even managed to take some video. The big question is, ***how should all of this content be organized into his new design?***

How do these bits of content fit into the design layout we did for Mark?

Organize your site's information

A website is all about **communicating information**. No matter how good your design is or how cutting edge your layout is, if your site doesn't speak to your audience, it won't be nearly as successful as a site that says something, and says that something clearly.

A huge part of how well your website communicates its content has to do with how its information is organized. If a site's content isn't organized well, all sorts of bad things can happen–like confused users leaving your site for someone else's. Organizing your site's information well (and logically) is the difference between good and bad navigation– which means the difference between your users finding what they want quickly and easily and your users being really confused.

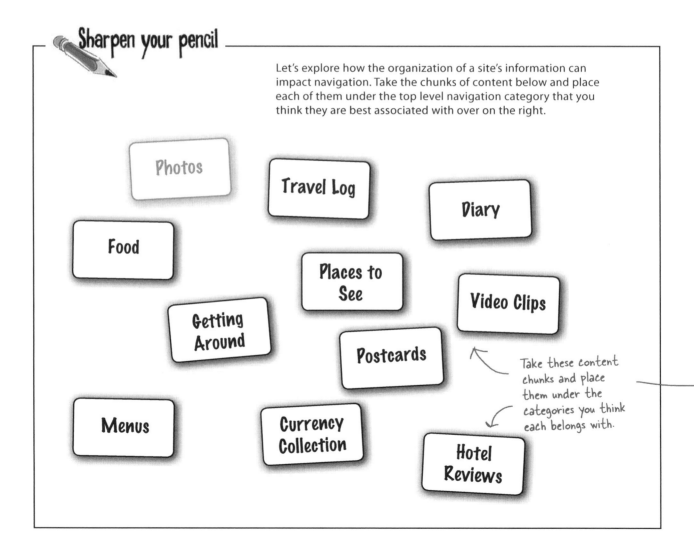

Sharpen your pencil

Let's explore how the organization of a site's information can impact navigation. Take the chunks of content below and place each of them under the top level navigation category that you think they are best associated with over on the right.

Photos

Travel Log

Diary

Food

Places to See

Video Clips

Getting Around

Postcards

Take these content chunks and place them under the categories you think each belongs with.

Menus

Currency Collection

Hotel Reviews

Sharpen your pencil

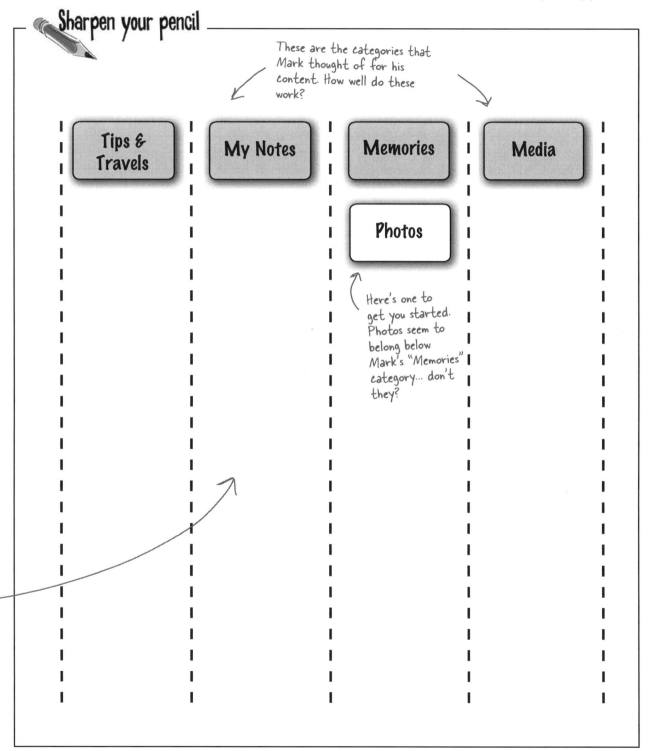

These are the categories that Mark thought of for his content. How well do these work?

Tips & Travels

My Notes

Memories

Media

Photos

Here's one to get you started. Photos seem to belong below Mark's "Memories" category... don't they?

Sharpen your pencil
Solution

So you needed to take the chunks of content and associate them with the most appropriate top level navigation category. Here's what we came up with... what does your solution look like?

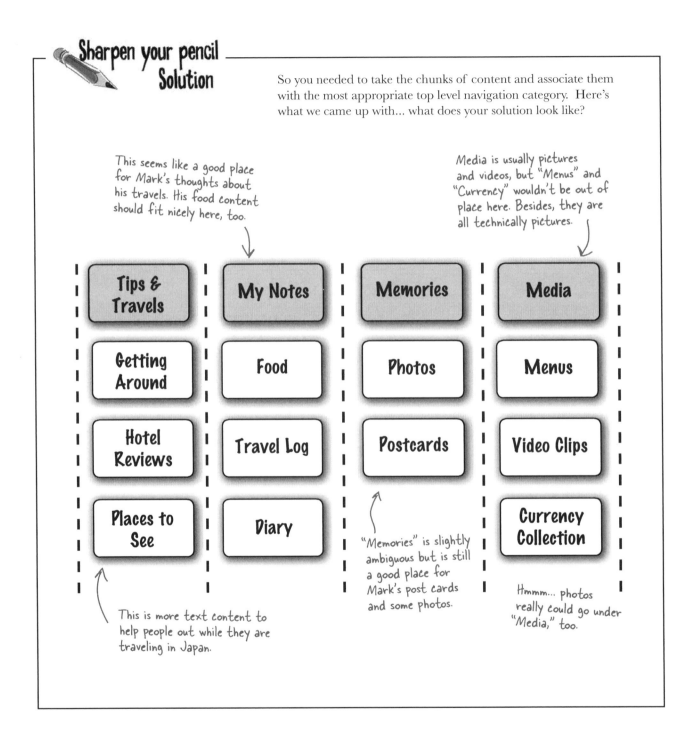

This seems like a good place for Mark's thoughts about his travels. His food content should fit nicely here, too.

Media is usually pictures and videos, but "Menus" and "Currency" wouldn't be out of place here. Besides, they are all technically pictures.

Tips & Travels

My Notes

Memories

Media

Getting Around

Food

Photos

Menus

Hotel Reviews

Travel Log

Postcards

Video Clips

Places to See

Diary

Currency Collection

This is more text content to help people out while they are traveling in Japan.

"Memories" is slightly ambiguous but is still a good place for Mark's post cards and some photos.

Hmmm... photos really could go under "Media," too.

These categories suck. Why aren't menus under Tips & Travels?

Ambiguous navigation confuses users

Thinking about what to name your main navigation categories is important and should not be a last-minute decision or an afterthought. Confusing categories will make it difficult for your users to find the information they're looking for and make your site look unorganized and haphazard. Let's take a closer look at Mark's top level categories:

"My Notes" doesn't really tell me what I am going to find on this page. What are the notes about? Travel? Food?

Tips & Travels	My Notes	Memories	Media

Mixing categories, especially unrelated ones, makes navigation confusing. Just because the category sounds good, doesn't mean users will understand it.

What can the user expect to find in "Memories"? Photos? Video? Shouldn't those be under "Media"?

"Media" isn't a bad choice for a category, but when you put your photos under "Memories," "Media" suddenly gets sort of confusing.

Sharpen your pencil

Go back to your solution on the previous page, and write in better, clearer category titles. You may also need to move around the chunks of content to match your new categories.

Sharpen your pencil
~~Solution~~
Better Solution

Having clear top navigation categories is the key to making information easier to find on your site. Let's see how some new main categories makes our organization more logical.

To avoid confusion, make this one category.

"Memories" is a little vague. Let's use "Souvenirs" instead. It's concrete and understandable.

~~Tips & Travels~~
Travel Tips

~~My Notes~~
Travel Diary

~~Memories~~
Souvenirs

Media

Getting Around	Food	Currency Collection	Photos
Hotel Reviews	Travel Log	Postcards	Video Clips
Places to See	Diary	Menus	Currency Collection
		Photos	Menus

"Travel Tips" is still a little ambiguous, but it will work given the options we have with Mark's content.

"Travel Diary" makes more sense given the types of content that will be found here.

"Photos" belongs under media now.

"Media" is a good category, but "Currency Collection" and "Menus" belong in Souvenirs.

there are no
Dumb Questions

Q: **How long is too long for a category name?**

A: In a perfect world you'd be able to find one word that describes all the content a user would find under a specific category. Unfortunately, that's not always the case. A good rule of thumb is to keep your category names short (one to two words), free of jargon, and as close to describing the content as possible.

Q: **But I know what the link means, isn't that all that matters?**

A: Actually, that doesn't matter at all. You aren't building a site for yourself; you're building a site for your users. Your number one goal is to make information on your site accessible and easy to find by your users. If visitors can't find what they came for, it makes no difference if you can.

Navigation headings should always be short, concise and reflect (as closely as possible) the content that a visitor will find when they click the link.

Q: **How can I tell if a category is ambiguous?**

A: Sometimes spotting category ambiguity is as easy as asking yourself if a user or visitor would understand what your categories mean without any background on the content or topic of your site. In some cases, it's not that easy, and you really have to step back and think about your content as a whole. If you have information on your site that loosely fits the theme or might be slightly extraneous, your category names will reflect that and won't immediately click with the user. This is why thinking hard about your content *before* you choose your categories is so critical.

Q: **What if I have content that fits in two different categories?**

A: Most likely, content fits into different categories because you haven't done a good job defining those categories. Content should only appear in one place on your site. Come up with five or six good categories, each of which is different enough that there's not a lot of overlap. If you're still having trouble, you may want to try a card sort.

Q: **What's a card sort?**

A: Good question. Keep reading...

You know, I'm not sure this new content organization works. It still feels disorganized to me.

Jim

Frank

Joe

Take your time with organizing your site. Navigation is built on your organization... and nobody likes confusing navigation options.

Jim: I actually think the categories are ok. This is what Mark gave us. Shouldn't we just go with it?

Joe: The organization isn't the best, but I think users will be able to find their way around. The headings are still a little confusing, but they're an improvement over the originals, and I don't think they'll get any better. Plus, I want to start coding. We shouldn't be spending so much time on something as trivial as categorization for a travel site.

Frank: But this is the foundation of our navigation!

Joe: What are you talking about?

Frank: Our navigation... isn't most site navigation just putting links and sub-pages to good categories?

Jim: I hadn't thought about it like that.

Joe: Well, what else can we do? We've already done one revision of the categories—or navigation, I guess—and like I said, it's not going to get much better.

Frank: I think we're too far into things to really know what problems we might have.

Jim: You mean, start from scratch?

Joe: Oh brother. We'll just end up right where we are now!

Frank: What if we don't just start over? What if we approach things in a completely different way?

Jim: Like how?

Frank: Let's build up an information architecture, not just a bunch of categories.

Joe: A what?

Frank: Information architecture. Here, let me show you...

Keep your site organized with information architecture (IA)

Information architecture is just a way to organize the content you already have into groups that are meaningful and logical both for you and for your users. Sometimes thinking about navigation, or categories, gets you too far into how a site is going to look.

Information architecture is all about taking a step back and really looking at what sort of content you've got... how does it all fit together? Take a look at this partial IA for a popular paint manufacturer, Krylon:

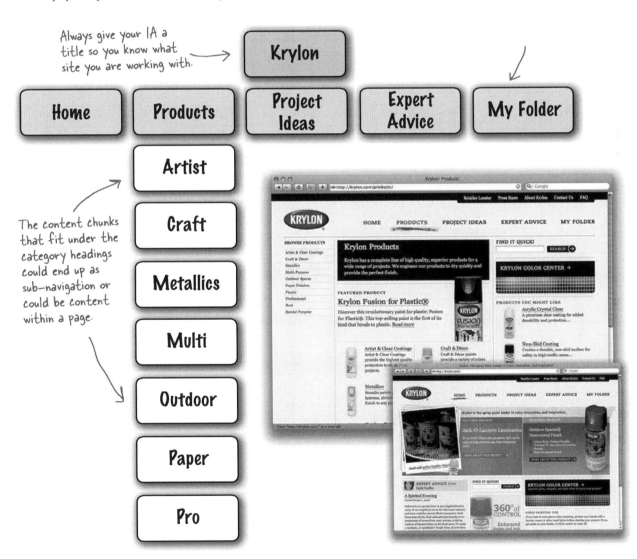

Always give your IA a title so you know what site you are working with.

Krylon

Home   Products   Project Ideas   Expert Advice   My Folder

Artist
Craft
Metallics
Multi
Outdoor
Paper
Pro

The content chunks that fit under the category headings could end up as sub-navigation or could be content within a page.

IA-The card sorting way

How exactly do you organize your site's information? Well, there are lots of ways. One of the best is something called card sorting.

Card sorting is a cheap and easy way to impose a structure on your site's information. It's also a great way to see how other people (maybe even your potential users) organize your site's information. Card sorting also takes a step back from XHTML or even the Web in general and lets you think about organization, not just navigation.

To run a successful card sort, you need:

1   A stack of 3x5 cards

2   A pen and a clear table surface (or the floor)

3   A solid idea of your site's content

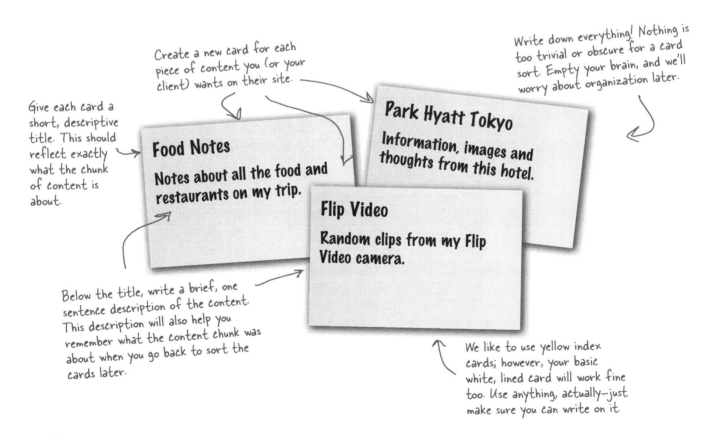

Create a new card for each piece of content you (or your client) wants on their site.

Write down everything! Nothing is too trivial or obscure for a card sort. Empty your brain, and we'll worry about organization later.

Give each card a short, descriptive title. This should reflect exactly what the chunk of content is about.

Food Notes

Notes about all the food and restaurants on my trip.

Park Hyatt Tokyo

Information, images and thoughts from this hotel.

Flip Video

Random clips from my Flip Video camera.

Below the title, write a brief, one sentence description of the content. This description will also help you remember what the content chunk was about when you go back to sort the cards later.

We like to use yellow index cards; however, your basic white, lined card will work fine too. Use anything, actually—just make sure you can write on it.

Card Sorts Exposed

This week's interview:
Getting Organized with Card Sorts?

Head First: Thanks for being with us, Card Sort. Glad to have you. You talk a lot about helping people organize their information, why have you been so successful?

Card Sort: Well, first of all, I think the main reason I help so much is that I just get people to write down all their ideas–good and bad. This way, nothing is left behind, and you don't end up in a situation where you're trying to squeeze content in at the last minute. Second, having the ability to physically move the cards around helps you visualize different scenarios for your content.

Head First: Is moving things around really that important? Seems like it might be a little trivial.

Card Sort: Not at all. It's probably the most valuable attribute of a card sort. It takes no time at all to completely rethink your content and navigation. Plus, you can have other people do the sort, too, and compare their arrangement to yours.

Head First: Wow, I never thought about that! Do you always have someone else do a sort?

Card Sort: Most of the time. It really helps to have a second opinion on things. Usually, having someone else perform the card sort leads to a content layout that you never would have thought of on your own.

Head First: Very cool. If I could, I'd like to go back to the cards. What exactly do people put on your index cards? Is it just random ideas, or is there some type of template you follow?

Card Sort: Well, I wouldn't go as far as saying they're just random ideas. You need to think of my index cards as content chunks–bits of information you want on your site. For example, if someone was building a personal site, their cards might include things like: "jobs," "hobbies," "family pictures," and "vacation." The cards can also be more detailed with terms like: "soccer," "Disney World photos," and "Grandparents."

Head First: So the cards can be specific or more general?

Card Sort: Yeah, because some may end up as category headings and some may end up as individual content chunks. The main goal is to get every conceivable content idea out of your head and onto the cards.

Head First: Ok, this is making more sense now. One last question about your cards. Are the descriptions really necessary?

Card Sort: Not always, but they're good to have– especially if you have lots of cards. You don't want to run into a situation where you're trying to remember what you meant when you wrote down a content chunk. More of the *getting your ideas down on paper* methodology.

Head First: That's great advice. Well, we're just about out of time. Thanks for talking to us today, Card Sort.

Card Sort: No problem, thanks for having me.

Its now time to do a card sort based on Mark's content. On each of the cards, write down a single chunk of information and a (very) brief description. Try to be as precise as possible. After you've filled out a card, set it aside–we'll come back to these cards in a bit. Continue doing this until you've got all of the possible content from Mark's site written down on the cards. You may need more cards than we provided, so use your own index cards if you need to.

Mark learned a lot about Japanese culture and also compiled a list of travel advice for others planning a trip to the country.

Mark bought a rail pass and traveled all over Japan. He visited Tokyo, Hiroshima, Hikone, Kyoto and Yokohama.

Food was on Mark's mind most of his trip. He brought back menus and took lots of notes about what he ate.

Mark took video with his flip camera and lots of pictures everywhere he went.

Content "chunk" title

Don't forget to give a brief description so you know exactly what each content "chunk" is about.

Don't be afraid to make lots of cards. For now, just get all your content down on the cards.

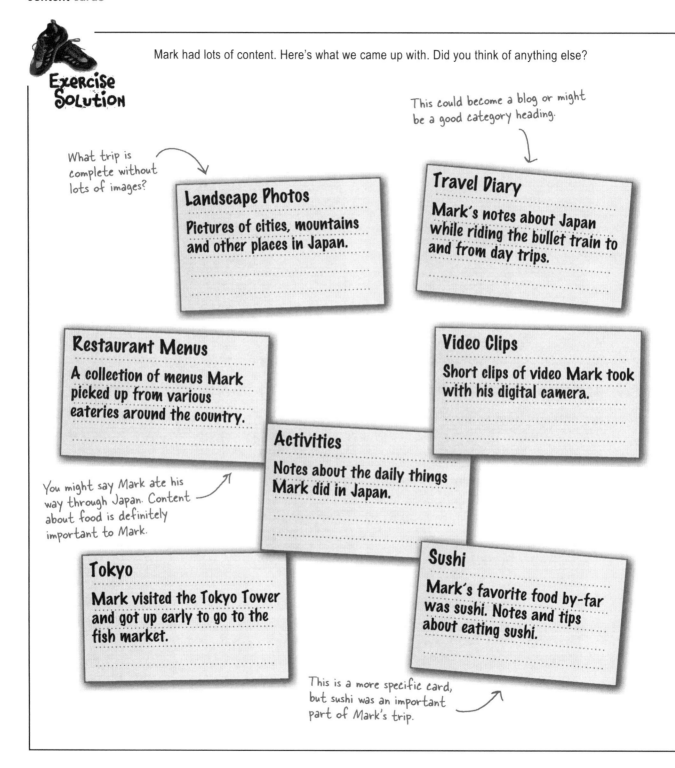

Mark had lots of content. Here's what we came up with. Did you think of anything else?

Exercise Solution

This could become a blog or might be a good category heading.

What trip is complete without lots of images?

Landscape Photos

Pictures of cities, mountains and other places in Japan.

Travel Diary

Mark's notes about Japan while riding the bullet train to and from day trips.

Restaurant Menus

A collection of menus Mark picked up from various eateries around the country.

Video Clips

Short clips of video Mark took with his digital camera.

Activities

Notes about the daily things Mark did in Japan.

You might say Mark ate his way through Japan. Content about food is definitely important to Mark.

Tokyo

Mark visited the Tokyo Tower and got up early to go to the fish market.

Sushi

Mark's favorite food by-far was sushi. Notes and tips about eating sushi.

This is a more specific card, but sushi was an important part of Mark's trip.

Since Mark really liked food, we came up with several food-related chunks. That lets us break things up a lot more.

Food Notes

Notes about all the food and restaurants Mark visited.

Advice and insight about traveling to Japan.

Travel

What it's like to travel to and around Japan. Trains, planes, cabs, etc...

Culture

The difference between American and Japanese culture.

Bars and Nightlife

A look at the bars and nightlife in and around Tokyo and Kyoto.

Learning Japanese

Quick Japanese language lessons for new travelers.

Hiroshima

About the trip to the site of the A-Bomb.

People Photos

Pictures of people and friends that Mark met along the way.

Mark visited some of Japan's most famous cities. We could probably have a card for each major city.

It's okay if your answers are different. We'll be using these cards in the rest of the chapter, but you're welcome to use your own, too.

Sort your cards into related stacks

Once you've finished filling out your cards, you need to sort
them into groups. The cards in each group should obviously be
related–and their grouping should make sense to you. Here's a
little hint: **These groups will eventually become sections
within Mark's website.**

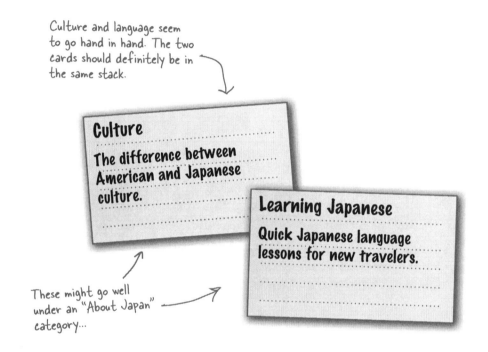

Culture and language seem
to go hand in hand. The two
cards should definitely be in
the same stack.

Culture

The difference between
American and Japanese
culture.

Learning Japanese

Quick Japanese language
lessons for new travelers.

These might go well
under an "About Japan"
category...

Exercise

Group the cards you made on the previous page into logical groups. Don't worry
if you have leftover cards—we'll deal with those in a bit.

Give your stacks names that are <u>short</u> and <u>descriptive</u>

After you've created your groups, it's time to give each group a name. The name has to be short and descriptive. These descriptions may end up becoming part of your main navigation, so keep them focused on the content, but broad enough to contain the content they describe.

Since you've already spent some time digging into Mark's content, try and come up with category headings that are different (and better) than what you came up with earlier in the chapter, back on page 76.

Exercise

Look at the stacks you made in the previous exercise and come up with short, descriptive titles for each stack. You can use an existing card or make a new one for the description. Write your new category names in the spaces below.

....

....

....

....

Take a picture of how you organized your cards. You can reference the picture later and still move your cards around into different arrangements.

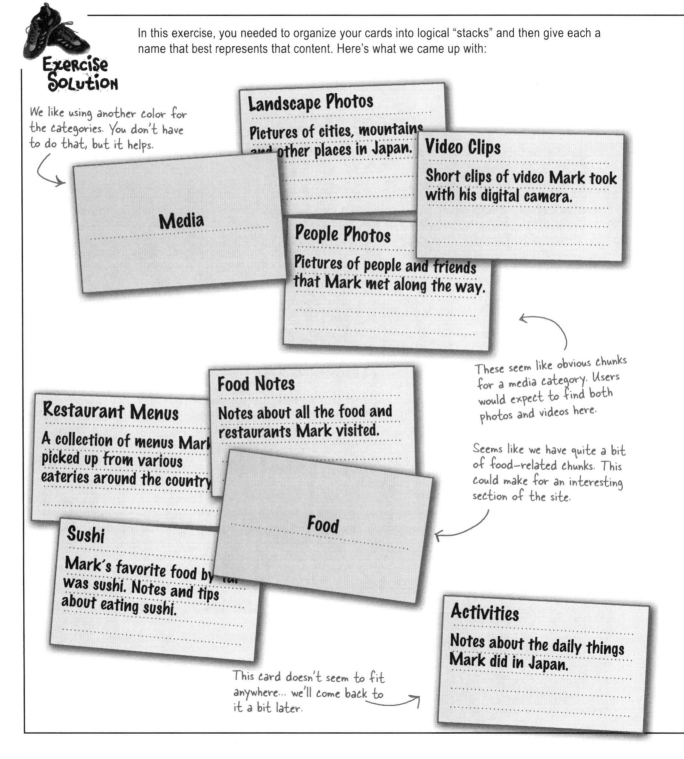

Exercise Solution

In this exercise, you needed to organize your cards into logical "stacks" and then give each a name that best represents that content. Here's what we came up with:

We like using another color for the categories. You don't have to do that, but it helps.

Landscape Photos

Pictures of cities, mountains and other places in Japan.

Video Clips

Short clips of video Mark took with his digital camera.

Media

People Photos

Pictures of people and friends that Mark met along the way.

These seem like obvious chunks for a media category. Users would expect to find both photos and videos here.

Food Notes

Notes about all the food and restaurants Mark visited.

Restaurant Menus

A collection of menus Mark picked up from various eateries around the country.

Seems like we have quite a bit of food-related chunks. This could make for an interesting section of the site.

Food

Sushi

Mark's favorite food by far was sushi. Notes and tips about eating sushi.

Activities

Notes about the daily things Mark did in Japan.

This card doesn't seem to fit anywhere... we'll come back to it a bit later.

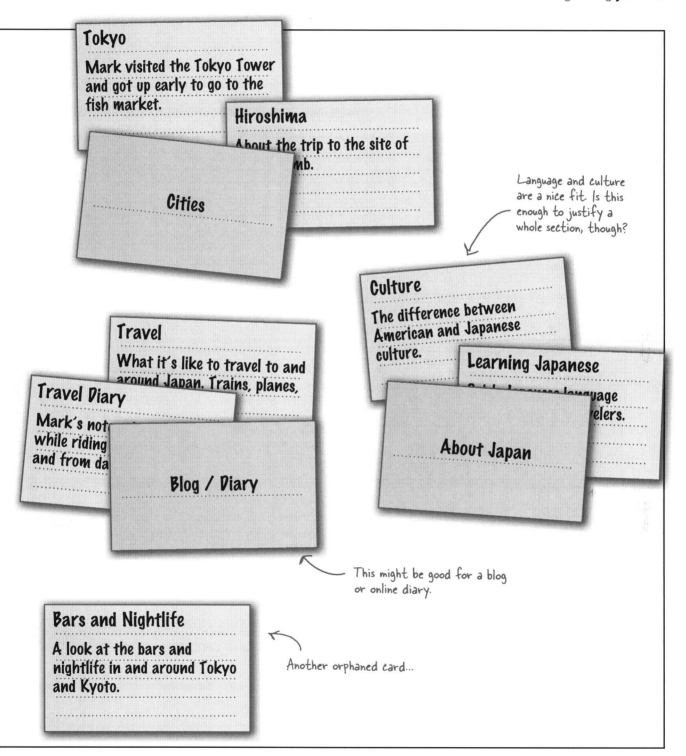

Tokyo

Mark visited the Tokyo Tower and got up early to go to the fish market.

Hiroshima

About the trip to the site of ____ mb.

Cities

Language and culture are a nice fit. Is this enough to justify a whole section, though?

Culture

The difference between American and Japanese culture.

Learning Japanese

_____ language ___elers.

About Japan

Travel

What it's like to travel to and around Japan. Trains, planes,

Travel Diary

Mark's not__ while riding and from da__

Blog / Diary

This might be good for a blog or online diary.

Bars and Nightlife

A look at the bars and nightlife in and around Tokyo and Kyoto.

Another orphaned card...

Hold on a second. I've got a bunch of cards that don't fit into my groups. What am I supposed to do with these?

Orphaned cards force you to ask yourself: "Is this content really necessary?"

In some cases, you'll find that cards don't fit anywhere–these are called **orphaned cards**. You might be wondering whether you've done something wrong, but don't worry. These cards are usually a sign that you are doing something right!

Orphaned cards come in two flavors. You can have orphaned cards that didn't fit into another pile; however, you think that the content is important enough to your site that you create a new group with your single orphaned card. Then there are cards that don't fit into another pile but are so different from the other cards that you couldn't come up with a group if you tried (let's call these the *really* orphaned cards). Including orphaned content that doesn't fit into your site's information architecture *always* results in confusion for your user.

What if, for example, the produce section at your local grocery store had a pile of toasters, a large display of beef jerky, and an entire wall of deodorant? Shoppers would get amazingly confused. We interact with the world around us based on the **predictability** of things. There is no reason whatsoever for deodorant (or toasters and beef jerky) to go in the produce section. The same holds true for the organization of a website's information. If random content appears in a section of the site where we never assumed it would be, we'll be confused–and our experience with the site will be negatively impacted.

So, what do you do with orphaned cards? You've got two choices. First, you could change the content in such a way that it fits into another one of your groups. However, more often than not, that strategy just isn't going to work. The other alternative is simply to recognize the fact that the content doesn't fit into your website and toss it out.

What do you think about these orphaned cards? Important? Not right for Mark's site? Too vague? Too specific?

Activities

Notes about the daily t
Mark did in Japan.

Bars and Nightlife

A look at the bars and nightlife in and around Tokyo and Kyoto.

Hey, why are we doing the sorting anyway? I thought that the whole point of User-Centered Design is that you don't design for yourself, you design for your user.

Friends don't let friends sort alone

Up until now, you've done the card sort all by your lonesome. But doing a card sort by yourself is **not** the (only) way to do things. Why? Well there's one really good reason: You aren't designing for yourself, you're designing for your audience! And if you aren't designing for yourself, why would you do a card sort by yourself?

Ideally, you want to run the exact same card sort with the exact same cards–but have someone else sort the cards. Try to choose someone from your target audience. If for some reason you can't find someone from your target audience, enlist someone else to help. At the very least, they will give you a second opinion on your site's information structure.

Exercise

Ask a friend to sort the cards you created. Give them a very basic introduction to Mark's site (careful, don't try to influence them to choose one particular information structure), and let them organize your cards. Did they do the sort the same way you did? What different decisions did they make? Ask why! The ultimate goal is to come up with an information architecture for Mark's site that will not only meet the needs of the site (and Mark), but those of the user as well. Write at least three things you learned from your friend's card sort below.

....

....

....

Get your camera out again! Now you should have two pictures of two totally different organizations of Mark's content.

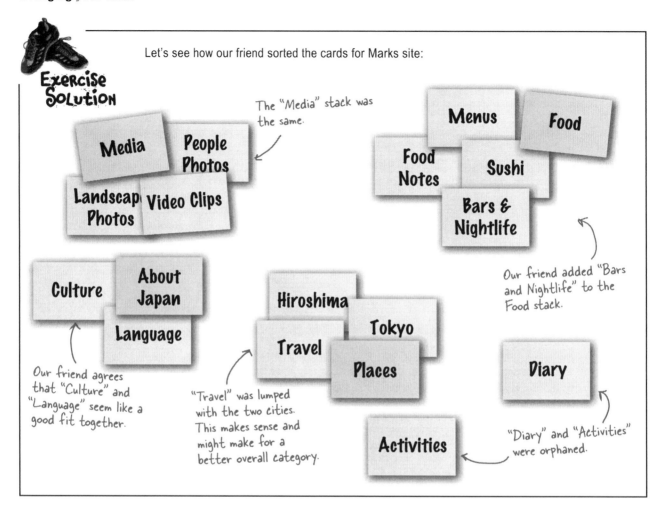

Let's see how our friend sorted the cards for Marks site:

EXERCISE SOLUTION

The "Media" stack was the same.

Media

People Photos

Landscape Photos   Video Clips

Menus

Food

Food Notes

Sushi

Bars & Nightlife

Our friend added "Bars and Nightlife" to the Food stack.

Culture

About Japan

Language

Our friend agrees that "Culture" and "Language" seem like a good fit together.

Hiroshima

Tokyo

Travel

Places

"Travel" was lumped with the two cities. This makes sense and might make for a better overall category.

Diary

Activities

"Diary" and "Activities" were orphaned.

Which card sort is right?

Getting a second opinion on your sorts is important and often results in organization that you may not have initially thought of. But how do you know which one is better or which one deserves more weight? Well, it depends. If five of your friends do the sort and all come up with similar results, you can bet that's probably the best way to organize things.

However, you're the web designer. Sometimes having two or three options and just tweaking your original sort is all you need. Make sure that when you're done, though, you feel good about the organization you've come up with. You (and Mark!) are going to have to live with it for a long time.

Arrange your cards into a site hierarchy

Once you're happy with your card stacks and titles, you need to put some structure in place. Lay your cards out like a site map. Just take a bunch of your leftover 3x5 cards and write the group names that you came up with. Spread those out on the table that you've been using. Then, line up each "content" card below the appropriate "section" card.

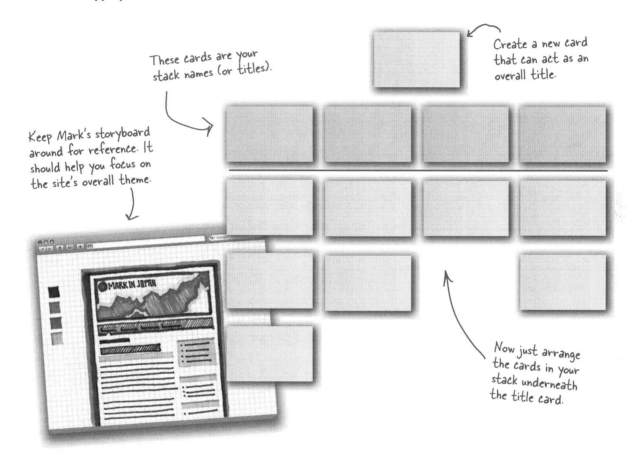

Create a new card that can act as an overall title.

These cards are your stack names (or titles).

Keep Mark's storyboard around for reference. It should help you focus on the site's overall theme.

Now just arrange the cards in your stack underneath the title card.

Exercise

Once you've gone through a few iterations of your sort and had a friend or two try it out, arrange your cards as an IA diagram and **take another picture**.

Exercise Solution

After considering the sorts our friends did and rethinking our original card sort, we came up with a final sort layout like this:

We removed the descriptions so everything could fit on the page...

Mark in Japan

A potential title for Mark's site

Media   **Food**   **Travel Notes**   **Blog**   **About Japan**

Landscape Photos   **Food Notes**   **Tokyo**   **Travel Diary**   **Culture**

People Photos   **Restaurant Menus**   **Hiroshima**   **Language**

Video Clips   **Sushi**

Bars & Nightlife

The photos and videos definitely belong under "Media."

We added "Bars and Nightlife" to the food category because it kept coming up when our friends did the sort.

We kept the cities in their own column but changed the heading to "Travel Notes" to better represent the results of our card sort.

Mark's travel diary will work perfectly as a blog.

All of our friends put culture and language in the same category. These are good chunks for a section about general information about Japan. This is also a place where Mark can add extra content if he wants to.

IA diagrams are just card sorts on paper

An IA diagram is a lot like the "on the table" site map you created (and photographed) in the last exercise, but it's also a lot more. An IA diagram not only shows the organization of your site's content, but it shows the hierarchical relationship between sections and subsections of that content. The good news is, because you already took the time and did a few card sorts, most of your work is done!

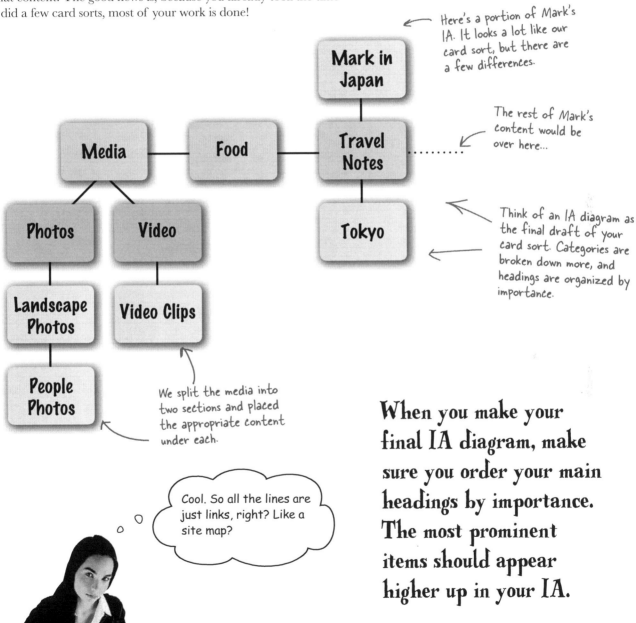

Here's a portion of Mark's IA. It looks a lot like our card sort, but there are a few differences.

The rest of Mark's content would be over here...

Think of an IA diagram as the final draft of your card sort. Categories are broken down more, and headings are organized by importance.

We split the media into two sections and placed the appropriate content under each.

Cool. So all the lines are just links, right? Like a site map?

When you make your final IA diagram, make sure you order your main headings by importance. The most prominent items should appear higher up in your IA.

IA diagrams are <u>NOT</u> just links between pages

IA diagrams are not about links—they're all about the hierarchical relationship between sections and subsections of content. If you were to try to create a diagram that showed links between sections, you would end up with a useless, spaghetti-looking mess that wouldn't give you any kind of information whatsoever about this vital hierarchical relationship between the site's content.

Think about it like this... most sites have links all over the place, cutting across categories and site sections. That would make for a pretty messy IA!

If IA were about links...

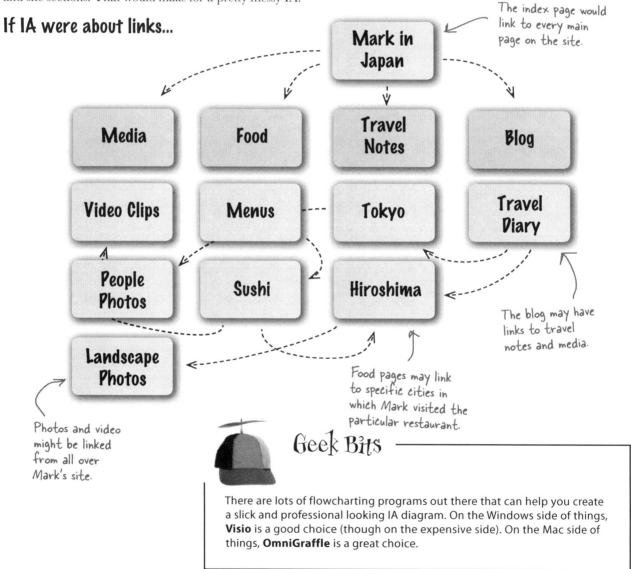

The index page would link to every main page on the site.

The blog may have links to travel notes and media.

Food pages may link to specific cities in which Mark visited the particular restaurant.

Photos and video might be linked from all over Mark's site.

Geek Bits

There are lots of flowcharting programs out there that can help you create a slick and professional looking IA diagram. On the Windows side of things, **Visio** is a good choice (though on the expensive side). On the Mac side of things, **OmniGraffle** is a great choice.

Based on your card sort, build an IA diagram of Mark's site. Remember, you aren't showing links between pages, you're showing the hierarchical relationship between sections and subsections.

Exercise

Add content chunks from your card sort—but be more detailed. Don't be afraid to add extra subcategories to better organize Mark's content.

About Japan

Culture

Don't forget to add a title to your IA diagram.

Sometimes you'll change your card sort a bit during IA. That's okay... it's about a good site organization, not avoiding changes to your original ideas.

EXERCISE
SOLUTION

Your job was to to build an IA diagram based on your card sorts. Here's what we came up with:

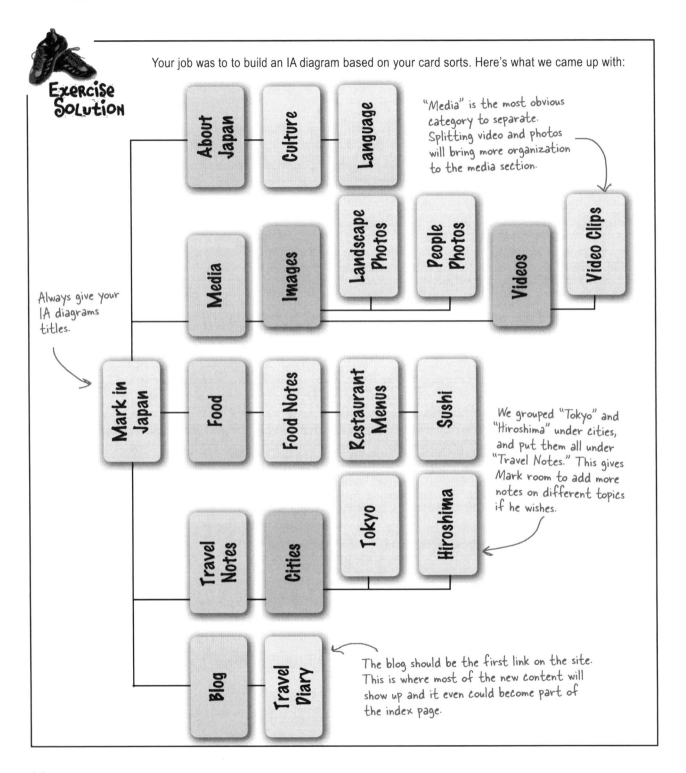

"Media" is the most obvious category to separate. Splitting video and photos will bring more organization to the media section.

Always give your IA diagrams titles.

We grouped "Tokyo" and "Hiroshima" under cities, and put them all under "Travel Notes." This gives Mark room to add more notes on different topics if he wishes.

The blog should be the first link on the site. This is where most of the new content will show up and it even could become part of the index page.

there are no
Dumb Questions

Q: Is all this work really needed just to come up with some navigation categories?

A: Well, it is if you want to do it properly. Some sort of thought needs to go into the design of your content and navigation. Hastily designed IA can have a disastrous effect on the success of a website. Even if you do shortened, "quickie" versions of card sorting and IA diagramming, your outcome is likely to be better than if you did nothing at all.

Q: What if I just want to skip right to the IA and not do a card sort?

A: That's better than nothing, but you will really have no way of sifting through and auditing your content. The reason a card sort is so important is that is helps you get rid of content that is irrelevant and makes you think about how all those content chunks relate to each other. IA diagrams can help with this, but they aren't as thorough as a card sort.

Q: If IA diagrams don't show link relationships, what does?

A: Most of the time, a site map is the best way to show what links are available on a site. The problem with this is that a site map can't really be made until the site is finished. During pre-production, your focus should be on organizing content and not building links. That work will come when you start to build out pages.

Q: Do all websites go through this same process?

A: Actually, most probably don't–and that's why so many sites on the Internet are so difficult to use. In so many cases, IA and content organization are a design afterthought, leading to unusable websites and content that's difficult to find. Skipping pre-production will only lead to frustrated users and dwindling hits.

Q: How does a site's theme relate to information architecture?

A: IA actually directly relates to your site's theme. The content of your site is what drives the overall theme, and the organization of that content is important. If the IA is bad or focus is put on the wrong content, it will not only confuse users, but your theme won't come across either.

Move from pre-production to production

Coming up with an IA diagram and doing all those card sorts may have seemed like a lot of work for a simple navigation. Mark will love you, though, especially when his users are easily navigating his site and finding all his content without any problems.

And now we've got a well-organized IA, a storyboard Mark likes, and a clear idea where we want to take the site. Let's lay down some markup and style!

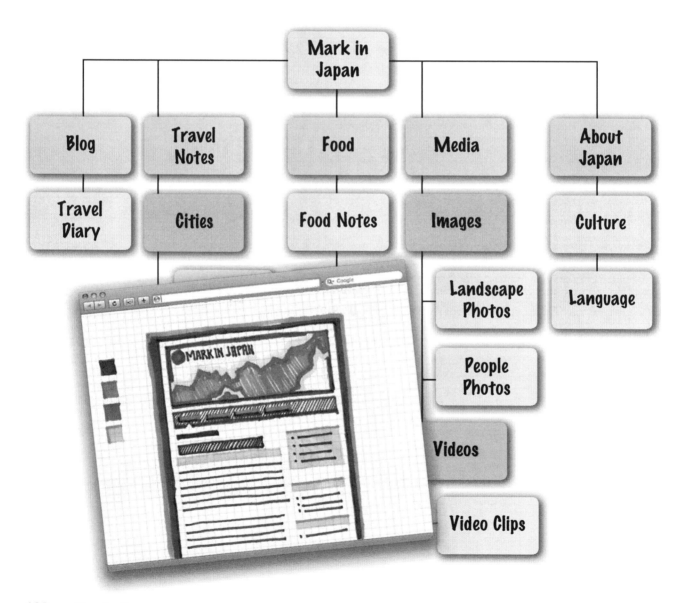

Build Mark's site structure

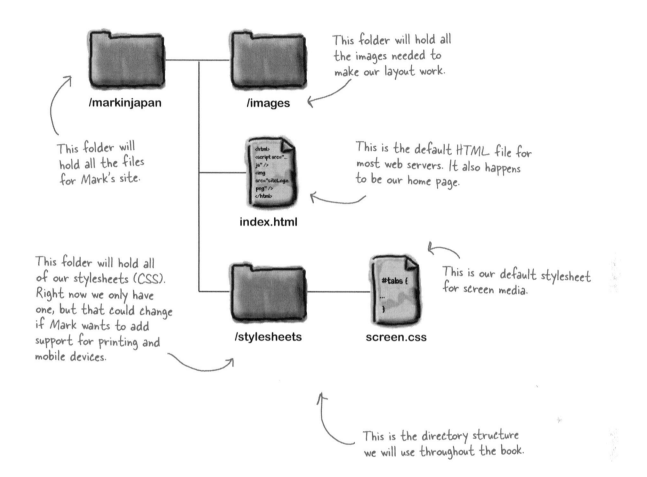

/markinjapan

This folder will hold all the files for Mark's site.

/images

This folder will hold all the images needed to make our layout work.

index.html

This is the default HTML file for most web servers. It also happens to be our home page.

This folder will hold all of our stylesheets (CSS). Right now we only have one, but that could change if Mark wants to add support for printing and mobile devices.

/stylesheets

screen.css

This is our default stylesheet for screen media.

This is the directory structure we will use throughout the book.

Create index.html first...

Using Strict XHTML means you won't be tempted to sneak style tags like <center> and <font> into your markup. You'll have a nice separation of content and style.

```
<!DOCTYPE html PUBLIC "-//W3C//DTD XHTML 1.0 Strict//EN"
        "http://www.w3.org/TR/xhtml1/DTD/xhtml1-strict.dtd">
<html xmlns="http://www.w3.org/1999/xhtml" xml:lang="en" lang="en">
<head>
   <title>Mark in Japan</title>
   <meta http-equiv="Content-Type" content="text/html; charset=utf-8" />
   <link rel="stylesheet" href="stylesheets/screen.css" type="text/css" media="screen" />
</head>
<body>
<div id="wrap">
   <div id="header">
      <h1>Mark in Japan</h1>
   </div>
   <div id="nav">
      <ul>
         <li><a class="active" title="Home" href="#">Home</a></li>
         <li><a title="Travel Notes" href="#">Travel Notes</a></li>
         <li><a title="Food from Japan" href="#">Food</a></li>
         <li><a title="Photos and Videos" href="#">Media</a></li>
         <li><a title="About Japan" href="#">About Japan</a></li>
      </ul>
   </div>
   <div id="content">
      <h2>Blog Header</h2>
      <p>Lorem ipsum dolor sit amet, consectetuer adipiscing elit. Pellentesque quis
         nisl eget est viverra placerat. Nam tincidunt ligula id turpis. Duis nunc.
         Nullam imperdiet quam ut magna.</p>
   </div>
   <div id="sidebar">
      <h3>Sidebar Header</h3>
      <ul>
         <li>Fusce diam. Pellentesque bibendum. Nulla viverra vestibulum justo.
            Pellentesque pulvinar sapien.</li>
         <li>Cras vestibulum elit id nibh hendrerit eleifend. Pellentesque id ante.
            Sed volutpat blandit mi.</li>
      </ul>
   </div>
   <div id="footer">
      <p>Copyright &copy; Mark in Japan, all rights reserved.</p>
   </div>
</div>
</body>
</html>
```

The "wrap" <div> is the container for all our content and will also allow us to center the page in the browser window.

The navigation is just an unordered list using the headers we came up with in pre-production.

For right now, just use dummy text to fill in the content and sidebar <div>'s.

We use another unordered list in the sidebar to help organize our content.

A footer gives us a place for more links and copyright information. Notice this is still within the main "wrap" <div>.

...and then screen.css for style

```
/* screen.css */
body {
        margin: 0;
        padding: 0;
        background: #026dc0 url('../images/bg.gif') repeat-x top;
        font-family: Helvetica, sans-serif;
        line-height: 1.4em;
}
h1, h2, h3, p, ul, li {
        margin: 0;
        padding: 0;
}
p, h2, h3 {
        margin: 0 0 10px 0;
}
ul {
        list-style-type: none;
}
#wrap {
        margin: 0 auto;
        margin-top: 40px;
        margin-bottom: 40px;
        padding: 10px;
        width: 780px;
        background: #fff;
        border: 10px solid #044375;
}
#header {
        background: url('../images/island_header.jpg') no-repeat;
        height: 250px;
}
#header h1 {
        padding: 30px 0 30px 30px;
        color: #fff;
        background: url('../images/dot.png') no-repeat 10px 50%;
        font-weight: normal;
        letter-spacing: -1px;
}
```

This background is just a 1px by 450px image that is repeated on the x-axis of the page. The end result is a nice gradient effect.

You can declare multiple elements in a rule that share common attributes.

The main styling for the "wrap" <div> includes a 10px border and "0 auto" margin that centers the page in the browser.

The background on the header is placed using CSS by moving the text over and setting the red dot as its background image.

Continued on the next page...

screen.css, continued...

```
#nav {
     margin: 10px 0 0 0;
     padding: 10px;
     background: #044375;
     border-top: 5px solid #033761;
}
#nav ul li {
     display: inline;
     margin: 0 10px 0 10px;
}
#nav a {
     color: #fff;
     text-decoration: none;
}
#content {
     margin: 10px 0 0 0;
     padding: 10px;
     float: left;
     width: 505px;
}
#sidebar {
     margin: 10px 0 0 0;
     padding: 10px;
     float: right;
     width: 225px;
}
#sidebar ul {
     margin: 0 0 40px 0;
}
#sidebar h3 {
     padding: 5px;
     background: #eee;
     border-bottom: 2px solid #ddd;
     font-weight: normal;
}
#footer {
     clear: both;
     padding: 10px;
     background: #eee;
     border-bottom: 2px solid #ddd;
}
```

Our navigation is just an unordered list that is displayed in an inline fashion instead of a block style. The "display: inline" changes this attribute.

On links, you must set the color on the elements itself. Links won't take the color from their parent <div>'s or elements.

The content and sidebar are both floated left and right, respectively, with widths that equal about 2/3 for the content and 1/3 for the sidebar.

Make sure you clear the footer so that it displays below both the content and sidebar <div>'s.

Don't worry, all this code can be downloaded from the Head First site.

Actually, you should download the site. We've provided all the images, too, so that your design looks as good as it does on the page. You can also see Mark's site online to compare your version with:

www.headfirstlabs.com/books/hfwd

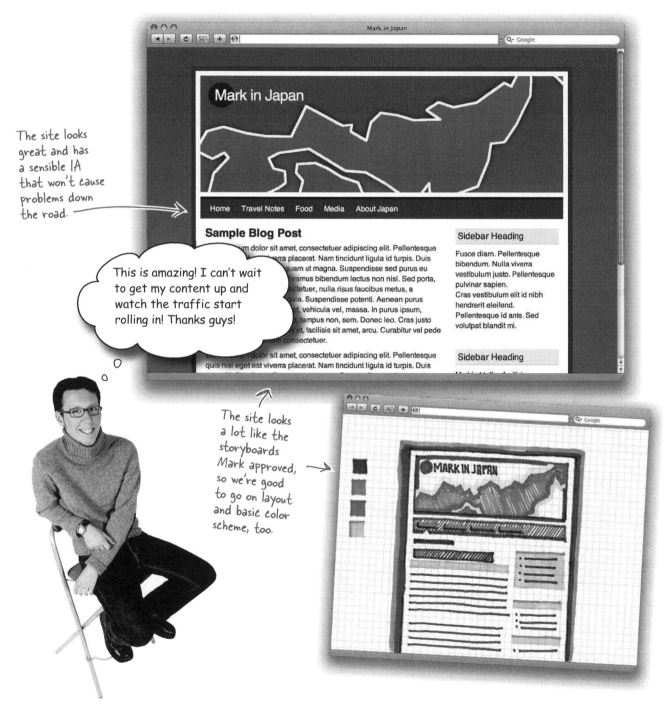

The site looks great and has a sensible IA that won't cause problems down the road.

> Mark in Japan
>
> Home   Travel Notes   Food   Media   About Japan
>
> **Sample Blog Post**
>
> um dolor sit amet, consectetuer adipiscing elit. Pellentesque
> rra placerat. Nam tincidunt ligula id turpis. Duis
> quam ut magna. Suspendisse sed purus eu
> amus bibendum lectus non nisl. Sed porta,
> ctetuer, nulla risus faucibus metus, a
> ula. Suspendisse potenti. Aenean purus
> , vehicula vel, massa. In purus ipsum,
> tempus non, sem. Donec leo. Cras justo
> et, facilisis sit amet, arcu. Curabitur vel pede
> n consectetuer.
>
> n dolor sit amet, consectetuer adipiscing elit. Pellentesque
> quis nisl eget est viverra placerat. Nam tincidunt ligula id turpis. Duis
>
> **Sidebar Heading**
>
> Fusce diam. Pellentesque
> bibendum. Nulla viverra
> vestibulum justo. Pellentesque
> pulvinar sapien.
> Cras vestibulum elit id nibh
> hendrerit eleifend.
> Pellentesque id ante. Sed
> volutpat blandit mi.
>
> **Sidebar Heading**

This is amazing! I can't wait to get my content up and watch the traffic start rolling in! Thanks guys!

The site looks a lot like the storyboards Mark approved, so we're good to go on layout and basic color scheme, too.

> MARK IN JAPAN

Pre-production to production: The complete process

①   **Gather all the your content.**

②   **Brainstorm a theme and visual metaphor ideas.**

Map of Japan
Sushi
Hiroshima
The Golden Palace

③   **Develop a visual metaphor and think about layout.**

④   **Build a storyboard (on paper).**

⑤   **Do a few card sorts and create an IA diagram.**

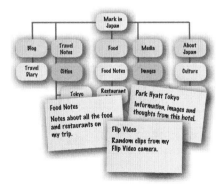

⑥   **Markup your content and style with CSS.**

Your Web Design Toolbox

You've got Chapter 3 under your belt, and now you've added card sorting, IA diagrams and information organization to your tool box. Next up? We'll dive into designing a site for your audience...

BULLET POINTS

- The point of a website is to communicate information–if that information is organized badly, your users will leave and not come back.

- The organization of a site's information has a direct impact on its navigation and usability.

- Card sorting is a cheap and easy technique used to impose an information structure on a site's content.

- Never rely upon your own card sort of a site's information–you aren't designing for yourself, you are designing for the site's audience.

- A card sort often results in orphaned cards–which are a clear indication of content that should either be rethought or discarded entirely.

- An information architecture (IA) diagram is a representation of the hierarchical relationship between sections and subsections of the site's information.

- Information architecture diagrams are not designed to show the links between pages in a site.

4 layout and design

Follow the Golden Rule

Since I started listening to Sue, and giving her two-thirds of my attention, the results have been unbelievable! I get so much more attention and knowledgeable button-clicking!

It pays to be a good listener... and to carry a pocket calculator.

We've been talking about **user-centered design** for a few chapters, but here's where you really put your listening skills to the test. In this chapter, you'll take your users' feedback and build a site that meets their needs. From **browsers** to **screen real estate**, it's all about giving your users what they really want. Not only that, you'll learn the secrets of the **rule of thirds**. Find out how a few easy presses of the *calculator*, a *ruler*, and some *gridlines* can turn your blase web page into a thing of **beauty**.

Design is about <u>audience</u>

The **design** and **layout** of your site is the lens though which your users view and experience your content. If you have a confusing layout, your users are going to have a bad experience. However, if you develop a design and layout that is both functional and aesthetically pleasing, your users are not only going to hang around your site longer, but they'll want to come back.

The first step on the road to putting together a design which appeals to your users is to actually **know your users**. It's a lot harder to come up with a design that meets their needs if you don't know who they are (and what makes them tick).

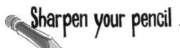

Sharpen your pencil

Who's your site's audience? Take a look at these two sites, and write down who you think the specific audience of each site is.

www.deliciousdays.com

....

....

....

....

....

....

Hop online to see these sites, and judge their audiences for yourself.

www.walmart.com

....

....

....

....

....

Sharpen your pencil
Solution

Let's take a look at the possible audiences for these sites.

High-end food photography turns meals into models and shows the site's passion for all things food.

www.deliciousdays.com

In-depth food writing makes Delicious Days more than just a site to find recipes.

Delicious Days audience is a group of people that see cooking as more than just something they have to do. These people might be described as "foodies" or see food as a form of art.

Walmart uses a very generic, centered, two-column design that seems to try and appeal to a wide audience.

www.walmart.com

The sidebar has links to all the products offered on the site—not favoring any particular group of items. Again, something for everyone.

Walmart's intended audience is not immediately apparent. Their site is generic and was most likely designed to appeal to a large group of people.

Your newest gig: RPM Records

A local record store—RPM Records—decides they want to redo their horrendous site that was created for them way back in 1998. They not only want to bring their site up to date, but they want something that really meets the needs of their customers. The kicker is that they are also one of the sponsors of an upcoming progressive music festival, and they would look really silly if they were still using their old site by the time the festival starts.

You've got to redo RPM, make it look great, and ensure current users can get around easily.

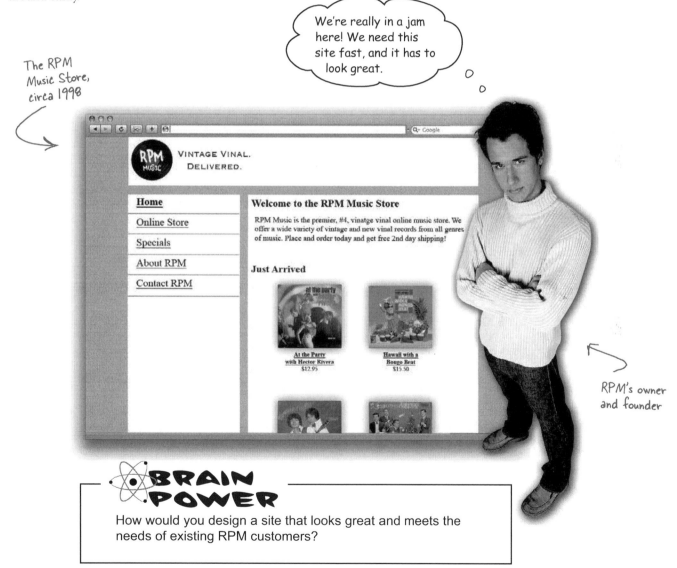

The RPM Music Store, circa 1998

We're really in a jam here! We need this site fast, and it has to look great.

RPM's owner and founder

BRAIN POWER

How would you design a site that looks great and meets the needs of existing RPM customers?

Pinpoint RPM's audience with <u>personas</u>

When you're designing for a specific audience, you've got to know what they like, and how they'd use a site. But you can hardly deal with hundreds—maybe thousands, even millions—of users all at once!

This is where a **persona** comes into the picture. A persona is a single user that stands in for all of your audience—a fictional user that has the most prominent characteristics of *all* your intended users. Those characteristics should relate to things that impact their web experience and browsing habits, like the browser your audience favors, or how long your audience spends online each week.

Give your persona a name – this helps to identify with them (as well as reference them).

The specific details of the persona help us understand how each user interacts with a specific website.

Name: **Ann**

Age: **28**

Internet Connectivity: **DSL**

Avg. time online/week for leisure: **15 hours**

Browser of choice: **Firefox**

Operating System: **Windows XP**

Screen Resolution: **800x600**

Occupation: **Student**

Details: **Ann considers herself very tech-savvy. She actively participates in social networks and online communities. She also regularly shops online. Her laptop (which is a little old, but all she can really afford right now) is her primary computer–and where she does all of her web browsing.**

Give all your personas an image. This attaches a face to a story and helps to reinforce the individuality of the user.

The most important part of a persona is the details. Give your user a story and a personality.

> This is what you call web design? Making up people out of thin air, and figuring out their hobbies? Come on!

Your personas should be based on <u>real</u> <u>data</u>.

So where exactly does all of the data used to build personas come from? Well, it can come from a lot of different places. Technical stuff (like operating system and browser) can come from server statistics. Information about how your users behave online can come straight from the users themselves—using tools like surveys and focus groups. The point is that when you build a persona, you are not pulling characteristics out of thin air.

Let's look at some data about the RPM users that we can use to build accurate personas for the new RPM site. The RPM owner had some old surveys he's given us to work with:

Data about RPM Music's users:

Age

18 - 24	32%
25 - 34	30%
35 - 44	22%
45 - 54	12%
55 - 64	4%

Age and gender give you the foundation on which to build the rest of your personas.

Gender

Female	35%

Operating Systems

Windows XP	75%
Windows Vista	10%
Mac OS X	13%
Other	2%

Browsers

Internet Explorer	65%
Firefox	22%
Safari	10%
Other	3%

All other data regarding the technology and browsing habits of RPM's users can help us create a more rounded and accurate persona.

Music Preference

Blues	5%
Classical	1%
Country	15%
Electronic	3%
Hip Hop/Rap	25%
Jazz	4%
Pop	30%
Rock	20%

Music Preference will tell us what our audience likes to listen to and help us decide on a theme and look and feel for the site, since it's so music-dependant.

Screen Resolution

800x600	43%
1024x768	42%

Internet Connection

Dialup	12%
DSL	55%
Cable	27%
T1 or higher	6%

These stats are from an old customer survey, and the logs from the RPM site web server.

Exercise

Based on the RPM user data, create two different personas for the RPM Music Store redesign. For the first persona, take the top value for each of the categories. For the second persona, use the secondary value.

Name: ....

Age: ....

Internet Connectivity: ....

Avg. time online/week for leisure: ....

Browser of choice: ....

Operating System: ....

Screen Resolution: ....

Occupation: ....

Details: ....

....

....

....

....

Make sure you add a picture. Paste in a Creative Commons photo, one you might have laying around, or anything you can find that seems to fit your persona.

Name: ....

Age: ....

Internet Connectivity: ....

Avg. time online/week for leisure: ....

Browser of choice: ....

Operating System: ....

Screen Resolution: ....

Occupation: ....

Details: ....

....

....

....

....

Make up some fictional details about your persona (including occupation) – this helps give the persona a more realistic feel.

Two personas means we can deal with more common traits of our audience, right? So we end up with more satisfied users.

Building two personas widens the audience you can build your site for.

When you are building a persona, you're creating a representation of the primary characteristics of your audience. But most of the time, your audience isn't composed of just one type of person. You'll have lots of users who do not fall in line with the characteristics that you identified for your first (primary) persona. This is where the secondary persona enters the picture.

A secondary persona represents the characteristics that are ***next in line*** behind the majority characteristics that you used to build your primary persona. So you design first for your primary persona, but then you can also work on meeting the needs of your secondary persona, too. The result? A site that meets more of your audience's needs and makes more of them happy.

---
there are no
Dumb Questions

Q: So do I always have to build 2 personas?

A: You don't have to, but it's a good idea. Audiences are diverse. You aren't always designing for one specific type of person. The second persona represents those audience members who are in the minority... but sometimes by only a percent or two.

Q: Can I build more than 2 personas?

A: Absolutely. If your audience is diverse enough (as shown by your audience research), it might be a good idea to have personas that represent other audience characteristics. Be aware, however, that you really don't need more than three. Too many personas just add confusion and detract from the project at hand.

Exercise Solution

Based on RPM user data, here are two personas (a primary one and a seconday one) we can use for the design and implementation of the RPM Music site.

Males represent the primary RPM users – by quite a large margin.

Jon falls into the largest age group of the RPM users (18–24).

Name: **Jon**
Age: **24**
Internet Connectivity: **DSL**
Music of Choice: **Pop**
Browser of choice: **Internet Explorer**
Operating System: **Windows XP**
Screen Resolution: **800x600**
Occupation: **Architect**
Details: **Jon is a busy guy and only spends about an hour a day outside of work online. He uses the family computer to read news and a few architectural blogs online. Occasionally, he buys books and music from Amazon when he can't make it out to the store.**

Jon is the "primary" persona for the RPM Music site and represents a typical user of the site. He will be the main focus throughout the design and development of the site.

Because Jon has a busy career, he has little time for Internet leisure. When he can, he uses Amazon, which means he's familiar with online shopping—especially for music.

You probably have something different here. Just make sure your details line up with the stats for the persona.

Susan fits into the second largest demographic of RPM Music users (24–34 year-olds) and, as a female, represents about 1/3 of the total visitors.

Susan connects to the Internet using a Cable line from her apartment. According to the server logs, this is the second most common way RPM users connect to the site.

Name: Susan
Age: 30
Internet Connectivity: Cable
Music of Choice: Rap/Hip Hop
Browser of choice: Firefox
Operating System: Mac OS X
Screen Resolution: 1024x768
Occupation: Student
Details: Susan is grad student and spends a fair amount of time online outside school. She is very tech-savvy and likes to shop and buy music online for her MP3 player. Her PC is a laptop so she can easily take notes in class and study outside her apartment.

1024x768 is pretty standard on laptops, and Mac OS X is an extremely popular operating system among college students.

Susan is the "secondary" persona for the RPM Music site and represents the second most common user of the site. She won't be the main focus throughout the design, but she's still important.

Let the personas be your guide...

So now you've got your two personas, and it's time to ask: "What would Jon do?" "How would Susan react?" Instead of designing for hundreds or thousands of faceless users, you're now designing for your personas... and *only* your personas.

So let's look at the old RPM site once more, in light of Jon and Susan. What do *they* think about the site?

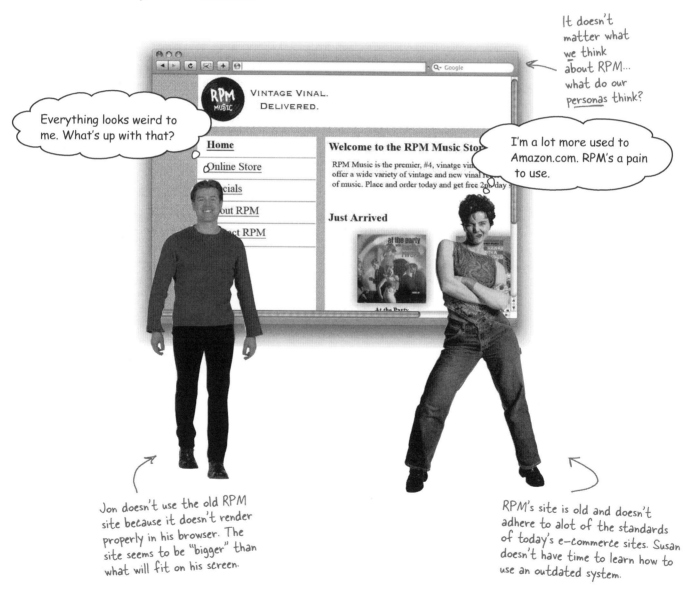

It doesn't matter what we think about RPM... what do our personas think?

Everything looks weird to me. What's up with that?

I'm a lot more used to Amazon.com. RPM's a pain to use.

Jon doesn't use the old RPM site because it doesn't render properly in his browser. The site seems to be "bigger" than what will fit on his screen.

RPM's site is old and doesn't adhere to alot of the standards of today's e-commerce sites. Susan doesn't have time to learn how to use an outdated system.

You know, I've been getting a lot of complaints about things looking "weird" or "too big." Do people need bigger monitors to use RPM?

Smaller displays limit screen real estate.

Jon uses an 800x600 screen resolution, which isn't very big... and, of course, if Jon uses that resolution, then most of the RPM users do, too.

With a lower resolution like 800x600, parts of the RPM site aren't showing up, and Jon's having to scroll all over the place just to see everything. Not so usable... and sure to cause problems.

It sounds like RPM's old site was designed without much regard for **screen real estate**... and that's the first thing we can try and fix.

BRAIN POWER

Is it better to design a site that looks perfect on one specific resolution—the most common one used by your audience—or a resolution that looks pretty good on lots of resolutions, but not quite perfect on any?

Resolution impacts design and layout

Screen resolution affects the screen real estate your site has to work with. Higher resolution means more available space... but also tends to make things look smaller to users.

Let's look at the old RPM site in several different resolutions:

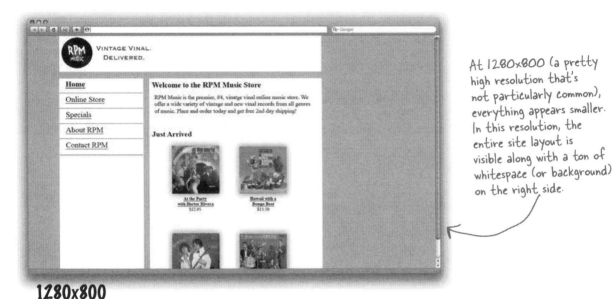

At 1280x800 (a pretty high resolution that's not particularly common), everything appears smaller. In this resolution, the entire site layout is visible along with a ton of whitespace (or background) on the right side.

1280x800

At 1024x768, the entire layout is still visible. However, the elements still appear pretty large, and the whitespace on the right isn't quite so prominent.

1024x768

800x600

The first thing you'll notice with the site at 800x600 is that everything appears larger. The layout is actually bigger than the available space in the browser window. There are scrollbars everywhere, and all the whitespace and background that appeared at higher resolutions on the right side are completely gone.

At a resolution of 640x480, the layout is absolutely huge — and the screen real estate simply can't contain it. Only the smallest portion of the layout is actually visible in the browser window. If you wanted to see the rest of the page, you would have to do a whole lot of scrolling.

640x480

Screen real estate determines how <u>MUCH</u> of your site will display in your user's browser

Think about screen real estate as the size of the canvas upon which you will build your website. But the thing is, that canvas size isn't fixed. Some users have large 30" displays, some have nothing but a tiny iPhone. Even worse, a lot of users actually access your site on multiple screens: a phone on the go, a 21" monitor at work, and a 14" AirBook at home.

Screen <u>RESOLUTION</u> also affects screen real estate

Then there's screen resolution. Even on a 21" monitor, users can choose their resolution: from 640x480 to 1600x1200, with a ton of different (and often unusual) choices in between. A higher resolution means that things appear smaller—and you'll have more virtual space for your site to work with. A lower resolution means that things on our site appear bigger, so you've got less virtual space to work with.

> I don't know about all that. I just know that the RPM site sucks. I love coming in and picking up some vinyl, but online... no way.

Your users don't care about screen real estate... they just want sites to "work."

Have you ever seen a site that has an opening message like, "Site best viewed in 1024x768?" Have you ever actually gone in and messed with your screen resolution based on one of those messages?

Yeah, not so much.

It's up to you, the web designer, to make sure a site looks right for your audience. You can't count on users changing their resolution or the device they use your site on... at least not if you (and your client) want to stay in business. So we've got to figure out a way to make RPM a lot easier to use for Jon, who's sporting an 800x600 screen resolution, and Susan, who's using 1024x768.

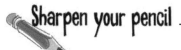

Sharpen your pencil

Below are methods for dealing with different screen resolutions. Take a look at each one and write down a pro and a con of each.

Methods

Use JavaScript in your page to automatically detect a user's current screen resolution, and direct them to a version of the RPM site that works best with that resolution.

Pros: ....
....
Cons: ....
....

Use JavaScript to load a CSS stylesheet appropriate for each user's screen resolution.

Pros: ....
....
Cons: ....
....

Design a single version of RPM that works fairly well with a wide variety of devices and screen resolutions.

Pros: ....
....
Cons: ....
....

Sharpen your pencil Solution

Your goal was to write one pro and one con for each of the different methods for managing screen resolutions. What did you come up with?

Methods

This is definitely the hardest of the three options. Seriously, who wants to design that many sites?

Use JavaScript in your page to automatically detect the user's current screen resolution, and direct them to a site that works best with that resolution.

Pros: Ability to handle a wide variety of screen resolutions.

Cons: If JavaScript is off, this method becomes useless.

Relying on JavaScript for a critical task like making sure your pages are displaying properly isn't such a good idea. If there's a script problem, or Javascript is off, both these techniques become useless.

Use JavaScript to load a CSS stylesheet appropriate for your visitor's screen resolution.

Pros: One site with multiple stylesheets is better than multiple sites.

Cons: Again, no JavaScript, no resolution detection.

This is a better strategy than a site for every device and screen resolution. Granted, you've got to create multiple CSS files, but you only have to create one XHTML file — which means less markup to maintain and update.

Design a single version of RPM that works fairly well with a wide variety of devices and screen resolutions.

Pros: No JavaScript or extra code.

Cons: You must decide on a "base" resolutions that you will design for.

This is the easiest way to go. Not only will you write less code, but you also won't be relying on JavaScript to handle resolutions. All you need to do is identify the smallest resolution that will work for your users and design for that. All larger resolutions will render the site properly, and smaller screens will generate scroll bars (but hopefully this is a tiny portion of your users).

I think I want to be forward thinking and shoot for 1024x768. Besides, a large chunk of my audience is already there

there are no
Dumb Questions

Q: I understand screen real estate, but I'm having some trouble with screen resolution. How exactly is the resolution of a screen measured?

A: Screen resolution is measured in horizontal and vertical pixels. So a small display may have a screen resolution of 640x480. This means that the monitor displays an area of 640 pixels wide and 480 pixels high. A resolution of 800x600 means 800 pixels wide and 600 pixels high, and so on. It's also important to note that it isn't just computer displays that measure their resolution in pixels. Televisions (LCDs, DLPs, etc.) all use the same method of representing screen resolution. For example, a 720px HD television has a screen resolution of 1280x720.

Q: Are there really that many screen sizes and screen resolutions that I need to think about when I'm designing my site?

A: Absolutely! Even when it comes to traditional desktop computers, you've got to be concerned with a wide variety of screen resolutions. Computer screens can range in resolution from the very small, 640x480, to the very large, 2560x1600. And that doesn't even count mobile devices (iPhones, cell phones, PSPs, etc.) and those other consumer devices that allow you to browse the Web (like the Nintendo Wii, for example). Ultimately, it all comes down to doing your research and knowing your target audience—and developing a persona that takes the important user characteristics into account. If you know that your primary persona generally views websites at a lower resolution, you don't have to worry too much about designing for higher screen resolutions and larger displays.

Q: Ok, I get the fact that I've got to worry about lots of different screen resolutions and display sizes. But is there one screen resolution that is most widely used?

A: It's all about your audience. If you've done your research and you know your audience, you can probably decide upon a target screen resolution that you can design for. However, if you don't know anything about your audience (or if your audience is very general), most web statistics agree that about 54% of users have a screen resolution of 1024x768. For more cool statistics, check out http://www.w3schools.com/browsers.

Q: How will I know if my site works on a certain screen resolution?

A: Test, test, test. Build your site, and then change the screen resolution on your display to test out your design. If you are designing for a specific resolution, build the site from the ground up in that resolution. If you are designing for another kind of device (mobile device, etc.), be absolutely sure you've got one of those devices around in order to test your site on it.

Build an XHTML and CSS foundation optimized for 1024x768

Standard XHTML Strict DOCTYPE

index.html

<div id="wrap"> will
be used to center our
layout in the browser.

This dummy text is just temporary so we
can make sure our page is setup properly.

rpm.css

```
/* rpm.css */
body {
     margin: 0;
     padding: 0;
     background: #fbf9ef;
     font-family: Helvetica, sans-serif;
     line-height: 1.4em;
}
p {
     margin: 0;
     padding: 0;
}
#wrap {
     margin: 0 auto;
     width: 900px;
}
```

This is a typical setup for the <body> tag.
Zero out the padding and margins, set a
background color and a font, and establish a
line height for site text.

margin: 0 auto will center our
dummy text in the browser.
This value will also allow your
site to adjust to different
screen resolutions.

A width of 900px is small enough to accommodate a
1024x768 screen but large enough for the content we
need for the RPM site.

TEST DRIVE

Create a very simple test page.

We don't have much to RPM yet, but go ahead and create `index.html` and `stylesheets/rpm.css`, and load them up in your web browser.

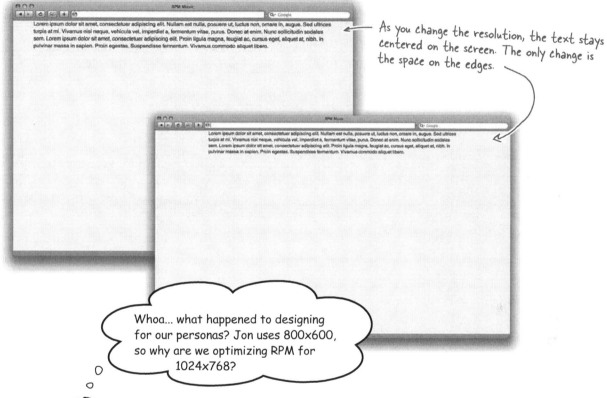

As you change the resolution, the text stays centered on the screen. The only change is the space on the edges.

Whoa... what happened to designing for our personas? Jon uses 800x600, so why are we optimizing RPM for 1024x768?

Knowing your audience lets you make <u>informed</u> decisions.

Jon uses 800x600, but if you check the RPM user survey back on page 115, 800x600 just barely nudges out 1024x768. Since we know that, we can build a site that actually looks ideal on 1024x768... but that also looks pretty good on 800x600, too. That's the power of personas: you'll have a good idea of how the decisions you make may affect your audience.

Hmmm. Latin text on a screen... not really what I had in mind. Let me give you a better idea what I'm looking for...

RPM Music 2.0

☐ Reach all my current customers.

☐ Update the look and feel of the site.

☐ Provide a blog, but as a secondary focus.

☐ Feature records on the home page.

Exercise

Which of the RPM site features have we addressed? Any of them? None of them? Check off any boxes you think we've handled (or at least worked on). Then write down your ideas about how to take on the remaining features for RPM Music 2.0.

....

....

....

....

....

This is terrible... we've spent all this time building personas and entering Latin text on a screen. Now the CEO thinks we've got nothing done. We're way behind...

Jim

Frank

Joe

Frank: I'm not so sure. I actually think we've got a good handle on his first requirement: "Reach all my current users."

Joe: You mean because we can get text to look right on 1024x768 and 800x600?

Frank: Well, that's part of it. But our personas—

Jim: Jon and Susan? Enough with the fictional characters already!

Frank: No, I'm serious. I really think if we can please them, we'll have reached RPM's core audience.

Joe: How do you please a persona? I mean, how do you *know* if you've designed for them?

Jim: Maybe you can send a fictional survey to their fictional address. Offer them a fictional gift for responding...

Frank: Okay, okay... yeah, we can't exactly ask Jon or Susan what they think. But we know they're young, that they've got modern computers...

Joe: ...so you're saying that if we design something that's pretty modern, then they'll like it?

Frank: Exactly.

Jim: Okay, just for a moment, let's say I buy into all this persona stuff. What is modern? I mean, how do you make a site look clean and hip and all that stuff? Isn't it just aesthetics? Like it's all in the mind of the designer?

Frank: Not at all. In fact, I was just reading about something pretty cool: the Golden Ratio.

Joe: Is that like the Golden Rule? Do unto others...

Frank: No, the Golden Ratio is a cool way to make sure a site looks pleasing to the eye. Let me show you...

Humans like things lined up and well-organized

What makes a beautiful site appealing to us? What makes an ugly site so unattractive? Well, most of the time, it's all about how our eyes perceive the elements on the site. There is nothing worse than a print document or a web page in which graphics and text have been thrown in haphazardly. Our eye needs predictability and a certain amount of visual logic when absorbing information.

Imagine if you laid out a grid on top of your favorite sites. Do things line up along a grid? Are there strong horizontal and vertical spaces that allow you to group the page into sections? Take a look at a grid-based site... and the old version of RPM:

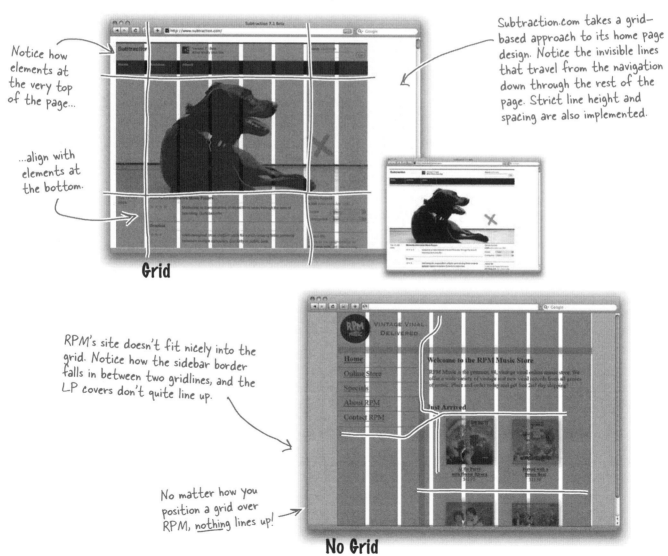

Notice how elements at the very top of the page...

...align with elements at the bottom.

Grid

Subtraction.com takes a grid-based approach to its home page design. Notice the invisible lines that travel from the navigation down through the rest of the page. Strict line height and spacing are also implemented.

RPM's site doesn't fit nicely into the grid. Notice how the sidebar border falls in between two gridlines, and the LP covers don't quite line up.

No matter how you position a grid over RPM, <u>nothing</u> lines up!

No Grid

How wide should my grid be? Use the Golden Ratio

The grid is one of the oldest graphic design tools out there. It's so old that it predates "modern" graphic design. Way back during the Renaissance, painters started using a grid based on the Golden Ratio in order to compose their paintings. Golden Ratio? What the heck is that? Well, if you take a length of a line and multiply by .62, you get a ratio that can be used to create a pleasing, natural-looking grid—that's the Golden Ratio!

The whole idea behind the Golden Ratio is to use a balance that we've all seen around us our whole lives, and put that balance into use on a website. The result? Sites just "feel" and "look" right to our eyes. Just take a look at a few examples of the Golden Ratio in action:

Da Vinci's Last Supper is a great example of art that utilizes the Golden Ratio.

The sidebar is the smaller number in the ratio.

The main content section is the larger number in the ratio and accounts for about 2/3 of the page.

The footer and header represent the full length of the block.

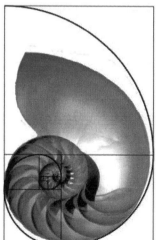

The nautilus shell is an example of the Golden Ratio showing up in nature.

The rule of thirds: A shortcut to the Golden Ratio

The Golden Ratio says that if you take the entire width of something, and multiply it by 0.62, you'll get a nice wide area that you can put content into. The remaining 0.38 is great for sidebars, extra content, things that the eye should look at second.

But multiplying by 0.62 isn't that handy unless you're carrying around a pocket calculator (*Head First Algebra*, anyone?). Fortunately, 0.62 is awfully close to 2/3... and the remaining 0.38 is pretty close to 1/3. So if you divide something into thirds, two of those thirds are perfect for your main content, and the remaining 1/3 is great for sidebars, navigation, blogs...

Here's what you should do:

Step 1: Take a piece of paper, and draw a rectangle to represent your site. Then divide your rectangle vertically by thirds (use a ruler, or just estimate carefully).

Step 2: Divide the rectangle horizontally by thirds. Now you've got a very loose grid.

Step 3: Divide each of your vertical columns into thirds. Now you've got a sort of grid-within-your-grid so that you can actually use the 2/3-to-1/3 ratio in smaller chunks of your site, too.

Step 4: Lay out your site, aligning things with your gridlines.

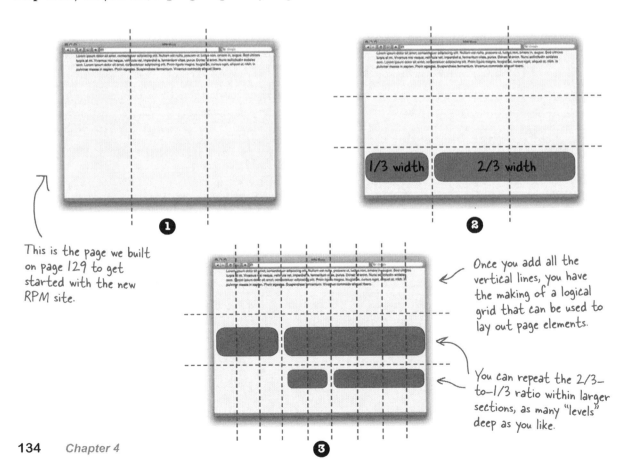

This is the page we built on page 129 to get started with the new RPM site.

1/3 width   2/3 width

Once you add all the vertical lines, you have the making of a logical grid that can be used to lay out page elements.

You can repeat the 2/3-to-1/3 ratio within larger sections, as many "levels" deep as you like.

RPM and the Golden Ratio: An (anti) case study

So if the eye really likes to see things in a 2/3-to-1/3 ratio, how does RPM's site stack up? We already know it doesn't really follow any particular grid alignment. But what if we overlay the 2/3-to-1/3 ratio graphically... what does it tell us about RPM?

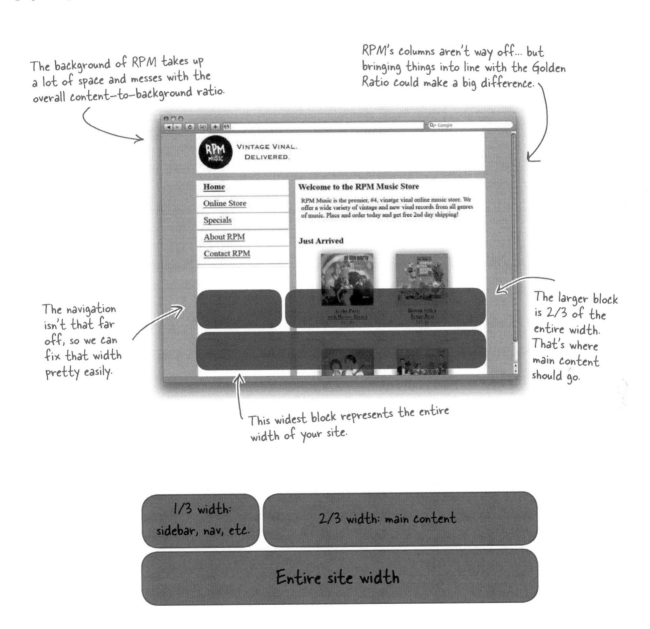

The background of RPM takes up a lot of space and messes with the overall content-to-background ratio.

RPM's columns aren't way off... but bringing things into line with the Golden Ratio could make a big difference.

The navigation isn't that far off, so we can fix that width pretty easily.

The larger block is 2/3 of the entire width. That's where main content should go.

This widest block represents the entire width of your site.

1/3 width: sidebar, nav, etc.

2/3 width: main content

Entire site width

Exercise

Based on the grid below, sketch out a storyboard for the RPM Music site. Try and keep up with how your elements are laying out, not only against the grid, but in relation to each other. Is an element part of the main content? Try and make it the 2/3 part of a 2/3-to-1/3 ratio. Just do your best... there's no perfect answer if you keep things in proportion.

This grid is based on a page width of 950px (each column is 30px with a spacer of 10px).

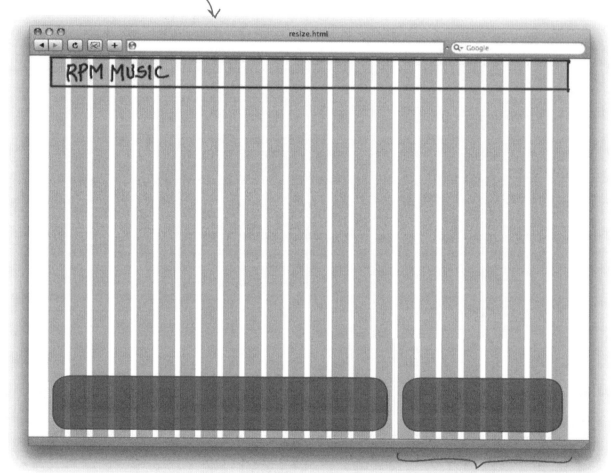

8 columns equals 1/3 of the layout.

> I think we have to do more than just make things the right proportion to each other. We've got to make the important things attract attention... so make them bigger, right?

Important content should "weigh" more.

You should already be putting your most important content into the 2/3 part of your 2/3-to-1/3 page ratios. But is that the only way to draw attention to something? Not at all!

When you're laying out your page, you're creating a balance between larger elements and smaller ones. The larger elements have more weight, and the smaller ones have less weight. Plus, there's how the elements relate to each other:

The page elements in this example feel balanced on the left and right side.

Because of the heavy weight in the left column, this example seems disproportionate.

When you are laying out your web page, you need to consider two kinds of balance: symmetrical and asymmetrical.

Symmetrical balance occurs when elements on either side of a line (either horizontal or vertical) have the same weight.

Asymmetrical balance occurs when the weight of a site's elements is not evenly distributed around a central line. So you've got one really large element only partially offset by other, smaller elements.

Exercise

Revisit your solution to the exercise on page 136. Is your layout symmetrical or asymmetrical? Do you think balancing (or unbalancing) your layout is an improvement? Make any changes you want to, and then turn the page to see what we came up with.

Exercise Solution

In this exercise, you had to draw a storyboard for the RPM Music site based on the browser grid. There's no right answer, as long as you came up with a balanced layout that follows the Golden Ratio.

The header will span the entire top of the page, and the upper left will hold the logo.

The navigation will take up 2/3 of the header <div> and be block-styled like tabs

Within the main content, we used the Golden Ratio again to split up text descriptions and album covers.

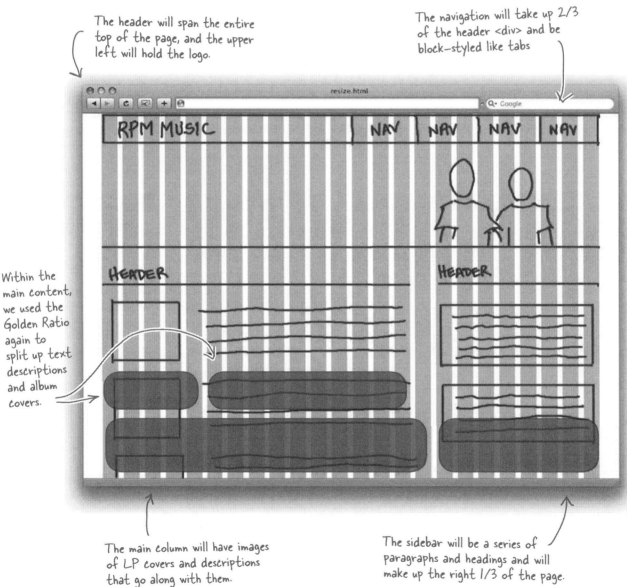

The main column will have images of LP covers and descriptions that go along with them.

The sidebar will be a series of paragraphs and headings and will make up the right 1/3 of the page.

Remember your personas?

Take a second and look back at your answer on page 138. Is it balanced? Symmetrical or asymmetrical is okay. Did you follow the Golden Ratio?

But that's not all you have to worry about. Remember, you should be designing for your personas, who have some pretty specific concerns.

Does your version of RPM highlight musical interests?

Name: Jon
Age: 24
Internet: DSL
Music: Pop
Browser: Internet Explorer
OS: Windows XP
Resolution: 800x600

Name: Susan
Age: 30
Internet: Cable
Music: Rap/Hip Hop
Browser: Firefox
OS: Mac OS X
Resolution: 1024x768

Browser issues aren't really relevant yet, but screen resolution certainly is.

Remember your client?

The RPM owner also had a lot of requirements. Did your vision of RPM 2.0 meet what he's looking for?

RPM Music 2.0

- ☑ **Reach all my current customers.**
- ☑ **Update the look and feel of the site.**
- ☑ **Provide a blog, but as a secondary focus.**
- ☑ **Feature records on the home page.**

Look over your RPM 2.0 ideas. Can you check off each of these boxes based on your design?

If you need to make changes to your design, go ahead! That's why we're working with paper, anyway.

So we're ready to dig into some XHTML, right? Can we use CSS to actually build a grid that we can align elements to?

There are CSS frameworks that provide grids for our content to "sit" against.

When you're actually building your page in XHTML, it's not always easy to line things up as well as you can with paper, pencil, and a ruler. Fortunately, there are a lot of cool CSS frameworks that will provide a grid for you. One of the best of these is Blueprint: http://www.blueprintcss.org/

You can Google "CSS framework" or "CSS grid framework" to find several other options.

One of the best things about Blueprint is that it provides an enormous amount of flexibility in terms of the types of layouts you can create. It also provides support for styling form elements and status messages—something you don't see in a lot of other frameworks.

Blueprint allows you to build grid-based layouts in just about any conceivable configuration.

Blueprint uses a page width of 950px, which is based on 24 30px columns with 10px spacing. This will give us a layout that fits nicely within a 1024x768 resolution.

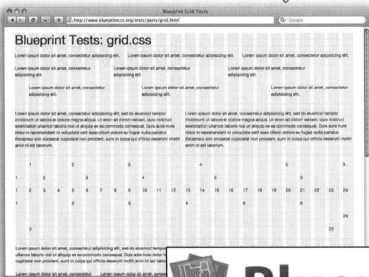

Add grid.css to your page, and you'll see this nice grid overlaying everything else on your page.

Blueprint

Set up RPM 2.0 with the Blueprint Framework

Make sure you've got the simple version of index.html and rpm.css from page 128. Then visit `blueprintcss.org` and download Blueprint. In the unzipped directory, you'll find a `/blueprint` folder that has all the files you need. You can drop the stylesheets in this folder right into the stylesheets folder of the RPM 2.0 site you're building:

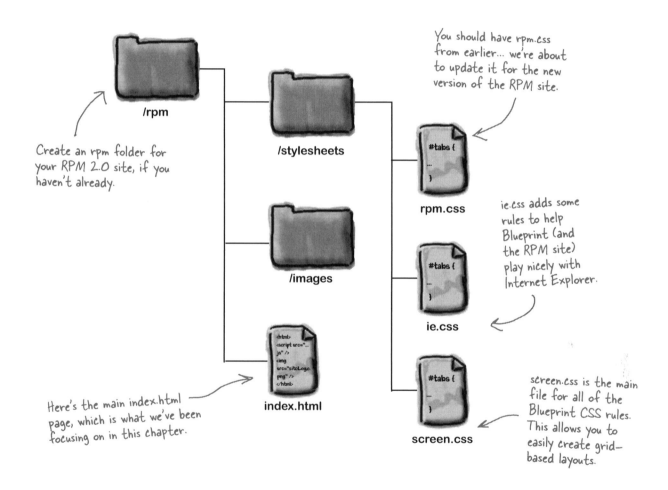

Create an rpm folder for your RPM 2.0 site, if you haven't already.

/rpm

/stylesheets

/images

index.html

Here's the main index.html page, which is what we've been focusing on in this chapter.

You should have rpm.css from earlier... we're about to update it for the new version of the RPM site.

rpm.css

ie.css adds some rules to help Blueprint (and the RPM site) play nicely with Internet Explorer.

ie.css

screen.css

screen.css is the main file for all of the Blueprint CSS rules. This allows you to easily create grid-based layouts.

Exercise

Go ahead and create any parts of this directory structure you don't have. Download Blueprint and add in its CSS files to your site structure. Then, link in ie.css and screen.css in your version of index.html. Use the examples that come with Blueprint as a model, especially for how ie.css is referenced.

Exercise Solution

Go ahead and create any parts of this directory structure you don't have. Download Blueprint and add in its CSS files to your site structure. Then, link in ie.css and screen.css in your version of index.html. Here's what you should have come up with:

Make sure you add the Blueprint CSS links <u>above</u> the rpm.css file. This way, our CSS rules overwrite any Blueprint CSS rules.

```
<!DOCTYPE html PUBLIC "-//W3C//DTD XHTML 1.0 Strict//EN"
        "http://www.w3.org/TR/xhtml1/DTD/xhtml1-strict.dtd">
<html xmlns="http://www.w3.org/1999/xhtml" xml:lang="en" lang="en">
<head>
  <title>RPM Music</title>
  <meta http-equiv="Content-Type" content="text/html; charset=utf-8" />
  <link rel="stylesheet" type="text/css" media="screen"
      href="stylesheets/screen.css" />
  <!--[if IE]>
    <link rel="stylesheet" href="stylesheets/ie.css" type="text/css"
        media="screen, projection">
  <![endif]-->
  <link rel="stylesheet" href="stylesheets/rpm.css" type="text/css"
          media="screen" />
</head>
<body>
  <div id="wrap">
    <p>Lorem ipsum dolor sit amet, consectetuer adipiscing elit. Nullam
      est nulla, posuere ut, luctus non, ornare in, augue. Sed ultrices
      turpis at mi. Vivamus nisi neque, vehicula vel, imperdiet a, fermentum
      vitae, purus. Donec at enim. Nunc sollicitudin sodales sem. Lorem
      ipsum dolor sit amet, consectetuer adipiscing elit. Proin ligula magna,
      feugiat ac, cursus eget, aliquet at, nibh. In pulvinar massa in sapien.
      Proin egestas. Suspendisse fermentum. Vivamus commodo aliquet libero.</p>
  </div>
</body>
</html>
```

screen.css is the main Blueprint file.

ie.css is for handling Internet Explorer differences.

The <!--[if IE]> comment only shows the ie.css file to browsers that identify themselves as Internet Explorer.

index.html

there are no
Dumb Questions

Q: What exactly is a framework?

A: These days "framework" is really just a buzzword in web design and development. A framework is just a set of tools, libraries, conventions, and best practices that are designed to abstract day-to-day, routine web design tasks into generic modules that can be reused. The goal of a good framework is to allow you to focus on tasks that are unique to your specific project, rather than more repetitive, mundane tasks (like laying out a grid in CSS!).

Q: I get that Blueprint is good, but are there other grid-based CSS frameworks?

A: Yup—there are lots and lots out there. Some of the most prominent are 960 and Yahoo UI (YUI) Grid CSS.

Q: 960? How does that measure up against Blueprint?

A: Like Blueprint, 960 (`http://960.gs/`) provides a great deal of flexibility in the types of layouts you can create. Unfortunately, it doesn't provide as much built in support for typographic styling as Blueprint. The cool thing about 960 is that the files package not only includes the necessary CSS files, but also includes some handy dandy extras, such as a paper template grid (based on the 960 framework) that you can use to sketch out your designs.

Q: What about YUI Grid CSS?

A: YUI Grids CSS (`http://developer.yahoo.com/yui/grids/`) is part of the Yahoo User Interface Library. Like Blueprint and 960, it provides a fair amount of flexibility in terms of the types of layouts you can create. Unfortunately, YUI Grids CSS is somewhat complicated, making its learning curve a little steep. On the plus side, the YUI Grids CSS site has the YUI Grids Builder tool, a visual, menu-based editor which allows you to rapidly create (and customize) layouts based on the YUI Grids CSS framework.

Q: I'm still a little confused about which framework to choose. Can you give me some more advice?

A: As with a lot of things, the framework you choose is entirely dependent on your needs. A good rule of thumb is to choose a framework that balances simplicity (especially if this is your first time using a framework) with flexibility, in terms of the number of different layouts you can build. Blueprint is the most popular and flexible out there. But, honestly, give them all a try. You might find one that better suits your needs. Remember, frameworks are all about alleviating your CSS workload. So whichever one you choose, make sure it works for you, and you don't work for it!

Use Blueprint CSS rules to style RPM 2.0

With Blueprint CSS rules available, now you can go to work on RPM 2.0's XHTML. Just use the `class` attribute on your `div`s, like this:

```
<div id="header" class="column span-24">
```

The column class is from Blueprint and lets the browser know to use Blueprint CSS rules for positioning this div.

So the "header" `div` will span 24 30-pixel columns here, which is the entire width of the page. Within that `div`, you might have other `div`s that have a span of span-16 and span-8, to get to your Golden Ratio.

Go ahead and make these additions to your copy of RPM's `index.html`:

```
<!DOCTYPE html PUBLIC "-//W3C//DTD XHTML 1.0 Strict//EN"
        "http://www.w3.org/TR/xhtml1/DTD/xhtml1-strict.dtd">
<html xmlns="http://www.w3.org/1999/xhtml" xml:lang="en" lang="en">
<head>
  <title>RPM Music</title>
  <meta http-equiv="Content-Type" content="text/html; charset=utf-8" />
  <link rel="stylesheet" type="text/css" media="screen"
        href="stylesheets/screen.css" />
  <!--[if IE]>
    <link rel="stylesheet" href="stylesheets/ie.css" type="text/css"
          media="screen, projection">
  <![endif]-->
  <link rel="stylesheet" href="stylesheets/rpm.css" type="text/css"
        media="screen" />
</head>
<body>
  <div id="wrap" class="container">

    <div id="header" class="column span-24 last">
      <div id="nav" class="column span-16 last">Site Navigation</div>
      <div id="mast" class="column span-24 last"></div>
    </div>

    <div id="content" class="column span-15 colborder last">Main Body Content</div>

    <div id="sidebar" class="column span-8 last">Sidebar Content</div>
  </div>


  <div id="footer">Footer Content</div>
</body>
</html>
```

Blueprint requires you to wrap your content in a div classed as "container".

Here, 16 is 2/3 of 24... so we're using the Golden Ratio.

15-to-8 is pretty much 2/3-to-1/3, with a column of spacer left over.

These two <div>s are placeholders for content we'll add soon.

Each major element of the site needs a class with an initial value of "column". This tells Blueprint how to position the element. The second value (span-xx) tells the framework how many columns to span the element.

index.html

We're still working with the index.html file.

Time to get your RPM groove on

Can I see what the site would look like with some of my records in place?

At the Party with Hector Rivera

Hector Rivera, the king of New York Latin Soul, really makes a splash with his 1966 release "At the Party" climbing into the R&B Top 40. This classic album will have you dancing all night long and is sure to become one of the favorite records in your collection.

Hawaii with a Bongo Beat

LeRoy Holmes has done it again with this Hawaiian-Nashville fusion album, sure to take you back to the islands or the country. Pick up this record and listen to your favorite tropical classics, like "The Moon of Manakoora" and the always delightful "Mahilini Mele." Great music for the whole family.

Dreamin' Wild

The hunky duo of Donnie and Joe Emerson bring you this psychedelic rock album for the ages. Their smash hit "Don't Go Lovin' Nobody Else" will have you humming for days. This is a collector's item and is only being offered for a limited time here at RPM Music. Get it while it's hot.

XMAS A Go Go

This week's mystery LP looks to be a great addition to any Christmas music collection. This just showed up one day in the RPM Music warehouse, and we've priced it to sell. Get your piece of mystery history with XMAS A Go Go.

Exercise

Add the above content to the main \<div> of the RPM site in the index.html file you've been working with. Think about ways to insert your content to match what it is: a bunch of similar items that aren't ordered, but may need to each be styled. You can download the album covers from Head First Labs:

`http://www.headfirstlabs.com/books/hfwd/ch04`

Fireside Chats

Tonight's talk: **Who's more important to the user? Content and Style discuss who matters more when it comes to the user's experience.**

Style:

You know, I really don't think that there's much to discuss here. I mean, the Internet is a visual medium, and people want something nice to look at. No one is going to care about the content if the site doesn't look good.

Content:

Nothing to discuss? How quickly you forget the humble origins of the World Wide Web. Berners-Lee proposed HTML to help researchers share and update information, specifically scientific research. Content was king back in the early days.

Yeah, back in the *way* early days. But today, style and design are the branding of a site. They're what gives a site its character and personality.

True, but even well-designed sites with the most cutting-edge CSS won't hold up without well-written content. Graphics and one of those fancy three-column layouts can only get you so far. I have to be clear, short, and easy to read. Otherwise, people lose focus. And don't even get me started on what happens if I can't answer the questions visitors are looking for. It's a lot of pressure!

Well there's just as much pressure on me. What about navigation? Huh? If I don't get people from one part of a site to another, they'd never even find you. Not to mention screen size, text size, and the usability of all these things I'm doing. It's quite a bit to manage and not as easy as you may think.

Navigation? An unordered list and some text links should do just fine. You graphic designers...

What is this, 1995? Unordered lists and text links without CSS? Boring.

Content:

<markup>
Style, are you still complaining about Content? Don't you remember when you were right there next to him? I helped you get there with tags like <font>, <i>, <b> and <table>.
</markup>

Style:

Hey, who invited this guy?

Content:

<markup>
Stylesheets are great, but remember how it used to be? Endlessly-nested tables, markup filled with hex colors, and the always lovable spacer GIF.
</markup>

Style:

I told you, we don't talk about that anymore. We were all young and stupid then, with a complete disregard for the separation of markup and style. By the way, where's Content?

Content:

Sorry, that **`markup`** guy has a tendency to follow me around sometimes. However, he makes a valid point. You used to be just tags in the HTML mess.

Style:

So that was good? Now that I live in CSS documents, I'm much more useful and not so bogged down by all the stuff that **`markup`** is doing. It's definitely better for me. If anything, I'm really doing you a favor, too. Now you get to stand alone... for whatever that's worth.

Content:

You have cleaned up the files quite a bit by moving into the `/stylesheets` directory. It really has given **`markup`** and me a chance to get to know each other better. It's amazing what you can do without all your meaningless style tags all over the place.

Style:

Is that supposed to be a compliment? You know, it has been a lot easier for me not having to deal with all your <p>s everywhere. Just don't forget to include me in your head.

Exercise
Solution

Here's how we marked up the album covers, descriptions, and titles in our version of RPM 2.0.
What did you do?

```
<body>
  <div id="wrap" class="container">
    <div id="header" class="column span-24 last">
      <div id="nav" class="column span-16 last">Site Navigation</div>
      <div id="mast" class="column span-24 last"></div>
    </div>
    <div id="content" class="column span-15 colborder last">
      <h3>New at RPM Music</h3>
      <ul>
        <li><div class="column span-4"><img alt="cover1"
              src="images/cover1.jpg" /></div>
          <h4>At the Party with Hector Rivera</h4>
          <p>Hector Rivera, the king of New York Latin Soul really makes a splash with
his 1966 release <em>At the Party</em>. Climbing into the R&amp;B Top 40, this classic
album will have you dancing all night long and is sure to become one of the favorite
records in your collection.</p>
        </li>
        <li><div class="column span-4"><img alt="cover2"
              src="images/cover2.jpg" /></div>
          <h4>Hawaii with a Bongo Beat</h4>
          <p>LeRoy Holmes has done it again with this Hawaiian-Nashville fusion album
sure to take you back to the islands&mdash;or the country. Pick up this record and
listen to your favorite tropical classics like "The Moon of Manakoora" and the always
delightful "Mahilini Mele." Great music for the whole family.</p>
        </li>
        <li><div class="column span-4"><img alt="cover3"
              src="images/cover3.jpg" /></div>
          <h4>Dreamin' Wild</h4>
          <p>The hunky duo of Donnie and Joe Emerson bring you this psychedelic rock
album for the ages. Their smash hit "Don't Go Lovin' Nobody Else" will have you humming
for days. This is a collector's item and is only being offered for a limited time here
at RPM Music. Get it while it's hot.</p>
        </li>
        <li><div class="column span-4"><img alt="cover4"
              src="images/cover4.jpg" /></div>
          <h4>XMAS A Go Go</h4>
          <p>This weeks mystery LP looks to be a great addition to any Christmas music
collection. This just showed up one day in the RPM Music warehouse and we've priced it
to sell. Get your piece of mystery history with XMAS A Go Go.</p>
        </li>
      </ul>
    </div>
    <div id="sidebar" class="column span-8 last">Sidebar Content</div>
  </div>
  <div id="footer">Footer Content</div>
</body>
```

This is really just a list of albums, so we used an unordered list (ul).

We put each album cover in a separate <div> so we can position these independent of the description text.

Album titles are in a heading element (h4) to indicate their importance and let us style them using our CSS.

index.html

Test Drive

How's RPM 2.0 looking?

Update your version of `index.html`, and load it up in your browser.

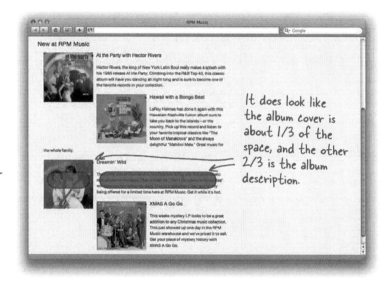

Hmmm... the records don't line up properly. We need to add some style to these lists to sharpen them up.

It does look like the album cover is about 1/3 of the space, and the other 2/3 is the album description.

Add some CSS to clean up the layout

Some simple additions to `rpm.css` should clean up things considerably:

```
p, ul, li, h1, h2, h3, h4 {
        margin: 0;
}
h3 {
        margin: 0 0 20px 0;
        padding: 0 0 5px 0;
        font-weight: bold;
        border-bottom: 1px solid #ccc;
}
ul {
        list-style-type: none;
}
#content, #sidebar {
        margin: 40px 0 20px 0;
}
#content h4 {
        font-weight: bold;
        font-size: 1.4em;
}
#content li p {
        margin: 0 0 70px 0;
}
```

Zero out the margin for some common page elements.

rpm.css

The ul and #content rules will help get our records straightened out. list-style-type: none will globally remove bullets from the album list. Usually bullets are good, but in this case we don't want them. The other important rule here is the bottom margin on #content li p. This rule makes sure each <li> stacks nicely on top of the others.

Test Drive

RPM 2.0(1) is ready to test.

Update your version of `rpm.css`, and reload the RPM site.

A bottom border and font styling clean up the section headers and separate them from headers within the content.

New at RPM Music

At the Party with Hector Rivera
Hector Rivera, the king of New York Latin Soul really makes a splash with his 1968 release *At the Party*. Climbing into the R&B Top 40, this classic album will have you dancing all night long and is sure to become one of the favorite records in your collection.

Hawaii with a Bongo Beat
LeRoy Holmes has done it again with this Hawaiian-Na... to take you back to the islands—or the country. Pick up ... your favorite tropical classics like "The Moon of Ma... delightful "Mahilini Mele." Great music for the whol...

Dreamin' Wild
The hunky duo of Donnie and Joe Emerson bring you this psychedelic rock album for the ages. Their smash hit "Don't Go Lovin' Nobody Else" will have you humming for days. This is a collector's item and is only being offered for a limited time here at RPM Music. Get it while it's hot.

XMAS A Go Go
This weeks mystery LP looks to be a great addition to any Christmas music collection. This just showed up one day in the RPM Music warehouse and we've priced it to sell. Get your piece of mystery history with XMAS A Go Go.

A little simplistic, but I like it. Sort of like Amazon.com, but I'd rather shop locally, anyway.

With a modest margin below the <p> tag on each of the record descriptions, the list lines up with the grid, and our layout is much more orderly.

Finish off the content and navigation markup

Let's add a little more content to show the RPM owner just how far
we've come. Make these changes to your copy of index.html:

> We're still using Blueprint. This time, we
> want the navigation to span 2/3 of
> the page. That's 16 of the 24 columns
> Blueprint provides.

```html
<body>
  <div id="wrap" class="container">
    <div id="header" class="column span-24 last">
      <h1 class="column span-8 last">RPM Music</h1>
      <div id="nav" class="column span-16 last">
        <ul>
          <li class="active"><a title="RPM Music home" href="#">Home</a></li>
          <li><a title="Music Store" href="#">Music</a></li>
          <li><a title="RPM Blog" href="#">Blog</a></li>
          <li><a title="About RPM Music" href="#">About</a></li>
          <li><a title="Shopping Cart" href="#">Cart</a></li>
        </ul>
      </div>
      <div id="mast" class="column span-24 last"><img alt="rpm guys"
          src="images/rpm_guys.jpg" /></div>
      <div id="subheader" class="column span-24 last">
        <h2>RPM Music is the #4 online, midwest, <em>shrink-wrap</em>
            music retailer</h2>
      </div>
    </div>
    <div id="content" class="column span-15 colborder last">
      <h3>New at RPM Music</h3>
      <ul>
        <!-- Album listings from earlier -->
      </ul>
    </div>
    <div id="sidebar" class="column span-8 last">
      <h3>From the Blog</h3>
      <p><strong>Nov 4</strong> &mdash; RPM is gearing up for the holiday season and
stocking up on lots of records for the post-Thanksgiving LP rush. We should be flush
with inventory and we suspect that we'll have some cool new specials to announce later
in the month. Check back soon for the holiday RPM madness.</p>
      <p><strong>Oct 20</strong> &mdash; We just received a mysterious package in
our warehouse full of Christmas albums that seem to have originated in Japan. We are
currently investigating their origins and if everything checks out, we'll have them up
on the site for purchase. Could be the makings of an RPM Music exclusive.</p>
      <p><strong>Oct 7</strong> &mdash; New specials are up on on the site as of last
night. Be sure to check out the LP's that offer free shipping.</p>
    </div>
  </div> <!-- end "container" div -->
  <div id="footer">
    <p>Copyright &copy; RPM Music, all rights reserved.</p>
  </div>
</body>
```

> These are sample blog entries. Later, we
> could pull these programmatically from
> the RPM blog, but for now, static text
> lets us show what things will look like.

> A quick copyright notice is all we need in the footer for right now.
> Notice that the footer <div> is outside the main container. This lets
> us span the footer across the entire bottom of the page.

index.html

We're using Blueprint to put in the Golden Ratio horizontally. But what about when we want a 2/3-to-1/3 ratio vertically?

Vertical ratios usually require images and CSS positioning.

It's relatively easy to get your horizontal ratios right using a CSS grid framework like Blueprint. But how do you get a vertical ratio going, like between a main header image and the rest of a site's content?

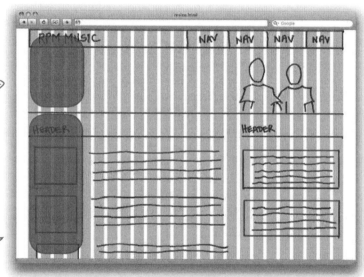

We want the main header image to take up 1/3 of the vertical space...

...and the content below to be 2/3 of the space.

You can start by sizing your image to take up about 1/3 of the typical user's vertical screen real estate. But then you're having to use a lot of different images, and possibly even the dreaded 1-pixel transparent spacer. And what about the parts of the page within the header: a navigation bar, the site logo, any headings... it can turn into a mess—fast.

A better solution is to put together a background image that has things in the correct proportions, like this:

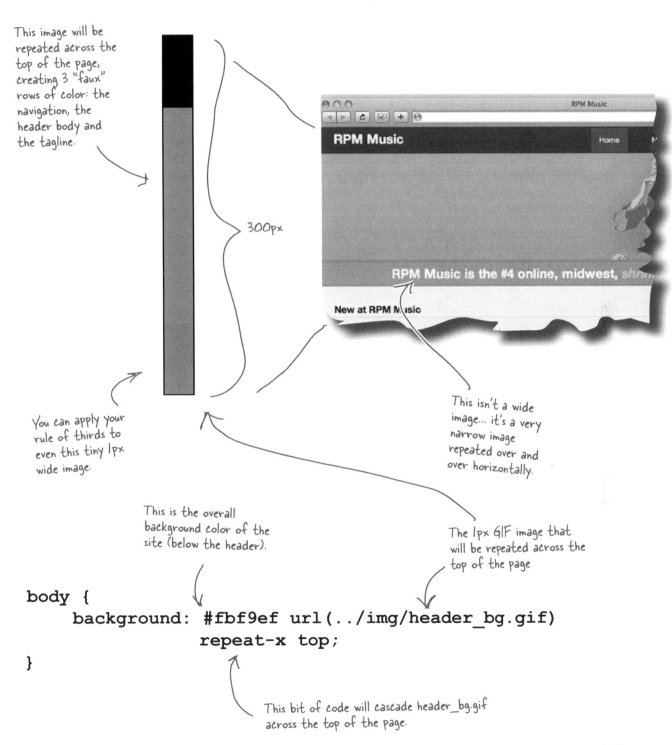

This image will be repeated across the top of the page, creating 3 "faux" rows of color: the navigation, the header body and the tagline.

300px

You can apply your rule of thirds to even this tiny 1px wide image.

This isn't a wide image... it's a very narrow image repeated over and over horizontally.

This is the overall background color of the site (below the header).

The 1px GIF image that will be repeated across the top of the page

```
body {
    background: #fbf9ef url(../img/header_bg.gif)
               repeat-x top;
}
```

This bit of code will cascade header_bg.gif across the top of the page.

Add layout and typographic details with some more CSS

Here are some more CSS rules to help clean up and format all the new XHTML you just added. Make these additions to rpm.css, too:

```css
body {
  margin: 0;
  padding: 0;
  background: #fbf9ef url(../images/header_bg.gif) repeat-x top;
}

p, ul, li, h1, h2, h3, h4 {
  margin: 0;
}

h3 {
  margin: 0 0 20px 0;
  padding: 0 0 5px 0;
  font-weight: bold;
  border-bottom: 1px solid #ccc;
}

ul {
  list-style-type: none;
}

#nav {
  height: 50px;
}

#nav ul {
  float: right;
}

#nav ul li {
  float: left;
  padding: 15px;
}

#nav ul li a {
  color: #fff;
  text-decoration: none;
  padding: 15px;
  font-size: 1.2em;
}

#nav ul li.active, #nav ul li:hover {
  background: #333;
}

#mast img {
  float: right;
}
```

Just adding a few CSS rules will give us a nice-looking, functional navigation that also makes the site easier to use.

This navigation positioning will get the "tabs" to stay on the right side of the layout.

A 15px padding on the nav li will give the <a> tag room to grow and form our blocks.

This will highlight whatever <a> tag is classed with "active." This lets users know what page they are on.

#mast img is the main image in the header. We want this to float over on the right side of the page.

rpm.css

```
#header h1 {
  padding: 10px 0 0 0;
  font-size: x-large;
  font-weight: bold;
  color: #fff;
}
#header h2 {
  margin: 8px 0 0 0;
  text-align: center;
  color: #fff;
  font-weight: bold;
}

#header h2 em {
  color: #ccc;
}

#content, #sidebar {
  margin: 40px 0 20px 0;
}

#content h4 {
  font-weight: bold;
  font-size: 1.4em;
}

#content li p {
  margin: 0 0 70px 0;
}

#sidebar p {
  margin: 0 0 10px 0;
}

#footer {
  border-top: 5px solid #928977;
  background: #a9a294;
}

#footer p {
  margin: 0 auto;
  padding: 10px;
  width: 950px;
  font-size: 1.2em;
  font-weight: bold;
  text-align: center;
}
```

The <h2> element in the header is the RPM tag line. This spans the entire page and is centered in the layout. We need a little top padding to get this to line up properly.

These rules for the footer will allow it to span the entire bottom of the site, outside of the grid container. Using the same width as the grid (950px) and centering the content with margin: 0 auto gives us the layout we're looking for.

Focus on design, not the CSS.

It's okay if you're not 100% sure on all these CSS rules. You can pick up *Head First HTML with XHTML & CSS* for more details. For now, focus on the look we're creating, and how it's balanced, organized, and follows the Golden Ratio.

Test Drive

RPM is ready to go live.

Update and , and download any images you don't already have from Head First
Labs. Then see what all your work has produced:

Now RPM looks like
it belongs on this
side of 1999, and it's
pleasing to the eyes.

This looks amazing! I never would have thought you could nail this so quickly... and I'm already getting positive responses from my customers.

BULLET POINTS

- A survey is an excellent way to get broad information about your audience.

- A persona is an archetype user that embodies and represents your audience.

- Screen real estate refers to the amount of space on the screen of the device that the designer has to work with.

- The lower your resolution, the larger items will be and the more screen real estate they will take up.

- A grid can provide order and visual logic when you are designing your layout on paper.

- The Golden Ratio can produce designs that are more pleasing to the eye.

- The rule of thirds is a quick and easy way to create grids that are based on the Golden Ratio.

- A CSS grid-based framework is a specialized CSS file that contains all of the necessary styles for laying your site out along a grid in CSS.

- The goal of a CSS grid-based framework is to allow the designer to focus on tasks that are unique to their specific project, rather than reinventing the wheel each time around.

- Block hover navs provide users with information as to where they will end up when they click on the link.

5 designing with color

Moving Beyond Monochrome

Now that my site has color, the checks keep rolling in. Who knew a tetradic scheme could be so profitable.

Color is the unsung hero of web design. A good color palette can draw your audience into your site, give them a powerful feeling of immersion, and keep them coming back for more. And when it comes to color and web design, it's not just about picking a **good color palette**, it's also about how you *apply* those colors. You can have a great color palette, but if you don't use those colors **thoughtfully**, people might avoid your site like the plague. By the end of this chapter, you'll not only be intimately familiar with the **impact** that color has on the web user, but you'll also be able to choose a great looking color palette that fits in—and even complements—your user-centered websites.

Help support your local music scene

The site you designed for RPM Music was a big hit. Sam, the store owner, has received such good feedback that he wants to extend his reach and create a new site called SampleRate that offers coverage of the local music scene—and he wants you to design his new website. The thing is, Sam has got it in his head that he wants the new site to be part of the 9Rules Music network (**http://9rules.com/music**). If this new site is chosen to be part of the network, it would mean a lot of exposure for the store and the site (and you as a designer).

Here's the storyboard we already worked up and got Sam to sign off on.

Sam, RPM owner and music afficionado

SampleRate is the perfect complement to RPM's online store. But the SampleRate site has to be top notch... I'm counting on you!

Sam loves the idea of some kind of guitar visual in the header.

The SampleRate design is fairly straightforward: one main column for content with a left-aligned sidebar for additional details.

9Rules: The blog network gold standard

In today's web, blogs are everywhere. The problem is that there are so many that it's hard to know where to find the good ones. That's where 9Rules comes into the picture. 9Rules (**http://9rules.com**) is a cross between a blog aggregator and a blog network. It syndicates the posts of its members (which are conveniently organized by topic categories, such as music, photography, science, design, and games) and provides a one stop shopping spot for those wanting to find top quality blogs.

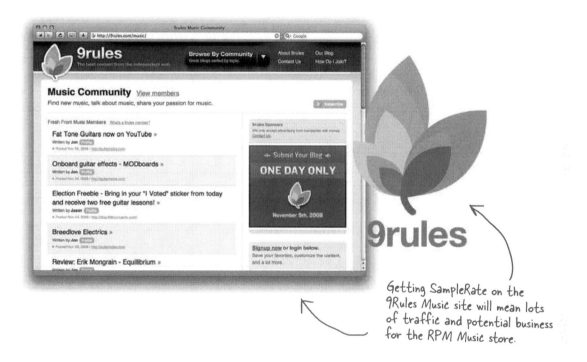

Getting SampleRate on the 9Rules Music site will mean lots of traffic and potential business for the RPM Music store.

So how do we get SampleRate onto the site? Periodically through the year, 9Rules has a 24 hour submission process. During this time, site owners can submit their blogs to be reviewed for membership. On average, 9Rules only accepts about 30 or 40 sites per submission round (out of thousands). The bottom line is that getting accepted into 9Rules is a huge deal and the goal of many designers, content producers, and bloggers.

It takes more than just a great design to get on 9Rules. What are three really effective way to get a site noticed online?

Sometimes your choices are a bit... limited

Sam loves your storyboards, but there's a catch: he's already got a logo for SampleRate that he loves. No matter what else you come up with, you've got to make the new SampleRate site mesh with the existing logo Sam's picked out.

That means we've got some choices taken care of for us, like colors. Take a look at the SampleRate logo... what will this dictate about our design?

This is the logo that Sam's set on using for the SampleRate site.

This is a take on a graphical EQ. For us, though, it sets the colors we've got to work with on the rest of the site.

Sam personally chose this typeface, so we may want to use that font within the site, too.

> Uh, I hate to bring up the obvious, but how can we learn anything about color when this is all in black and white?

You've got a good point.

We didn't need to do this whole book in color (that just means we'd have to charge you more, and who wants that?), but obviously this becomes a problem when we do have to talk about color. And now's the time to talk about color. So we're providing this chapter in color for free online. Head on over to www.headfirstlabs.com/books/hfwd, where you'll be able to download the color version of this chapter.

Color has an emotional impact

Now that you've got this chapter in color, how did you **feel** when you first looked at the SampleRate logo? No matter whether you liked it or hated it, you probably felt something. That's because **color creates emotion**. For example, red is associated with excitement, purple is dignified and stately, yellow is cheerful, and blue is associated with comfort and security.

When we're designing a site that involves strong colors, we've got to think about the emotions those colors generate. Pages that use color well have a feeling that you don't get from sites that don't consciously use color as a design element or that use color poorly. You should treat color as an element, one that's just as important as navigation, images, or content.

Take a look at these bold colors and the sites that use them. You can't help but have a reaction... and that's what we want with SampleRate: a strong, **positive** reaction!

Exercise

Take a look at these four screenshots and write down what you feel when you look at them. Use any kind of descriptive words you want. Excited, playful, happy, sad, curious—whatever you *feel*.

❶ freshairapps.com

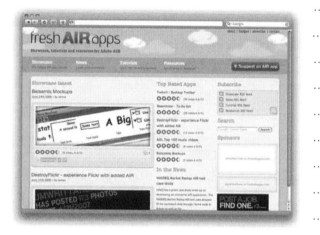

....
....
....
....
....
....
....
....

❷ bigbluedev.com

....
....
....
....
....
....
....
....
....

❸ caxtonstreetfestival.com.au

❹ le-moulin-desauvage.com

"This site does a really good job of reinforcing its visual metaphor with color. The light blue color and clouds play off the fact that the site's called Fresh Air Apps, and the whole page has a very light and airy feel."

Color is probably the single most important design element on this page. Without the light blue (representing the sky), the page loses its "airy" feel and the entire visual metaphor breaks down.

"The whole color scheme is based off the lobster. The deep red really grabs my attention. I also like the wood grain as the background for the content—kind of like a cutting board. This site makes me hungry!"

The red in this site takes the color of the lobster and uses it as the foundation color for the whole page. The page is bright, fun, and represents the content perfectly.

The color wheel (where it all begins)

Before we can even think about what colors we're going to use for SampleRate, let's get acquainted with the mother of all color tools in the design world: **the color wheel**. The color wheel (or *color circle* as it's sometimes called) is a circular diagram that displays different colors and shows the relationship between those colors.

Those relationships are key... and the color wheel lets us choose colors that go well together. Let's start by finding some of the colors in the SampleRate logo on the color wheel:

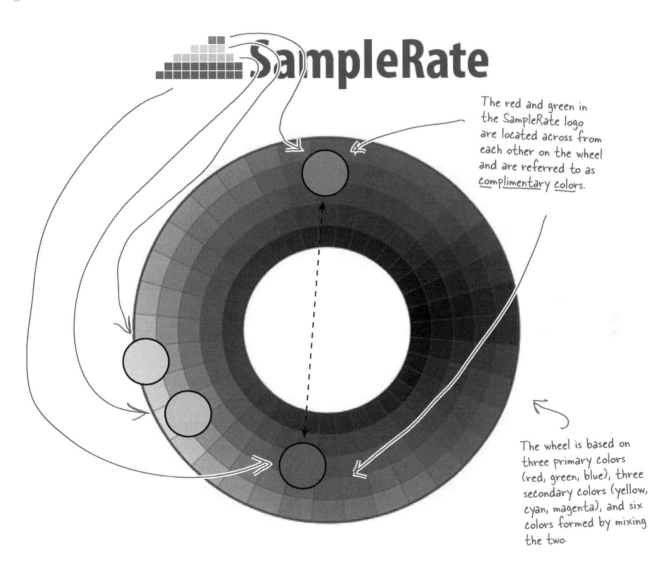

The red and green in the SampleRate logo are located across from each other on the wheel and are referred to as <u>complimentary</u> <u>colors</u>.

The wheel is based on three primary colors (red, green, blue), three secondary colors (yellow, cyan, magenta), and six colors formed by mixing the two.

Sharpen your pencil

Take a look at the sites below and circle each site's main colors on the accompanying color wheel. Once you've circled the colors, try drawing lines between them. Notice any patterns?

Circle every major color represented in the site. Don't worry if the color's not exact, just get as close as you can on the wheel.

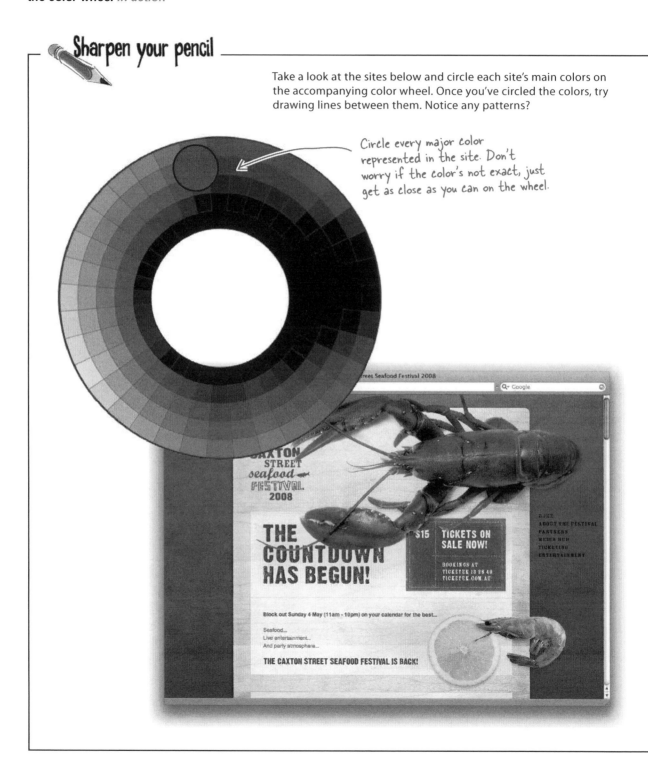

Connect your colors on the wheel in different ways. Any common themes?

Use the color wheel to choose colors that "go together"

You might already be thinking, "Yeah, the color wheel is cool and all, but how do I use it to actually pick colors that work together and don't look like a dog barfed on my web page?" This is where **color schemes** come into the picture. Color schemes are more than just collections of colors. A color scheme is a certain grouping of colors that goes well together.

And here's the kicker: all good color schemes start with a single color and your handy-dandy color wheel.

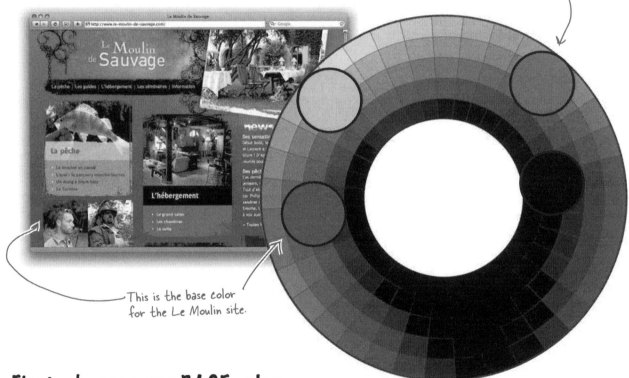

Sometimes you'll hear an individual color in a scheme called a "swatch" of color.

This is the base color for the Le Moulin site.

First, choose your <u>BASE</u> color

The site above has a fairly deep green all over the place. That's the **base color** of the site: the color that most represents the visual metaphor and that all other colors are based on. For SampleRate, we'll need to begin by choosing a base color. Then, we base everything else—other colors, their depth, their hue—off of that base color.

But don't get too stressed out! There's no right or wrong base color... and you can always abandon a scheme that you end up not liking and start over.

Use the <u>triadic scheme</u> to create usable color patterns

Color schemes come in all shapes and sizes—and they all have fancy-sounding names (monochromatic, analogous, complementary, triadic, tetradic, etc.). Don't worry, once you get past their names, they're really just pretty simple ways to pick different kinds of color palettes that you can use for your site. Think of color schemes as just another helpful tool in your web design toolbox.

The **triadic color scheme** is one of the most commonly used color schemes around. Triadic uses **three** colors, *equally spaced* around the color wheel. So once you pick your base color, you can just draw an equalateral triangle (three equal sides), and pick your other two colors:

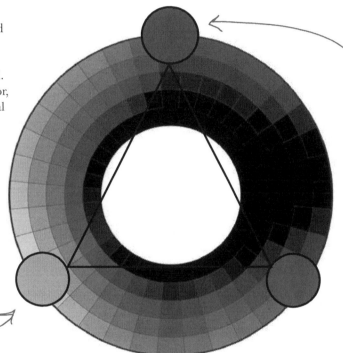

When using the triadic scheme, each color should be equally spaced around the wheel. For you math buffs out there, that's 120 degrees all the way around.

Because all the colors in a triadic scheme are equally spaced around the wheel, <u>any</u> color in the palette can be the base.

Exercise

Create a three-color palette based on the SampleRate logo that Sam provided. Make sure you start with a base color and build your palette from there.

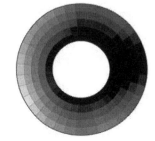

Exercise Solution

We used the deep green as our base color... and came up with the palette below. What colors did you choose? Did the combinations surprise you?

The base color

This green seems like a logical choice for a base color. Plus it's easy to match on our color wheel.

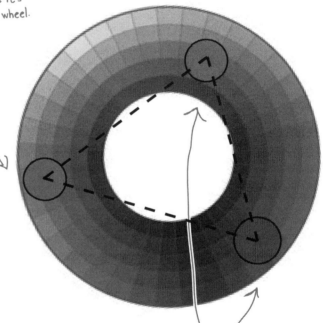

Both these colors are about the same distance from our base color.

BRAIN POWER

Did it surprise you that some of the colors in your triadic scheme were so different from the SampleRate logo? Do you think that's a problem?

Get started on the SampleRate markup

Our standard XHTML
Strict header

```
<!DOCTYPE html PUBLIC "-//W3C//DTD XHTML 1.0 Strict//EN"
        "http://www.w3.org/TR/xhtml1/DTD/xhtml1-strict.dtd">
<html xmlns="http://www.w3.org/1999/xhtml" xml:lang="en" lang="en">
<head>
  <title>Sample Rate</title>
  <meta http-equiv="Content-Type" content="text/html; charset=utf-8"/>
  <link rel="stylesheet" href="stylesheets/screen.css" type="text/css"
        media="screen" />
</head>
<body>
  <div id="header">
    <div id="logo"><img alt="sample rate logo" src="images/samplerate2.gif" /></div>
  </div>
  <div id="nav">
    <ul>
      <li><a class="active" title="title" href="#">Home</a></li>
      <li><a title="title" href="#">Archive</a></li>
      <li><a title="title" href="#">Music</a></li>
      <li><a title="title" href="#">About</a></li>
      <li><a title="title" href="#">Contact</a></li>
    </ul>
  </div>
  <div id="wrap">
    <img id="masthead" alt="header image" src="images/gitfiddle.jpg" width="740px" />
    <div id="content">
      <h1>Heading One</h1>
      <p>Lorem ipsum dolor sit amet, consectetuer adipiscing elit. Fusce
        consequat arcu in mauris.</p>
      <h1>Heading Two</h1>
      <p>Lorem ipsum dolor sit amet, consectetuer adipiscing elit. Fusce
        consequat arcu in mauris.</p>
    </div>
    <div id="sidebar">
      <p>Lorem ipsum dolor sit amet, consectetuer adipiscing elit. Fusce
        consequat arcu in mauris.</p>
    </div>
    <div id="footer">
      <p>Copyright &copy; SampleRate and RPM Music, all rights reserved.</p>
    </div>
  </div>
</body>
</html>
```

Make sure to include your stylesheet, which should be
located in a directory called /stylesheets.

This is the guitar image that the owner
wanted to see on the site.

You may want to
add some more
dummy text to fill
out the page as we
add color and style.

index.html

Typing-challenged? Go online!

If you don't want to type all this in, you can download
the SampleRate files from the Head First Labs website.
You may want to work through these examples on your
own, though... who knows what you might learn in the process?

Create the basic page layout with CSS

```
body {
        margin: 0;
        padding: 0;
        font-family: Verdana, sans-serif;
}
h1 {
        margin: 0 0 5px 0;
}
p {
        margin: 0 0 20px 0;
        line-height: 1.4em;
}
#header {
        margin: 0;
        padding: 20px 0 10px 0;
}
#header #logo {
        margin: 0 auto;
        width: 800px;
}
#nav {
        background: #ccc;
}
#nav ul {
        margin: 0 auto;
        width: 800px;
        list-style-type: none;
}
#nav ul li {
        display: inline;
}
#nav ul li a {
        text-decoration: none;
}
#nav ul li a.active {
}
#wrap {
        margin: 0 auto;
        width: 800px;
}
#masthead {
        margin: 20px 20px 0 20px;
}
```

```
#content {
        float: right;
        margin: 10px 0 0 0;
        padding: 0 20px 0 20px;
        width: 540px;
}
#sidebar {
        float: left;
        margin: 20px 0 0 0;
        padding: 0 20px 0 20px;
        width: 180px;
}
#footer {
        clear: both;
        text-align: center;
}
#footer p {
}
```

screen.css

This CSS will serve as the frame for our layout. Later, we'll add more color and some detail to let Sam really get a feel for our design.

Content chunks below floated <div>'s must be cleared so they appear <u>below</u> those elements.

Like we've done before, use margin: 0 auto to center the layout in the browser.

Remember, this it the board Sam liked... here's what we're going for.

Great, I've got circles on my pretty little color wheel. How do I turn that into CSS? I need those funny hex values, right?

We need a <u>digital</u> color wheel.

CSS requires hexadecimal values for all but the most basic colors. Hex values are 6 characters long, like #572266. A hex value tells the browser how much red, green, and blue to display. So we need a way to take the values we chose on the color wheel and turn them into hex.

Fortunately, there's a program perfect for the job: Kuler (available at **kuler.adobe.com**). Kuler not only has a digital color wheel and hex-conversion tool, it lets you check out other people's palettes and even export your own palettes.

Kuler allows you to select different patterns and see how the colors work together.

Our familiar color wheel

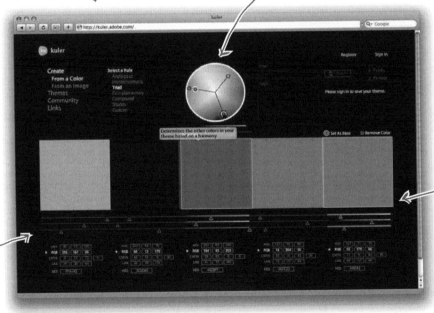

Sliders allow you to make small adjustments to colors, and Kuler automatically adjusts your other colors to fit the color scheme you've chosen.

Stop! Go load Kuler by going to kuler.adobe.com now. You'll see it throughout the rest of the chapter.

Color output is given in multiple formats, including HEX and RGB.

Kuler Up Close

Kuler's color wheel lets you interactively select base colors and then build palettes with different schemes.

The slider view lets you adjust colors with more detail and also displays the selected color in multiple formats.

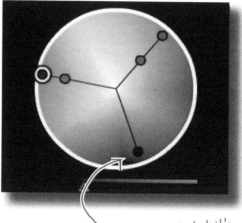

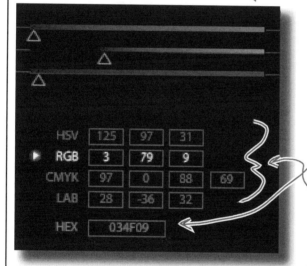

Kuler doesn't show a triangle, but it's the same idea: the triadic scheme uses three colors, equally spaced on the wheel.

Kuler displays the hex value for a color, as well as its hue-saturation-value (HSV), red-green-blue (RGB), and cyan-magenta-yellow-black (CMYK) values. You can even get LAB values from Kuler.

HSV	125	97	31
▶ RGB	3	79	9
CMYK	97	0	88	69
LAB	28	-36	32
HEX	034F09		

Some of Kuler's features require an Adobe ID.

Watch it!

In order to take advantage of Kuler's more advanced features (especially the social stuff), you need to have an Adobe ID. Don't worry, signing up is easy, fast, and free.

Exercise

Use Kuler to take the base color you selected in the previous exercise and build a digital color palette based on the triadic scheme. Once you have your palette, add the hex color values to your SampleRate CSS file and see how they work together. Use your colors for the background colors of the various <div>s in the SampleRate site.

There are more <div>s than colors in a three-color triadic scheme. Try picking some extra colors that are a little lighter or darker than your main three colors to fill out SampleRate.

SampleRate minus any color is pretty bland.

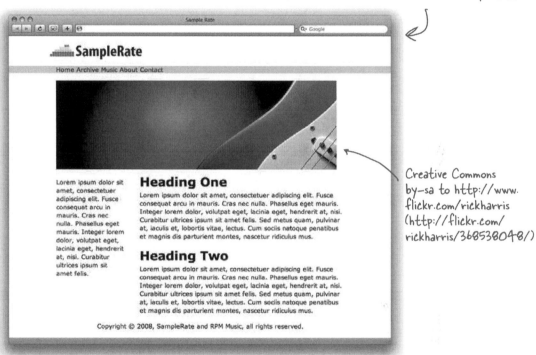

Creative Commons by-sa to http://www.flickr.com/rickharris (http://flickr.com/rickharris/368538048/)

Kuler's a lot more accurate than choosing colors by hand. You might get different colors than we did back on page 172 when we chose colors by hand.

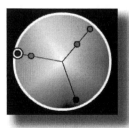

The handle with the white ring represents your base color in Kuler.

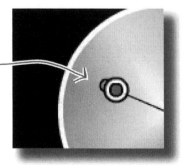

Exercise Solution

Your job was to pick some colors on the color wheel and fill in the CSS for SampleRate using those colors. What did you come up with? Here are the colors we chose:

#572266   #59ad41   #427236 (Base)   #945737   #ad6c49

Each color in this palette is represented in the wheel below. Even though this is a triadic scheme, five colors are possible because 2 of them are lighter shades of two triadic colors.

Our "base" green ended up as the background color for the page.

```
body {
        margin: 0;
        padding: 0;
        font-family: Verdana, sans-serif;
        background: #427236;
}


#header {
        margin: 0;
        padding: 20px 0 10px 0;
        background: #ad6c49;
}

#nav {
        background: #59ad41;
}

#wrap {
        margin: 0 auto;
        width: 800px;
        background: #fff;
}
```

Light brown for the header.

Light green for the navigation.

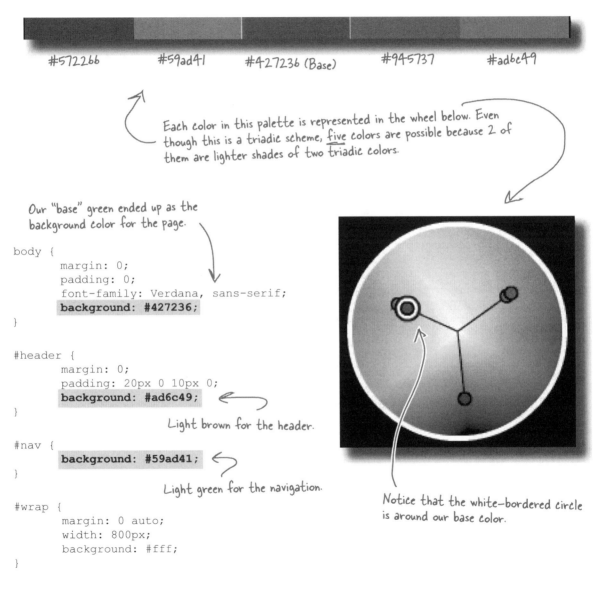

Notice that the white-bordered circle is around our base color.

The SampleRate logo still has a white background. Once we finalize a color palette, we can change the logo so that it matches the header.

I don't know, the site just feels... heavy and oppressive. Do you think you can fix that?

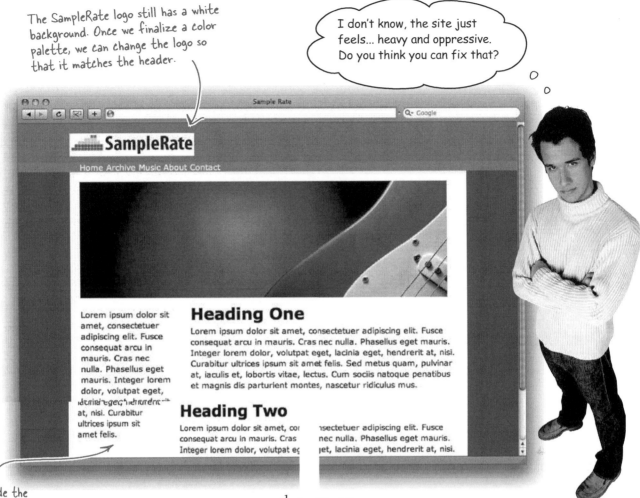

We made the wrap <div> background white so the content of the page stands out a bit better... that makes it more readable.

there are no Dumb Questions

Q: What happened to our blue color?

A: Good question. We just couldn't find a natural place to use that color, although it might work well for the link color for text. Just because your scheme results in three colors, you're not bound to use them. Always trust your judgment over a color wheel or best practice. Ultimately, you're the designer!

Q: Where did that light green come from?

A: Kuler gives you lots of varying colors when you're choosing a scheme, including lighter and darker versions of colors you've already chosen. Those additional colors will go well with your scheme, and that's where our light green came from.

Q: My version of SampleRate looks totally different!

A: Good! Your sites should reflect your choices and your client's tastes.

The opposite of heavy is... light

Sam thinks SampleRate looks heavy. That's not surprising... remember, color causes people to feel things more than any other type of web element. So what do we do about a site feeling heavy? Well, we try and make the site feel *lighter*.

The great thing about the triadic color scheme (or any other type of color scheme) is that as long as you stick to the general location of a color on the color wheel, you can change its saturation. **Saturation** is just a fancy design term for the darkness or lightness of a color. So we can lighten the saturation of our color scheme... it's the same colors, but a lighter feeling result.

The feel of this site really changes as the color saturation is adjusted.

To change the palette as a whole, move all the colors the same distance closer or further away from the center of the color wheel.

Closer to the center results in a darker color.

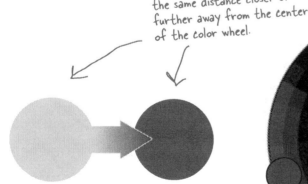

Further from the center results in a lighter color.

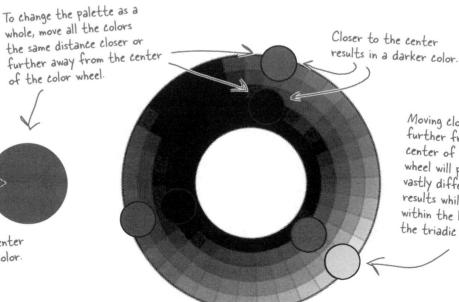

Moving closer and further from the center of the color wheel will produce vastly different results while remaining within the bounds of the triadic scheme.

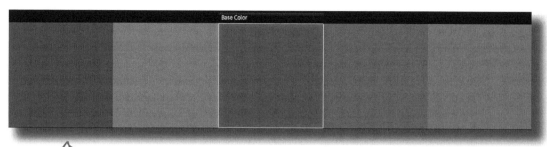

Each color in this palette is represented in the wheel below. Even though this is a triadic scheme, five colors are possible because 2 of them are lighter shades of two triadic colors.

You can grab the circles and move them around on the wheel. Because you have "Triad" selected, you don't have to worry about messing up your scheme.

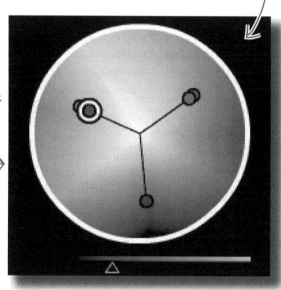

Select a Rule
Analogous
Monochromatic
Triad
Complementary
Compound
Shades
Custom

Remember, we're still using the Triadic (Triad) color scheme.

Sharpen your pencil

Adjust the saturation of the colors on the SampleRate site and change the values in your CSS file, starting with the colors below. How do the new colors change the feel of the site?

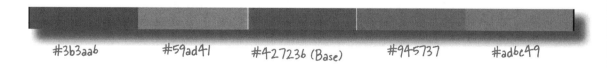

#3b3aa6 #59ad41 #427236 (Base) #945737 #adbc49

Create a richer color palette with the tetradic color scheme

When people find a site boring, that may mean the colors are too light... but we already know that Sam doesn't like a darker triadic color scheme for SampleRate. So if you can't go darker, consider adding colors. In other words, go from a three-color scheme to a four-color scheme.

One of the most common four-color schemes is the **tetradic color scheme**. The tetradic color scheme (which is sometimes also called the **double complementary scheme**) is the richest of all the schemes because it uses four colors arranged into two complementary color pairs.

Be careful, though. Four different colors is a lot to deal with, and you can't use all four colors equally or your site will look like a mess. But for adding some extra complexity and energy to a site, a fourth color can really make a difference.

Colors in a <u>tetradic</u> scheme are in pairs across from one another and about 20 degrees to the left or right of the other pair.

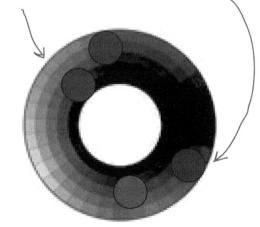

Exercise

Create a new color palette for SampleRate based on a more complex color scheme like tetradic (split complimentary). Use Kuler to find the hex values for the colors you choose.

1 Choose a swatch from the logo colors to set as the base color of your palette (any one that you like, it really doesn't matter).

2 Set this as the base color in Kuler and play around with the controls until you find a palette you like (make sure you select the "Compound" option from the Rule menu).

We're going to use tetradic, but if you want to experiment with another color scheme, go for it!

You should see this setup when you work with compound color schemes in Kuler. Notice the four handles on the color wheel you can adjust now.

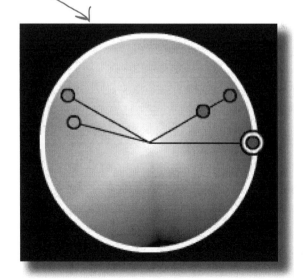

Exercise Solution

We used a tetradic scheme based on the dark green in the SampleRate logo. Kuler gave us four colors in the tetradic scheme, and we also took a lighter swatch of one of the greens Kuler provided for a little more variety.

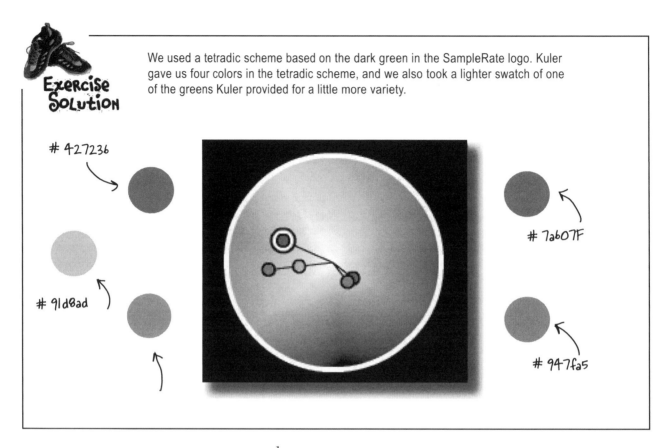

427236

91d8ad

7ab07F

947fa5

there are no
Dumb Questions

Q: **Are there only two color schemes? Triadic and tetradic?**

A: No, there are a bunch of others. Most of the them are simpler schemes: monochromatic, analogous, complementary, and split complementary. All of the schemes follow the same general principles as triadic and tetradic. They find colors related to each other by certain angles that go well together. For more information on these and other color schemes, check out http://www.color-wheel-pro.com/color-schemes.html

Q: **Do I really need to use a color scheme to create a good color palette? Seems like a lot of work to go through when I can just pick some colors off the color wheel.**

A: Sure, you could randomly choose some colors off of the color wheel for your color palette. However, most of the time you are going to get at least two colors that clash. Color schemes are based on solid color theory that has been around for ages. They are designed specifically to help you create harmonious color combinations.

Q: **What if I want lighter colors than the ones available on the color wheel?**

A: Color wheels can either get progressively lighter or darker as you get closer to the center. If lighter colors are what you're after, just drag your colors toward the center of the wheel. Or you can adjust the hue or opacity of a darker color until you've got the lighter swatch you're looking for.

> So once we've chosen our colors, aren't there some rules we can apply to make sure we use them correctly on the page?

There's no golden rule for color placement.

Although there's definitely a Golden Ratio!

There really isn't a set of rules that will always work for all sites. What looks great for one site's structure could look awful for another site's layout and design. On top of that, you've got to match your site's theme and visual metaphor.

But there are definitely some ***principles*** you can apply:

Create contrast

If you want to separate different areas of your layout (say a main column and sidebar), use **contrasting** colors. This contrast creates a border between two areas. That border lets users know that the two areas are different and probably have different functions or uses within the context of the site.

adipiscing elit. Fusce consequat arcu in mauris. Cras nec

The background of the page and the text area use highly-contrasting colors. This makes the content of the page clearly separate from the overall site background.

Emphasis-o-matic

If you want to emphasize certain areas of your layout, use the most dominant color in your color palette. If you surround an important area of content (like a header or page title) with the palette's dominant color, that area will be emphasized.

Home

Here contrast and a dominant color are used. There's a contrast between the Home tab and the dark background. But the tab is emphasized against the very dominant brown background.

Let's update the SampleRate CSS

Here is the completed CSS for the SampleRate site. The colors for the design are
blank (and represented by the grey bars). Get the CSS linked up with your XHTML
and double check the layout. We'll add the color in the next few pages.

*All the blanks are places we
need colors... we'll add those in
over the next few pages.*

```css
body {
        margin: 0;
        padding: 0;
        font-family: Verdana, sans-serif;
        color: #333;
        background: ...............;
}
h1 {
        margin: 0 0 5px 0;
}
p {
        margin: 0 0 20px 0;
        line-height: 1.4em;
}
#header {
        margin: 0;
        padding: 20px 0 10px 0;
        background: ...............;
}
#header #logo {
        margin: 0 auto;
        width: 800px;
}
#nav {
        background: ...............;
}
#nav ul {
        margin: 0 auto;
        padding: 20px 10px 20px 10px;
        width: 800px;
        list-style-type: none;
}
#nav ul li {
        display: inline;
}
#nav ul li a {
        padding: 10px 20px 20px 20px;
        text-decoration: none;
        color: #fff;
        font-weight: bold;
}
```

```css
#nav ul li a.active {
        background: #eee;
        color: #333;
}
#wrap {
        margin: 0 auto;
        width: 800px;
        background: #eee;
        border-left: 10px solid ...............
        border-right: 10px solid ...............
}
#masthead {
        margin: 20px 20px 0 20px;
        border: 10px solid #ddd;
}
#content {
        float: right;
        margin: 10px 0 0 0;
        padding: 0 20px 0 20px;
        width: 540px;
}
#sidebar {
        float: left;
        margin: 20px 0 0 0;
        padding: 0 20px 0 20px;
        width: 180px;
}
#footer {
        margin: 20px 20px 0 20px;
        padding: 10px 20px 10px 20px;
        clear: both;
        background: ...............;
        text-align: center;
        color: #fff;
}
#footer p {
        margin: 10px 0 0 0;
        font-size: small;
}
```

*Borders around the
main <div> provide
some contrast.*

Write the hex values for your colors in the spaces where you think the color fits best. Think about contrast and the best way to make the content stand out. We'll build these colors into our actual design in just a few pages. Remember, white space is your friend! Use `#ffffff` for white.

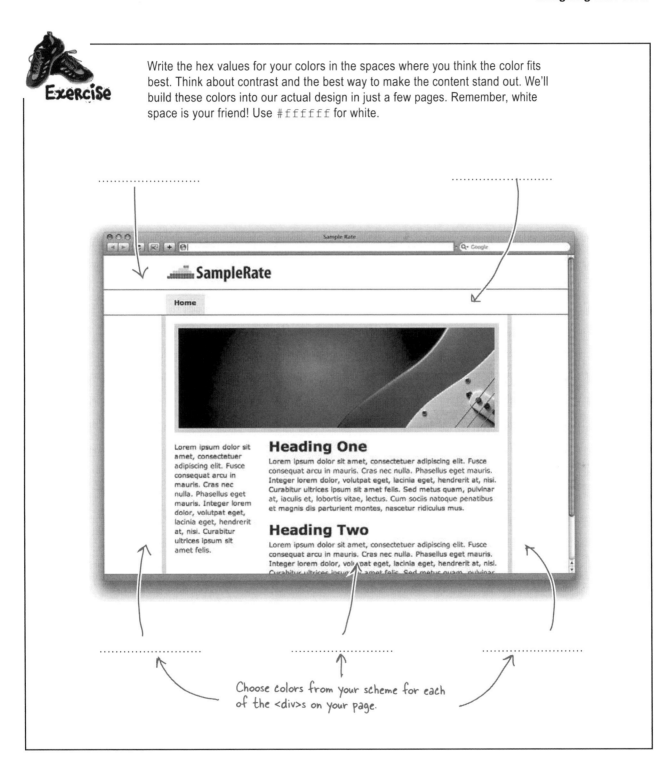

Choose colors from your scheme for each of the <div>s on your page.

Exercise Solution

Here's the layout we came up with. What do you like? What don't you like?

#ffffff
→ We thought keeping the logo on a white background makes it pop out better.

We used the color pulled from the logo on the header, which ties the logo into the rest of the page.

#447236 ←

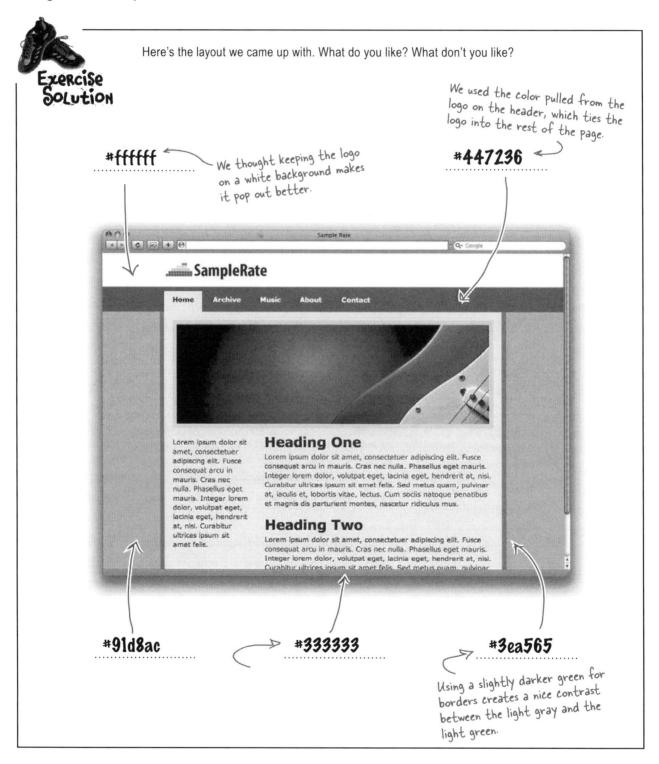

#91d8ac

#333333

#3ea565
Using a slightly darker green for borders creates a nice contrast between the light gray and the light green.

Hey, that's really nice! I like it... but listen, I did some branding research, and everyone thinks my logo is too "analog." So I've got a new one—much more Web 2.0. You can fix the site to use this, right?

The new "Web 2.0" version of the SampleRate logo is complete with gradients and bold fonts. The icon has also been slightly reworked.

Exercise

We've got a whole new logo! Your job is to update your color palette to fit the new design and add the new hex color codes to your SampleRate CSS file.

1 Select a base color from the new logo (your choices are a bit more limited this time).

....

Write the hex code of the base color you chose here (use Kuler).

2 Use Kuler to develop a color palette that meets the new SampleRate site's needs (and that of the site's content). Write the hex color codes you chose in the blanks below:

....

3 Update your CSS file to reflect the new colors. Experiment as much as you like!

Your Web Design Toolbox

Color, tetradic, triadic, split complementary... lots of new terms, and you've handled them all. Go back to the other sites you've worked on and update them with color, too.

- Color has a powerful impact on your site's visitors.

- Use the color wheel to choose colors for your site's design.

- Color schemes are tools to help you choose a harmonious color palette.

- The triadic color scheme has three colors spaced equally from around the color wheel.

- The triadic color scheme is popular because it provides strong visual contrast while retaining balance, color richness, and harmony.

- The triadic scheme is not as contrasting as some other schemes.

- The tetradic color scheme has 4 colors arranged into two complementary color pairs.

- The tetradic color scheme is the richest of all the schemes.

- The drawback to the tetradic scheme is that it's sometimes hard to harmonize.

- Use a tool like Kuler to crate a color palette (and get the hex values of the colors in the palette.)

"In 2 seconds, click 'Home'."

Thanks to my on-bike navigation, I'm no longer getting lost on my evening rides.

What would the Web be without navigation?

Navigation is what makes the Web such a powerful information medium. But here's the thing: navigation is a lot more than just whipping up some cool-looking buttons and slapping them into your design. Building smart navigation starts with your information architecture and continues through your entire design process. But how does it work? How do you really make sure your users never get lost? In this chapter, we'll look at different styles of navigation, how IA guides your page links, and why icons (alone) aren't always iconic.

School's back in session

The College of New Media at Mackinac State University has a bit of a problem. They've just paid a bundle to a web design firm to redo their site. The new site looks great... but nobody can find anything anymore! Professors can't find their papers and documents, teaching assistants can't even figure out what classes they're teaching, and new students need to register for the next semester's classes... now.

The college needs you to unravel their navigation nightmare, and do it fast. Otherwise they're going to lose students *and* faculty!

We don't need a new design, but this navigation deal is a mess.

MSU's Registrar, awash in complaints and confusion

This is the College of New Media's new website.

Exercise

Take a look at the screenshot of the current CNM site. First circle all the different areas of navigation. Then list any problems you find in the blanks below the screenshot. Be thorough and remember, both students and faculty are using this site.

Don't forget to describe the problems you find here.

1 ....
....
....

2 ....
....
....

3 ....
....
....

4 ....
....
....

Exercise
Solution

Your job was to find all the potential navigation problems on the CNM website. What did you come up with?

Each numbered item refers to a problem we wrote down below.

① **The titles of these links leave users wondering what to expect when they click them.**

② **These look like icons for the different programs. Not sure what they mean though.**

③ **It looks like the designers skipped the navigation. Needs some style work.**

④ **Will this always be a title? Will more navigation show up here? I'm confused...**

Most of this is about crappy link names, right? Can't we just go in and fix those?

The first step to good <u>navigation</u> is good <u>IA</u>

The names of your links are more than just helpers for your users. They're actually the categories that organize your entire site. And most of the time, a bad link name means someone wasn't thinking about navigation way back at the information architecture stage.

Let's see what the CNM IA diagram looks like:

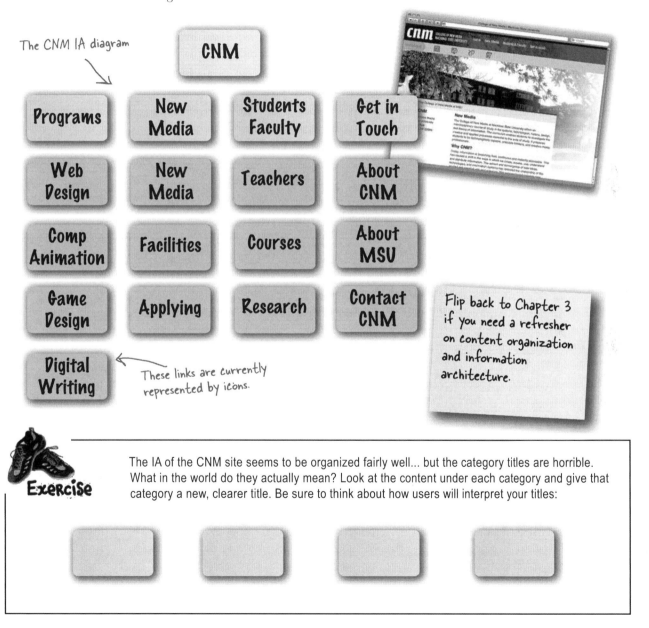

The CNM IA diagram

CNM

Programs | New Media | Students Faculty | Get in Touch

Web Design | New Media | Teachers | About CNM

Comp Animation | Facilities | Courses | About MSU

Game Design | Applying | Research | Contact CNM

Digital Writing

These links are currently represented by icons.

Flip back to Chapter 3 if you need a refresher on content organization and information architecture.

Exercise

The IA of the CNM site seems to be organized fairly well... but the category titles are horrible. What in the world do they actually mean? Look at the content under each category and give that category a new, clearer title. Be sure to think about how users will interpret your titles:

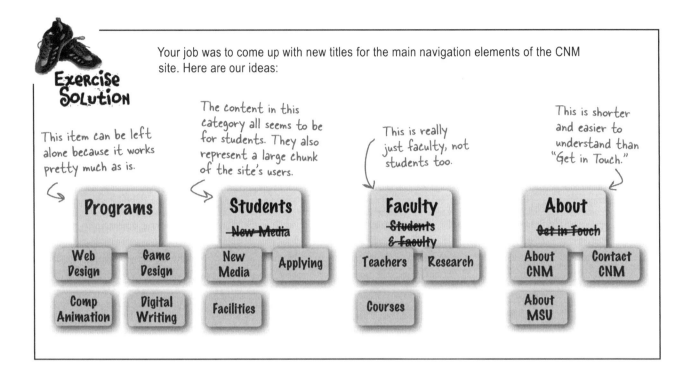

Exercise Solution

Your job was to come up with new titles for the main navigation elements of the CNM site. Here are our ideas:

This item can be left alone because it works pretty much as is.

The content in this category all seems to be for students. They also represent a large chunk of the site's users.

This is really just faculty, not students too.

This is shorter and easier to understand than "Get in Touch."

Programs
- Web Design
- Game Design
- Comp Animation
- Digital Writing

Students
~~New Media~~
- New Media
- Applying
- Facilities

Faculty
~~Students & Faculty~~
- Teachers
- Research
- Courses

About
~~Get in Touch~~
- About CNM
- Contact CNM
- About MSU

What's really in a name, anyway?

The names that you give your navigational elements (links, buttons, etc.) have a direct impact on the usability of your site. In other words, *names are a really big deal* on the Web. You should put a lot of thought into the name you use for each of your IA categories and navigational elements. Here are some general guidelines to help you come up with good names:

1 **Keep names <u>short</u>**. Make sure that your names are as short as possible. You want your user to be able to scan a name quickly. One word is ideal. Only use two if you really need that extra word. Avoid using words like "the" or "a" in names, too. Those are just a waste of space.

2 **Keep names <u>descriptive</u>**. Make sure that the name you choose is as clear and straight to the point as possible. You don't want your users to look at a link and be confused. If you're not 110% sure what a name means, your users sure won't be, either.

Test Drive

① **Download the College of New Media site files from the Head First Labs site.**

Visit http://www.headfirstlabs.com, find the Web Design link, and click through to the Chapter 6 sample files.

② **Update the main CNM navigation links.**

```
<!DOCTYPE html PUBLIC "-//W3C//DTD XHTML 1.0 Strict//EN"
        "http://www.w3.org/TR/xhtml1/DTD/xhtml1-strict.dtd">
<html xmlns="http://www.w3.org/1999/xhtml" xml:lang="en" lang="en">
<head>
   <title>College of New Media | Mackinac State University</title>
   <meta http-equiv="Content-Type" content="text/html; charset=utf-8"/>
   <link rel="stylesheet" href="stylesheets/screen.css"
         type="text/css" media="screen" />
</head>
<body>
   <div id="header">
     <img alt="cmn logo" src="images/cnm_logo.png" />
     <p id="nav">
       <a class="active" title="CNM Home" href="index.html">Home</a>
       <a title="#" href="#">Students</a>
       <a title="#" href="#">Faculty</a>
       <a title="#" href="#">About</a>
     </p>
   </div>
   <!-- rest of HTML -->
</body>
</html>
```

Update the links in the navigation paragraph to reflect your new category titles from the IA diagram.

③ **Check out the site and make sure things look right.**

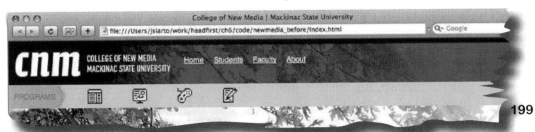

I've been taking a close look at these nav links. They're just in <a> tags, right? Should we do anything to make those links related to each other? They're all navigation, right?

The Web is both <u>VISUAL</u> and <u>SEMANTIC</u>.

We've mostly been focusing on how sites look, but there's another element to the Web: the semantic Web. Right now, our navigation links look good, but they've got no meaning. Really, those links are a list of items that are all part of the site's navigation.

What we need is a way to give some semantic meaning to our list of links. Of course, XHTML gives us a couple of list elements, so let's start there:

Give the <ul> a unique ID so that we can style it differently from other lists that may appear on the site.

By giving the link of the page we are currently on an active state, we can add a style that helps users know what page they are on.

This id also uniquely identifies this list as a list of navigation elements: that's semantic meaning.

```
<ul id="navigation">
  <li><a class="active" title="Home" href="index.html">Home</a></li>
  <li><a title="My Blog" href="/blog/">Blog</a></li>
  <li><a title="My Portfolio" href="portfolio.html">Portfolio</a></li>
  <li><a title="Contact us" href="contact.html">Contact</a></li>
</ul>
```

A standard link tag goes in between each list item creating the list of links.

This is what the link list will look like with no CSS applied.

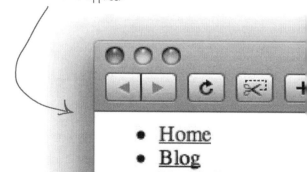

there are no
Dumb Questions

Q: Why do semantics matter if things look good on screen?

A: Good question. For one thing, you can write much more specific and functional CSS rules if you're identifying sections of your site semantically. But even more importantly, semantics are a big deal when disabled users access your site. We'll talk a lot more about site accessibility in Chapter 8, so hold that thought a little longer.

Sharpen your pencil

Before we can start updating the look and feel of the CNM navigation, we need to get the main nav into an unordered list. Take a look at the main XHTML and CSS for the site file and update the markup and rules to work with an unordered list.

```
<!DOCTYPE html PUBLIC "-//W3C//DTD XHTML 1.0 Strict//EN"
        "http://www.w3.org/TR/xhtml1/DTD/xhtml1-strict.dtd">
<html xmlns="http://www.w3.org/1999/xhtml" xml:lang="en" lang="en">
<head>
   <title>College of New Media | Mackinac State University</title>
   <meta http-equiv="Content-Type" content="text/html; charset=utf-8"/>
   <link rel="stylesheet" href="stylesheets/screen.css"
        type="text/css" media="screen" />
</head>
<body>
   <div id="header">
      <img alt="cmn logo" src="images/cnm_logo.png" />
```

```
   </div>
   <!-- etc. -->
</body>
</html>
```

index.html

Add the new navigation link list to the header of the CNM site.

```
#nav {

}
```

Once you change the markup, you need to adjust the CSS so that your navigation looks the same. Add some rules to get the navigation looking like it did before you changed the markup.

```
#nav li a {

}
```

screen.css

Sharpen your pencil
Solution

Now that you've got a good idea about the primary and secondary navigation, it's time to put your newfound knowledge to work.

```
<!DOCTYPE html PUBLIC "-//W3C//DTD XHTML 1.0 Strict//EN"
        "http://www.w3.org/TR/xhtml1/DTD/xhtml1-strict.dtd">
<html xmlns="http://www.w3.org/1999/xhtml" xml:lang="en" lang="en">
<head>
  <title>College of New Media | Mackinac State University</title>
  <meta http-equiv="Content-Type" content="text/html; charset=utf-8"/>
  <link rel="stylesheet" href="stylesheets/screen.css"
        type="text/css" media="screen" />
</head>
<body>
  <div id="header">
    <img alt="cmn logo" src="images/cnm_logo.png" />
    <ul id="nav">
      <li><a class="active" title="CNM Home" href="index.html">Home</a></li>
      <li><a title="#" href="#">Students</a></li>
      <li><a title="#" href="#">Faculty</a></li>
      <li><a title="#" href="#">About</a></li>
    </ul>
  </div>
  <!-- etc. -->
</body>
</html>
```

index.html

We changed the <p> tags to <ul>s and added the appropriate <li>s to each link.

```
#nav {
    float: left;
    width: 460px;
    height: 75px;
    font-size: 1.4em;
}
```

We floated the whole navigation to the left so it appears next to the logo in the upper left corner.

```
#nav li a {
    color: #fff;
    float: left;
    padding: 20px 20px 20px 0;
}
```

Like the nav <ul>, we floated each link to the left so that they appear inline instead of in block form (which is the default).

screen.css

Test Drive

Update your versions of index.html and screen.css, and take the new CNM site for a test drive. How do things look? Better? Worse? The same?

> Well this is clearer, but people are still getting lost. I don't think people even notice those links up top.

Sharpen your pencil

Where else could the links go? Write down at least three ideas for a different style and/or location for the CNM's site navigation.

1. ....
2. ....
3. ....

Approach #1: Horizontally-tabbed navigation

Many of today's modern, standards-based designs feature horizontally-tabbed navigation systems. This type of design works great with a one or two-column layout (though they tend to get a little stretched out the wider a layout gets). A horizontally-tabbed navigation system also works great for your primary navigation because if the links are put at the top of your page, they attract the attention and focus of your user. Tabs also give the impression of the site having different sections—which it does.

Here's what horizontal tabs usually look like in XHTML and CSS:

```
<ul id="navigation">
  <li><a class="active" title="Home" href="index.html">Home</a></li>
  <li><a title="My Blog" href="/blog/">Blog</a></li>
  <li><a title="My Portfolio" href="portfolio.html">Portfolio</a></li>
  <li><a title="Contact us" href="contact.html">Contact</a></li>
</ul>
```

Like before, these links are in a list and semantically marked as navigation.

| Home | Blog | Portfolio | Contact |

A simple, horizontal navigation.

```
#navigation {
      margin: 0;
      padding: 10px;
      list-style-type: none;
      border-bottom: 1px solid #ccc;
}
#navigation li {
      display: inline;
}
#navigation li a {
      text-decoration: none;
      padding: 10px;
      color: #777;
}
#navigation li a.active, #navigation li a:hover {
      background: #eee;
      border-top: 2px solid #ddd;
      color: #333;
}
```

This rule changes the <li> tags from a block element to an inline element, allowing them to appear next to each other instead of on top of one another.

The active and hover states allow us to define rules that change the navigation when the link has an "active" class or when it's hovered over with the mouse.

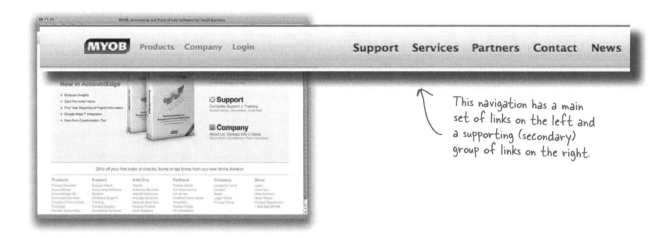

This navigation has a main set of links on the left and a supporting (secondary) group of links on the right.

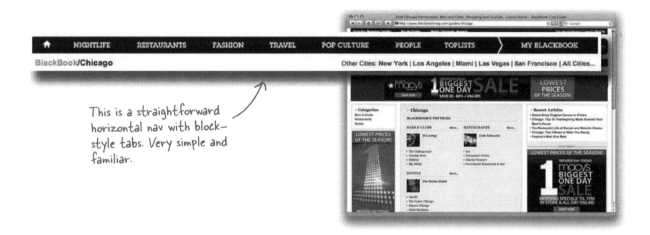

This is a straightforward horizontal nav with block-style tabs. Very simple and familiar.

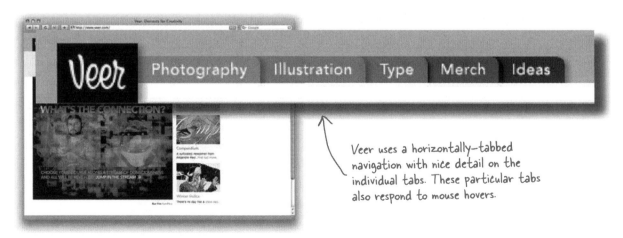

Veer uses a horizontally-tabbed navigation with nice detail on the individual tabs. These particular tabs also respond to mouse hovers.

Approach #2: Vertical navigation

Vertical navigation designs are just as popular as horizontal ones—and show up in a lot of two-column designs. Vertical navigation isn't inherently better than horizontal navigation designs; it's just a different way to display your site links.

You can't always go with vertical navigation, though. Some single-column designs just don't play nicely with vertical navigation... but with most designs, you can go horizontal or vertical.

Here's what vertical navigation looks like in XHTML and CSS:

Notice that the XHTML stays the same... all the styling and positioning is done in CSS.

```
<ul id="navigation">
  <li><a class="active" title="Home" href="index.html">Home</a></li>
  <li><a title="My Blog" href="/blog/">Blog</a></li>
  <li><a title="My Portfolio" href="portfolio.html">Portfolio</a></li>
  <li><a title="Contact us" href="contact.html">Contact</a></li>
</ul>
```

```
#navigation {
      margin: 0;
      padding: 0;
      list-style-type: none;
      width: 200px;
}

#navigation li {
      border-bottom: 1px solid #ccc;
}

#navigation li a {
      text-decoration: none;
      color: #777;
      display: block;
      padding: 10px;
}

#navigation li a.active, #navigation li a:hover {
      background: #eee;
      color: #333;
}
```

Just by slightly changing your CSS, you can create a whole different navigation layout.

In our CSS, the <li>s are displayed normally (not inline), and our <a> tags are displayed as blocks. This allows us to create nice block rollovers and active states.

It can't get any simpler than this. Short, stacked, easy to find and read.

This is almost like a vertical tab. The nav runs the length page, and when a link is active, it's background matches the body content.

there are no
Dumb Questions

Q: Is it better to put vertical navigation on the left or right side of my page?

A: Lots of usability studies show there doesn't seem to be any real difference if you put your navigation on the left or the right side. If your layout works better with the navigation on the left, you should put it there. If your layout works better with a nav on the right, then that's okay too.

> I don't want to radically change our design, so let's stick with horizontal navigation. But can you make the links a lot more obvious? It seems so confusing right now...

Inconsistent navigation confuses users.

We base the way in which we interact with the world around us on the predictability of events. Every day millions of people pull up to a red light, wait for it to turn green, and then continue driving. But what if you pulled up to a red light and instead of it turning green, it turned blue? You'd probably have absolutely no clue what to do.

Navigation works in a similar way. When a navigational system works right, people rely on it. In the CNM system, the navigation isn't what users are expecting. That's because it probably violates at least one of the following three principles:

1 Navigation should be in a place users expect it to be: usually the top of a page or along either side.

2 Links should look like links. They should appear to be "clickable" for users.

3 Links should be clearly identified and separate from each other.

Sharpen your pencil

How does the CNM site navigation hold up to the principles above? Next to each principle, write down some notes about that principle relating to the current CNM navigation.

Exercise

Using the header overlays below, sketch three different navigation designs for the CNM site. Think about consistency and how familiar your scheme is going to feel for a typical user.

Exercise Solution

How did your navigation design go? Were you able to come up with some ideas that clearly followed the three navigation principles we looked at back on page 208?

❶

Tabs would be a familiar option for users, but they wouldn't quite work with the overall theme of the site.

Tabs are intuitive, clearly clickable, and distinct from one another. That's why they're so popular for navigation.

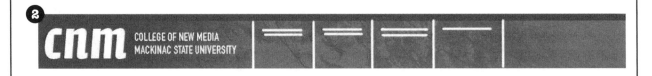

❷

These are a lot like tabs, and the dividing lines make each link look more clickable to an average user.

This block-style navigation is a nice fit with the CNM site and will be quick and easy to implement.

❸

This navigation is close to what CNM already has. It's basically a cleaned up version with a rounded background on the active and hover states.

The big change here was making sure the links stood out more and were more obviously something that could be clicked on.

I really like the tabs. Why don't we go with those, and just update the rest of the page's design to match a tabbed look?

Frank

Jim   Joe

Joe: I thought the registrar said they really liked the current design and just wanted to fix the navigation?

Frank: Besides, I think navigation should fit into your design, not make you change it.

Jim: Why not? I thought we all agreed that navigation should start way back when we're doing IA. So doesn't navigation have to influence our design?

Frank: Well, when we were doing IA, we just needed to make sure our category titles were short—

Joe:—and descriptive.

Frank: Right. But that's got nothing to do with how navigation actually looks on the page.

Jim: So we're stuck with the current design?

Joe: I'm not sure we're stuck with it. It's pretty nice, you know? I just don't think we need to mess with something that's working already.

Frank: Exactly. We're not getting paid to do all that extra design work.

Jim: Hmm. That's true. And I don't suppose the school would give us extra cash out of the goodness of their heart, huh?

Frank's talking about this option for navigation.

Frank: Probably not. I think going with a simple, block-style of navigation is our best bet.

Joe: That's where we just have some dividing lines between our navigation links, right?

Frank: Exactly.

Jim: So why do you call it *block* navigation?

Frank: Let me show you... it's all about the CSS we'll need to create that sort of a navigation menu...

Know your role in a web design gig. You'll rarely get paid for doing "extra" work unrelated to your core assignments.

Block elements are your friends

Block elements (like paragraphs and headings) literally form a block from one side of the page to the other. And by default, block elements are as tall as the content they contain.

This is why when you apply a background image to a heading. The image stretches well beyond the text within the element.

We've got our links in block elements already—those `<li>`s we added earlier:

```
<ul id="nav">
  <li><a class="active" title="CNM Home" href="index.html">Home</a></li>
  <li><a title="#" href="#">Students</a></li>
  <li><a title="#" href="#">Faculty</a></li>
  <li><a title="#" href="#">About</a></li>
</ul>
```

Each of these `<li>`s is a block element.

But we need to make the navigation lists behave like inline elements so that they line up next to each other horizontally. We can accomplish this using CSS by changing the list to display inline or floating the list items left or right:

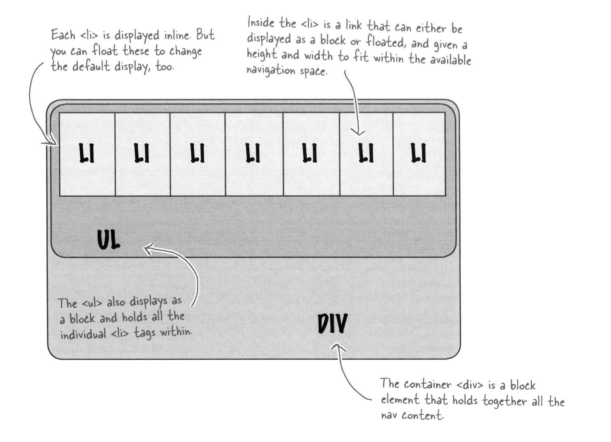

Each `<li>` is displayed inline. But you can float these to change the default display, too.

Inside the `<li>` is a link that can either be displayed as a block or floated, and given a height and width to fit within the available navigation space.

The `<ul>` also displays as a block and holds all the individual `<li>` tags within.

The container `<div>` is a block element that holds together all the nav content.

Let's float the block navigation on the CNM site

If we think of each `<li>` in our navigation as a block, then we just need some CSS to style those blocks. We can add borders to separate each block and make sure each block is positioned related to the previous block.

Make these changes to your version of `screen.css`:

screen.css

```
#nav {
    float: left;
    width: 460px;
    height: 75px;
    font-size: 1.4em;
}

#nav li a {
    float: left;
    width: 104px;
    height: 65px;
    padding: 10px 0 0 10px;
    color: #fff;
    text-decoration: none;
    border-right: 1px solid #777;
}

#nav li a.active {
    background: #222;
}
```

Because the #nav (<ul>) is a block element, it's going to want to wrap below the header logo. To fix this, we need to float the <ul> left and give it a fixed width so it displays next to, not below, the header logo.

Like the <ul>, the links need to float to the left to mimic a block style. We'll give the links a fixed height and width that will give the nav items a consistent look regardless of the length of the text.

A dark background on the "active" class will give the current page link a distinctive look and let users know where they are in the site.

This CSS gives us a simple, clean navigation that catches the user's eye. All the links are now clearly separated from each other too.

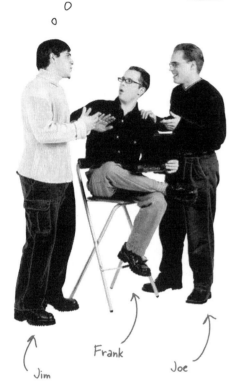

Jim

Frank

Joe

Alright, you had a good point about using block navigation. It looks nice. But I bet you'll agree with me on this... those little icons are terrible!

Here's what Jim's referring to... these are just below the header of the CNM site. ↙

Frank: Yeah, no argument there. What are those?

Joe: I tried clicking on them. They're actually navigation.

Frank: Really? Where'd they take you?

Joe: To different degree program sub-sites. One was video games—

Jim: Oh, I bet that was the little icon that looks like a game controller, right?

Joe: Right. But another was...

Frank: Wait, let me guess. If the icons are good, I should be able to figure this out for myself, right?

Joe: Ha, I guess. Good luck though.

Frank: Let's see. It's a school for new media, so... web design. Was one of them web design?

Joe: Wow, nice call.

Jim: Wait a second... ***which*** icon stands for web design, Frank?

Frank: Hmm. Honestly? I have no idea...

Jim: My point exactly. We've *got* to do something about those icons. I didn't even know you could click on them at first!

Confusion is the enemy of good web design. If something's confusing to you, it will probably be <u>VERY</u> confusing to your users.

Icons don't <u>SAY</u> anything... they just look pretty

Yes, icons are cool little design elements. The problem is, when used for navigation, they can cause some serious problems. What does an icon mean? What happens if you click on it? Where will the site take me?

Even this is debatable.

What one icon represents to you might be completely different from what it represents to another person. And if you use an icon as a navigational element, your users might get the wrong impression about where they will end up if they click the icon. The end result? The user's taken somewhere they didn't mean to go, and now they're a lot more likely to move on to another site.

Take the icons on the CNM site... how clear are their meanings?

Sharpen your pencil

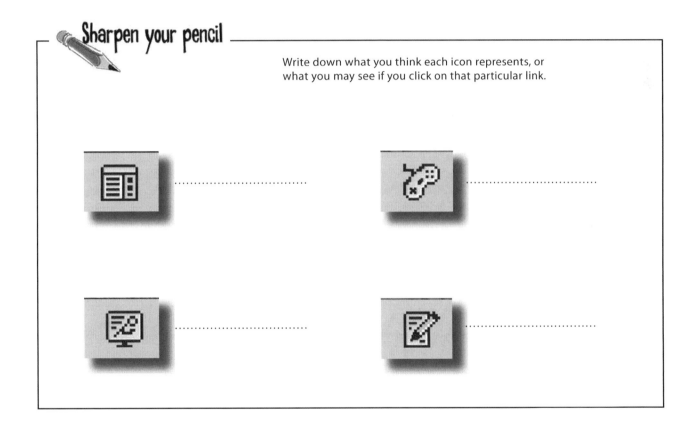

Write down what you think each icon represents, or what you may see if you click on that particular link.

Sharpen your pencil
Solution

Here is what the College of New Media says each of the icons mean. How close were you? If you got even two of these right on, then you get the Ambiguous Icon Detective award for the day...

This icon represents a web page and is meant to indicate the web design program at CNM.

 **Web Design**

The gamepad was used to represent the video game design program. CNM thinks this is a totally obvious icon.

 Game Design

Computer Animation

This icon is supposed to represent a man running on a computer screen. It links to the computer animation program.

Digital Writing & Rhetoric

This is a commonly used icon—the classic pen and paper. In this case, it represents the digital writing and rhetoric program.

Woah, those icons are in all of our promotional material. We can't lose those... it's just not an option.

When in doubt, __ADD TEXT.__

Sometimes you're gonna get stuck with a bad display element, or perhaps just some meaningless or confusing icons. If you're not able to make major changes, one easy fix is to simply add text, clarifying the icons or explaining how to use a particular page element.

A little bit of clarifying text goes a long way to let a user know what to click or where to go on a page.

Add icons to your text, not the other way around

Right now the four CNM icons are little images inserted into the XHTML. If we want to add text descriptions of those icons, we'd need to squeeze the text between each icon, potentially resize the icon, align the text with the image... and things get pretty complicated fast.

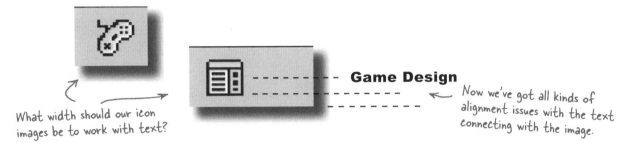

What width should our icon images be to work with text?

Now we've got all kinds of alignment issues with the text connecting with the image.

So what can we do? Suppose we started with text, like "Web Design" and "Computer Animation." The icons are meant to be links, so we can surround the text with <a> tags. But once we've got <a> tags, we can style those with CSS.

This <a> tag can by styled now...

...and put into a list for some semantic meaning.

With stylable elements to work with, we can get around all the position issues and actually insert the icons as background images to the <li> text items. That means the <li> will grow to the right size, and since each link is in an <li>, everything will naturally line up properly.

We can set the background image property of each <li> to the appropriate icon and make sure things line up just right.

By default, an image in the background property will repeat. Use the "no-repeat" value to make an image only display once, and then position it centered on the left side of an element.

```
background: #dddddd url('web_design-icon.gif') no-repeat left center;
```

Update the CNM XHTML to use textual links

Let's open up `index.html` and remove the icon images from the XHTML. We need a new unordered list, with `<li>`s and `<a>`s for each link. We'll use the textual link name, and then in a moment we can update our CSS to style each link.

Go ahead and make these changes to your copy of `index.html`:

```
<!DOCTYPE html PUBLIC "-//W3C//DTD XHTML 1.0 Strict//EN"
       "http://www.w3.org/TR/xhtml1/DTD/xhtml1-strict.dtd">
<html xmlns="http://www.w3.org/1999/xhtml" xml:lang="en" lang="en">
<head>
   <title>College of New Media | Mackinac State University</title>
   <meta http-equiv="Content-Type" content="text/html; charset=utf-8"/>
   <link rel="stylesheet" href="stylesheets/screen.css" type="text/css"
       media="screen" />
</head>
<body>
   <div id="header">
     <img alt="cmn logo" src="images/cnm_logo.png" />
     <ul id="nav">
       <li><a class="active" title="CNM Home" href="index.html">Home</a></li>
       <li><a title="#" href="#">Students</a></li>
       <li><a title="#" href="#">Faculty</a></li>
       <li><a title="#" href="#">About</a></li>
     </ul>
   </div>
   <div id="subnav">
     <ul>
       <li class="option">Programs</li>
       <li><a class="webdesign" href="#">Web Design</a></li>
       <li><a class="animation" href="#">Computer Animation</a></li>
       <li><a class="game" href="#">Game Design</a></li>
       <li><a class="writing" href="#">Digital Writing &amp; Rhetoric</a></li>
     </ul>
   </div>
   <!-- etc... -->
</body>
</html>
```

This list item has a special class so that we can style it differently from the rest of the links. This will act almost like a title for the sub-navigation.

The # signs are just placeholders for links. When we have files to link to, we'll replace the # sign.

This link list should be very similar to the main nav link list. Just make sure that you give the container <div> a different id.

Each link has its own class, so we can assign the right icon to the background.

index.html

Now we can style our new block elements...

Now you can add these rules to `screen.css` to style the `subnav`
and related elements:

```
#subnav {
      margin: 0;
      padding: 0;
      background: #d2dbc0;
      height: 46px;
}
```

For the sub-navigation, we gave an ID to the
`<div>` that contains the link list. This gives us a
little more flexibility with styling.

```
#subnav ul {
      list-style-type: none;
}
```

We need to get rid of the default bullet points—those
aren't going to work here.

```
#subnav ul li {
      float: left;
      margin: 0;
      padding: 15px 10px 15px 10px;
      font-size: 1.4em;
}
```

screen.css

This is the rule for the special list item that
acts like our subnav heading. Notice the use of
the background image to make the faux arrow.

```
#subnav li.option {
      text-transform: uppercase;
      background: #b2bf99 url('../images/option_li_bg.gif') no-repeat right;
      padding: 15px 25px 15px 10px;
      color: #7f8e62;
}
```

```
#subnav li a {
      padding: 10px 0 10px 35px;
      color: #333;
      text-decoration: none;
}
```

Each link has its own class which allows us to assign
a different background image to each. Make sure
you use the no-repeat vlaue so you don't tile the
image in the background.

```
#subnav li a.webdesign {
      background: url('../images/webdesign_icon.png') no-repeat left center;
}
```

```
#subnav li a.animation {
      background: url('../images/animation_icon.png') no-repeat left center;
}
```

```
#subnav li a.game {
      background: url('../images/game_icon.png') no-repeat left center;
}
```

```
#subnav li a.writing {
      background: url('../images/writing_icon.png') no-repeat left center;
}
```

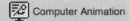 PROGRAMS | Web Design Computer Animation 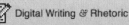 Game Design | Digital Writing & Rhetoric

Test Drive

Fire up your browser. Suddenly those confusing icons are clear, and you've managed to keep the icons intact... something the registrar thought was pretty important.

Primary navigation shouldn't change...
...but secondary navigation SHOULD

Primary navigation is the navigation that provides links to the main sections of the site. So with CNM, our primary navigation is the top-level blocks, with Home, Students, Faculty, and About displayed. These links should be displayed on most (if not all) of the pages in your site.

This is our primary navigation.

Secondary navigation is navigation that links to subsections of the site. Secondary navigation should apply to what's going on with the page and where the user is *at a specific time.*

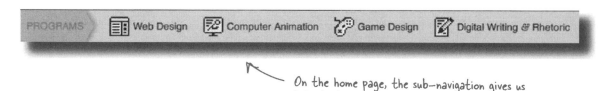

On the home page, the sub-navigation gives us links to the various course programs available.

Suppose someone clicks the Faculty link on the CNM page. The primary navigation links still make sense, but the secondary navigation—the program links—probably don't anymore. What about on the About page... should those links appear there?

Exercise

Create a page for each main section of the site: Students, Faculty, and About (you've already got Home as index.html). Just copy and rename index.html over to three more files. Then for each new page, change the title to match what that page is about.

Next, use the IA diagram on page 198 to update the secondary navigation on each new page (don't worry about the main text content for now).

Primary navigation applies to your ENTIRE site.

Secondary navigation applies to the CURRENT SECTION of a site you're on.

Each sub-page gets its own secondary navigation

Open up the page you created for the Students section. We called ours
`students.html`. We need to change the title and update the secondary
navigation based on the CNM's IA diagram:

```
<!DOCTYPE html PUBLIC "-//W3C//DTD XHTML 1.0 Strict//EN"
        "http://www.w3.org/TR/xhtml1/DTD/xhtml1-strict.dtd">
<html xmlns="http://www.w3.org/1999/xhtml" xml:lang="en" lang="en">
<head>
    <title>Students | College of New Media</title>
    <meta http-equiv="Content-Type" content="text/html; charset=utf-8"/>
    <link rel="stylesheet" href="stylesheets/screen.css" type="text/css"
        media="screen" />
</head>
<body class="page">
    <div id="header">
        <img alt="cmn logo" src="images/cnm_logo.png" />
        <ul id="nav">
          <li><a title="CNM Home" href="index.html">Home</a></li>
          <li><a class="active" title="#" href="students.html">Students</a></li>
          <li><a title="#" href="#">Faculty</a></li>
          <li><a title="#" href="#">About</a></li>
        </ul>
    </div>
    <div id="subnav">
      <ul>
        <li class="option">Students</li>
        <li><a href="#">New Media</a></li>
        <li><a href="Our facilities">Facilities</a></li>
        <li><a href="Apply to the CNM">Applying to CNM</a></li>
      </ul>
    </div>
    <div id="wrap">
      <p class="crumbs">Welcome to The College of New Media at MSU</p>
      <div id="content">
        <p>Content</p>
      </div>
      <div id="sidebar">
        <p>Sidebar</p>
      </div>
      <div id="footer">
          <p>Copyright &copy; College of New Media at Mackinac State University</p>
      </div>
    </div>
</body>
</html>
```

The title of the page should match the link name and possibly provide a little extra detail.

We added a "page" class so we can style section pages differently than the main index.html page.

Primary navigation applies to the entire site, so it stays the same even on different sections.

We keep the option class and change the label name to Students (which is our current active nav element). The rest of the <ul> is just <li>s based on the IA for this part of the CNM site.

students.html

Let's style the navigation with our CSS

Now that we've got some actual secondary navigation in place, we can add some CSS rules to style the sectional pages. Each sectional page will have a body with a class of "page," so we can style those separately.

```
#subnav {
     margin: 0;
     padding: 0;
     background: #d2dbc0;
     height: 46px;
}

#subnav ul li {
     float: left;
     margin: 0;
     padding: 15px 10px 15px 10px;
     font-size: 1.4em;
}

#subnav li.option {
     text-transform: uppercase;
     background: #b2bf99 url('../images/option_li_bg.gif') no-repeat
right;
     padding: 15px 25px 15px 10px;
     color: #7f8e62;
}

#subnav li a {
     padding: 10px 0 10px 35px;
     color: #333;
     text-decoration: none;
}

.page #subnav li a {
     padding: 15px;
}

.page #subnav li a.active {
     background: #b2bf99;
}
```

Notice the .page declaration? That's telling CSS to only apply these rules if the <body> has a class="page". This lets us style body elements for sectional pages differently than for the main index.html page.

This padding will make sure that our active and hover states fill the whole block.

This dark green will give the hover and active states a nice effect for secondary links.

This is the same CSS that we used for the rest of the site. Now it handles section pages too.

#tabs {
...
}

screen.css

Test Drive

Create `students.html` and update `index.html` to link to your new section page. Be sure and update your CSS. Create pages for the Faculty and About sections, too.

Then it's time to try things out again. This time open up `index.html` and select one of the main links: Students, Faculty, or About. On each sub-page, you should see secondary navigation that matches the site's IA. You also should get a nice green color when you hover over a link:

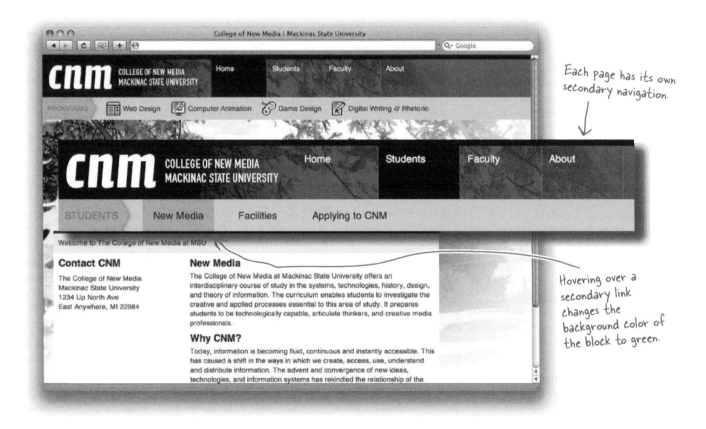

Each page has its own secondary navigation.

Hovering over a secondary link changes the background color of the block to green.

Your Web Design Toolbox

You're over halfway done and you've tackled navigation. Your sites are well-organized and people can actually get around in them. Up next: writing for the Web. Sounds easy, right? Just wait until you read on...

BULLET POINTS

- Use your site's information architecture as the foundation for navigation.

- Primary navigation is the navigation that provides links to the main sections of the site. Secondary navigation is navigation that links to subsections of the site.

- When naming your navigational elements, make sure you use labels that are both short and descriptive.

- Horizontal navigation designs work particularly well with one and two-column layouts.

- If your site has a vertical design for its primary navigation, make sure that you don't put secondary navigational elements higher on the page.

- The goal of navigation is to tell your users where they are in the overall architecture of your site and provide them with the means to make decisions about where they want to go from there.

- In order to avoid confusion, make sure you keep your navigation consistent across your entire site.

- Make sure that your users can learn your navigation system quickly.

- Breadcrumb trails give the user a visual indication as to the location of their current page in the site's overall information architecture.

- Never use icons (on their own) as navigational elements—what an icon means to you could be completely different from what it means to someone else.

- If you want to use icons as navigational elements, make sure you also use text in order to provide a clear indication of where your users will end up if they click on the link.

7 writing for the web

Yes, you scan!

Wow, these articles are great. I wish they were available online so we didn't have to share this paper.

Writing for the Web is just like any other kind of writing, right? Actually, writing for the Web is *completely different* than writing for print. People don't read text on the Web like they read text on a printed page. Instead of reading text from left to right, beginning to end, they **scan** it. All of the text on your site needs to be quickly *scannable* and *easily digestible* by the user. If not, *users won't waste their time* on your site, and they'll go somewhere else. In this chapter, you'll learn a bevy of tips and tricks for writing scannable text from scratch and making existing text easy to scan.

Sharpen your pencil

Text on a screen reads differently than text on page. This is kind of a big deal when it comes to writing for the Web. But don't take our word for it, give it a try.

First, read the text at **www.headfirstlabs.com/books/hfwd/chapter07/text/ index.html** and keep track of how long it takes (write down your time below).

Now, read the version below and make a note of how long it takes.

Coleco Industries, which was originally named the Connecticut Leather Company, was founded in West Hartford, Connecticut in 1932 as a shoe leather company by Russian immigrant Maurice Greenberg. Moving into plastic molding in the 1950's, Coleco eventually sold off their leather business, and became a publicly traded company. By the beginning of the 1960s, the company was one of the largest manufacturer of above-ground swimming pools. In 1976, after an unsuccessful attempt to enter the dirt-bike and snowmobile market, they released Telstar, a clone of the home PONG unit being sold and marketed by Atari.

Despite the fact that Coleco was certainly not the only company releasing home PONG clones, they enjoyed moderate success and went on to produce nine more varieties of the Telstar unit. Unfortunately, in 1978, as the home video game market moved to programmable, cartridge based game units, Coleco was forced to dump over one million obsolete Telstar machines at a nearly crippling cost of more than 20 million dollars.

Coleco president Arnold Greenberg ignored this near disaster and directed his Research and Development team to begin work on a new home videogame system, the ColecoVision, which he felt would set the standard in graphics quality and expandability.

Time to read online version: ....

Time to read print version: ....

Which took longer? ....

Why? ....

....

Aww. C'mon, just because I read the online text a little slower doesn't mean that people always read slower on the web!

Jim   *Frank*   *Joe*

Frank: Woah, hold on there, buddy. Actually, it does. See, text on screen reads slower than text on a printed page. People read about 15% slower on the Web than they do from a print document.

Jim: You're kidding. All the time? Wow. That's quite a bit slower.

Frank: And that's not all. Move your eyes really close to your computer monitor. What do you see?

Jim: Ack, that's nasty. The text gets blurry and fuzzy on my screen.

Frank: Exactly. You read slower on screen because computer display devices have a far lower resolution than print does.

Joe: Oh, I get it. I read slower because my eyes are trying to make up for the blurry text?

Frank: Exactly. And you'll probably experience eye strain faster than you would if you were reading from a print document. So people read text on screen differently than they do other kinds of text to avoid eye strain and headaches.

Jim: But they don't know you're doing that? Reading slower?

Joe: Did you realize you were doing it?

Jim: Huh. No, I guess not. But how does this help me write text for my websites?

Frank: Users *scan* your text, looking for keywords, sentences, and paragraphs that are meaningful to them. So if you write text that's specifically designed to be scannable, your users will read your faster and understand and retain your message better.

Joe: That sounds like the holy grail of copywriting. Are you sure you've got this right, Frank?

Frank: Yup. Scannable text gives users a better experience on your site—which means they'll stay longer and come back more often. And that's the whole goal of user-centered design: giving your users what they want and keeping them coming back for more.

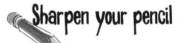

Sharpen your pencil

Grab a stopwatch and take exactly 20 seconds to read the block of text on this page. Then answer the questions below the text. But don't cheat: look at the questions only *after* you've read the text.

This clunky machine is a ColecoVision.

Coleco Industries, which was originally named the Connecticut Leather Company, was founded in West Hartford, Connecticut in 1932 as a shoe leather company by Russian immigrant Maurice Greenberg. Moving into plastic molding in the 1950's, Coleco eventually sold off their leather business, and became a publicly traded company. By the beginning of the 1960s, the company was one of the largest manufacturers of above-ground swimming pools. In 1976, after an unsuccessful attempt to enter the dirt-bike and snowmobile market, they released Telstar, a clone of the home PONG unit being sold and marketed by Atari.

Despite the fact that Coleco was certainly not the only company releasing home PONG clones, they enjoyed moderate success and went on to produce nine more varieties of the Telstar unit. Unfortunately, in 1978, as the home videogame market moved to programmable, cartridge based game units, Coleco was forced to dump over a million obsolete Telstar machines at a nearly crippling cost of more than 20 million dollars.

Coleco president Arnold Greenberg ignored this near disaster and directed his Research and Design team to begin work on a new home videogame system, the ColecoVision, which he felt would set the standard in graphics quality and expandability.

1 What was the name of the home PONG clone that Coleco released?

....

2 What was the name of the man who founded Coleco?

....

3 Who was the president of Coleco in the 1970's?

....

Now try the same thing with this block of text. Don't cheat!
Be sure to read the text before you look at the questions.

The Release of the ColecoVision

ColecoVision was released in the summer of 1982 at a retail cost of $199, featuring several noteworthy advancements:

- The ability to display 32 sprites on-screen at the same time

- A 16 color on-screen palette out of a total of 32

- Three channel sound

Donkey Kong: The Key to the ColecoVision's Success

The key to this new system's success was its included cartridge. In the case of the ColecoVision, Coleco successfully negotiated the right to release the smash arcade hit Donkey Kong.

Donkey Kong: Legal Problems with Universal

While amazingly popular, Coleco's release of Donkey Kong with the ColecoVision was not without its problems. Universal City Studios Inc., believing that Donkey Kong infringed upon their own King Kong, threatened both Nintendo and Coleco with legal action. With a large sum of money already invested in the license, Arnold Greenberg agreed to pay Universal 3% of the net sale price of the game.

Coleco Caves and Nintendo Fights Back

Unlike Coleco, Nintendo fought the lawsuit, offering numerous in-court demonstrations of gameplay vs. movie plot. Nintendo argued that in a previous case, Universal had argued that King Kong's characters and plot were in the public domain. Nintendo successfully argued its claim and was awarded $1.8 million in damages. This prompted Coleco to file as well, earning back a portion of the royalties they had previously paid to Universal.

1 **How many sprites could the ColecoVision display on screen?**

....

2 **What game was included with the ColecoVision?**

....

3 **Who sued Nintendo & Coleco over copyright infringement?**

....

Sharpen your pencil
Solution

So you took exactly 20 seconds to read two blocks of text and answer questions on each. How did you do?

1 **What was the name of the home PONG clone that Coleco released?**

Telstar

This was buried in the first paragraph. Did you find it?

2 **What was the name of the man who founded Coleco?**

Maurice Greenberg

You may have got this one easily. That's because the answer was early in the first paragraph of text.

3 **Who was the president of Coleco in the 1970s?**

Did you get as far as this bit of info in twenty seconds?

---

1 **How many sprites could the ColecoVision display on screen?**

32

This was in the first bullet, so it's easy to recall.

2 **What game was included with the ColecoVision?**

This was repeated several times as well as starting the second and third headlines.

3 **Who sued Nintendo & Coleco over copyright infringement?**

Universal

Again, easy to get, as it was in a headline. Your eye was automatically drawn to the bold text.

Text written specifically to be scannable is easier to quickly read and understand. One of the blocks of text was written for scannability, one wasn't. Which do you think it was?

Build a better online newspaper

A local alternative newspaper was so impressed with the successful launch of the **RPM** record store site that they've decided to hire you to create an online version of their print newspaper.

Although the paper's always had well-written articles, they've been struggling lately to keep their readers. The Editor-in-Chief also wants to cover more than just news on the paper's website. He thinks adding hip articles on computing and gaming pop culture (geek chic) will appeal to readers. The biggest challenge for this project isn't layout—it's writing text for the Web. This new site's the last chance to save their paper, so they really need your help...

> I can't thank you enough for taking on this project. Before things get started, could you show me a concept on paper for how the site will look?

Editor-in-Chief of the
Hipster Intelligencer

Hipster Intelligencer Online: project specs

Before you get started, the paper's sent over some specs. This will help you refine the look and feel of the site you're building for them.

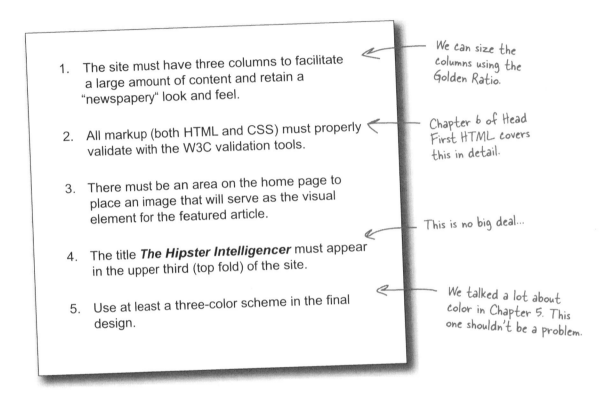

1. The site must have three columns to facilitate a large amount of content and retain a "newspapery" look and feel.

   We can size the columns using the Golden Ratio.

2. All markup (both HTML and CSS) must properly validate with the W3C validation tools.

   Chapter 6 of Head First HTML covers this in detail.

3. There must be an area on the home page to place an image that will serve as the visual element for the featured article.

4. The title **The Hipster Intelligencer** must appear in the upper third (top fold) of the site.

   This is no big deal...

5. Use at least a three-color scheme in the final design.

   We talked a lot about color in Chapter 5. This one shouldn't be a problem.

The problem is TEXT

None of these specs look like that big of a deal. However, there's one major issue *not* in these specs: the Hipster is mostly text—lots and lots of text. So we've got to build a text-heavy site that still feels usable and hip.

Based on the specifications for the site's design provided by the Editor-in-Chief of the Hipster Intelligencer, use this handy-dandy browser template to put together a polished storyboard.

Exercise

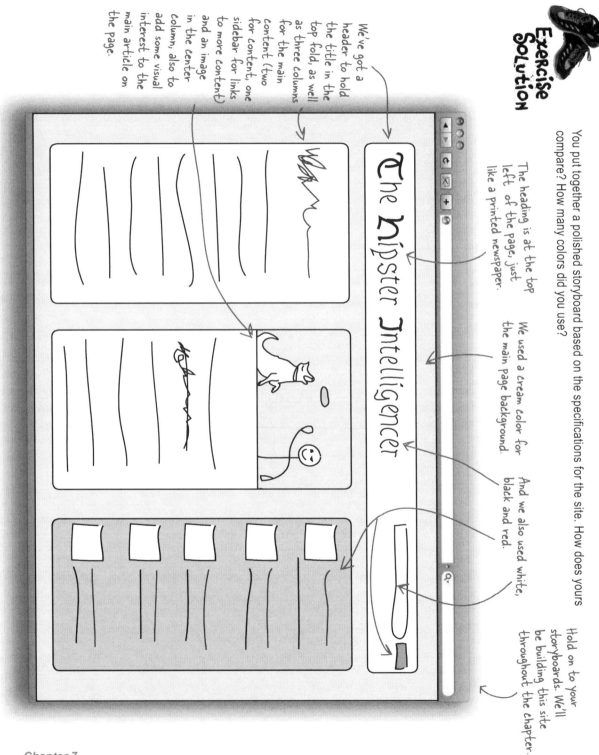

Exercise Solution

You put together a polished storyboard based on the specifications for the site. How does yours compare? How many colors did you use?

The heading is at the top left of the page, just like a printed newspaper.

We used a cream color for the main page background.

And we also used white, black and red.

Hold on to your storyboards. We'll be building this site throughout the chapter.

We've got a header to hold the title in the top fold, as well as three columns for the main content (two for content, one sidebar for links to more content) and an image in the center column, also to add some visual interest to the main article on the page.

The Hipster Intelligencer

Ready Bake Code

Here's some basic HTML and CSS to get you started implementing your storyboard.

```
<!DOCTYPE html PUBLIC "-//W3C//DTD XHTML 1.0 Strict//EN"
        "http://www.w3.org/TR/xhtml1/DTD/xhtml1-strict.dtd">
<html xmlns="http://www.w3.org/1999/xhtml" xml:lang="en" lang="en">
<head>
  <title>The Hipster Intelligencer</title>
    <meta http-equiv="Content-Type" content="text/html; charset=utf-8"/>
    <link rel="stylesheet" href="hipster.css" type="text/css" media="screen" />
</head>
<body>
  <div id="wrap">
    <div id="header">
    </div>
    <div id="content">
      <div id="main">
      </div>
      <div id="center">
      </div>
      <div id="sidebar">
      </div>
    </div>
  </div>
</body>
</html>
```

Don't forget to link your CSS file!

These <div>s will hold our content and graphics. We'll position them with the CSS at right.

```
/* The Hipster CSS File */

body {
}
/*
Add global rules here (h1, h2, p, ul, etc...)
*/
#wrap {
}

#header {
}

#content {
}

#content #main {
}

#content #center {
}

#content #sidebar {
}
```

CSS comments: The browser just ignores these, so go ahead and type whatever you want.

Remember the # sign represents an id in the HTML file.

Stop! Be sure and create these two files before you move on.

Now we need some content so we can add some style...

> Wow, this is coming along great! Could you use this article I've written to show me how content will look in the design?

The Hipster Intelligencer

DAILY HIPSTER NEWS + EVENTS

Website copy

In 1973, Gary Gygax, a game designer from Lake Geneva, Wisconsin, and Don Kaye founded Tactical Studies Rules in order to publish the rules for Cavaliers and Roundheads, a miniature war game based in the English Civil War. While Cavaliers and Roundheads was the initial focus of Tactical Studies Rules, Gygax and Kaye also wished to publish the rules for Dungeons & Dragons, a fantasy miniature role playing game developed by Gygax whose rules were based on Chainmail, a medieval miniature game developed by Gygax and Jeff Perren in 1971. As Cavaliers and Roundheads began generating revenue for Tactical Studies Rules, the partnership was expanded to include Dave Arneson and Brian Blume. While Dave Arneson was brought into the partnership as a game designer, and left shortly thereafter, Brian Blume entered as a funder. Blume believed that Cavaliers and Roundheads was not generating enough revenue, and encouraged Gygax and Kaye to focus their efforts on releasing Dungeons & Dragons.

There is considerable debate as to the contributions that Dave Arneson made to the initial development of Dungeons & Dragons. While Arneson has labeled himself "The Father of Role-playing," and has said that he was responsible for writing

Don't worry! All this text is available online

Check out **www.headfirstlabs.com/books/hfwd/chapter7/copy.html** to get the full text you'll need to complete your site.

TEST DRIVE

Now that you've got the framework for your site built in markup, add the content that the Editor-in-Chief has provided to the main content section of your HTML page. Remember, you can download all the copy from the Head First website.

Place the editor's copy in the main <div> and don't forget to enclose paragraphs in <p> tags.

```
. . .
    <div id="content">
     <div id="main">



    </div>
    <div id="center">
. . .
```

Open the new Hipster page in your browser. How does it look?

---

there are no
Dumb Questions

Q: Do people really read that much more slowly online?

A: Yup. Lots of scientific studies have come to the same conclusion, but you did your own experiment with the 20-second reading test and found the same thing, right?

Q: Hmm. Okay, but that two blocks of text didn't seem all that different to me. How come I remembered so much more from the second one?

A: It's all thanks to chunking—breaking down content into smaller easier to read and understand bits. Sounds simple, but it's a killer tip for getting people to read more of your site. We'll take a look at how over the next few pages.

Q: So you mean I can apply these principles to my blog? It's not just for online newspapers and long articles?

A: Absolutely! You can apply this to your blog or any other text you know folks will have to read on a computer screen.

◄ ► C ⌧ + ⬢ http://www.headfirstlabs.com/books/hfwd/chapter7/copy.html Q▾

In 1973, Gary Gygax, a game designer from Lake Geneva, Wisconsin, and Don Kaye founded Tactical Studies Rules in order to publish the rules for Cavaliers and Roundheads, a miniature war game based in the English Civil War. While Cavaliers and Roundheads was the initial focus of Tactical Studies Rules, Gygax and Kaye also wished to publish the rules for Dungeons & Dragons, a fantasy miniature role playing game developed by Gygax whose rules were based on Chainmail, a medieval miniature game developped by Gygax and Jeff Perren in 1971. As Cavaliers and Roundheads began generating revenue for Tactical Studies Rules, the partnership was expanded to include Dave Arneson and Brian Blume. While Dave Arneson was brought into the partnership as a game designer, and left shortly thereafter, Brian Blume entered as a funder. Blume believed that Cavaliers and Roundheads was not generating enough revenue, and encouraged Gygax and Kaye to focus their efforts on releasing Dungeons & Dragons.

There is considerable debate as to the contributions that Dave Arneson made to the initial development of Dungeons & Dragons. While Arneson has labeled himself *The Father of Role-playing*, and has said that he was responsible for writing the game in its entirety, Gygax contends that he himself was primary responsible for the development of Dungeons & Dragons, and Arneson's involvement, while important, was contributory. After Tactical Studies Rules was dissolved, and TSR Hobbies, Inc. was formed, Arneson continued to receive credit for his involvement in the development of Dungeons & Dragons, as well as royalties per his contract.

In 1975, after the highly successful release of Dungeons & Dragons, Don Kaye died of a stroke. The immediate result was that Blume and Gygax dissolved Tactical Studies Rules and founded a new company named TSR Hobbies, Inc. The board of directors for TSR Hobbies, Inc. consisted of Brian Blue, Gygax, and Kevin Blume, Brian Blue's younger brother who has received shares from Melvin Blume, Brian and Kevin's father, who had purchased shares in the company. Brian Blume acted as President of Creative Affairs, while Kevin Blume acted as President of Operations, and Gygax acted as the company's CEO and President. Unlike the equal partnership of Tactical Studies Rules, Brian Blume & Kevin Blume owned a majority of the new company's shares.

Initially, TSR Hobbies, Inc. experienced phenomenal success in both the United States and abroad. Unfortunately, despite the fact that the Dungeons & Dragons brand was becoming more popular and widely recognized, the Blume's began to greatly overextend the company's reach. They not only moved into domains such as boardgames and toys, but they began to diversify in remarkably unrelated areas. Perhaps the best evidence of this was the unapproved acquisition of Greenfield Needlewomen, a needlepoint business owned by one of the Blume's relatives. In addition, TSR Hobbies, Inc was remarkably overstaffed (the result of the Blume's nepotism). Further, Kevin Blume had grossly overprinted millions of copies of the previously successful multi-path Dungeons & Dragons adventure books, all of which could not be sold. In an effort to mitigate the mounting financial problems, TSR Hobbies, Inc was restructured into four companies: TSR, Inc., TSR Ventures, TSR International, and TSR Entertainment. TST Inc. continued to manufacture the company's core Dungeons & Dragons role playing products. TSR Ventures focused on the production of plastics and toys in Asia. TSR International was established to manage overseas business, distribution and sales there, licensing and production. TSR Entertainment, which later changed its name to Dungeons & Dragons Entertainment Corporation, was entertainment markets, such as movie and television. Unfortunately, TSR Dungeons & Dragons cartoon. Upon multiple occasions, Gygax had said as keeping foreign income away from US taxation.

money as a result of mismanagement. Eventually, both Kevin and after being accused of misusing corporate funds and accumulating late acquisitions. In the wake of the Blume's departure from the board regained partial control of the company. However, unbeknownst to secret negotiations with Lorraine Williams, a potential investor who Gygax had brought into the company as an officer, to acquire their majority stock. When Williams finally acquired a controlling stake in the company, Gygax attempted to have the sale declared illegal. Unfortunately, the attempt failed, and Gygax sold his remaining stock to Williams and used the capital to form a new company entitled New Infinity Productions.

The departure of Gygax from TSR irreparably changed the face of the company. TSR successfully expanded into areas such as magazines, paperback fiction, and comic books. In addition, the company released popular new role-playing settings including Dragonlance, Ravenloft, Forgotten Realms, and Greyhawk, all of which have had an enduring impact on the tabletop roleplaying landscape.

However, the company was unable to adapt to the continued fragmentation of the tabletop RPG community as new products were released by other companies. In addition, in an effort to compete in the emergent collectible card game market, TSR released a series of products, such as Dragon Dice and Spellfire, which simply did not sell. The downward financial spiral was aggravated by the fact that, as their products continued to perform poorly in the marketplace, TSR began to legally attack those who it believed infringed on its intellectual property. The targets of these legal actions included not only other corporations and businesses, but individuals fans involved in authoring fan fiction and D&D fan modules. The result of these actions was that TSR was widely perceived as directly attacking its customers.

In 1997, as TSR approached receivership, the company and all of its intellectual property were acquired by Wizards of the Coast. Ironically, Wizards of the Coast, which was now widely considered to be the preeminent tabletop role playing game company had been responsible for publishing Magic: The Gathering, the game whose remarkable success had been responsible for TSR's failure in the collectible card game market. After the sale to Wizards of the Coast, which continues to publish Dungeons & Dragons to this day, TSR was slowly dismantled. In 2003 the final TSR trademarks were allowed to expire by Wizards of the Coast.

Despite its almost constant legal and financial troubles, TSR had a lasting impact on both digital and non-digital games. One might easily argue that TSR has had more impact on the entertainment game industry (digital or non-digital) than any other company in the history of games. Not only are many computer role playing games based on the archetypes and mechanics first introduced in Dungeons & Dragons, but many of the luminaries in the history of digital games were greatly influenced by TSR and its various products. TSR's products have long since passed into the realm of popular culture.

Founded in 1973 by Gary Gygax and Don Kaye as an eventual means to publish, sell, and distribute the rules of Dungeons & Dragons, TSR went on to become one of the most noteworthy companies in the entertainment game industry. While Dungeons & Dragons went on to have a significant lasting impact on both digital and non-digital games, TSR, as a corporate entity, is perhaps best known for its financial woes and the bitter conflict that arose over ownership of the company and its intellectual property.

Uh oh... so much for readable text online!

Yikes! Look at the length of that scroll bar.

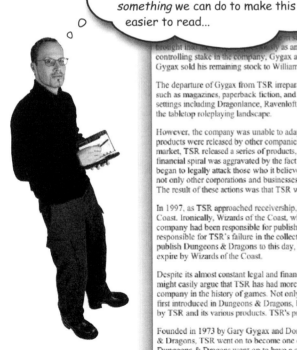

Wow. That online version's long and wordy. There's got to be *something* we can do to make this easier to read...

Improve your content with the Inverted Pyramid

A low percentage of people scroll beyond the information that's initially visible in their browser window. Even if your users are willing to scroll, most of them decide whether they want to read the page based on what they see in the browser window when the page loads.

To account for this, you should structure your text like an **inverted pyramid**. Start with a short conclusion so that users can quickly get the gist of the page, and add detail afterward. This way, users can stop reading at any time and still be confident that they've already read the important pieces of information.

Put the most important stuff at the top of your text. Users should be able to read your first paragraph and get the idea of the whole piece.

Importance

Main Heading

A little body text to give the user some context and a brief introduction to the page content.

- Then maybe a few bullet points
- that contain the highlights
- of the page content.

Another heading

Some more body text that gives the user more detail about the content of the page.

And so on...

Content that's progressively less important, even though it's still well-written. Stuff that's not essential to the user's understanding of the article can go down here.

Exercise

Here are two pieces of text. One was written using the inverted pyramid, the other was not. Read both, but stop reading when you feel that you've gotten the gist of what the article contains.

1

Avalon Hill, now owned by Hasbro and operating as a division of Wizards of the Coast, was a tabletop game company specializing in war games and strategic board games. They were not only responsible for pioneering many of the key concepts of modern tabletop wargaming–such as the hex grid and zones of control–they were also responsible for publishing some of the most recognizable titles in the board game industry such as Civilization, Axis and Allies, Runequest, and Dune.

In 1958, Charles Roberts founded Avalon Hill in order to capitalize on the success of his game Tactics. Self-published in 1952, Tactics was particularly noteworthy because it was based on actual war tactics and scenarios. As such, Tactics is considered to be the first modern tabletop war game. Shortly after the company was founded, it released Tactics II, the sequel to Roberts' original game. Shortly after the release of Tactics II, Avalon Hill published Gettysburg, which is widely considered to be the first tabletop wargame based upon an actual historical battle.

Avalon Hill enjoyed moderate growth through the 1980s and early 1990s. However, during the mid 1990s, the board game industry as a whole began suffering a downturn in sales. Not only had overall sales of their board games decreased, but the company had also lost the rights to two of their most popular games, Civilization and 1830, in a legal battle with the computer game publisher Microprose. In the summer of 1998, Eric Dott, president of Monarch Avalon, Inc. (the parent company of Avalon Hill), sold the rights to all Avalon Hill titles, all back stock, and the name company itself to Hasbro, Inc. Hasbro continued to publish games under the Avalon Hill name. In late 1999, Avalon Hill was made a division of Wizards of the Coast, who had been purchased by Hasbro earlier that year. Wizards of the Coast continues to release games under the Avalon Hill name, including Axis & Allies, Betrayal at House on the Hill, RoboRally, and Risk 2210 A.D.

2

Warhammer, which is currently in its 7th edition, is played using player-selected armies of 25 mm - 28 mm plastic or metal miniatures. The game rules (as well as storyworld material) are published and released in a series of books (some of which are core to gameplay, while some of which are supplementary). The game itself is generally played on a surface, the standard size of which is 4x6 feet. While the game can be played with just the miniatures, players will often use model scenery, such as trees, buildings, and topography, in order to add realism and depth to their game. Each unit (either a single miniature or a group of miniatures) has a point value based on their power or skills. Players build (or "draft") an army based on an overall point value set by the game type. For instance, a 700 point game means that each player can build an army totally 700 points or less. Movement across the playing surface, which is turn-based, is measured in inches and combat between units is accomplished through use of six-sided dice. Victory in Warhammer is most often determined by victory points, which earned by killing enemy units and meeting scenario based special objectives.

It's important to note that Warhammer is not a collectible game. As a result, miniatures are not sold using a closed-box, random model. Players simply pick and choose the miniatures they want to have in their armies, and buy them individually or in large sets. It is also important to note that Warhammer miniatures do not come pre-painted. It is the responsibility of the player to paint their own miniatures. As such Warhammer is somewhat of a niche product as it requires specialized skills to fully experience the game. In addition, unlike other pre-painted tabletop miniature games, such as WizKids' HeroClix, Wizards of the Coast's Star Wars Miniatures, or Fantasy Flights Games' Mutant Chronicles CMG, the Warhammer community has a unique system (which is both formal and informal) that recognizes particularly talented miniature painters. Generally speaking, Warhammer is most commonly played in game stores, hobby stores, and comic stores. In addition, Games Workshop organizes a Grant Tournament season each year in which players compete against one another for community-wide recognition and prizes.

Which was easier to read?

Can you identify the text written using the inverted pyramid?

How do you think the inverted pyramid makes text easier to read?

Exercise Solution

You read two pieces of text until you felt you'd gotten the gist of what each article contained. Which one did you stop reading first? Let's take a look at the first two sentences of each opening paragraph:

Text block **1** was written with the inverted pyramid.

Importance

1 Avalon Hill, now owned by Hasbro and operating as a division of Wizards of the Coast, was a tabletop game company specializing in war games and strategic board games. They were not only responsible for pioneering many of the key concepts of modern tabletop wargaming–such as the hex grid and zones of control– they were also responsible for publishing some of the most recognizable titles in the board game industry such as Civilization, Axis and Allies, Runequest, and Dune.

We learn a lot about what we can expect in this article from the first two sentences.

2 Warhammer, which is currently in its 7th edition, is played using player-selected armies of 25 mm - 28 mm plastic or metal miniatures. The game rules (as well as storyworld material) are published and released in a series of books (some of which are core to gameplay, while some of which are supplementary).

Boring stats like the size of plastic miniatures aren't good opening material. No inverted pyramid here!

Copy Magnets

Organize these chunks of text from the Editor-in-Chief's copy using the inverted pyramid. Remember to keep the most important information at the top.

Despite the restructuring, TSR, Inc. continued to lose money as a result of mismanagement. Eventually, both Kevin and Brian Blume were removed from the board of directors after being accused of misusing corporate funds and accumulating large debt in the pursuit of unapproved and inappropriate acquisitions. In the wake of the Blumes' departure from the board of directors, Gygax assumed the role of CEO and regained partial control of the company. However, unbeknownst to Gygax, Kevin and Brian Blume were in secret negotiations with Lorraine Williams, a potential investor who Gygax had brought into the company previously as an officer, to acquire their majority stock...

Initially, TSR Hobbies, Inc. experienced phenomenal success in both the United States and abroad. Unfortunately, despite the fact that the Dungeons & Dragons brand was becoming more popular and widely recognized, the Blumes began to greatly overextend the company's reach. They not only moved into domains such as board games and toys, but they began to diversify in remarkably unrelated areas. Perhaps the best evidence of this was the unapproved acquisition of Greenfield Needlewomen, a needlepoint business owned by one of the Blume's relatives...

the company was unable to adapt to the continued fragmentation of the tabletop RPG community as new products were released by other companies. In addition, in an effort to compete in the emergent collectible card game market, TSR released a series of products, such as Dragon Dice and Spellfire, which simply did not sell...

In 1973, Gary Gygax, a game designer from Lake Geneva, Wisconsin, and Don Kaye founded Tactical Studies Rules in order to publish the rules for Cavaliers and Roundheads, a miniature war game based in the English Civil War. While Cavaliers and Roundheads was the initial focus of Tactical Studies Rules, Gygax and Kaye also wished to publish the rules for...

Copy Magnets Solution

You organized chunks of copy from the Editor-in-Chief using the inverted pyramid. How do you think users would react to the text as it is here?

In 1973, Gary Gygax, a game designer from Lake Geneva, Wisconsin, and Don Kaye founded Tactical Studies Rules in order to publish the rules for Cavaliers and Roundheads, a miniature war game based in the English Civil War. While Cavaliers and Roundheads was the initial focus of Tactical Studies Rules, Gygax and Kaye also wished to publish the rules for...

Initially, TSR Hobbies, Inc. experienced phenomenal success in both the United States and abroad. Unfortunately, despite the fact that the Dungeons & Dragons brand was becoming more popular and widely recognized, the Blumes began to greatly overextend the company's reach. They not only moved into domains such as board games and toys, but they began to diversify in remarkably unrelated areas. Perhaps the best evidence of this was the unapproved acquisition of Greenfield Needlewomen, a needlepoint business owned by one of the Blume's relatives...

Despite the restructuring, TSR, Inc. continued to lose money as a result of mismanagement. Eventually, both Kevin and Brian Blume were removed from the board of directors after being accused of misusing corporate funds and accumulating large debt in the pursuit of unapproved and inappropriate acquisitions. In the wake of the Blumes' departure from the board of directors, Gygax assumed the role of CEO and regained partial control of the company. However, unbeknownst to Gygax, Kevin and Brian Blume were in secret negotiations with Lorraine Williams, a potential investor who Gygax had brought into the company previously as an officer, to acquire their majority stock...

the company was unable to adapt to the continued fragmentation of the tabletop RPG community as new products were released by other companies. In addition, in an effort to compete in the emergent collectible card game market, TSR released a series of products, such as Dragon Dice and Spellfire, which simply did not sell...

Scannable web copy

☑ has content ordered by the inverted pyramid

This still seems too long. I really don't want to read all that text...

Compress your copy

One of the easiest things you can do to make text more web-friendly is *remove unnecessary content*. If your text's clear and concise, your users will spend less time reading and will be happier.

They won't realize why, but you just saved them strained eyes!

So what's the best way to write less but still keep the relevant content in your article? It's a matter of careful editing. Get to the point quickly with *short words and phrases* and concise *two to three sentence paragraphs*.

Reduce adverbs (words that change other words and often end in -*ly*, like "~~a really~~ly big moose") and replace passive phrases with active phrases ("~~the brain was hydrated by eight glasses of water a day~~" vs. "hydrate your brain with eight glasses of water daily"). You'd be surprised how many words don't have to be included in copy for it to make sense.

When you're done, *re-read your copy*. If you can't work out what it says, what hope do your users have of understanding it?

Sharpen your red pen

Take the article that the Editor-in-Chief gave you and edit it down so it's shorter.

The full text to edit is available at www.headfirstlabs.com/books/hfwd/chapter7/copy_edited.html

The Hipster Intelligencer
DAILY HIPSTER NEWS + EVENTS

Website copy

In 1973, Gary Gygax, a game designer from Lake Geneva, Wisconsin, and Don Kaye founded Tactical Studies Rules in order to publish the rules for Cavaliers and Roundheads, a miniature war game based in the English Civil War. While Cavaliers and Roundheads was the initial focus of Tactical Studies Rules, Gygax and Kaye also wished to publish the rules for Dungeons & Dragons, a fantasy miniature role playing game developed by Gygax whose rules were based on Chainmail, a medieval miniature game developped by Gygax and Jeff Perren in 1971. As Cavaliers and Roundheads began generating revenue for Tactical Studies Rules, the partnership was expanded to include Dave Arneson and Brian Blume. While Dave Arneson was brought into the partenership as a game designer, and left shortly thereafter, Brian Blume entered as a funder. Blume believed that Cavaliers and Roundheads was not generating enough revenue, and encouraged Gygax and Kaye to focus their efforts on releasing Dungeons & Dragons.

There is considerable debate as to the contributions that Dave Arneson made to the initial development of Dungeons & Dragons. While Arneson has labeled himself "The Father of Role-playing," and has said that he was responsible for writing the

247

Sharpen your red pen
~~Solution~~
Solution

You edited the article that the Editor-in-Chief gave you so it's shorter. What else will you need to do?

Don't worry, the "After" looks longer because all the stuff you deleted hasn't been taken out yet, it just has a line through it.

Before

In 1973, Gary Gygax, a game designer from Lake Geneva, Wisconsin, and Don Kaye founded Tactical Studies Rules in order to publish the rules for Cavaliers and Roundheads, a miniature war game based in the English Civil War. While Cavaliers and Roundheads was the initial focus of Tactical Studies Rules, Gygax and Kaye also wished to publish the rules for Dungeons & Dragons, a fantasy miniature role playing game developed by Gygax whose rules were based on Chainmail, a medieval miniature game developed by Gygax and Jeff Perren in 1971. As Cavaliers and Roundheads began generating revenue for Tactical Studies Rules, the partnership was expanded to include Dave Arneson and Brian Blume. While Dave Arneson was brought into the partnership as a game designer, and left shortly thereafter, Brian Blume entered as a funder. Blume believed that Cavaliers and Roundheads was not generating enough revenue, and encouraged Gygax and Kaye to focus their efforts on releasing Dungeons & Dragons.

There is considerable debate as to the contributions that Dave Arneson made to the initial development of Dungeons & Dragons. While Arneson has labeled himself *The Father of Role-playing*, and has said that he was responsible for writing the game in its entirety, Gygax contends that he himself was primary responsible for the development of Dungeons & Dragons, and Arneson's involvement, while important, was contributory. After Tactical Studies Rules was dissolved, and TSR Hobbies, Inc. was formed, Arneson continued to receive credit for his involvement in the development of Dungeons & Dragons, as well as royalties per his contract.

In 1975, after the highly successful release of Dungeons & Dragons, Don Kaye died of a stroke. The immediate result was that Blume and Gygax dissolved Tactical Studies Rules and founded a new company named TSR Hobbies, Inc. The board of directors for TSR Hobbies, Inc. consisted of Brian Blue, Gygax, and Kevin Blume. Brian Blume's younger brother who has received shares from Melvin Blume, Brian and Kevin's father, who had purchased shares in the company. Brian Blume acted as President of Creative Affairs, while Kevin Blume acted as President of Operations, and Gygax acted as the company's CEO and President. Unlike the equal partnership of Tactical Studies Rules, Brian Blume & Kevin Blume owned a majority of the new company's shares.

Initially, TSR Hobbies, Inc. experienced phenomenal success in both the United States and abroad. Unfortunately, despite the fact that the Dungeons & Dragons brand was becoming more popular and widely recognized, the Blume's began to greatly overextend the company's reach. They not only moved into domains such as boardgames and toys, but they began to diversify in remarkably unrelated areas. Perhaps the best evidence of this was the unapproved acquisition of Greenfield Needlewoman, a needlepoint business owned by one of the Blume's relatives. In addition, Kevin Blume had grossly overprinted millions of copies of the previously successful multi-path Dungeons & Dragons adventure books, all of which could not be sold. In an effort to mitigate the mounting financial problems, TSR Hobbies, Inc was restructured into four companies: TSR, Inc., TSR Ventures, TSR International, and TSR Entertainment. TST Inc. continued to manufacture the company's core Dungeons & Dragons role playing products. TSR Ventures focused on the production of plastics and toys in Asia. TSR International was established to manage overseas business, distribution and sales there, licensing and production. TSR Entertainment, which was headed up by Gygax and later changed its name to Dungeons & Dragons Entertainment Corporation, was responsible for leveraging TSR's IP in other entertainment markets, such as movie and television. Unfortunately, TSR Entertainment's only success was the short lived Dungeons & Dragons cartoon. Upon multiple occasions, Gygax has said that the separate corporations were Blume's attempt at keeping foreign income away from US taxation.

Despite the restructuring, TSR, Inc. continued to lose money as a result of mismanagement. Eventually, both Kevin and Brian Blume were removed from the board of directors after being accused of misusing corporate funds and accumulating large debt in the pursuit of unapproved and inappropriate acquisitions. In the wake of the Blume's departure from the board of directors, Gygax assumed the role of CEO and regained partial control of the company. However, unbeknownst to Gygax, Kevin and Brian Blume were in secret negotiations with Lorraine Williams, a potential investor who Gygax had brought into the company previously as an officer, to acquire their majority stock. When Williams finally acquired a controlling stake in the company, Gygax attempted to have the sale declared illegal. Unfortunately, the attempt failed, and Gygax sold his remaining stock to Williams and used the capital to form a new company entitled New Infinity Productions.

The departure of Gygax from TSR irreparably changed the face of the company. TSR successfully expanded into areas such as magazines, paperback fiction, and comic books. In addition, the company released popular new role-playing settings including Dragonlance, Ravenloft, Forgotten Realms, and Greyhawk, all of which have had an enduring impact on the tabletop roleplaying landscape.

However, the company was unable to adapt to the continued fragmentation of the tabletop RPG community as new products were released by other companies. In addition, in an effort to compete in the emergent collectible card game market, TSR released a series of products, such as Dragon Dice and Spellfire, which simply did not sell. The downward financial spiral was aggravated by the fact that, as their products continued to perform poorly in the marketplace, TSR began to legally attack those who it believed infringed on its intellectual property. The targets of these legal actions included not only other corporations and businesses, but individuals fans involved in authoring fan fiction and D&D fan modules. The result of these actions was that TSR was widely perceived as directly attacking its customers.

In 1997, as TSR approached receivership, the company and all of its intellectual property were acquired by Wizards of the Coast. Ironically, Wizards of the Coast, which was now widely considered to be the preeminent tabletop role playing game company had been responsible for publishing Magic: The Gathering, the game whose remarkable success had been responsible for TSR's failure in the collectible card game market. After the sale to Wizards of the Coast, which continues to publish Dungeons & Dragons to this day, TSR was slowly dismantled. In 2003 the final TSR trademarks were allowed to expire by Wizards of the Coast.

Despite its almost constant legal and financial troubles, TSR had a lasting impact on both digital and non-digital games. One might easily argue that TSR has had more impact on the entertainment game industry (digital or non-digital) than any other company in the history of games. Not only are many computer role playing games based on the archetypes and mechanics first introduced in Dungeons & Dragons, but many of the luminaries in the history of digital games were greatly influenced by TSR and its various products. TSR's products have long since passed into the realm of popular culture.

Founded in 1973 by Gary Gygax and Don Kaye as an eventual means to publish, sell, and distribute the rules of Dungeons & Dragons, TSR went on to become one of the most noteworthy companies in the entertainment game industry. While Dungeons & Dragons went on to have a significant lasting impact on both digital and non-digital games, TSR, as a corporate entity, is perhaps best known for its financial woes and the bitter conflict that arose over ownership of the company and its intellectual property.

After

(marked-up/struck-through version of the above text)

Scannable web copy

- ☑ has content ordered by the inverted pyramid
- ☑ has been edited so it's shorter

The full marked up text is available at:
www.headfirstlabs.com/books/hfwd/
chapter7/copy_edited_markedup.html

there are no
Dumb Questions

Q: So if people don't like to read on the Web, what's the point in editing my text down? Won't users just go ahead and print it to read offline?

A: Sure, some users print pages for future reference, but think about how you use the Web. When did you last print a page to read later? Most people surfing the Net want quick answers, so it pays to give them text that's quick to read.

Q: Wait. Won't that mean they spend less time on my site, not more?

A: Actually, no. Sure, the occasional browser who was looking for something specific will read the page then head on out never to be seen again, but the majority of users are hooked by good content. Once you've got them hooked, you can feed them more content with carefully placed links to related articles.

Q: So this inverted pyramid thing... How do I work out what's most important about my content so I can present that to users after a general introduction?

A: There are no hard and fast rules. If it's content you wrote, you should have a good idea of the two or three main points you want readers to take away. If it's content you received from someone else, read it through and see if you can find the main takeaways.

Q: So if my content's ordered by importance, how do I know when to stop?

A: If some bit of content's so far down the importance line that you're not sure whether to include it, that may be enough of a hint to get rid of the text. Of course, if you're still not sure, be the user. Imagine you're reading the text. Does that last little bit of detail help you understand the main gist of the text? If it doesn't, you know what to do: Dump it!

Q: So how much content should I have removed when I edited my text? You made some changes I didn't even think of...

A: There's no perfect answer to this, but if you follow the rules to create 2-3 sentence paragraphs and remove unnecessary words, you'll find your text will be significantly shorter. Shoot for around 80% of your original text's length.

Practice will help here, but you can learn a lot by looking at other sites like yours to compare their writing style. Chances are, if you're following the rules, you're already seeing places where they could slim down their content a little!

The inverted pyramid and editing are useful tools, but so is re-reading. Once you're done editing, take another pass through and see if you can shave off just a little bit more.

TEST DRIVE

Update your XHTML so that it contains only your edited text. Let's test it out in the browser... are we getting any closer?

The Hipster Intelligencer

http://www.headfirstlabs.com/books/hfwd/chapter7/copy_edited.html

In 1973, Gary Gygax and Don Kaye founded Tactical Studies Rules (TSR) to publish the rules for Cavaliers and Roundheads, a game based in the English Civil War. Cavaliers and Roundheads was the initial focus of TSR, but Gygax and Kaye also wished to publish the rules for Dungeons & Dragons, a role playing game developed by Gygax. As Cavaliers and Roundheads began generating revenue for TSR, the partnership was expanded to include Dave Arneson and Brian Blume. Dave was brought into the partnership as a game designer, but soon left, while Brian Blume entered as a funder. Blume believed that Cavaliers and Roundheads was not generating enough revenue, and encouraged Gygax and Kaye to focus their efforts on releasing Dungeons & Dragons.

In 1975 Don Kaye died of a stroke. The immediate result was that Blume and Gygax dissolved TSR and founded a new company named TSR Hobbies, Inc. The board of directors for TSR Hobbies, Inc. consisted of Brian Blume, Gygax, and Kevin Blume. Brian was President of Creative Affairs, Kevin was President of Operations, and Gygax was the company's CEO and President. Unlike the equal partnership of TSR, brothers Brian and Kevin owned a majority of the new company's shares.

TSR Hobbies, Inc. experienced phenomenal success in both the United States and abroad. But the Blumes began to overextend the company's reach. They moved into domains such as boardgames and toys, and began to diversify into unrelated areas. The best evidence of this was the unapproved acquisition of Greenfield Needlewomen, a needlepoint business owned by one of the Blumes' relatives. Also, Kevin Blume had printed millions of copies of the previously successful multi-path Dungeons & Dragons adventure books, which couldn't be sold.

In an effort to mitigate the mounting financial problems, TSR Hobbies, Inc was restructured into four companies: TSR, Inc., TSR Ventures, TSR International, and TSR Entertainment. TSR Inc. continued to manufacture the company's core Dungeons & Dragons role playing products. TSR Ventures focused on the production of plastics and toys in Asia. TSR International was established to manage overseas business, distribution, sales and licensing, and production. TSR Entertainment was responsible for leveraging TSR's IP in other entertainment markets, such as movie and television. Unfortunately, TSR Entertainment's only success was the short lived Dungeons & Dragons cartoon. Gygax claimed the separate corporations were Blume's attempt at keeping foreign income away from US taxation.

Despite the restructuring, TSR, Inc. continued to lose money as a result of mismanagement. Eventually, both Kevin and Brian Blume were accused of misusing corporate funds and accumulating large debt in the pursuit of unapproved and inappropriate acquisitions and removed from the board of directors. After the Blumes' departure from the board of directors, Gygax assumed the role of CEO and regained partial control of the company. But Kevin and Brian Blume were in secret negotiations with Lorraine Williams—a potential investor who Gygax had brought into the company previously as an officer—to acquire the majority stock. When Williams finally acquired the controlling stake in the company, Gygax tried to have the sale declared illegal. The attempt failed, and so Gygax sold his remaining stock to Williams and used the capital to form a new company called New Infinity Productions.

The departure of Gygax from TSR irreparably changed the face of the company. TSR successfully expanded into areas such as magazines, paperback fiction, and comic books. In addition, the company released popular new role-playing settings including Dragonlance, Ravenloft, Forgotten Realms, and Greyhawk, all of which have had an enduring impact on the tabletop roleplaying landscape.

In 1997, as TSR approached receivership, the company and all of its intellectual property were acquired by Wizards of the Coast. Ironically, Wizards of the Coast, had published Magic: The Gathering, the game whose remarkable success had been responsible for TSR's failure in the collectible card game market. After the sale, TSR was slowly dismantled. In 2003 Wizards of the Coast allowed the final TSR trademarks to expire. Wizards of the Coast continues to publish Dungeons & Dragons to this day.

Despite its almost constant legal and financial troubles, TSR had a lasting [...] could argue that TSR had more impact on the entertainment game industry than any other company in the hist[...] ed on the archetypes and mechanics first introduced in Dungeons & Dragons, but TSR and its various [...] ave long since passed into the realm of popular culture.

That's much better, but it still looks like way too much in my browser. All that text on screen's a little overwhelming.

How would you fix this?

You're a web user. What do other sites do to break up content and make it manageable?

Jim →

Frank →

So we still need to break the text down some, huh? How about using a list to make the content more scannable?

Jim: How would that work? Doesn't a list just add a bunch of different-sized chunks of text for user's eyes to scan?

Frank: Lists break up large blocks of text into smaller chunks that are easier for the user to read. And they give the user's eyes something to lock onto when they scan the page. Let me show you how it works. I'll write out some text then show you how it can be broken down into a list.

Lists do a great job of breaking up text and making the content on your page more scannable. Lists can break up paragraphs that seem to have lots of list-type items in them, and lists can even break larger paragraphs into smaller chunks, essentially building a list of paragraphs. Lists can be used in the main content body, sidebars, navigation, forms, and pretty much everywhere else on your page.

Jim: That's not bad, actually. Looks like the first paragraph of an article about lists, using the inverted pyramid to get all the important points up top.

Frank: Ha ha. Yes, well, you know, I've been paying attention. So anyway, like you say, this text isn't *bad*. But it could be ***much*** quicker to scan and read—

Jim: —in a list?

Frank: You betcha. Just like this:

Use a list when:
- You need to make your text scannable
- Paragraphs or sentences have "listable" elements
- Large blocks of text can be broken into 1 or 2 sentence chunks

Breaking text into a list allows readers to quickly glance at the text and extract information.

Jim: Neat. Those bullets summarize three sentences of your text into just three bullet points. But what about the rest of the text?

Frank: [writing]

Lists can be used in different ways all over your site. Try them in:
- Your main content
- Sidebars
- Navigation and Headers

Long Exercise

Visit the following sites and annotate these screenshots. Which of these sites use the inverted pyramid? Why do you think any of the sites wouldn't use the inverted pyramid? Do any of the sites use lists and bullets? Why or Why not?

slashdot.org

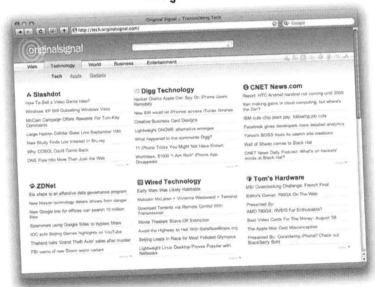

tech.originalsignal.com

newsvine.com

digg.com

Long Exercise Solution

Which of these sites use the inverted pyramid? Why do you think any of the sites wouldn't use the inverted pyramid? Do any of the sites use bullets? Why or Why not?

Slashdot and Newsvine use the inverted pyramid to present content to their users.

slashdot.org

Slashdot uses a list—paragraph hybrid. Posts are displayed in a list ordered by date. Each article excerpt has a title and a quote on a dark green background that catches your eye and moves it down the page.

newsvine.com

Newsvine doesn't use lists as its main layout tool but does a great job of placing them in sidebars and extra content. Notice the bullets in each of the three columns.

Digg, everyone's favorite technology aggregator, is one giant list. The most recent, most popular "diggs" act as bullets to grab your eye, and they provide a nice clickable link to the story.

digg.com

These are our answers. Yours may be a little different, but check the sites again if your annotations are a LOT different than ours.

Original Signal breaks its content into two sets of lists. The first lists the header for each site. The second is a list below each site's heading with the most recent stories first.

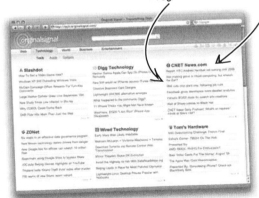

tech.originalsignal.com

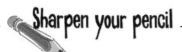

Sharpen your pencil

Take this paragraph from the Editor-in-Chief's copy you already edited and make it more readable by turning it into a list.
Hint: You can use a sentence or two to explain what the list is.

> The departure of Gygax from TSR irreparably changed the face of the company. TSR successfully expanded into areas such as magazines, paperback fiction, and comic books. In addition, the company released popular new role-playing settings including Dragonlance, Ravenloft, Forgotten Realms, and Greyhawk, all of which have had an enduring impact on the tabletop roleplaying landscape.

Don't worry about HTML yet. Just rewrite this text as a list.

Sharpen your pencil
Solution

You made this edited paragraph more readable by turning it into a list. Leaving a sentence or two to explain what the list is helps give the user context.

> The departure of Gygax from TSR irreparably changed the face of the company. TSR successfully expanded into areas such as magazines, paperback fiction, and comic books. In addition, the company released popular new role-playing settings including Dragonlance, Ravenloft, Forgotten Realms, and Greyhawk, all of which have had an enduring impact on the tabletop roleplaying landscape.

This content already uses the inverted pyramid (most important content first), but now it's broken down even further into lists.

The departure of Gygax from TSR irreparably changed the face of the company. TSR successfully expanded into areas such as:

Notice how a little text before each list gives the list some context.

- Magazines
- Paperback fiction
- Comic books

These lists items are fragments, so they don't need punctuation, but notice that the first word after each bullet is capitalized.

In addition, the company released popular new role-playing settings, including:

- Dragonlance
- Ravenloft
- Forgotten Realms
- Greyhawk

The content that we used to create the lists already listed a number of items, so it was perfect for, uh, lists!

All of these have had an enduring impact on the tabletop role-playing landscape.

The last sentence needed a small edit now that it follows a list.

Scannable web copy	
☑	has content ordered by the inverted pyramid
☑	has been edited so it's shorter
☑	breaks down content even more with lists

Add lists to your XHTML

Go ahead and edit the rest of your text to add lists where appropriate. When you're done, alter your XHTML so that it uses lists, too. You can use unordered and ordered lists to give you bulleted or numbered list items:

Unordered list

```
<p>My favorite Seinfeld episodes</p>
<ul>
    <li>The Chinese Restaurant</li>
    <li>The Pez Dispenser</li>
    <li>The Yada Yada</li>
    <li>The Junior Mint</li>
    <li>The Big Salad</li>
    <li>The Fuscilli Jerry</li>
    <li>The Rye</li>
    <li>The Merv Griffin Show</li>
</ul>
```

Ordered list

```
<p>Top 10 reasons to move to Chicago</p>
<ol>
    <li>Lake Michigan</li>
    <li>The "Chicago-stlye" hot dog</li>
    <li>The "El"</li>
    <li>Millenium Park</li>
    <li>Wrigley Field (even if you don't like the
    <li>The Bean</li>
    <li>The Sears Tower</li>
    <li>Really Deep-dish Pizza</li>
    <li>The Midwest accent</li>
    <li>intelligentsia Coffee</li>
</ol>
```

Stop! Create lists in your XHTML before you move on.

TEST DRIVE

So you've applied the inverted pyramid to your article, edited it some, and now you've added lists. How's it looking?

Here's our XHTML with lists. Check it out for yourself at www.headfirstlabs.com/books/hfwd/chapter7/copy_edited_lists.html

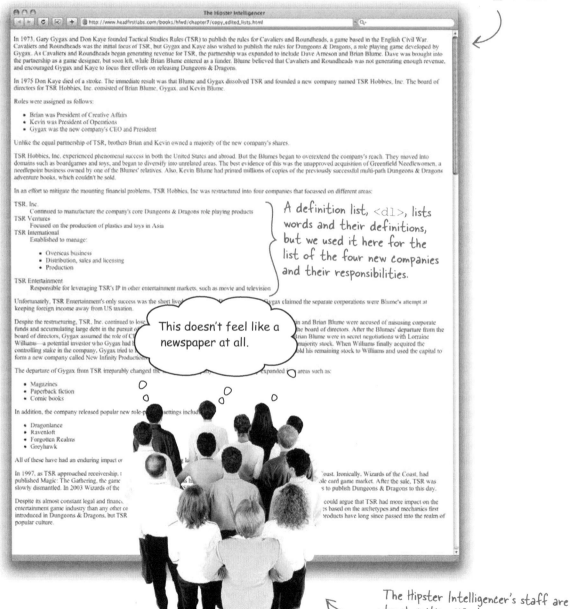

A definition list, `<dl>`, lists words and their definitions, but we used it here for the list of the four new companies and their responsibilities.

This doesn't feel like a newspaper at all.

The Hipster Intelligencer's staff are tough critics. What can you do to improve the look of the copy?

Headings make your text *even* more scannable

So you've used lists to break down some paragraphs and sentences into bullets, but what else can you do to help users scan your content? **Headings** are a great way to make blocks of text more scannable.

Headings reduce large blocks of text into more manageable chunks, and they announce exactly what that chunk of text is about—which lets your users decide whether they want to invest their time in reading that bit of text.

Exercise

Here's the home page of the *New Yorker*, `www.newyorker.com`.

Circle *all* the headings and lists. Take your time... try not to miss anything.

Exercise Solution

Did you find *all* the headings and lists?

The main site heading appears on every page and gives the users context if they arrived there through a search engine or any place else that wasn't the home page.

The subscription section is an unordered list, <ol>. There's no bullet, but it's clearly still a list.

The site navigation is also an unordered list that's set to display inline.

The table of contents mixes headings in a list!

Another unordered list holds links to articles related to the lead story.

Today's date is a heading on the top left of the page.

Sidebar headers let the user know where the links go or why this content is different from the main column.

Notice also how the sidebar breaks down linked content into a list.

Another two headings announce more feature content towards the bottom of the top fold to encourage users to scroll down.

Sub-headings in the body text help to break up the page and emphasize ancillary content...

...and that content's linked via another heading.

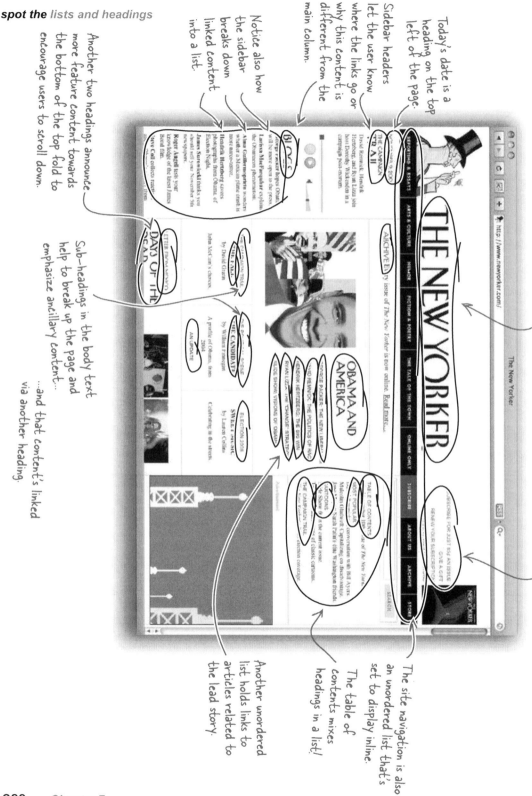

Exercise

Now that you've got a good idea why headings are important (and what makes a good heading), it's time to try headings out on your own.

Write a short heading for each of the blocks of text below. Remember to create headings that are straight to the point and scannable.

....

Acoustic guitars are used in a variety of different genres across the globe. Because of the long history of the acoustic guitar, there are many different kinds; some kinds are rarely considered guitars, such as the ukulele, which was based on the four-stringed braginho or cavaquinhos from Portugal.

....

The Protestant movement may have commenced earlier, but the publication of Ninety-Five Theses by Martin Luther in 1517 spurred on the revolution within the Church. Luther attacked the Church's theology, which, he believed, misrepresented the Bible and placed too much authority in the hands of the clergy, and he wished to reform the Church. After being excommunicated, Luther published many books on Reform. Luther's works were most influential in Germany and Scandinavia.

....

The surface of Mars is a lot like a desert on Earth; it is very dry and dusty, but it is also very cold. There are a lot of loose rocks and dunes of fine sand. Crater impacts mark the surface, but these are not as common as on the Moon. One of the craters is the huge Hellas Planitia. It is about half the size of the continental United States. The southern half of the planet has more craters than in the north. The south is also higher in elevation.

You wrote headings that are straight to the point and scannable for the blocks of text. Is this enough to give the copy that newspaper feel that the Hipster Intelligencer's staff wanted?

This text isn't just about acoustic guitars, but the different types of guitar that have evolved around the world.

Acoustic Guitar Types

Acoustic guitars are used in a variety of different genres across the globe. Because of the long history of the acoustic guitar, there are many different kinds; some kinds are rarely considered guitars, such as the ukulele, which was based on the four-stringed braginho or cavaquinhos from Portugal.

This text is about Luther and his role in the Protestant movement, so if you have a heading that focuses on either, that's probably fine.

Martin Luther

The Protestant movement may have commenced earlier, but the publication of Ninety-Five Theses by Martin Luther in 1517 spurred on the revolution within the Church. Luther attacked the Church's theology, which, he believed, misrepresented the Bible and placed too much authority in the hands of the clergy, and he wished to reform the Church. After being excommunicated, Luther published many books on Reform. Luther's works were most influential in Germany and Scandinavia.

Yup, this one's definitely about geographical elements and Mars. Sometimes headings are no-brainers.

The Geography of Mars

The surface of Mars is a lot like a desert on Earth; it is very dry and dusty, but it is also very cold. There are a lot of loose rocks and dunes of fine sand. Crater impacts mark the surface, but these are not as common as on the Moon. One of the craters is the huge Hellas Planitia. It is about half the size of the continental United States. The southern half of the planet has more craters than in the north. The south is also higher in elevation.

there are no
Dumb Questions

Q: Doesn't adding a bunch more small items on the page make it longer? Won't that strain my users' eyes more than a shorter page?

A: No. In fact, lists help your users scan the page faster and take in more information, more easily. Lists break down sentences and paragraphs that contain a lot of information into easy-to-read chunks. Lists might add a little to the length of a page, but your users will be happy to scroll down if the content's relevant to them. And since you've already edited your text so it follows the inverted pyramid structure, they'll know right away if the page is relevant to them.

Q: When should I use lists? You had a couple I didn't have, and I added some in that you didn't. What gives?

A: Lists are great for breaking long paragraphs down into two or three more manageable chunks. If you broke down more paragraphs than we did, that's fine, but be careful not to overuse lists. It's good to try and keep a balance between short, focused sentences and lists. Both help keep your users interested.

Q: What about the definition list in your solution, what made you decide to use that where you did?

A: Definition lists aren't just for definitions! Sure you can use them to give a word or phrase and provide a definition, but we chose to use the `<dl>` to list each of the four new companies and their responsibilities.

Q: What if I didn't catch all the lists and headings in the New Yorker exercise?

A: Hey, don't be too hard on yourself! Seriously, there are a *lot* of headings and lists on that page. If you didn't catch them all, it's no big deal. Just keep practicing, and soon you'll be writing web copy like a pro—and recognizing the same tricks at work on other people's sites, too.

Keep practicing. The more web copy you write and edit, the better you'll be at slimming text down and making it scannable.

 **Long Exercise**

Use your newfound expertise to write headings for the first four sections of your copy.

....

In 1973, Gary Gygax and Don Kaye founded Tactical Studies Rules (TSR) to publish the rules for Cavaliers and Roundheads, a game based in the English Civil War. Cavaliers and Roundheads was the initial focus of TSR, but Gygax and Kaye also wished to publish the rules for Dungeons & Dragons, a role playing game developed by Gygax. As Cavaliers and Roundheads began generating revenue for TSR, the partnership was expanded to include Dave Arneson and Brian Blume. Dave was brought into the partnership as a game designer, but soon left, while Brian Blume entered as a funder. Blume believed that Cavaliers and Roundheads was not generating enough revenue and encouraged Gygax and Kaye to focus their efforts on releasing Dungeons & Dragons.

....

In 1975 Don Kaye died of a stroke. The immediate result was that Blume and Gygax dissolved TSR and founded a new company named TSR Hobbies, Inc. The board of directors for TSR Hobbies, Inc. consisted of Brian Blume, Gygax, and Kevin Blume.

Roles were assigned as follows:

- Brian was President of Creative Affairs
- Kevin was President of Operations
- Gygax was the new company's CEO and President

Unlike the equal partnership of TSR, brothers Brian and Kevin owned a majority of the new company's shares.

....

TSR Hobbies, Inc. experienced phenomenal success in both the United States and abroad. But the Blumes began to overextend the company's reach. They moved into domains such as board games and toys, and began to diversify into unrelated areas. The best evidence of this was the unapproved acquisition of Greenfield Needlewomen, a needlepoint business owned by one of the Blumes' relatives. Also, Kevin Blume had printed millions of copies of the previously successful multi-path Dungeons & Dragons adventure books, which couldn't be sold.

In an effort to mitigate the mounting financial problems, TSR Hobbies, Inc. was restructured into four companies that focussed on different areas:

TSR, Inc.
Continued to manufacture the company's core Dungeons & Dragons role playing products

TSR Ventures
Focused on the production of plastics and toys in Asia

TSR International
Established to manage:

- Overseas business
- Distribution, sales and licensing
- Production

TSR Entertainment
Responsible for leveraging TSR's IP in other entertainment markets, such as movie and television

Unfortunately, TSR Entertainment's only success was the short lived Dungeons & Dragons cartoon. Gygax claimed the separate corporations were Blume's attempt at keeping foreign income away from US taxation.

Now write the headings for the rest of your article, and when you're done, change your XHTML file to match.

When you've done that, download the content for the center `<div>` and sidebar.

`www.headfirstlabs.com/books/hfwd/chapter7/center.html`

`www.headfirstlabs.com/books/hfwd/chapter7/sidebar.html`

and add headings and lists for those, too.

LONG EXERCISE SOLUTION

You should now have headings for all of your copy including the center and sidebar `<div>`s.

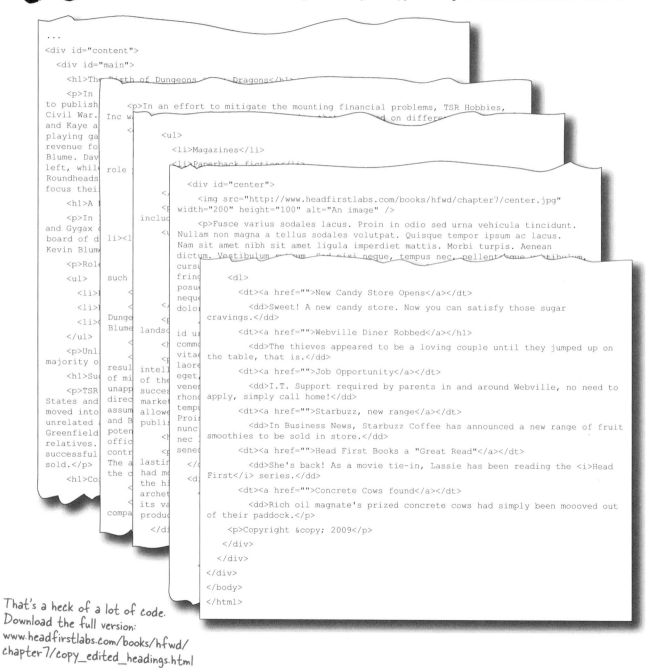

```
...
<div id="content">
  <div id="main">
    <h1>The Birth of Dungeons      Dragons</h1>
    <p>In
to publish          <p>In an effort to mitigate the mounting financial problems, TSR Hobbies,
Civil War.    Inc w                                      ed on differe
and Kaye a
playing ga          <ul>
revenue fo             <li>Magazines</li>
Blume. Dav
left, while            <li>Paperback fiction
Roundheads    role
focus thei             <div id="center">
    <h1>A              <img src="http://www.headfirstlabs.com/books/hfwd/chapter7/center.jpg"
    <p>In     include  width="200" height="100" alt="An image" />
and Gygax
board of d    li><l    <p>Fusce varius sodales lacus. Proin in odio sed urna vehicula tincidunt.
Kevin Blum             Nullam non magna a tellus sodales volutpat. Quisque tempor ipsum ac lacus.
    <p>Role            Nam sit amet nibh sit amet ligula imperdiet mattis. Morbi turpis. Aenean
    <ul>      such     dictum. Vestibulum          nisi neque, tempus nec, pellent      tibulum,
        <li>           cursu
        <li>  <         frin       <dl>
        <li>  Dunge    posu          <dt><a href="">New Candy Store Opens</a></dt>
    </ul>     Blume    neque          <dd>Sweet! A new candy store. Now you can satisfy those sugar
    <p>Unl             dolo   cravings.</dd>
majority o    id u           <dt><a href="">Webville Diner Robbed</a></h1>
    <h1>Su    resul  comm          <dd>The thieves appeared to be a loving couple until they jumped up on
    <p>TSR    of the vita   the table, that is.</dd>
States and    unapp  laore          <dt><a href="">Job Opportunity</a></dt>
direc  succes eget          <dd>I.T. Support required by parents in and around Webville, no need to
moved into    assum  marke  vener  apply, simply call home!</dd>
unrelated     and B  allowe rhond          <dt><a href="">Starbuzz, new range</a></dt>
Greenfield    poten  publis tempu          <dd>In Business News, Starbuzz Coffee has announced a new range of fruit
relatives.    offic         Proi   smoothies to be sold in store.</dd>
successful    contr  <       nunc          <dt><a href="">Head First Books a "Great Read"</a></dt>
sold.</p>     The a  lastir nec           <dd>She's back! As a movie tie-in, Lassie has been reading the <i>Head
    <h1>Co    the c  had m  sened  First</i> series.</dd>
                     the hi </           <dt><a href="">Concrete Cows found</a></dt>
                     archet <d           <dd>Rich oil magnate's prized concrete cows had simply been moooved out
                     its v  of their paddock.</p>
compa  produ          <p>Copyright &copy; 2009</p>
    </di          </div>
        </div>
    </div>
  </body>
</html>
```

That's a heck of a lot of code.
Download the full version:
www.headfirstlabs.com/books/hfwd/
chapter7/copy_edited_headings.html

TEST DRIVE

How are those headings and lists looking in the browser?

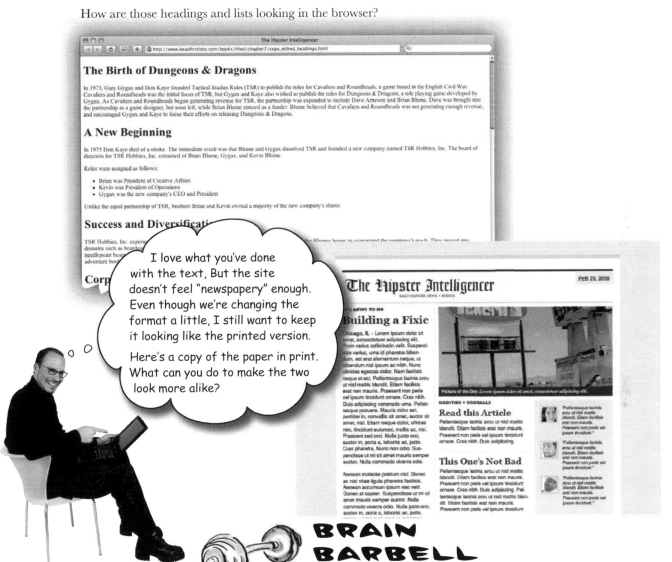

> I love what you've done with the text, But the site doesn't feel "newspapery" enough. Even though we're changing the format a little, I still want to keep it looking like the printed version.
>
> Here's a copy of the paper in print. What can you do to make the two look more alike?

BRAIN BARBELL

Newspapers have a distinct typographic look and feel. Go pick up your local paper and think about how the type looks. Is it serif or sans-serif? Are the lines spaced far apart or close together? What about the look of the newspaper's typography makes it look "newspapery"?

Mix fonts to emphasize headings and other text

Using a different font for your site can dramatically change the feel and emotion of the design. On top of that, different fonts can make your text more readable and make life easier for your users. There are two distinct categories of fonts for the Web: **serif** and **sans-serif**.

A mix of serif and sans-serif fonts can add a nice touch to pages and help separate content from headings. It also allows you to render serif fonts at a larger size and keep the body content in a sans-serif that can be safely displayed in a smaller size.

Serif fonts used as large headings can create nice contrast from body content.

Because sans-serif fonts are easier to read at smaller sizes, they work well for main content sections.

Geek Bits

Serif fonts look like Times New Roman and are defined by the small projections—or "serifs"—that extend off the main stroke of the character.

Sans-serif means "without (sans) serif" and is composed of font families like Helvetica and Arial. Sans-serif fonts are easier to read on screen because the relatively low resolution of computer monitors makes serif fonts look blurry, especially at smaller sizes.

This doesn't mean you can't use serif fonts on the Web; they just need to be used properly and rendered large enough so that they can be easily read by your users.

Hmm. That's not exactly what I'd call "subtle." Couldn't we introduce some variation by making the headings different sizes?

We could, but be careful. Do you mean text size or heading level?

The <u>level</u>, not the <u>size</u>, of a heading conveys importance

HTML comes out of the box with six different header levels: `<h1>` through `<h6>`. With no stylesheet (just the naked markup), most browsers will render `<h1>` in the largest text and `<h6>` in the smallest.

Remember, HTML's a markup language and isn't intended to convey style information. The different heading levels are used to **signify importance** in your content. A level one heading `<h1>` is the most important heading, `<h2>` is the next-most important, and so on.

When you're marking up your sites, remember to make main headings `<h1>` or `<h2>` and make other sub-headings a lower heading level. This will ensure that the site is semantically correct and search engines are interpreting your content correctly. (Remember, the bots can't actually see your design.)

> Using CSS, an `<h6>` tag can display larger than an `<h1>`. Always remember that the heading number is a function of <u>importance</u>, not <u>size</u>.

Heading Level 1
Heading Level 2
Heading Level 3
Heading Level 4
Heading Level 5
Heading Level 6

BRAIN BARBELL

Just because you *can* style the lower-level headings in larger fonts with CSS, does that mean you *should*?

Fireside Chats

Tonight's talk: **Serif and Sans-serif discuss readability and who makes the better web font.**

Serif:

I've been around a lot longer than you, Sans-serif. I've worked with newspapers and books for years, so I can't understand why I wouldn't be a perfect fit for the Web...

Like you're so readable at small sizes. Plus, the user can resize the text in their browser. Everyone knows that. And what do you mean *I look blurry on a computer monitor*. Most folks have those fancy screens anyway.

That was a low blow. I thought this was supposed to be a civilized conversation? Can you back any of that up with proof, big guy?

Oh, uh, okay, point taken. But you have to admit that there are some nice-looking serif fonts, including **Georgia**, which was made specifically for the Web.

Sans-serif:

Listen, just because you're easier to read in a book or magazine, doesn't mean you're better for the Web. All those little "serifs," as you call them, make you look blurry on screen. And don't even get me started on how you look at small font sizes. Not. Even. Legible.

Oh man. First of all, not everyone knows how to resize text in their browser, and there's a *huge* difference between screen and print resolution. Those fancy flat screen monitors still don't even come close to matching the resolution of text printed on a page. Ever try to read a whole book on your fancy computer monitor? The eye strain would be so bad, you'd never finish. Why make that worse with a serif font?

www.webstyleguide.com/type/face.html

Serif:

It is kind of nice being the default browser font. I couldn't ask for better publicity right out of the gate. But you know, **Helvetica**'s out there spreading the good word on sans-serif, and **Verdana**'s made some noise on the Web lately.

Sans-serif:

Even I'm a fan of Georgia, especially for headings. But you're *everywhere* these days.

You're okay when you sit down face-to-face. You could do wonders for my pages if I use you in the right place...

Exercise

Okay, you're on to the final stretch. Here's what's left to do:

☐ Change up your XHTML to use the different heading levels.

Don't rely on your CSS to show what level each heading is. Be semantic.

☐ Create CSS styles for the different heading levels

☐ Use CSS to style the main content text.

☐ Do you like how your lists look out of the box? If not, use CSS!

Keep this page open and tick off each to-do as you complete it.

Exercise Solution

You changed up your XHTML and added CSS styles for your headings, body text, and maybe even lists, but how did you do? Why not tell us!

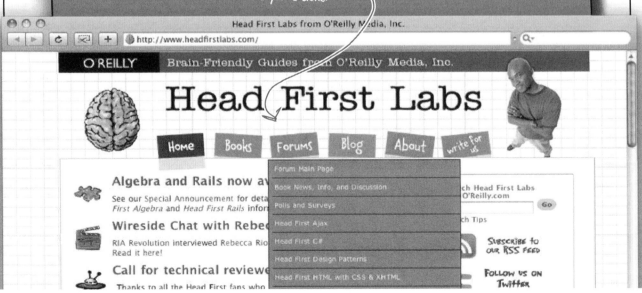

Your Web Design Toolbox

You've got Chapter 7 under
your belt, and you now know
the ins and outs of writing good
web content. You should be able to
write organized, scannable web text.
But there's still more... keep reading!

BULLET POINTS

- People read text off of a screen 15% slower than off a printed page.

- The low resolution of monitors (compared to a printed page) often results in eye straining–making it uncomfortable to read text off a screen.

- On the Web, people don't read text like they do on a printed page. Instead, they scan it, looking for keywords, sentences, and paragraphs that are meaningful to them.

- Write your text like an inverted pyramid —with a general summary at the beginning and detail after. The idea is that users can stop reading at any time and still be confident in the fact that they've already gotten the most important pieces of information.

- Always write at least 15% less text for a website than you would for a print document.

- Use lists to break up large blocks of text and give the user's eye something to latch onto when they are scanning your page.

- Headers make text more scannable. Not only do they break up large blocks of text, but they also tell the user what the paragraph is about.

- Sans-serif fonts are easier to read on a screen than serif fonts, especially at smaller font sizes.

8 accessibility

Inaccessibility Kills

> Look, I just need two more days... I've got my ALT tags done. Will that hold you over? Please, I just need to order my <div>s, and you'll have everything you want...

Who's missing out on experiencing your website right now?

You may have a beautiful, well-laid out, easily navigable site... but that doesn't mean everyone's enjoying it. Whether it's someone who's visually-impaired or just a user who has trouble distinguishing blues from greens, your site must be **accessible**. Otherwise, you're losing users and hurting your business. But don't worry: *accessibility isn't difficult!* By **planning the order of your markup**, using **ALT** attributes and **LONGDESC** tags, and **thinking about color**, you'll widen your audience immediately. Along the way, you may even get **WCAG certified**. What's that? Turn the page, and find out...

Audio-2-Go: inaccessible accessibility

Audio-2-Go is a site that sells audio books for the blind and visually impaired. But the owner's got a problem: his site doesn't work for those who can't see! It turns out that the firm who did his site didn't know anything about accessibility, and now he's losing customers faster than you can say, "But I can't **see** what your site looks like!"

It's up to you to take Audio-2-Go to its audience: those who depend on accessibility every day.

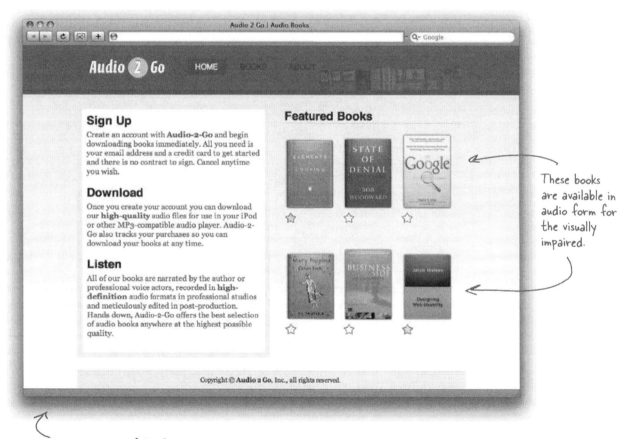

These books are available in audio form for the visually impaired.

Do you see this site in full color at high-resolution? Then you're probably <u>not</u> in Audio-2-Go's core audience!

Accessibility means making your site work for <u>EVERYONE</u>

So what exactly is accessibility? When a website can't be used by someone with a disability, the site's inaccessible. When your site can be used by someone with a disability, then your site is **accessible**.

So, basically, accessibility is both the process and the techniques used to create a site that can be used by someone with a disability. Web accessibility usually deals with visual, auditory, physical, speech, cognitive, and neurological disabilities. And on the Web, accessibility also includes designing for older individuals whose abilities are changing due to age.

Accessibility is thinking about how <u>DISABILITIES</u> affect how people experience and enjoy <u>YOUR</u> website.

This site is a real pain to use without a mouse. Nobody thought about my disability...

It sure seems like nobody considered I'd be using a screen reader for this site...

Both these users are having problems using the Audio-2-Go site.

Poor motor skills in his hands

Legally blind

How does your site <u>READ</u>?

When you think about disabilities, one of the first things you probably think about is the visually impaired or the blind. Those disabilities have a huge effect on how your site is perceived. All your visuals become more or less irrelevant... in how they *look*, but not in how they *sound*.

The majority of people who are blind use a **screen reader** to browse the Web. A screen reader is a piece of software that reads the text of a website out loud. While there are quite a few screen readers on the market, the most popular is JAWS (http://www.freedomscientific.com/jaws-hq.asp), a Windows-only product. Mac users often use VoiceOver, a screen reader built right into the Mac OS X operating system (http://www.apple.com/macosx/features/voiceover/).

Regardless of the product, a screen reader literally reads your page out loud.

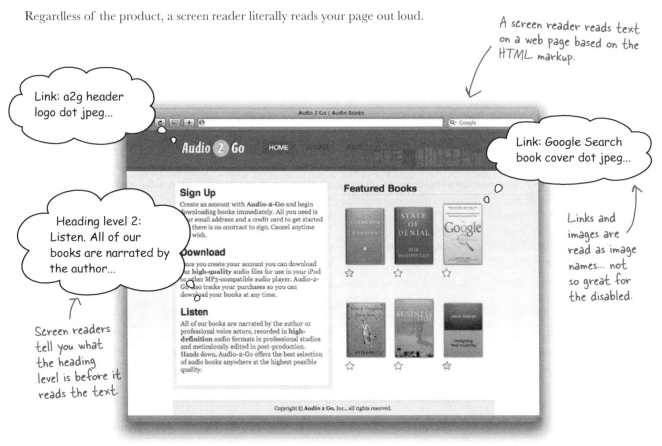

A screen reader reads text on a web page based on the HTML markup.

Link: a2g header logo dot jpeg...

Link: Google Search book cover dot jpeg...

Heading level 2: Listen. All of our books are narrated by the author...

Links and images are read as image names... not so great for the disabled.

Screen readers tell you what the heading level is before it reads the text.

Sharpen your pencil

You can't begin to understand accessibility until you experience a website as someone who is blind or visually impaired does. Open up JAWS (they've got a great free demo) if you are on a Windows machine, or VoiceOver if you are on a Mac, and turn your screen reader loose on your favorite website. Oh... and before you start the reader, **make sure you close your eyes.**

Now that you've got a bit of an idea about how the blind and visually impaired experience the Web, its time to see how Audio-2-Go's website measures up. Open up your screen reader and turn it loose on the Audio-2-Go website (http://www.headfirstlabs.com/books/hfwd/ audio2go/). Write down three things you learned about the site, and then what you think the overall site is about... based just on what you heard from the screen reader.

What is Audio-2-Go about?

1 ....
....

2 ....
....

3 ....
....

What are your thoughts about the overall site?

....
....
....
....

A site's message should be clear...to <u>EVERYONE</u>

Audio-2-Go's message isn't so clear verbally, is it? The whole point of a website is to communicate something to your audience. That means your job is to make sure your content is just as clear to someone using a screen reader as it is to a sighted user. But when you "listen" to Audio-2-Go, a lot's lost in translation.

Here's what a few visually impaired users thought about the Audio-2-Go site:

> My reader started listing what sounded like image names, or maybe filenames. Aren't there any books on this site?

Without your help, a screen reader will read image names, which is pretty confusing.

> I had no idea where I was. I never even heard the name of the page... just some text and a bunch of weird sounding names.

Titles, headings, and descriptions are vital for screen readers.

> I heard a bunch of book names, and then some information about signing up. That was confusing... shouldn't I hear that introduction text before hearing a bunch of book names?

The order of your markup matters a LOT to screen readers... and can have a big effect on confusing visually impaired visitors.

Face it: computers are stupid!

If you want to get a handle on screen readers and accessibility in general, you have to accept that **computers are stupid!** A computer or a piece of software can't figure out that your image really represents a book, and that humans want to know the title of that book. So even though your page displays a book and an image that looks like a book, that's not what a computer sees.

A human can look at a picture and describe what they see in clear descriptive terms.

Awww... It's a cute orange kitten with big eyes.

DCS1243.jpg...

Without any other information, all a computer sees is a filename and an extension.

BRAIN BARBELL

How can you tell the computer what your image really is in a way you think a screen reader might understand?

A computer will read your image's ALT text

So what happens when a screen reader comes upon an image? Most of the time it simply reads the filename... which is absolutely no good to someone who is blind or visually impaired. Fortunately, img elements have an attribute that lets you provide your own description: the alt attribute. If a screen reader sees an image with an alt attribute, the reader reads the value of the alt attribute *instead of* the image name. Perfect, right?

Well, only if your alt text is any good.

Fortunately, good alt text is pretty easy to create. You want a short, descriptive, clear phrase. In other words, just succinctly describe the image:

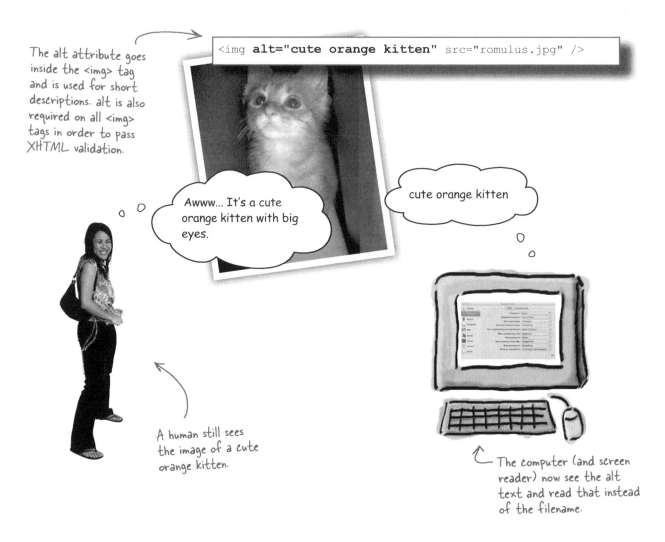

The alt attribute goes inside the <img> tag and is used for short descriptions. alt is also required on all <img> tags in order to pass XHTML validation.

```
<img alt="cute orange kitten" src="romulus.jpg" />
```

Awww... It's a cute orange kitten with big eyes.

cute orange kitten

A human still sees the image of a cute orange kitten.

The computer (and screen reader) now see the alt text and read that instead of the filename.

Exercise

Create an <img> tag based on the information for each image and the alt text that was provided by the owner.

Filename: `audio2go-logo.jpg`

Description: Audio-2-Go header logo

Write in the full <img> tag here.

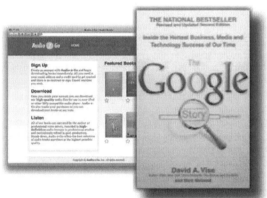

Filename: `googlestory.jpg`

Description: The Google Story: An inside look into one of the World's greatest technology startups.

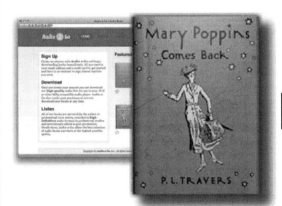

Filename: `poppins.jpg`

Description: Mary Poppins by P.L. Travers

TEST DRIVE

Try out the Audio-2-Go site with a screen reader.

Download the code for the Audio-2-Go site from the Head First Labs website. Open up index.html in your text editor and add the alt tags from the last page. Then fire up your screen reader and check out the Audio-2-Go site again. Any better?

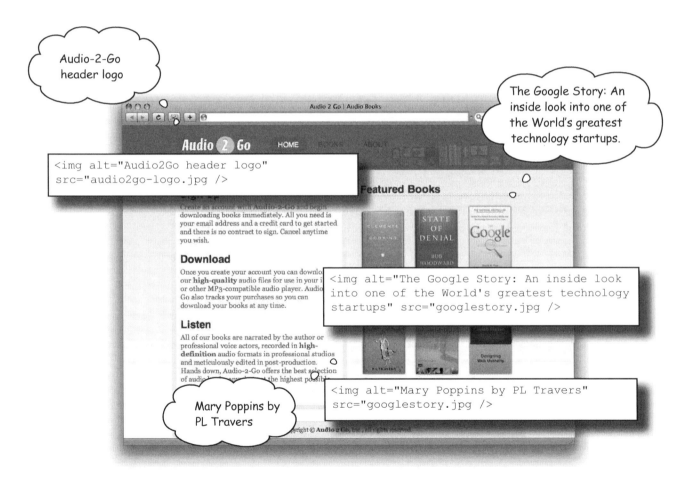

Audio-2-Go header logo

The Google Story: An inside look into one of the World's greatest technology startups.

```
<img alt="Audio2Go header logo"
src="audio2go-logo.jpg />
```

```
<img alt="The Google Story: An inside look
into one of the World's greatest technology
startups" src="googlestory.jpg />
```

```
<img alt="Mary Poppins by PL Travers"
src="googlestory.jpg />
```

Mary Poppins by PL Travers

I thought alt text was supposed to be short. Isn't that description of the Google Story book a bit long? It's gonna take like 10 minutes just to read the home page. Just 'cause people are visually disabled, doesn't mean they've got hours to sit around listening, right?

EVERYONE's time is valuable.

Nobody wants to see or hear a page that's filled with text that's not relevant. Lengthy alt values are going to bog down your page and give information that's not really needed. What we need is a way to provide additional information about an element, but let a viewer or listener choose whether they want to access that additional information.

The `longdesc` attribute lets you do just that. `longdesc` gives screen readers an option to go to additional information about an element... like a *longer description* (`longdesc`... makes sense, right?):

A short alt text gives a concise description of an image.

```
<img alt="cute orange kitten"
     longdesc="romulus.html" src="romulus.jpg" />
```

longdesc indicates a page that has more detail... lots of cloying details about that cute orange kitten are available, but only if a user wants that information.

cute orange kitten

Would you like more information?

Most screen readers let you choose to hear the longdesc page of information.

Convert your long ALT text to a LONGDESC

Let's convert the too-long `alt` text for the Google book to a `longdesc`...
complete with a separate XHTML page. Here's what you should do:

❶ Add a LONGDESC attribute to the Google book image tag.

Now the alt text is short and to the point.

longdesc is added and points to a page with more information.

```
<img alt="The Google Story" longdesc="googlestory.html"
    src="googlestory.jpg" />
```

❷ Create an HTML file called googlestory.html and add a longer description.

The file you reference in longdesc should be normal XHTML.

```
<!DOCTYPE html PUBLIC "-//W3C//DTD XHTML 1.0 Strict//EN"
        "http://www.w3.org/TR/xhtml1/DTD/xhtml1-strict.dtd">
<html xmlns="http://www.w3.org/1999/xhtml"
        xml:lang="en" lang="en">
<head>
  <title>The Google Story</title>
  <meta http-equiv="Content-Type"
        content="text/html; charset=utf-8"/>
</head>
<body>
  <p>The Google Story: An inside look into one of the
      World's greatest technology startups.</p>
</body>
</html>
```

Make sure you properly mark up your content. Remember, this is still an HTML file... Let's keep things valid!

A longdesc page looks pretty bland... but these are meant to be read more than seen.

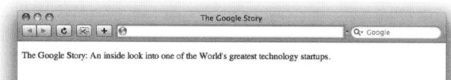

Test Drive

Give Audio-2-Go another screen-reading try.

Add the `longdesc` attribute to the image for The Google Story and create the corresponding XHTML file to hold the actual description. Save your files and give Audio-2-Go's main page one more run through with a screen reader.

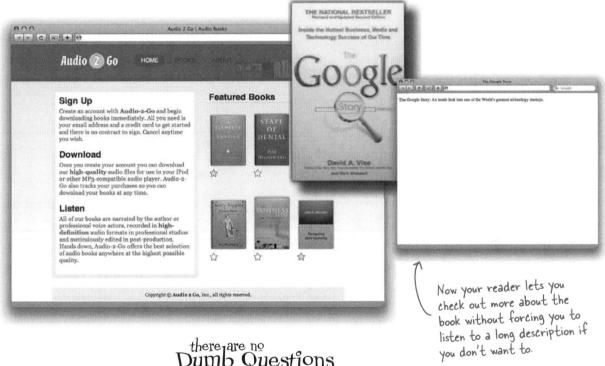

Now your reader lets you check out more about the book without forcing you to listen to a long description if you don't want to.

there are no Dumb Questions

Q: Does the page with the full text description need to have the same design as the site?

A: Nope. Description pages will only be viewed by users with screen readers. So all you need is (semantically correct) marked up text. No CSS required.

Q: Will sighted users see the LONGDESC link?

A: `longdesc` is only "visible" for people using screen readers. Sighted users won't even know it's there unless they view the source code for your page.

Q: Does longdesc work with all screen readers?

A: Unfortunately, `longdesc` is only recognized by newer screen readers. Older screen readers didn't have the feature built into them. Thankfully, current versions of JAWS, by far the most popular screen reader, support `longdesc`.

Your improvements are making a difference for <u>SOME</u> Audio-2-Go customers

Legally blind

Poor motor skills in his hands

Mouseless users are still having lots of trouble getting around Audio-2-Go. There's still work to do on the site.

Accessibility is not just about screen readers

`alt` and `longdesc` attributes will get you a long way toward accessibility... but visually impaired users aren't your only audience. Lots of folks out there have trouble with a mouse, or just prefer using the keyboard. That changes everything.

The Web without a mouse? Yup, it's going on more than you might think. And that means you've got to check your site out *without* a mouse.

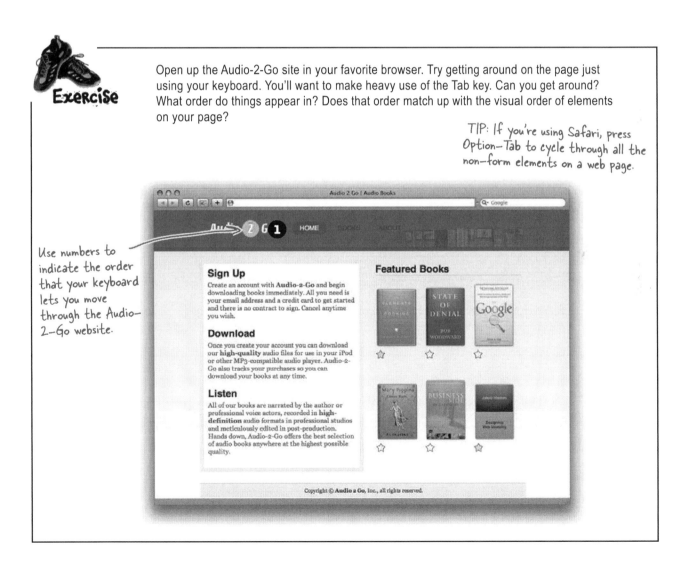

Exercise

Open up the Audio-2-Go site in your favorite browser. Try getting around on the page just using your keyboard. You'll want to make heavy use of the Tab key. Can you get around? What order do things appear in? Does that order match up with the visual order of elements on your page?

TIP: If you're using Safari, press Option-Tab to cycle through all the non-form elements on a web page.

Use numbers to indicate the order that your keyboard lets you move through the Audio-2-Go website.

Exercise Solution

Your job was to check out Audio-2-Go with only your keyboard. How did your actual results line up with what your eyes were telling you? Did the Tab key do what you expected? Here's the order of elements we cycled through:

The header and the main navigation come first. That's good... just what we want since they're at the top of the page.

Tabbing from the heading takes us to the books. That doesn't seem right... what about all the intro text on the left of the page?

Hmm... this text should come after the top section... but it comes last in the tab order.

BRAIN POWER

Try using Audio-2-Go without a mouse *and* without your eyes. Does the tab order seem more or less important to you when "viewing" the site through a screen reader?

Tabbing through a page should be <u>ORDERLY</u>

Whether you're sighted or not, the Tab key should take you through a web page in the same order that your eyes would. That means the tab order should flow top-to-bottom, left-to-right. That's the way most sites are laid out and the way we process sites visually.

For Audio-2-Go, then, we need to make sure the left-side text (Sign Up, Download, and Listen) comes before the book offerings. That gives users more context and tracks with what they might be seeing visually. All we need to do to fix this problem is add a `tabindex` attribute to our elements and explicitly order our elements:

The books are items in a list. So for each book link, we provide a tabindex attribute.

```
<h2>Featured Books</h2>
<ul>
  <li><a href="books/1" tabindex="7">
    <img alt="the elements of cooking" src="images/elements.png" /></a>
    <br /><img alt="star" src="images/star_high.png" /></li>
  <li><a href="books/2" tabindex="8" >
    <img alt="state of denial" src="images/sod.png" /></a>
    <br /><img alt="star" src="images/star_medium.png" /></li>
  <li><a href="books/3" tabindex="9" >
    <img longdesc="google.html" alt="the google story" src="images/google.png" /></a>
    <br /><img alt="star" src="images/start_medium.png" /></li>
  <li><a href="books/4" tabindex="10" >
    <img alt="mary poppins" src="images/mp.png" /></a>
    <br /><img alt="star" src="images/star_medium.png" /></li>
  <li><a href="books/5" tabindex="11" >
    <img alt="business of creativity" src="images/creativity.png" /></a>
    <br /><img alt="star" src="images/star_high.png" /></li>
  <li><a href="books/6" tabindex="12" >
    <img alt="designing web usability" src="images/dwu.png" /></a>
    <br /><img alt="star" src="images/star_medium.png" /></li>
</ul>
```

These books will come after any elements with a lower tabindex and before any elements with a higher tabindex.

Exercise

All of the Audio-2-Go site needs a tabindex overhaul. Open up index.html and give a tabindex to all the elements that you feel need one. Keep trying out your page using just your keyboard until you're sure you've got the page just right.

Exercise Solution

Below is the majority of the Audio-2-Go index.html markup (we skipped the parts that aren't relevant). Here's how we ordered things using tabindex... did you come up with the same markup?

These got tabbed to first, but we added explicit tab indexes just to be sure.

```
<ul id="nav">
  <li><a tabindex="1" title="homepage" href="index.html">Home</a></li>
  <li><a tabindex="2" title="browse books"
         href="books.html">Home</a></li>
  <li><a tabindex="3" title="about Audio2Go"
         href="about.html">About</a></li>
</ul>
...
<div id="featured-books">
  <ul>
    <li><a tabindex="7" href="/books/1">
      <img alt="the elements of cooking" src="elements.jpg" /></a></li>
    <li><a tabindex="8" href="/books/2">
      <img alt="state of denial" src="sod.jpg" /></a></li>
    <li><a tabindex="9" href="/books/3">
      <img alt="the google story" src="google.jpg" /></a></li>
    <li><a tabindex="10" href="/books/4">
      <img alt="mary poppins" src="mp.jpg" /></a></li>
    <li><a tabindex="11" href="/books/5">
      <img alt="business of creativity" src="creativity.jpg" /></a></li>
    <li><a tabindex="12" href="/books/6">
      <img alt="designing web usability" src="dwu.jpg" /></a></li>
  </ul>
</div>
...
<div id="info">
    <h2><a tabindex="4" href="signup">Signup</a></h2>
    <p> Create an account with <strong>Audio-2-Go</strong> and begin
downloading books immediatly. All you need is your email address and
a credit card to get started and there is no contract to sign. Cancel
anytime you wish.</p>
    <h2><a tabindex="5" href="download">...</a></h2>
    <p>...</p>
    <h2><a tabindex="6" href="listen">...</a></h2>
    <p>...</p>
</div>
```

These appear early in the markup but need to be ordered later for keyboard users.

We've left off the star images to save space... don't worry, they're still in our markup.

These links are further down in the markup, but this text should be tabbed to before the markup just above it (the book links).

TEST DRIVE

What does a keyboardless Audio-2-Go feel like now?

Update index.html to use correct `tabindexes`. Then reload `index.html` and try working through it without a mouse.

Remember, if you're using Safari, you need to Option-Tab to make use of the built-in tab sequence.

The tab sequence should start with the page header and navigation.

The sequence should then jump to the page instructions (so users know what the site's about).

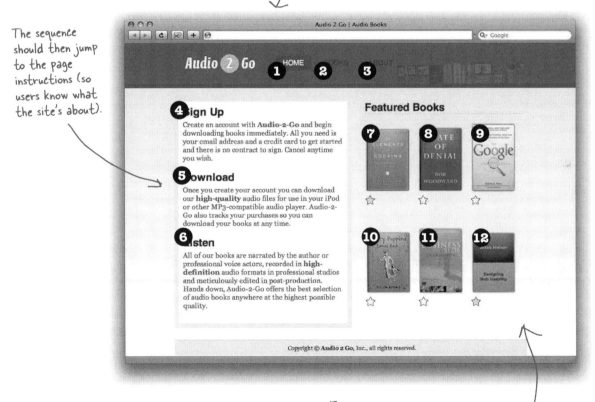

Finally, the tab sequence should step through each of these books.

Audio-2-Go is now a <u>LOT</u> more ACCESSIBLE

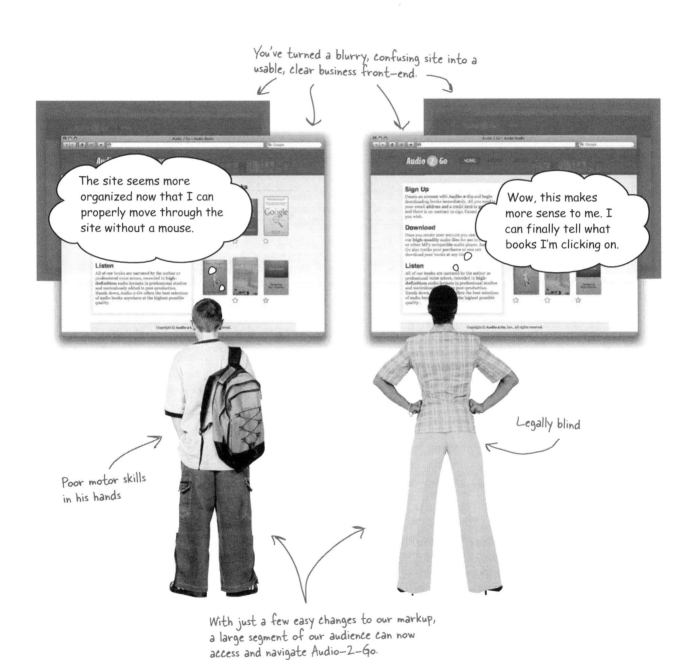

there are no
Dumb Questions

Q: So without a tabindex, fields go in the order of my markup?

A: Exactly. Browsers tab through elements in the order they are detailed in your XHTML, regardless of your CSS style.

Q: So why not just put things in my XHTML in the order they'll appear on the online page?

A: That's not a bad idea... in fact, we'll talk about that a little later. Although with CSS making it easy to change display order, using tabindexes still isn't a bad idea.

Q: The tabindex attribute can be geared toward people who prefer a keyboard over a mouse because they've got less motor control over their hands. But what about people that have no use of their hands whatsoever?

A: There are lots of web users who for one reason or another—such as paralysis or amputation—simply cannot use a mouse. Instead, they'll use alternate input systems like pointing devices such as a head-mouse, head-pointer or mouth-stick; voice-recognition software; or an eye-gaze system. Most of these systems will also pick up on your tabindexes... so that makes a logical tab order even more important.

Q: Not everyone who's got a visual impairment is blind. Does accessibility apply to these people as well?

A: Absolutely. Visual disabilities not only include total blindness, but also include people who have types of low vision (also known as "partially sighted"). This includes poor acuity (vision that is not sharp), tunnel vision (seeing only the middle of the visual field), central field loss (seeing only the edges of the visual field), and clouded vision.

Q: Do visual disabilities include color blindness?

A: Yup. Basically, color blindness is a lack of sensitivity to certain colors—such as red/green or blue/yellow. Sometimes color blindness results in the inability to perceive any color whatsoever.

Q: Do we have to pay any attention to hearing disabilities?

A: Both deafness and hard of hearing are things that someone who is designing an accessible website needs to worry about. This is especially important when you're working on websites that include rich media content, such as video or audio.

Q: What other kinds of disabilities should be considered when designing an accessible website?

A: Two disabilities to consider are cognitive and neurological. These include learning disabilities, such as dyslexia, attention and focus disorders, such as ADD, developmental disabilities that impact intelligence, and even memory disorders (things like unreliable short-term memory, missing long-term memory, or even the inability to recall language).

Q: How do you deal with all the cognitive and neurological disorders?

A: There are simple strategies that let you address cognitive and neurological disorders when designing an accessible website. For those with developmental disabilities, include graphics and images as an alternate way of communicating information. Also, sites with clear visual logic (something we covered back near the beginning of the book) help enormously to address many of the problems experienced by people with a wide variety of cognitive and neurological issues.

This whole accessibility thing is creating a lot of extra work. Is it really worth it?

Accessibility is ALWAYS worth the extra time.

It's really easy to ask yourself why you should care about accessibility. It's unlikely that your audience will have disabilities that impact how they experience your site, right? Is this really that big of a deal?

Actually, *you almost certainly have someone with a disability trying to access your site.* The U.S. Census Bureau categorizes **19.6% of the U.S. population** as having some sort of disability. And if that's not convincing, consider just a few more reasons why accessibility is essential!

❶ The law requires you to be accessible

Section 508 of the U.S. Federal Rehabilitation Act *requires* that federal agencies make their electronic and information technology, including websites, accessible to people with disabilities. In addition, many universities are requiring that all of their official web content be accessible.

❷ Everyone benefits from accessibility

Many of the enhancements and techniques used to make websites accessible to people with disabilities benefit those users *without* disabilities. Accessible websites are often easier to navigate, more user-friendly, and download faster.

❸ Accessibility can help your business

Design studios with a strong understanding of accessibility will have an enormous advantage over those that don't. For example, federal agencies who are required to abide by accessibility standards are sometimes unable to do so themselves. This means that if you have experience with designing accessible websites, you'll have the opportunity to win those jobs.

❹ Accessibility is the right thing to do

Accessible websites represent an important step toward independence for many of the disabled. They provide crucial access to fundamental governmental and educational services and information that would otherwise be unavailable to individuals with certain disabilities. Designing with accessibility in mind makes the Web a better place for everyone.

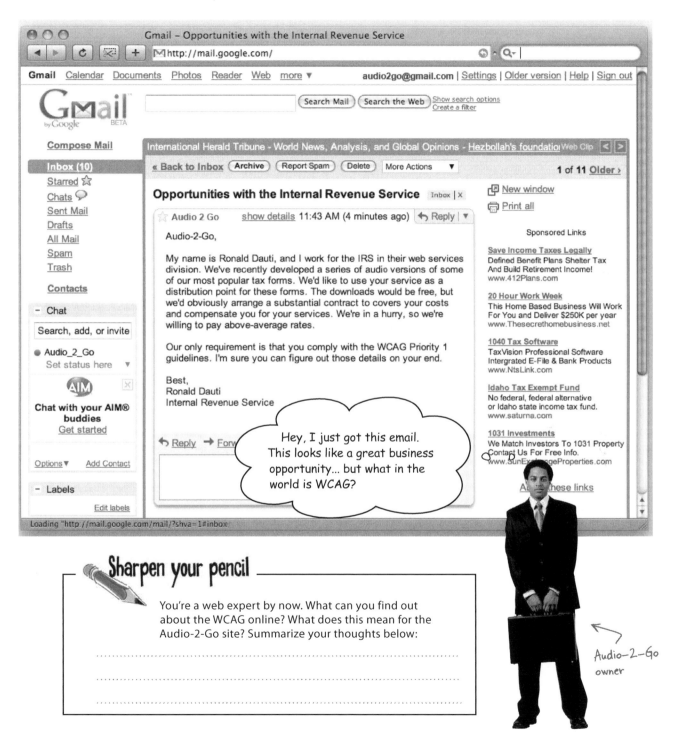

Hey, I just got this email. This looks like a great business opportunity... but what in the world is WCAG?

Sharpen your pencil

You're a web expert by now. What can you find out about the WCAG online? What does this mean for the Audio-2-Go site? Summarize your thoughts below:

Audio-2-Go owner

WCAG Priority 1

WCAG stands for Web Content Accessibility Guidelines. The W3C, the folks who come up with most web standards, have defined a set of guidelines that will allow you to build accessible sites. Follow the WCAG guidelines and your site will be a lot more accessible than if you don't.

WCAG Priority 1 is the set of guidelines that the W3C considers as a baseline requirement. Ignore Priority 1 and you'll definitely leave out some part of a disabled audience. Here's what the Priority 1 guidelines look like:

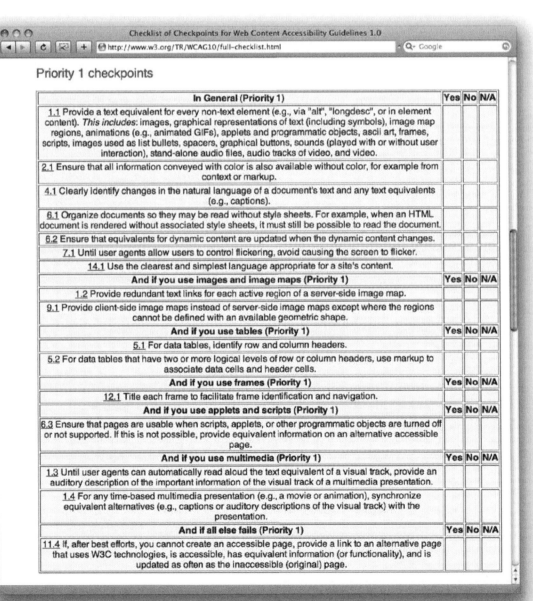

http://www.w3.org/TR/ WCAG10/full-checklist.html

This document has Priority 2 and 3, too. Audio-2-Go just has to meet the Priority 1 guidelines.

Whoa... that list is huge! It's going to take forever to make the Audio-2-Go site WCAG Priority 1 compliant... and we've already done so much work, anyway.

The WCAG is <u>exhaustive</u>... but your <u>changes</u> may not need to be.

The WCAG has to cover every conceivable possibility on almost every type of site possible. That means it deals with lots of things that may not affect your site.

On top of that, lots of the WCAG checkpoints are things you should already be doing, like "Use the clearest and simplest language appropriate for a site's content." So many of these checkpoints may already be done! To meet Priority 1, you just have to take care of **applicable checkpoints** that aren't already **complete**.

Sharpen your pencil

Take a look at the checklist on the previous page or visit the WCAG checkpoints online at http://www.w3.org/TR/WCAG10/full-checklist.html. Below, write any changes you think need to be made to Audio-2-Go to fulfill the Priority 1 checkpoints.

....

....

....

....

....

....

**Sharpen your pencil
Solution**

Your job was to figure out what we still needed to do with
Audio-2-Go to make it WCAG Priority 1 compliant.

1.1 Provide a text equivalent for every non-text element (e.g., via "alt", "longdesc", or in element content). *This includes*: images, graphical representations of text (including symbols), image map regions, animations (e.g., animated GIFs), applets and programmatic objects, ascii art, frames, scripts, images used as list bullets, spacers, graphical buttons, sounds (played with or without user interaction), stand-alone audio files, audio tracks of video, and video.

We've already done this by providing alt and longdesc attributes to our images.

2.1 Ensure that all information conveyed with color is also available without color, for example from context or markup.

This includes graphics and icons. Those stars that represent ratings on each book could be a problem... and what does the site look like without color?

6.1 Organize documents so they may be read without style sheets. For example, when an HTML document is rendered without associated style sheets, it must still be possible to read the document.

This is sort of like tabindexes... it's about order. But this time, the order has to make sense in the markup itself. We've got some problems here.

To Do

~~Provide a text equivalent for all non-text elements.~~

All color information must be displayed without color as well.

Organize documents so they can be read without stylesheets.

Here's the Audio–2–Go To–Do list we came up with. How does it compare with the list of things you thought we needed to do?

there are no Dumb Questions

Q: What is the difference between WCAG Priority 1 and Section 508?

A: There are a few main differences. First, WCAG is a recommendation that was written by the W3C, the Internet's governing body. Although the W3C has no authority to enforce its recommendation, it is considered the standard in making sure sites are accessible to individuals with disabilities. Section 508 is a US Government requirement that is based on the WCAG Priority 1 standards. 508 requires all government agencies and companies that do business with the government to comply with the law. 508 is not enforceable in the private sector as long as a company isn't doing business with the government.

Q: Can you be arrested for not complying with WCAG?

A: Not at all. WCAG is strictly a guide for making your website accessible. Plus, the W3C doesn't have authority to arrest you (or fine you, for that matter). Still, ignoring WCAG is like ignoring a part of your audience, and that's not a good thing. Even a few days spent on accessibility can have a huge impact on your site.

Q: Who decides if my site meets the guidelines?

A: For the most part, you decide. If you have followed along with guidelines and made an effort to make your site as accessible as possible to users with disabilities, you can call yourself accessible. Because Section 508 is a law, there are online services you can use that check and make sure your code is accessible. They will often allow you to post "badges" on your site that advertise the fact that your site meets the 508 requirement. Similar services are also available for the WCAG.

Ignoring accessibility is ignoring a part of your AUDIENCE. It hurts you, your site, and your users.

Think about accessibility as a <u>CRITICAL PART</u> of every website that you design.

Color shouldn't be your <u>ONLY</u> form of communication

You already know that color has an emotional impact. It'd be hard to imagine a site *without* color... but that's just how some people view at least a part of your website. That's why you must convey everything on your site with more than *just* color.

The rating stars for each book are colored based on the rating. Color is the only means of getting that meaning, which violates WCAG.

8% of males in the United States have some type of color blindness. The disability is far more common in men than in women.

Life through web-safe eyes...

You've probably heard about web-safe colors before. Those are the colors that most people say are going to look consistent on different resolutions and monitors. Here's a palette of web-safe colors:

Life through color-blind eyes...

But is this palette really "web-safe"? Take a look a the same palette through the eyes of someone with color blindness:

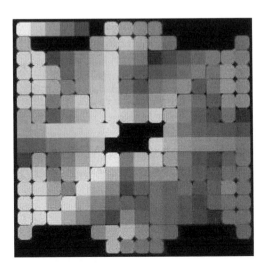

These two palettes look completely dissimilar... which one do your users see?

BRAIN POWER

How do you think color blindness can affect your choice of color palette? Do the triadic and tetradic color palettes offer any help in dealing with color blindness?

* These images are from a scan of a Visibone book
(http://www.visibone.com/products/browserbook.html).

Audio-2-Go, via color-blind eyes

Let's take a look at Audio-2-Go through a few different sets of eyes.
Depending on the cones available to the viewer, our nicely designed
Audio-2-Go site can look totally different:

Here is the original color scheme viewed
by someone with no color blindness.

Original

This view shows a diminished color
scheme, but most of the elements
are still distinguishable.

Deutanopia (no green cones)

This is a rarer type of color blindness that affects yellow tones. The stars are completely useless in this view... which definitely violates WCAG Priority 1.

Tritanopia (no blue cones)

Protanopia looks very similar to Deutanopia when comparing the Audio-2-Go site. The page looks bland, and the stars seem to blur together a fair bit.

Protanopia (no red cones)

Those stars are a real problem

So the stars at Audio-2-Go are a problem. It's not bad that they're in color, but it's bad that they *only* convey information through color. Remember one of the easiest ways to fix bad graphics or navigation? **Add text!**

So for the ratings, we can simply add in a textual rating. Then, we can add the stars as a background image, just like we did with navigation back in Chapter 6:

```
<div id="featured-books">
  <ul>
    <li><a tabindex="7" href="/books/1">
      <img alt="the elements of cooking" src="elements.jpg" /></a><br />
      <span class="rating high">Rating: 8</span>
    </li>
    <li><a tabindex="8" href="/books/2">
      <img alt="state of denial" src="sod.jpg" /></a><br />
      <span class="rating medium">Rating: 5</span>
    </li>
    <li><a tabindex="9" href="/books/3">
      <img alt="the google story" src="google.jpg" /></a><br />
      <span class="rating medium">Rating: 6</span>
    </li>
    <li><a tabindex="10" href="/books/4">
      <img alt="mary poppins" src="mp.jpg" /></a><br />
      <span class="rating low">Rating: 3</span>
    </li>
    <li><a tabindex="11" href="/books/5">
      <img alt="business of creativity" src="creativity.jpg" /></a><br />
      <span class="rating high">Rating: 9</span>
    </li>
    <li><a tabindex="12" href="/books/6">
      <img alt="designing web usability" src="dwu.jpg" /></a><br />
      <span class="rating medium">Rating: 6</span>
    </li>
  </ul>
</div>
```

Add a line break and a span to hold the rating number.

index.html

We'll class the span "rating" and then give it another class depending on the rating (low, medium and high, respectively).

---

there are no Dumb Questions

Q: So we can't use visual indicators, like the stars, anymore?

A: You definitely can. You just can't **only** use visual indicators. So if you use the visual of a thermometer, you'd need to put a textual description next to that thermometer.

Background images are ^still^ your friend

Now we can add the stars back into the page using CSS and the
`background` property. So we need to make some additions to our
stylesheet `screen.css`:

We need a new high-level class for ratings.

```
#featured-books li .rating {
    padding: 4px 0 4px 30px;
    font-family: Helvetica, sans-serif;
    font-size: small;
    text-transform: uppercase;
}
.high {
    background: url('../images/star_high.png') no-repeat left;
}
.medium {
    background: url('../images/star_medium.png') no-repeat left;
}
.low {
    background: url('../images/star_low.png') no-repeat left;
}
```

The rating class needs a 30px left padding to clear the way for the star.

Depending on the class, we will display the appropriate colored star.

screen.css

TEST DRIVE

Color without <u>depending</u> on color?

Update your versions of index.html and screen.css. Then reload the Audio-2-Go page
and check out the featured ratings of the books.

We can tick off this checkpoint now.

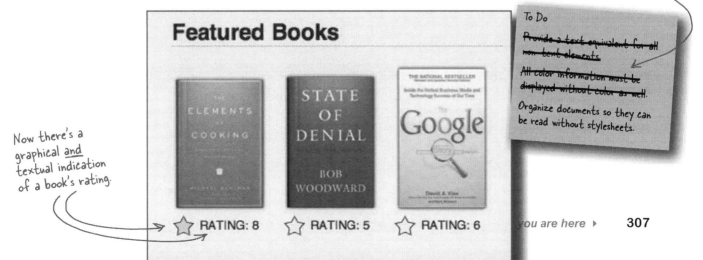

Now there's a graphical <u>and</u> textual indication of a book's rating.

To Do

~~Provide a text equivalent for all non-text elements.~~

~~All color information must be displayed without color as well.~~

Organize documents so they can be read without stylesheets.

There's more to ordering than just tabindexes

You've already used the `tabindex` attribute to make sure that the Tab key moves through your document in the right order. But the WCAG goes further: since there are certain accessibility devices that don't use standard keyboards, your actual ***markup*** has to be in order.

In other words, to meet WCAG Priority 1, you've got to order your XHTML in the sequence your content should be viewed, regardless of any CSS *and* tabindexing.

> **To Do**
>
> ~~Provide a text equivalent for all non-text elements.~~
>
> ~~All color information must be displayed without color as well.~~
>
> Organize documents so they can be read without stylesheets.

Header
Sidebar
Featured Links
Masthead
Content
Footer

← This site has its content below almost everything else... which might look great styled with CSS, but won't satisfy WCAG requirements.

The ordering of things here is difficult to follow.

Here's the same sequence of elements, but ordered how you'd want someone to view or hear the content.

Header
Masthead
Content
Sidebar
Featured Links
Footer

Just because your XHTML is standards compliant doesn't mean your XHTML meets this WCAG checkpoint.

Having your site validate as valid XHTML just means that your markup is correct and without errors. The WCAG checkpoints make sure that you are using that markup to make your site as accessible to as many people as possible. The two are related but not at all the same.

Watch it!

Exercise

It's time to tick off another Priority 1 checkpoint with Audio-2-Go. Here are the relevant parts of the Audio-2-Go index.html. It's up to you to re-order the content. Good luck!

The tabindexes give you some ordering... but the actual markup isn't in the right sequence.

```html
<ul id="nav>
  <li><a tabindex="1" title="homepage" href="index.html">Home</a></li>
  <li><a tabindex="2" title="browse books"
         href="books.html">Home</a></li>
  <li><a tabindex="3" title="about Audio2Go"
         href="about.html">About</a></li>
</ul>
...
<div id="featured-books">
  <ul>
    <li><a tabindex="7" href="/books/1">
      <img alt="the elements of cooking" src="elements.jpg" /></a></li>
    <li><a tabindex="8" href="/books/2">
      <img alt="state of denial" src="sod.jpg" /></a></li>
    <li><a tabindex="9" href="/books/3">
      <img alt="the google story" src="google.jpg" /></a></li>
    <li><a tabindex="10" href="/books/4">
      <img alt="mary poppins" src="mp.jpg" /></a></li>
    <li><a tabindex="11" href="/books/5">
      <img alt="business of creativity" src="creativity.jpg" /></a></li>
    <li><a tabindex="12" href="/books/6">
      <img alt="designing web usability" src="dwu.jpg" /></a></li>
  </ul>
</div>
...
<div id="info">
  <h2><a tabindex="4" href="signup">Signup</a></h2>
  <p> Create an account with <strong>Audio-2-Go</strong> and begin
downloading books immediatly. All you need is your email address and
a credit card to get started and there is no contract to sign. Cancel
anytime you wish.</p>
  <h2><a tabindex="5" href="download">...</h2>
  <p>...</p>
  <h2><a tabindex="6" href="listen">...</h2>
  <p>...</p>
</div>
```

Hint: You may want to remove the tabindexes and use Tab to see how your page is "naturally" ordered.

index.html

Your job was to rearrange the chunks of the Audio-2-Go page so that it has a more logical flow when rendered without a stylesheet. Here's what we did.

```
<ul id="nav>
  <li><a tabindex="1" title="homepage" href="index.html">Home</a></li>
  <li><a tabindex="2" title="browse books"
         href="books.html">Home</a></li>
  <li><a tabindex="3" title="about Audio2Go"
         href="about.html">About</a></li>
</ul>
```

```
<div id="info">
  <h2><a tabindex="4" href="signup">Signup</a></h2>
  <p> Create an account with <strong>Audio-2-Go</strong> and begin
downloading books immediatly. All you need is your email address
and a credit card to get started and there is no contract to sign.
Cancel anytime you wish.</p>
  <h2><a tabindex="5" href="download">...</h2>
  <p>...</p>
  <h2><a tabindex="6" href="listen">...</h2>
  <p>...</p>
</div>
```

```
<div id="featured-books">
  <ul>
    <li><a tabindex="7" href="/books/1">
      <img alt="the elements of cooking" src="elements.jpg" /></a></li>
    <li><a tabindex="8" href="/books/2">
      <img alt="state of denial" src="sod.jpg" /></a></li>
    <li><a tabindex="9" href="/books/3">
      <img alt="the google story" src="google.jpg" /></a></li>
    <li><a tabindex="10" href="/books/4">
      <img alt="mary poppins" src="mp.jpg" /></a></li>
    <li><a tabindex="11" href="/books/5">
      <img alt="business of creativity" src="creativity.jpg" /></a></li>
    <li><a tabindex="12" href="/books/6">
      <img alt="designing web usability" src="dwu.jpg" /></a></li>
  </ul>
</div>
```

← Flipping the "info" <div> and "featured-books" <div> makes the page display in the proper order when a stylesheet is disabled or unavailable.

TEST DRIVE

We don't need no stinkin' tabindexes.

Rearrange the order of your index.html and then reload the page. Things should look the same, but now we're WCAG compliant.

> Hey, doesn't this mean we don't need all those tabindexes now?

WCAG Priority 1 makes tabindex unnecessary.

With your markup ordered correctly, go ahead and remove all the `tabindex` attributes from your `index.html`. Not only are they unnecessary, they'll let you ensure that you've ordered things correctly by using the Tab key.

Using the Tab key is a great way to verify your site stays in order even when you add new sections.

We've got another item we can cross of our list. We're done, right?

To Do

~~Provide a text equivalent for all non-text elements.~~

~~All color information must be displayed without color as well.~~

~~Organize documents so they can be read without stylesheets.~~

Sharpen your pencil

What WCAG checkpoints need to be taken care off on the Books page? Look back through the checklist on page 298 (or online), and see if there are any additional checkpoints that might apply... write what you think you need to do in the to do list below.

These all have to be handled for the Top Titles page as well.

> **To Do**
>
> Provide a text equivalent for all non-text elements.
>
> All color information must be displayed without color as well.
>
> Organize documents so they can be read without stylesheets.
>
> ....
> ....

Hint: The Top Titles list is a table.

Exercise

Now that you know what needs to be done to the Books page, open up `books.html`. It should be in your chapter download files. Update the XHTML to be WCAG compliant, and meet all priority 1 checkpoints. Then turn the page to see if you caught everything.

Exercise Solution

Your job was to update the `books.html` XHTML to be WCAG compliant and meet all priority 1 checkpoints.

> **To Do**
>
> Provide a text equivalent for all non-text elements.
>
> All color information must be displayed without color as well.
>
> Organize documents so they can be read without stylesheets.
>
> All tables need row and column headings.

Did you get this one? Since the Books page has a table, we've got to add table headings.

```
<!DOCTYPE html PUBLIC "-//W3C//DTD XHTML 1.0 Strict/
          "http://www.w3.org/TR/xhtml1/DTD/xhtml1-s
<html xmlns="http://www.w3.org/1999/xhtml" xml:lang=
<head>
  <title>Books | Audio 2 Go</title>
  <meta http-equiv="Content-Type" content="text/htm
  <link rel="stylesheet" href="stylesheets/screen.c
        type="text/css" media="screen" />
</head>
<body>
  <div id="wrap">
    <div id="header">
      <h1><img alt="Audio 2 Go logo" src="images/a
      <ul id="nav">
        <li><a title="Audio 2 Go home" href="index
        <li><a class="active" title="Audio books"
              href="books.html">Books</a></li>
        <li><a title="About Audio 2 Go" href="#">About</a></li>
      </ul>
    </div>
    <div id="book-list">
      <h2>Top Titles</h2>
      <table cellpadding="0"
      <tr>
        <th>Book Title</th>
        <th>Price</th>
      </tr>
      <tr>
        <td>The Black Swan</td>
        <td class="price">$19.99</td>
      </tr>
      <tr>
        <td>Presentation Zen</td>
        <td class="price">$12.99</td>
      </tr>
      <tr>
        <td>The Digital Photography Book</td>
        <td class="price">$12.99</td>
      </tr>
      <tr>
        <td>Mac OS X Leopard: The Missing Manual</td>
```

5.1 For data tables, identify row and column headers.

We just need another table row, with a heading for each column.

```
            <td class="price">$15.99</td>
        </tr>
        <tr>
            <td>The iPhone Developer's Cookbook</td>
            <td class="price">$19.99</td>
        </tr>
        <tr>
            <td>slide:ology</td>
            <td class="price">$7.99</td>
        </tr>
        <tr>
            <td>The Numerati</td>
            <td class="price">$11.99</td>
        </tr>
        <tr>
            <td>Spore: Official Game Guide</td>
            <td class="price">$21.99</td>
        </tr>
    </table>
</div>
<div id="featured-books">
    <h2>Featured Books</h2>
    <ul>
        <li><a href="books/1"><img alt="the elements of cooking"
               src="images/elements.png" /></a>
           <br /><span class="rating high">Rating: 8</span></li>
        <li><a href="books/2"><img alt="state of denial" src="images/sod.png" /></a>
           <br /><span class="rating medium">Rating: 5</span></li>
        <li><a href="books/3"><img alt="the google story" src="images/google.png" /></a>
           <br /><span class="rating medium">Rating: 6</span></li>
        <li><a href="books/4"><img alt="mary poppins" src="images/mp.png" /></a>
           <br /><span class="rating low">Rating: 3</span></li>
        <li><a href="books/5"><img alt="business of creativity"
               src="images/creativity.png" /></a>
           <br /><span class="rating high">Rating: 9</span></li>
        <li><a href="books/6"><img alt="designing web usability"
               src="images/dwu.png" /></a>
           <br /><span class="rating medium">Rating: 6</span></li>
    </ul>
</div>
<div id="footer">
    <p>Copyright &copy; <strong>Audio 2 Go</strong>, Inc., all rights reserved.</p>
</div>
  </div>
</body>
</html>
```

This page was already ordered correctly with headings, then the Top Books list, and then the features. So we didn't need to do any re-ordering.

This is the same change we made to the main page: we need text, not just images, for the book ratings.

TEST DRIVE

Test Audio-2-Go's accessibility.

It's all well and good to implement accessibility measures, but you also need to test your site. So how can you do this? Well, there are a couple of ways:

Get a copy of the assistive technologies in question (like a screen reader) and take the site for a test drive yourself. Or, even better, you can use software, such as Cynthia Says, that automatically checks a site for WCAG compliance (**http://www.contentquality.com/**).

Update both the home page and the Books page and see how Audio-2-Go looks.

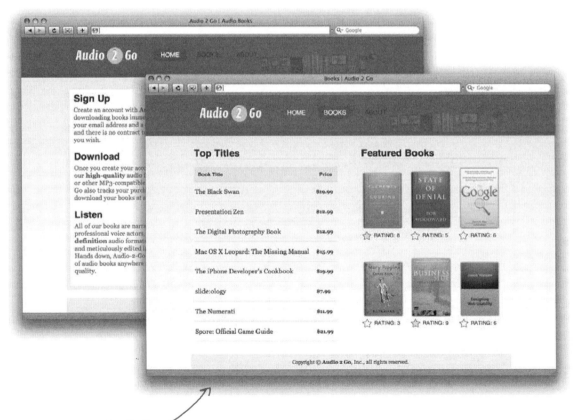

Give Audio-2-Go a test with the Cynthia Says validator.

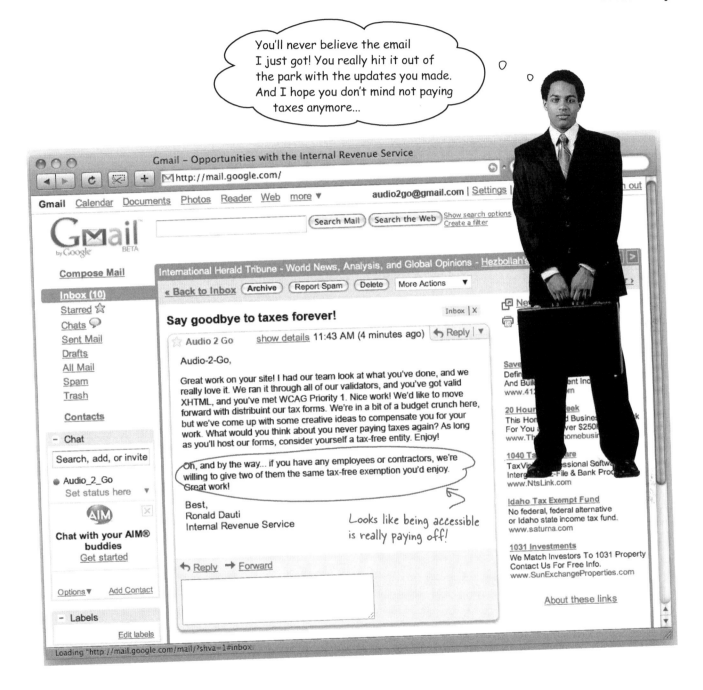

BULLET POINTS

- Accessibility is both the process and the techniques used to create a site that can be used by someone with a disability.

- A screen reader is a piece of software used by the blind and the visually impaired that reads the text of a website aloud.

- The `alt` attribute (which is part of the `img` element) allows you to provide an alternate text description for an image—which is read by the screen reader.

- `longdesc` is an attribute of the `img` element which provides a link to a page which contains a text description of an image that is too long for an `alt` attribute.

- People who have lost motor control of their hands often use the Tab key instead of a mouse to move from link to link on a web page.

- `tabindex` lets you manually set the position of a specific link in a tab sequence.

- The Web Content Accessibility Guidelines (WCAG) from the W3C were the first major effort to establish guidelines for accessible design—it consists of fourteen guidelines, each with three checkpoint levels.

- You don't have to worry about items on the WCAG checklist that don't apply to your site.

- Organize the markup of your page so that it reads logically if it were not rendered with a stylesheet.

- Make sure that all information conveyed with color is also available without color.

- If you use tables in your site, make sure that columns and rows have headers.

- Use software like Cynthia Says to check the accessibility of your site.

9 listen to your users

The Pathway to Harmonious Design

Ever since I started really listening to my users, people just can't stay away from my site. I barely have time to look at the stats over a cola these days!

Good design is all about really listening to your users.

Your **users can tell you what's wrong** with your site, **what's right** with your site, **how you can fix things** (if necessary) and *how you can improve your site*. There are lots of ways you can listen to your users. You can **listen to them in groups** (using tools like surveys), listen to them **individually** (with tools such as usability tests), and listen to their **collective actions on your site** (with tools such as site metrics and statistics). Whatever method you use, its all about "hearing" what your users are saying. If you do, your site will meet the needs of your audience and be that much better for it.

Problems over at RPM

I keep on getting angry emails from my customers. They're all complaining about the same problems with the site. You built the site for me—now I'm going to have to ask you to fix it so it works... properly this time!

The (not so happy) RPM Music Store Owner

RPM Music

RPM Music   Hom

RPM Music is the #4 online, midwest,

New at RPM Music

Gmail
by Google   BETA

Where are you guys

Bummed Customer <bummed@yahoo.com>
To: rpmmusic@gmail.com

RPM Dudes-

Just saw the new site, looks great! One question though: I
to find any of your contact information or a map to your sto
from out of town and really wanted to swing by and checko
selection. Seems like that should be on there somewhere. I
missed it. Anyway, would have loved to come out and see
today, maybe next time.

Thanks,
Bummed

RPM Music <rpmmusic@gmail

Gmail
by Google   BETA

Problems with the new site   Sat, Aug 23, 2008 at 4

C. Customer <custc@hotmail.com>
To: rpmmusic@gmail.com

RPM-

All of a sudden your site changed! It looks all crazy now. The
sections of the pages don't look like the are in the right place, and
things don't make sense. Can you fix this? I want to keep buying
stuff from you guys, but with a website looking like this, it's a
little difficult.

Thanks,
Concerned Customer

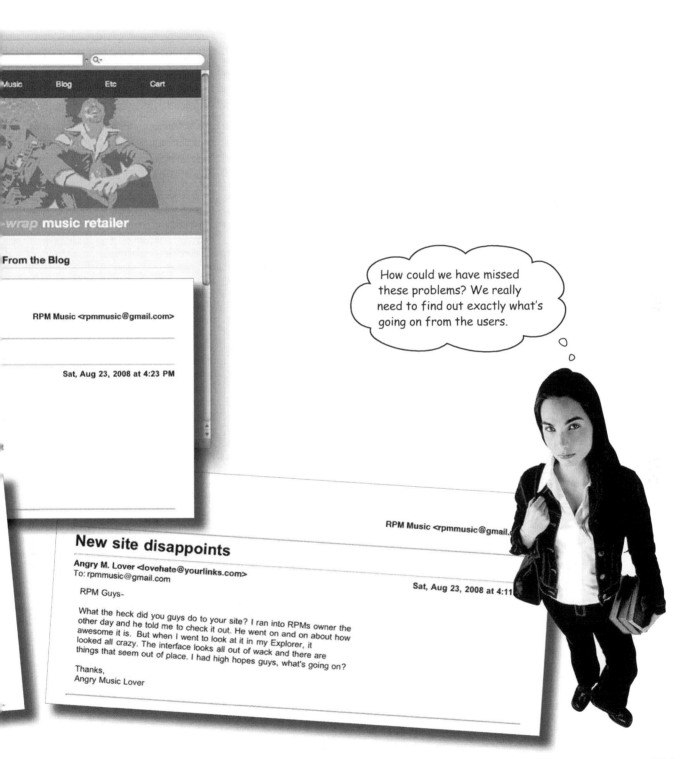

Music   Blog   Etc   Cart

-wrap **music retailer**

From the Blog

RPM Music <rpmmusic@gmail.com>

Sat, Aug 23, 2008 at 4:23 PM

How could we have missed these problems? We really need to find out exactly what's going on from the users.

RPM Music <rpmmusic@gmail.

New site disappoints

Angry M. Lover <lovehate@yourlinks.com>
To: rpmmusic@gmail.com

Sat, Aug 23, 2008 at 4:11

RPM Guys-

What the heck did you guys do to your site? I ran into RPMs owner the other day and he told me to check it out. He went on and on about how awesome it is. But when I went to look at it in my Explorer, it looked all crazy. The interface looks all out of wack and there are things that seem out of place. I had high hopes guys, what's going on?

Thanks,
Angry Music Lover

Let your audience speak to you through focus groups and surveys

When you're designing, redesigning, or fixing a site, you need to be able to ask your audience questions. Who are they? How often do they use the Web? What kind of computer do they use? What do they like about the site's current design? Do they like the site's proposed new design?

This is where focus groups and surveys come into the picture. Both are great tools for giving your audience a "voice"—letting them give their opinions, answer your questions, and even give feedback in unexpected ways. It's important to know that surveys and focus groups have different strengths and weaknesses, and those could impact which you use. Let's take a look at some pros and cons of both:

Remember, as we talked about in Chapter 4, surveys are a great tool for building personas at the beginning of your design process.

	PROS	CONS
Surveys	Require a relatively short time commitment from survey participants	Require a lot of advanced planning
	Can be administered to a huge amount of people	Written surveys may present problems for lower-level readers
	Can be administered in lots of ways (paper, online, by phone, in person)	Survey questions might be misinterpreted
	Participants can often complete the survey at their own leisure	
Focus Groups	Allow participants to build on each other's ideas	Require larger time commitment from participants
	Collects information on a very specific topic from those who have a stake in the topic	Usually require compensation for the participants
	Benefits from a trained facilitator	Public environment may intimidate some participants
		Requires a trained facilitator

Sharpen your pencil

Read through each of the scenarios below and decide which method (**survey** or **focus group**) would be best for getting the information you need to make your design decisions.

Write your answer on the dotted line.

Scenario 1

You've been hired to design a website for a local community access television station. The client wants to add all sorts of cool—but bandwidth intensive—Flash interactivity and video. You're worried that this extra media might be too much for the site's users.

You need to find out what kind of computers the TV station's viewers use (make, model, operating system, etc.), as well as their connection speed (dial-up, DSL, Cable, etc.) so that when they come to use the site, it doesn't fall over under the pressure of serving all that rich media content.

....

Scenario 2

You're doing some volunteer design work for a local inner-city community center. You really don't know that much about the site's users—gender, age, computer types, etc.—and you really need to find out so that you can target the design at the right level. The director of the community center did tell you that some of your users might have a low literacy rate.

....

Scenario 3

You and some friends are launching a new social network for web designers and developers. You're at the point where you've got a couple of different visual designs (really polished storyboards), and you need to get some specific feedback on what your potential audience thinks of the site's design. You're also pretty sure that your audience (who are designers themselves) will probably be up for sharing some their great design ideas with you.

....

 Sharpen your pencil
Solution

Let's take a look at whether a survey or focus group is the best choice for each of the scenarios. How will you implement your choice?

Scenario 1

You've been hired to design a website for a local community access television station. The client wants to add all sorts of cool—but bandwidth intensive—Flash interactivity and video. You're worried that this extra media might be too much for the site's users.

You need to find out what kind of computers the TV station's viewers use (make, model, operating system, etc.), as well as their connection speed (dial-up, DSL, Cable, etc.) so that when they come to use the site, it doesn't fall over under the pressure of serving all that rich media content.

Surveys are perfect for getting lots of information from a large group of people.

Survey

Scenario 2

You're doing some volunteer design work for a local inner-city community center. You really don't know that much about the site's users—gender, age, computer types, etc.—and you really need to find out so that you can target the design at the right level. The director of the community center did tell you that some of your users might have a low literacy rate.

This is a tough one. The kind of information you need is probably more suited to a survey, but the literacy issue might require a focus group if users are put off by filling out forms.

Focus Group OR Survey

Scenario 3

You and some friends are launching a new social network for web designers and developers. You're at the point where you've got a couple of different visual designs (really polished storyboards), and you need to get some specific feedback on what your potential audience thinks of the site's design. You're also pretty sure that your audience (who are designers themselves) will probably be up for sharing some their great design ideas with you.

This is perfect for a small focus group. Open-ended feedback and group discussion is exactly what you need.

Focus Group

Surveys and focus groups aren't free

When you're deciding whether to use surveys or focus groups to find out about your users, there's another thing to consider: **cost**. If you start out doing user testing with the comparative costs of surveys and focus groups in mind, that may help you decide which is the right route.

Survey Costs

Time is money, as they say.

$ Time spent designing the survey

$ Printing and mailing (if you are conducting a paper survey)

$ Time spent processing and interpreting the results

$ Possible compensation to survey participants

You can't just open the door and grab the nearest person — you need to put a lot of time and effort into recruiting people who are representative of your site's audience.

Focus Groups Costs

$ Time spent planning the focus group schedule

$ Recruiting participants

$ Rent space to hold focus group (if you don't already have it)

$ Equipment rental (projector, screens, recording devices, etc.)

$ Food and/or compensation for participants

$ Time spent processing and evaluating the results

$ Any additional supplies

$ Cost of a trained moderator

A moderator will run the focus group—they're highly skilled at what they do and generally don't come cheap.

It's customary to give focus group participants something for their time. That doesn't have to be money, but do you have the budget for pizza and drinks for all the participants you'd like to invite?

Sharpen your pencil

Now that you've got a good idea of the pros and cons of surveys and focus groups (and how much they could cost), write down the method you'd use to get feedback from the RPM Music site users. Also write down why you chose that method.

....

....

....

....

Sharpen your pencil
Solution

Which method for gathering feedback from the RPM Music users is probably the best, and why? Here's what we thought:

Not all clients will want to go the cheapest route. User feedback is vital to getting the design of a site right.

A Survey!

We need to get information from as many of the RPM Music customers as cheaply as possible (remember, we need to make the owner happy). Also, using a survey will allow us to collect information on browsers and operating systems — which might just provide a solution to our problem.

RPM is a web store, so it makes sense to provide users with a survey to fill out while they're online.

You're going to use a survey to try to get at the root of the problem? Ok, that sounds good. You can use my customer database to get in contact with my customers.

Surveys are cheap and effective, especially when you give participants the option of completing them online.

Surveys Exposed

This week's interview:
An online survey tells all

Head First: Welcome, Online Survey. We're very excited to be talking to you today outside of the World Wide Web.

Online Survey: I know, this is very exciting! It's been years since I've appeared in ink.

Head First: So tell us, why the big move to the Internet? All those tags and hypertext seem a bit overwhelming.

Online Survey: Well, it just seemed like the right move. I mean, sure, the initial setup took a little time, but after that I could just sit back and watch the data come pouring in.

Head First: Did you find that you received more attention as a web page than you did when you were printed on paper as a bubble sheet, say?

Online Survey: Oh, definitely. People have bad memories of filling out all those bubble sheets in high school. Also, being available online makes it easy for people to take me at their leisure. No pressure, you know. Oh! And if it's a long survey, they can save their answers and come back later.

Head First: Well that's convenient. So where do you keep all that data? If people aren't writing it down, where does it go?

Online Survey: Sometimes I just send an email with the answers. Most of the time, though, I keep everything in a database so that I can go back later and quickly see the results.

Head First: Wow! That seems technical. How do you manage all that without losing your cool?

Online Survey: Well I'm going to let you in on a little secret. I'm no wiz-bang programmer or database analyst, so if it's a complicated survey, I just use one of the many free survey tools available. They help me set up the questions, format, and even process the data, and then they send me the results. In the end, I come out looking like the hero.

Head First: Interesting. Don't you feel like you're cutting corners if you don't do all the work yourself?

Online Survey: Hey, if you want to spend all day writing code and HTML tags, that's your business. But time is money, buddy, and I just want to get my questions answered. I don't have time to deal with all those details. Not only does an online survey save my users time, it also saves me time.

Head First: Well that seems fair, and who can pass up all those colorful charts and graphs?

Online Survey: Not this guy. Believe me, going online was the best move of my life. We wouldn't be talking if it wasn't for the Web.

Head First: That's true! We're glad to have you. Thanks again for talking to us. I'm sure we'll be seeing you soon in some reader poll or career questionnaire.

Online Survey: You bet. Thanks for having me.

Ask the right questions in your surveys

So you're going with a survey, but there's a problem. What questions are you going to ask, and **how** will you ask them? Oftentimes online surveys either ask the wrong questions or ask questions that return unreliable data. You really need to invest some time in crafting your survey questions so that you get the best possible data you can. Let's take a look at what makes a good survey question.

Give your users an A, B, C, and D and make the options clear and concise.

☑ **A good survey question has specific answer choices.**

☑ **A good survey question does not lead the participants to any particular answer.**

☑ **A good survey question is short.**

☑ **A good survey question is easy to read and understand.**

If you confuse your users, they aren't going to provide you with accurate information. Pay close attention to how you word the questions.

☑ **A good survey question asks for knowledge or an opinion, but never both at once.**

there are no Dumb Questions

Q: What if I want to ask an open-ended question?

A: Just don't provide answer choices, and phrase the question so it's clear that you want the participant to answer in their own words. Open-ended questions are great for getting **qualitative data**. Qualitative data is data that isn't numerical in nature. So if you were to ask survey participants what operating system they use, your results would be numerical (58% Windows XP, 5% Windows Vista, 30% Mac OS, 7% Linux). But if you asked survey participants to describe the technical problem they are having with a website, each of the responses will be different, and the results will not be numerically based. If you ask an open-ended question, be prepared for more work when you put your results together. Each response will be different, and you won't get the same statistical (numerical) results that you'd get with other kinds of questions.

Exercise

Now that you've seen what makes for a good (and not so good) survey question, it's time to put your skills to the test. Below you'll find some survey questions that could use a little work. Have a look at them and write down the problems with each question.

1 **Which is your browser of choice?**

A. Internet Explorer 6

B. Internet Explorer 7

C. Internet Explorer 8

....

....

....

2 **Does your current CMS publish W3C-compliant markup?**

A. Yes

B. No

C. I don't publish with a CMS

....

....

....

3 **There are many people who believe that designing with web standards is a waste of time—are you one of these people?**

A. Yes

B. No

....

....

....

4 **Do you believe that the current single column layout website in question is bad and should be changed to a two-column layout?**

A. Yes

B. No

....

....

....

Exercise Solution

Let's take a look at the survey questions and see what we can do to make them better.

1 **Which is your browser of choice?**

A. Internet Explorer 6

B. Internet Explorer 7

C. Internet Explorer 8

The question isn't bad, but the possible answers are misleading.

The problem with this question is that it's biased. Biased questions encourage your participants to respond to the question in a certain way. They may contain terms or may be worded in a way that leads the participant to a specific answer. Here all of the associated options are Internet Explorer (though different versions). What if the respondent uses a different browser? Well, their only option would to choose "Other," if it were available as option D. That would ultimately skew the results (because you won't get any differentiation between browsers besides Internet Explorer). This question may also mislead participants into choosing Internet Explorer just because they have it in their system (as opposed to being their primary browser).

A better browser question might be...

The question is simple and direct. We don't have to change much here.

1 **Which is your browser of choice?**

A. Internet Explorer

B. Firefox

C. Safari

D. Mozilla

E. Opera

F. Other

To make sure this question is not biased, we need to offer choices for different browsers (not just IE).

Does your current CMS publish W3C-compliant markup?

A. Yes

B. No

C. I don't publish with a CMS

> Although this question if focused and simple, it falls into a common trap. The terms "CMS" and "W3C-compliant" are only used by a small group of people within web technology circles. Even though some users may recognize the terms, most won't and you risk confusing and frustrating your survey participants. Avoid using jargon in your questions and always try to write to the broadest audience possible.

Less jargon = better understanding = accurate responses

 Does your website code validate as standard XHTML or HTML?

A. Yes

 B. No

C. I don't know

Even without the jargon, it's good to give users an "I don't know" choice just in case.

there are no Dumb Questions

Q: How do I know if I'm using jargon? And how can I get rid of it in my questions?

A: Jargon is pretty subjective. What is jargon to one person isn't necessarily jargon to another. There are two things you can do to make sure your questions are clearly written. First, re-read your questions and think about your audience—try to phrase things as simply as possible. Second, give your questions to someone who isn't familiar with the subject matter. They'll tell you if they don't immediately understand something you've written.

⟶ More questions over the page...

Exercise Solution

Let's take a look at the survey questions and see what we can do to make them better.

❸ **There are many people who believe that designing with web standards is a waste of time—are you one of these people?**

A. Yes

 B. No

Read the question again. It's a strong opinion that you're being asked to agree or disagree with, and that could lead your respondents' answers.

This question's problem is that it assumes what it asks. This is a type of biased question that leads your participants to agree or respond in a certain way.

Let's not assume...

❶ **Do you agree or disagree that designing with web standards is a waste of time?**

A. Agree

B. Disagree

 C. Undecided

Don't lead the question with an opinion. This will always skew the results and make the survey less credible.

4 Do you believe that the current single-column layout website in question is bad and should be changed to a two-column layout?

A. Yes

B. No

The problem with this question is that it's two questions. Participants won't know which to answer. What if they agree with one but not both, or disagree with part or all of the question... How do they answer then? This can make them feel frustrated and could lead them to quit the survey without finishing it.

Just ask <u>one</u> question

 4 Do you like or dislike the current one-column layout in the website in question?

A. Like

B. Dislike

C. Undecided

If you offer yes and no options, always give an "undecided" option to cover respondents without a strong opinion either way.

Instead of asking two things in one question, ask two questions.

 5 Do you believe that the layout of the website in question should be changed to a two-column layout?

A. Yes

B. No

C. Undecided

These questions will be easier to understand and will result in more accurate data.

Sharpen your pencil

It's time to start building your user survey to help RPM Music. Write five technical questions to start with (what kind of browser users prefer, what kind of computer they have, etc.), then ask five demographic/usage questions (gender, age, how many hours/week do they use the web, etc.). Make sure you write questions that have answer choices, are short and straight to the point, and don't lead the respondent.

Technical survey questions:

A little example question to get you started

1

How do you connect to the Internet?

A. Dialup

B. DSL

C. Cable

D. T1 or LAN

E. I don't know

2

3

4

5

6

Demographic/usage questions:

1 How many hours/week do you spend on the internet?
A. 0 – 5 hours
B. 6 – 10 hours
C. 11 – 15 hours
D. 16 – 20 hours
E. 20+ hours

2

3

4

5

6

Sharpen your pencil
Solution

Let's take a look at some possible technical and demographic/usage questions you could ask RPM's users.

Possible technical questions:

2

What is your primary browser?
A. Internet Explorer
B. Firefox
C. Safari
D. Opera
E. Other

This is an important question because some browsers have peculiarities in how they render CSS.

3

What is your computer's operating system?
A. Windows XP
B. Windows Vista
C. Mac OS X
D. Linux
E. Other

Even if the users don't know what browser they use to surf the Net, we may be able to work out which browser they're likely to be using since all operating systems come with one installed by default.

4

What is the resolution of your computer monitor?
A. 800x600
B. 1024x768
C. 1280x1024 (or above)
D. I don't know

As you discovered back in Chapter 4, screen resolution can have a big impact on how your users view your site, so it's important information to have.

Possible demographic/usage questions:

2

What is your gender?

A. Male

B. Female

> Gender's one of those questions that all surveys ask, regardless of their subject matter.
>
> Depending on the site's content, gender can play a large or small part in your design decisions.

3

Do you buy music online (downloadable or shrink-wrapped)?

A. Yes

B. No

C. Don't know

> Do your users even buy music online? This may seem like an obvious question, but if you don't know, ask!
>
> This is a question that is great for the RPM Music site but wouldn't work with other kinds of sites.

4

How many hours per week do you spend online?

A. 0 – 5

B. 6 – 10

C. 11 – 15

D. 16 – 20

E. 21 – 25

F. 26 +

> The amount of time a user spends on the Web speaks to their experience online—which impacts how they use your site.

The final RPM Music user survey

Here's the completed survey ready to upload to the site
(or use a survey service to conduct it for us).

1. What is your primary browser?

    A. Internet Explorer

    B. Firefox

    C. Safari

    D. Other

These questions will help us get a better idea of the types of technology our visitors use to access the RPM Music site.

2. What is your computer's operating system?

    A. Windows XP

    B. Windows Vista

    C. Mac OS X

    D. Other

3. What is the resolution of your computer monitor?

    A. 800x600

    B. 1024x768

    C. 1280x1024 (or above)

    D. I don't know

4. How do you connect to the Internet?

    A. Dialup

    B. DSL

    C. Cable

    D. T1 or higher

5. What is your gender?

    A. Male

    B. Female

6. What is your age?

    A. 18- 24

    B. 25 - 34

    C. 35 - 44

    D. 45 - 54

    E. 55 - 64

    F. 65+

7. How many hours per week do you spend online?

    A. 0 - 5

    B. 6 - 10

    C. 11 - 15

    D. 16 - 20

    E. 21 - 25

    F. 26+

8. Do you purchase music online (downloadable or shrink-wrapped)?

    A. Yes

    B. No

9. Please provide any other feedback about the new RPM Music site:

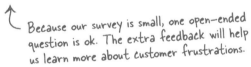

Because our survey is small, one open-ended question is ok. The extra feedback will help us learn more about customer frustrations.

there are no Dumb Questions

Q: Is there a limit to the number of open-ended questions I can include?

A: Not really. Open-ended questions are a great way to get specific answers and feedback from your users. However, because there are no answer choices, they take more time to analyze and interpret and can sometimes be vague or not answered at all. Also keep in mind that these types of questions take longer to answer and require more commitment from your users.

The results are in!

Let's take a look and see how our users responded to the RPM Music online survey.

Browsers

Internet Explorer	65%
Firefox	22%
Safari	10%
Other	3%

As expected, Internet Explorer is the most used browser.

Operating Systems

Windows XP	75%
Windows Vista	10%
Mac OS X	13%
Other	2%

Screen Resolution

800x600	10%
1024x768	48%
1280x1024 +	38%
Don't know	4%

Internet Connection

Dialup	12%
DSL	55%
Cable	27%
T1 or higher	6%

The results in this column are also very typical for other sites and the Internet as a whole.

Gender

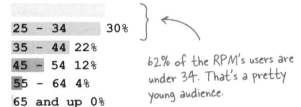

Female	35%

Age

25 - 34	30%
35 - 44	22%
45 - 54	12%
55 - 64	4%
65 and up	0%

62% of the RPM's users are under 34. That's a pretty young audience.

Hours per week spent online

0 - 5	12%
6 - 10	21%
16 - 20	18%
21 - 25	10%

Looks like the RPM audience spends a fair bit of time on the Net every week, too. That means they'll be more savvy about how websites work than if the results had skewed towards lower weekly hours.

Do you purchase music online?

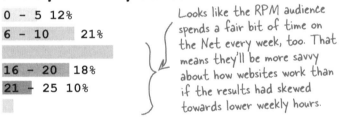

Yes	68%

Responses to the open-ended question:

> I love the new site. It really reflects the vibe of the store. It would be really nice if I could buy digital tracks—ya know, like iTunes—instead of just getting the CD shipped to me.

> I don't really use the site that much. I'd rather just come into the store. I really like talking with the people who work there as well as other customers. I guess the site is ok—it looks good—I just won't use it that much.

> The new site looks all crazy now. Parts of the pages don't look like they're in the right place, and things don't make sense. Can you fix this? I want to keep buying stuff from you guys, but it's a little difficult with a messy site.

> When I went to look at the site in Explorer, it looked all weird. The interface looks all out of whack... there are things that probably shouldn't be where they are.

Now that the results from the survey are in, start thinking about how all the information relates to each other. Finding patterns and connections can help shed some light on why RPM's users are having trouble with the site.

OK, looking at the results from the survey, it seems like our IE users are saying they're having the most trouble. Is there something wrong with the code?

Jim

Frank

Frank: Not necessarily. Browsers are the lens that you see the Web through–and not all browsers are created equally.

Jim: Oh, is one "brand" better than another? Is that why a lot of the RPM users seem to be using Internet Explorer?

Frank: No, actually. What I mean is that some of the browsers have peculiarities (in some cases, you might even call them bugs) that result in pages looking slightly different on one browser than they do on another.

Jim: Oh, I see. And since we want all of our users to have the same experience regardless of what browser they have, we need to take the peculiarities of each browser into account when we're designing the site...

Frank: Exactly. This is where web standards come in (sort of).

Jim: How so?

Frank: Web standards are part of the big cross-browser compatibility picture. Because the W3C works collaboratively with browser developers (among other people and companies), web standards are (mostly) baked right into the browsers themselves. So when you design to web standards, you can be fairly confident that your site will look the same browser to browser. But some browsers have peculiarities—

Jim: Bugs.

Frank: Ok, bugs—that won't display standards based XHTML and CSS the same way.

Jim: Oh, I see. So what browser do we design for?

Frank: Well, first off, you should always use standards compliant CSS and XHTML. That'll solve a bunch of your problems right away. You should be intimately familiar with your users. What browsers do they use?

Jim: We know that now. Most of them use IE and Firefox.

Frank: Exactly. Design for those two browsers in particular. Finally, there are some code-based workarounds—you may have heard of them already, they're also known as CSS "hacks"—that will help you bypass cross-browser computability problems (just like the ones the RPM Music site is experiencing). So we need to go look up some stats...

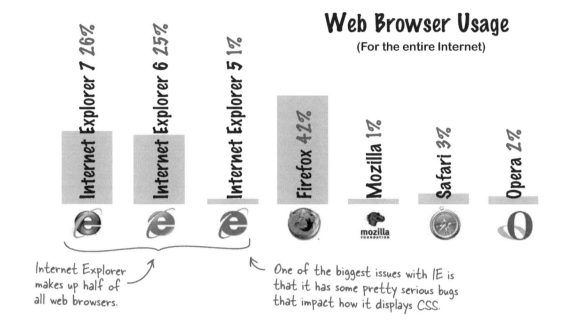

Web Browser Usage
(For the entire Internet)

Internet Explorer 7 26%

Internet Explorer 6 25%

Internet Explorer 5 1%

Firefox 42%

Mozilla 1%

Safari 3%

Opera 2%

Internet Explorer makes up half of all web browsers.

One of the biggest issues with IE is that it has some pretty serious bugs that impact how it displays CSS.

---

there are no Dumb Questions

Q: What if I don't have an easy way to find out what browsers my visitors are using?

A: If you can't get ahold of reliable browser statistics for your site, you can always use generic stats.

Q: Where can I get generic browser stats?

A: There are lots of sources out there. Probably the most reliable are the statistics compiled by the W3C (www.w3schools.com/browsers/browsers_stats.asp). The thing you have to realize is that no web statistics are completely accurate, and they may not be reflective of your users. But in the absence of any other kind of data, this is a start.

Q: If I don't have a specific browser on my computer, how do I test to make sure the design looks right?

A: Good question. Not everyone has every browser on every operating system available for testing designs. The best thing to do is to check your site on all browsers available for your system. For example, if you're using Windows XP, check your design on Internet Explorer and Firefox (available as a free download). This will be a good start and probably get you 90% there. To check the rest of the browsers out there, use a service like Browsershots (http://browsershots.org), which will take screenshots of your site on every browser/operating system combination and then allow you to download the results.

Fix RPM's CSS bug by moving the hover property

IE 6 doesn't handle the :hover pseudo-property very well (actually, at all). We need to move our "active" class to the link tag instead of the list item and update our CSS file to apply the background to the correct element.

IE6 only supports :hover on link and anchor tags

When we mouseover nav items, we should see a background appear. Because IE6 doesn't support the :hover property on anything besides links, our navigation won't work properly in that browser.

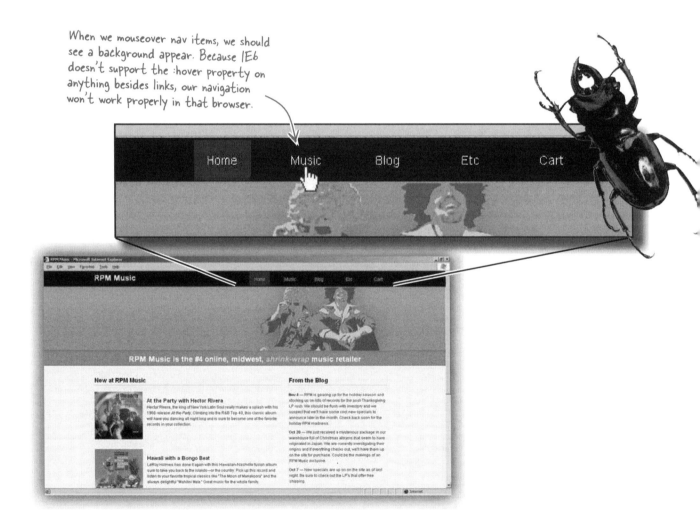

Exercise

Fix the RPM site by moving the "active" class from the <li> tag to the <a> tag in the XHTML markup. Make sure you also update the CSS file to reflect your changes.

1 Open up the index.html file and move the "active" class in the navigation to the link tag.

```
<li class="active"><a title="RPM Music home"
href="#">Home</a></li>
<li><a title="Music Store" href="#">Music</a></li>
<li><a title="RPM Blog" href="#">Blog</a></li>
<li><a title="More RPM Music" href="#">Etc</a></li>
<li><a title="Shopping Cart" href="#">Cart</a></li>
```

2 Open rpm.css and change the location of the :hover pseudo-property to the correct element.

```
#nav ul li.active, #nav ul li:hover {
        background: #333;
}
```

3 Launch the site in a browser and make sure everything looks as it should. If you're running Internet Explorer 6, you should see that the hover now appears properly.

One of the biggest issues with IE is that it has some pretty well-known bugs that impact how it displays CSS.

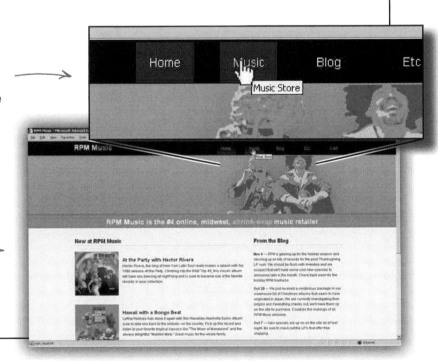

Exercise Solution

Let's take a look at the quick fix for the RPM :hover problem.

The XHTML

Place the active class in the link tag. Not only is this semantically correct, but it won't mess with IE6.

Don't forget to change the XHTML for the other pages as well.

```
<li class="active"><a class="active" title="RPM Music home" href="#">Home</a></li>
<li><a title="Music Store" href="#">Music</a></li>
<li><a title="RPM Blog" href="#">Blog</a></li>
<li><a title="More RPM Music" href="#">Etc</a></li>
<li><a title="Shopping Cart" href="#">Cart</a></li>
```

Nice work! I think this is going to put an end to the frustrated emails from users.

The CSS

```
#nav ul li.active, #nav ul li:hover
#nav ul a.active, #nav ul a:hover {
    background: #333;
}
```

Both the active and hover states share the same background color, so they can appear in the same rule.

Replace the <li> element with the <a> element to correspond with the changes we made in the XHTML.

Wait, what about the emails from users who were having trouble finding info on the site... Surely you're not going to fix that with CSS, too?

User Testing: Let your users tell you how they use your site.

If you want to know how your audience is actually *using* your site, you need to do some **user testing**. User testing, also known as usability testing, lets you evaluate a website by testing it out on actual users.

You don't have to wait until you have a finished product to do usability testing – you can do it at any time during the design process.

You'll see where users go, which pages they spend the most time on, where they get confused, how they move from point A to point B on the site, and a lot more. User testing can identify known problems, locate unknown problems, and pinpoint usage patterns that could inform a redesign.

But you don't just have to watch users interacting with your site, you can give them tasks and evaluate how they accomplish each task. Always remember it's the site you're evaluating, not the user. This is important because you don't want to give your participants (who are taking time out of their schedule to help you) the perception that you're testing them.

I think we should have paid more attention to the people who are actually using the site. We need to go back and do some usability testing on the RPM site–and do it quickly.

Jim

Frank

Joe

Frank: Good idea, Joe. We really should have baked usability testing right into our design process from the get go, but there's no reason we can't test the site after the fact. Usability testing's a great way to figure out a design problem because you're looking at how actual users are using your site.

Jim: Okay, I hate to rain on your parade, but testing sounds expensive...

Joe: I have a friend who works in professional user testing. It's big business, and her company doesn't just do websites—they user test all kinds of products. But professional companies like that cost tens, even hundreds, of thousands of dollars.

Jim: See that's what I was afraid of. Why so much?

Joe: They often have dedicated usability labs with computers that capture every keystroke and mouse movement, microphones that record every user comment, cameras that record the entire test, and even eye tracking devices that record where the user's eye was focused at any given time. Plus, they've also got a horde of experts who can process all of the data from the tests and provide comprehensive reports and recommendations.

Frank: That's a bit out of our budget. Any chance your friend shared a few of her secrets, Joe?!

Joe: Actually, she didn't need to. Just because you don't have a fancy lab doesn't mean you can't do useful usability testing. There are lots of budget-minded techniques we can use to test how real people use the RPM website.

Frank: So she did share some secrets after all?

Joe: Nope. All you really need to do your own usability testing is a solid plan, a computer, a few people to run the test and some willing participants. There's even been some pretty impressive and inexpensive software—like Silverback, http://silverbackapp.com—that's been coming onto the market recently. These applications can help you do some pretty sophisticated user testing without a crazy expensive lab.

Frank: Great, then let's get to it. RPM's users are waiting...

BE the user

Your job is to play the user and perform a task that would typically appear on a standard usability test. Follow the instructions below and write your impressions of the process in the space below.

Task #1: Using www.expedia.com, what would be the least expensive business class ticket price for a single adult flying from Detroit (MI) to Houston (TX), from any airport, departing on November 1st in the morning and returning November 4th in the evening?

Don't forget to write down the prices of the flights.

Behind the Scenes

In a real usability test, you wouldn't have to write down your thoughts or findings. Instead, you would just "think out loud," and someone else would write down or record what you said.

BE the user solution
Your job is to play the user and perform a task that would typically appear on a standard usability test. Follow the instructions below and write your impressions of the process in the space below.

You might get different results, but these should be close.

Task #1: Using www.expedia.com, what would be the least expensive business class ticket price for a single adult flying from Detroit (MI) to Houston (TX), from any airport, departing on November 1st in the morning and returning November 4th in the evening?

Selecting dates and times for the flight was pretty straightforward. The "Morn" and "Eve" options should be at the top of the dropdown list. If you don't know the exact airport, Expedia asks you to choose one. That particular screen is crowded and the "submit" button is hard to find. Switching from Economy to Business class was easy, but that option should also be on the home page.

We had both negative and positive experiences with the site. Picking the flights was straightforward, but option switching became a problem.

Sometimes the interface works well but something is missing or feels out of order.

The building blocks of budget usability testing

So what exactly do you need to do a decent usability test on a budget? Here are the basics:

 Plan: You've got to have a plan. What are your goals (what do you want to accomplish with the usability test)? How are you going to accomplish those goals? What are your tasks going to be? Who are you going to recruit to be your participants? If you don't have a solid plan, your usability test will be a mess from the get go.

 Moderator Script: A moderator script is basically the script for the entire usability test. How it will run, what the tasks are, and what needs to be told to the participants.

 Moderator: The moderator is the person who runs the usability test. They talk to the participant, tell them what they need to do, and give them clarification if they need it.

 Note Taker: The note taker is the person who records what the user does, what they say, etc. They basically collect the data that will be analyzed after the test is finished.

 Computer: You'll need a computer with an internet connection and necessary software for the test (browsers, plugins, etc.).

 Space: You need somewhere to run the test. If you don't have a lab, this could be your office, a quiet coffee shop or even the corner of a local library.

 Participants: You need someone to actually participate in the test. The more people the better. These participants should be drawn from your audience. It won't do you any good to select participants who would never use your site. You also need to compensate participants— give them something for their time. This may be cash ($50 is not uncommon for an approximately 3 hour session) or a gift certificate from somewhere (everyone loves Amazon).

Use a moderator script to organize the test

If you want to get the best results from your user test, you need to make sure you're well organized and that the test runs smoothly. That means knowing the exact sequence in which everything happens, what you're going to say to the participants, and what tasks you're going to have them perform—and that's what's in a moderator script.

Moderator Scripts dissected

Schedule

30 minutes - Instructions and pre-study questions

1 hour - Usability test and task assignments

15 min - Post-study questions and participant Q&A

A schedule will keep you on track and make sure the test runs as smoothly as possible.

When you do the usability test, you'll actually read this portion to your participants

Study Overview

Thank you for agreeing to participate in our study. We're very interested in your feedback about booking air travel online. We're trying to understand how people interact with multiple air travel websites during typical scenarios.

In this session, we'll first discuss why and how you use the Internet in your daily life and how you might use air travel websites in particular. Then I'll ask you to complete one task scenario on two air travel websites, dealing with looking up airfare prices for a specific destination.

As you're completing the scenarios, please speak aloud to let me know what you are doing. I'll also ask you to point out anything you encounter that's unexpected or surprising. When you've completed the scenarios, I'll ask you a series of questions about the websites and how you interacted with them. Then, I'll ask you some questions after you have filled out a brief feedback questionnaire.

Remember that this is an evaluation of the website's ease of use and not of your individual performance. Do you have any questions at this point?

Background Interview

A background interview provides information about the participant's general internet usage as well as their experience with the kind of site that's being tested. So, questions would include:

- What time(s) of day do you tend to use the Internet?

- What types of work or school-related activities do you perform using the Internet?

- What are the main issues you have when you visit websites in general?

- What is a scenario in which you might use a website like the one being tested?

*Do the background interview with your participants **before** you run the test.*

Task Instructions

These are the tasks that the user will perform, which you will observe them complete and record what they do. The tasks you come up with are the "test" portion of a usability test.

Sharpen your pencil

Think of some user tasks for the RPM Music site that a typical user might go through. Write your tasks below.

1 ....
....

2 ....
....

3 ....
....

Sharpen your pencil
Solution

Let's take a look at some possible tasks (that a typical music site user might do), which you can use for your RPM Music usability test.

1 Locate the contact information and directions to RPM Music

2 Find the name of this month's featured artist

3 Search for Chicago's Greatest Hits and place an order with RPM Music (test payment information will be provided)

Make sure that the tasks you pick don't focus exclusively on one section of the site or one specific feature. Variety will improve the results of the test.

These questions cover the participant's experience during the test and their opinions about the site in question.

Post-study Questions

Post-study questions are designed to get the participants overall impressions of the site (or sites) being tested. Questions could include the following:

• To what extent did the content of the website meet your expectations?

| Not at all | A Little | Neutral | Somewhat met | Very much so |

• Overall, how easy was it to understand the organization of the website's screens, especially the menu levels and the flow of the screens?

| Very difficult | Difficult | Neutral | Easy | Very Easy |

MODERATOR SCRIPT CONSTRUCTION

Now that you've got all the parts of your moderator script, put it all together in a document. Fill in any missing pieces, and you should be good to go.

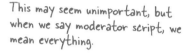

This may seem unimportant, but when we say moderator script, we mean everything.

1 Write a quick schedule and study overview that includes what you're going to say to your participants about the test

2 Write a quick background interview to find out a little more about your participants.

Age, technical proficiency, etc. These will be your demographics that will allow you to look for trends in your users.

3 Come up with some tasks that you think might help you solve some of the site's problems.

4 Finish up the script with some post-study questions that tie the user test together and get some final thoughts from the participant.

5 Gather and have ready any consent forms you may need for the test.

This is only necessary if you're doing this for a large company or university. In our case, we're just using friends—so we don't have to worry about this.

MODERATOR SCRIPT CONSTRUCTION SOLUTION

Let's take a look at what your RPM Music usability test moderator script might look like.

SCHEDULE

30 minutes – Instructions and pre-study questions
1 hour – Usability test and task assignments
15 min – Post-study questions and participant Q&A

Make sure you're staying on track and not wasting your friends time.

STUDY OVERVIEW

Thank you for agreeing to participate in our study. We are very interested in obtaining feedback about the RPM Music website and online store.

In this user test you will be asked to complete a series of tasks on the RPM Music website that will help us evaluate the efficiency and usability of the site. After the task portion of the test, you will be asked to complete a short survey about the site and your experience using the online store. While taking the test, please be sure to "think out loud" so that our moderators can record your reactions to the tasks. Finally, the moderators will not be able to assist or speak with you once the test starts. Do you have any questions at this time?

Use this script so you don't forget to tell your participant something.

BACKGROUND INTERVIEW

A background interview provides information about the participant's general internet usage, as well as their experience with the kind of site that is being tested. So, questions would include:

● What time(s) of day do you tend to use the Internet?

● What types of work or school-related activities do you perform using the Internet?

● What are the main issues you have when you visit websites in general?

● What is a scenario in which you might use a website like the one being tested?

Basic technical information

Task Instructions

◉ Locate the contact information and directions to RPM Music

◉ Find the name of this month's featured artist

◉ Search for Chicago's Greatest Hits and place an order with RPM Music (test payment information will be provided)

↖ Two to three tasks is enough—your friends probably have places to be.

Post-study Questions

◉ To what extent did the content of the website meet your expectations?

　Not at all　　　A Little　　　Neutral　　　Somewhat met　　　Very much so

◉ Overall, how easy was it to understand the organization of the website's screens, especially the menu levels and the flow of the screens?

　Very difficult　　　Difficult　　　Neutral　　　Easy　　　Very Easy

Great, I've got a moderator script. But what exactly do I do with it? Don't I need someone to actually interview?

Exercise

Remember the Expedia task you did earlier in the chapter? Now it's your turn to have a friend or family member perform the task, so you can get a taste of what it's like to be the moderator. Make sure you have them speak out loud and record your observations below.

Task #1: Using www.expedia.com, what would be the least expensive business class ticket price for a single adult flying from Detroit (MI) to Houston (TX), from any airport, departing on November 1st in the morning and returning November 4th in the evening?

Wait a second, should we really be using our friends? What if they aren't part of the target audience?

Friends and family can be a problem

When you're doing usability testing on a small budget, you're probably thinking that it would be easy to grab some friends or family and have them do the test. And you might also be thinking that you could persuade them to skip the compensation (because they are friends and family, y'know). The problem is that when you use friends and family for a usability test, you introduce bias into your study.

Because they're close to you, they might not be willing (either consciously or unconsciously) to give you unbiased feedback. Also, when you're choosing your participants, you need to choose people who would actually use the site. It's more than likely that the people close to you aren't part of the intended audience of the site, and, therefore, if you choose them, you may not get the results you need.

Probably not a good idea to use your mom. She'll be too nice.

there are no Dumb Questions

Q: How many participants do I need for a user test?

A: The more participants you get, the better (and more representative) your results will be. If you only have one or two participants, you're really only testing it on them. The results won't be representative of a large population; they'll just be their own opinions.

Q: No, really, how many participants do I need?

A: There's no real right answer for that question. The more the better. But, generally speaking, you should shoot for a minimum of 8-10.

Q: What if I can't recruit that many participants? Should I just avoid the user test entirely?

A: No, even a usability test with a small number of people (or even one) is beneficial.

The results of the usability test-what the users are telling you

I'm confused. Why don't you have a contact section? You have a whole page about the company but never tell me *where* you are.

Overall, I thought the site was ok... I had a hard time finding the contact information-it took me forever! Who puts contact information under an etc link?

Users who can't find what they're looking for probably won't come back.

The design is nice, and I think it's a huge improvement over the old site. I especially like the blog-it's cool to hear what you guys are up to.

I just kept on getting lost. And "etc"? What is up with that?

The new design rocks. I still wish you could purchase music digitally, though. Shrinkwrap was so 1999.

Some positive feedback on the design. Gotta love that.

A simple problem...

Looks like our users are a little confused by the navigation menu. They're having trouble finding the contact information because it's buried below a nav item that's incredibly confusing. This should be an easy fix...

The rest of the navigation seems to be getting users to what they are looking for.

The users are right. What does "etc" mean? This could be anything and is confusing our users. How are they expected to know that our contact info is below this link? We need to change up the link text.

RPM Music

RPM Music

| Home | Music | Blog | Etc | Cart |

RPM Music is the #4 online, midwest, *shrink-wrap* music retailer

New at RPM Music

At the Party with Hector Rivera
Hector Rivera, the king of New York Latin Soul really makes a splash with his 1966 release *At the Party*. Climbing into the R&B Top 40, this classic album will have you dancing all night long and is sure to become one of the favorite records in your collection.

Hawaii with a Bongo Beat
LeRoy Holmes has done it again with this Hawaiian-Nashville fusion album sure to take you back to the islands—or the country. Pick up this record and listen to your favorite tropical classics like "The Moon of Manakoora" and the always delightful "Mahilini Mele." Great music for the whole family.

From the Blog

Nov 4 — RPM is gearing up for the holiday season and stocking up on lots of records for the post-Thanksgiving LP rush. We should be flush with inventory and we suspect that we'll have some cool new specials to announce later in the month. Check back soon for the holiday RPM madness.

Oct 20 — We just received a mysterious package in our warehouse full of Christmas albums that seem to have originated in Japan. We are currently investigating their origins and if everything checks out, we'll have them up on the site for purchase. Could be the makings of an RPM Music exclusive.

Oct 7 — New specials are up on on the site as of last night. Be sure to check out the LP's that offer free shipping.

Test Drive

One simple fix later...

```
<ul>
        <li><a class="active" title="RPM Music home" href="#">Home</a></li>
        <li><a title="Music Store" href="#">Music</a></li>
        <li><a title="RPM Blog" href="#">Blog</a></li>
        <li><a title="More RPM Music" href="#">About</a></li>
        <li><a title="Shopping Cart" href="#">Cart</a></li>
</ul>
```

Much better. Just tell them what they can expect when they click the link.

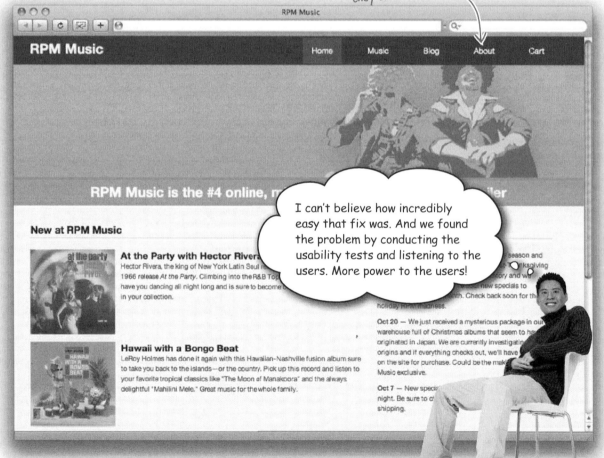

> I can't believe how incredibly easy that fix was. And we found the problem by conducting the usability tests and listening to the users. More power to the users!

Site stats give your users (another) voice

Site statistics are a handy way to find out more about what your users are doing—which pages they're hitting (and how often), which are their favorite pages, where they're coming from (referrers), and what searches they might be running while they're on the site.

You can get at your site statistics by using an application (either on your server or on another server) that captures, measures, and reports all sorts of information on your site's traffic. This process is often also called website analytics. Whatever name you use, website statistics or analytics, it's a great way to get information about how your site's being used by your audience. Let's see how RPM's stats are looking.

Website analytics tools

Mint

Mint (http://haveamint.com/) is a cool little application created by the legendary web designer/developer Shaun Inman (www.shauninman.com/) that sits on your web server and captures traffic data—which is then displayed in Mint's customizable dashboard. The great thing about Mint is it can be extended by plugins called Peppers. These Pepper plugins and widgets (which are available at the Pepper Mill http://haveamint.com/peppermill/) are developed by all sorts of people all over the web and will work seamlessly with your Mint install.

Mint only costs $30/per site you install it on.

Google Analytics

Google Analytics (http://analytics.google.com) is a free service offered by Google that generates detailed statistics about the visitors to a website. Although Google Analytics can provide detailed information about page views, referrers, browser versions, etc., it's geared more towards marketers than designers or developers.

Google Analytics works based on a system called "page tagging," in which a little bit of Javascript is inserted into every page on the site. Every time that page loads, the JavaScript collects anonymous visitor data, sends it back to the Google mothership for processing, and then displays it in a handy dandy dashboard format (at the Google Analytics site).

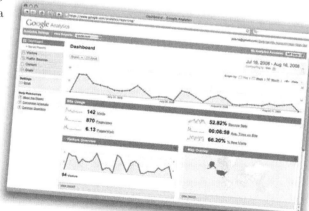

Google Analytics is free and has great data visualization, like line and bar graphs.

Sharpen your pencil

Take a look at the analytics dashboard and see if you can identify possible problems with the RPM site. Write down your top three observations below.

> Ok, let's take a look at RPM's site stats with Google Analytics and see what the users are "telling" us.

....

....

....

....

Top Content – Google Analytics

https://www.google.com/analytics/reporting/top_content

Export ▼ | Email | Add to Dashboard

Content
- Overview
- **Top Content**
  - Content by Title
  - Content Drilldown
  - Top Landing Pages
  - Top Exit Pages
  - Site Overlay
- Site Search

Goals

Settings
- Email

Help Resources
- ? About this Report
- ? Conversion University
- ? Common Questions

Graph by: Day | Week | Month | ─●─ Pageviews

July 28, 2008   August 4, 2008   August 11, 2008   August 18, 2008

35 URLs were viewed a total of 258 times

Content Performance

? Pageviews **258** % of Site Total: 100.00%	? Unique Pageviews **210** % of Site Total: 100.00%	? Time on Page **00:00:42** Site Avg: 00:00:42 (0.00%)	? Bounce Rate **75.54%** Site Avg: 75.54% (0.00%)
? % Exit **53.88%** Site Avg: 53.88% (0.00%)	? $ Index **$0.00** Site Avg: $0.00 (0.00%)		

Views: ▦ ▤ ≣

URL	Pageviews ↓	Unique Pageviews	Time on Page	Bounce Rate	% Exit	$ Index
1. /	111	93	00:01:30	75.56%	71.17%	$0.00
2. /music/	22	16	00:00:57	0.00%	54.55%	$0.00
3. /blog/	19	18	00:00:56	82.35%	78.95%	$0.00
4. /blog/rpm-relaunches-new-store.html	13	10	00:00:03	0.00%	7.69%	$0.00
5. /blog/the-problem-with-file-sharing.html	11	8	00:00:03	0.00%	9.09%	$0.00
6. /cart/	10	6	00:00:03	0.00%	0.00%	$0.00
7. /music/popular/	8	8	00:00:04	0.00%	0.00%	$0.00
8. /music/new/	8	4	00:00:23	0.00%	37.50%	$0.00
9. /etc/contact.html	5	5	00:01:00	75.00%	80.00%	$0.00
10. /etc/	5	5	00:00:02	0.00%	0.00%	$0.00

Find URL: containing ⊞ [ ] Go

Show rows: 10   Go to: 1   1 - 10 of 35 ▲ ▼

Sharpen your pencil
Solution

What do the RPM site stats tell us about usage patterns? Let's have a look.

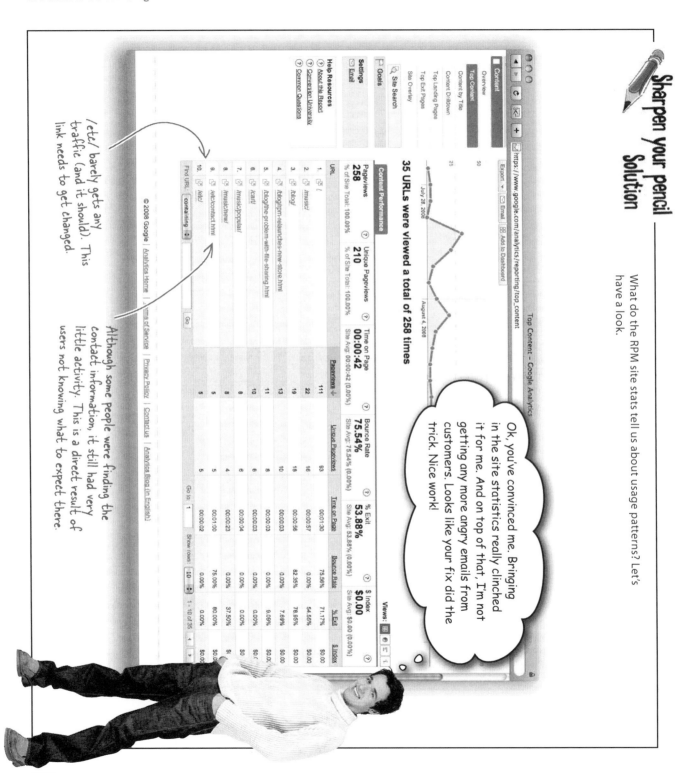

35 URLs were viewed a total of 258 times

Ok, you've convinced me. Bringing in the site statistics really clinched it for me. And on top of that, I'm not getting any more angry emails from customers. Looks like your fix did the trick. Nice work!

/etc/ barely gets any traffic (and it should). This link needs to get changed.

Although some people were finding the contact information, it still had very little activity. This is a direct result of users not knowing what to expect there.

Your Web Design Toolbox

You've got Chapter 9 under your belt, and now you've added usability testing to your tool box. Usable sites down; next up: evolving your sites to the next level.

BULLET POINTS

- Surveys are great for collecting information on a broad range of topics from a large number of people.

- Survey questions should be unbiased and uncomplicated.

- Open-ended questions are designed to provide qualitative data, but they can be complicated to deal with because each response will be different, and you won't be given the same kind of nice, statistical (numerical) results that you'd get with other kinds of questions.

- Some browsers have peculiarities that make a website look slightly different from how you designed it.

- If you design with web standards, you'll avoid most cross browser compatibility problems.

- Usability testing is designed to evaluate how real people use your site.

- Usability testing can be done cheaply.

- A usability test is task-based—you ask your participants to perform a task and you evaluate how they accomplish it.

- A moderator script is the blueprint for a usability test.

- Recruiting friends and family to do your usability test can introduce bias into your study and impact the reliability of your results.

- Site statistics (site analytics) provide usage data about your website, such as page views, referrers, popular pages, and browsers.

10 evolutionary design

Keeping your site fresh

I'm so excited to be able to post pictures to my new blog! Our visitors will be thrilled...

So you've built a bunch of awesome websites.

Now it's time to kick back, relax, and watch the visitor numbers grow, right? Whoa, not so fast. *The Web never stops evolving*—and your site needs to keep up. You can **add new features**, **tweak the design**, or even **do a complete redesign**. An ever-changing site reflects your growing skills—which means *your site is always your best PR tool*.

Your portfolio so far...

That's a good-looking collection of sites you've got there. Take a moment to look over them and feel proud of yourself. You've covered a lot of ground since chapter 1.

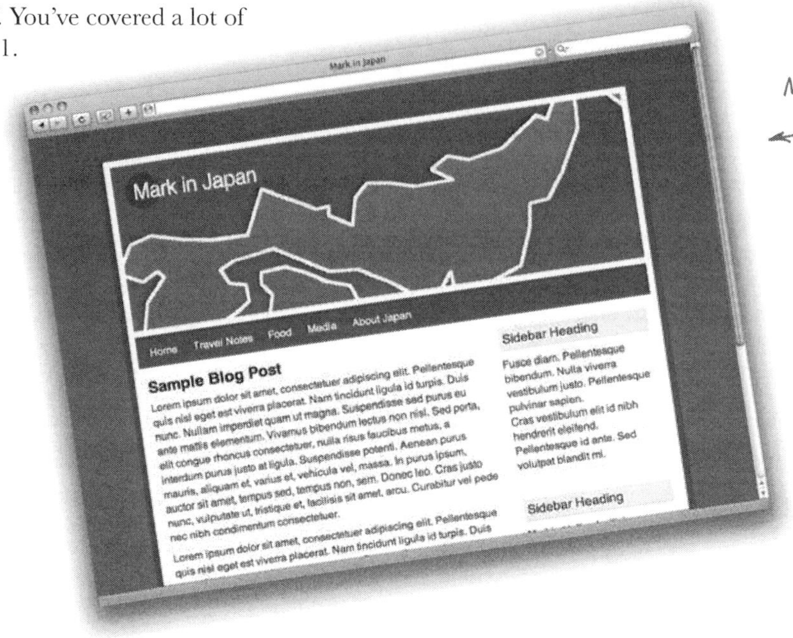

Mark's Japan Travel site

The Audio-2-Go site

The RPM Music store

College of New Media navigation overhaul

Red Lantern's site

But although it's beautiful, you can't sit around admiring your portfolio all day. There's *always* more work to be done...

Keeping your site and content fresh keeps your users coming back

If you're a web designer (either individually or as part of a larger studio), your site is your own best PR. It doesn't just showcase your project work, but it also highlights your skills, aesthetic, and design sensibilities. So you need to make sure that your site always represents your best and most progressive work.

This also means that you can't let your site linger with the same content (and features) for too long. A site that remains unchanged sends a message to your users. It says "Hey, I haven't changed in forever; there must be something wrong with the company." Fresh content will sent a positive message to your users and keep them coming back.

Revisting Red Lantern

Red Lantern's doing great. Working with Jane, you've got some truly impressive projects under your belt, and you've helped establish Red Lantern's reputation for being an innovative and cutting edge design studio. But to keep that reputation intact, you need to make sure the Red Lantern site's up-to-date, too. Now's the perfect time go back and revamp.

Keeping Red Lantern's site current should be no trouble with your web design skills, and I've brought in a junior graphic designer to help out.

Red Lantern To-Do List...

☐   Freshen up the look and feel of the site.

☐   Make the site more cross-browser compatible.

☐   Get better user feedback.

☐   Communicate better with users.

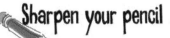

Sharpen your pencil

The new graphic designer at Red Lantern has been hard at work on a couple of update ideas for the site. What do you think of them?

We've left space for you to make notes on the pros and cons of each below.

Pros

....

....

....

Cons

....

....

....

Pros

....

....

....

Cons

....

....

....

Sharpen your pencil
Solution

What did you think of the graphic designer's ideas for the Red Lantern site? Are there elements of one (or both) you could use in a redesign?

Pros   Retains the site's original theme.

The logotype's updated.

Cleaner all-around layout, but the changes are subtle. It's not too obviously a redesign.

Cons   Does it look *too* similar?

The portfolio lists the same sites as before.

The header's the same.

Pros   Tabs highlight the navigation.

Cleaner all-around layout.

Updated logotype.

Cons   There's too little contrast between the background and main content.

Similar header image.

Design looks bland.

Positioning the tagline over the header image draws attention to it, but subtly, since the image is screened and still visible behind.

Subtle rounded corners at the top of the page.

A single column better highlights the sites in the portfolio since each of them now has more whitespace to the left and right.

This design gives a larger section of the page to the main content.

I like the first design best. It's new, but not too revolutionary. And it meets all of our needs.

Web design is about <u>evolution</u>, not revolution

Jane's right. Changing your site radically every three or four months can be problematic. First off, if you're doing client work, a complete overhaul of your site's design three or four times a year is going to suck up an amazing amount of time and resources—resources that would be better used on client projects.

Second, your users are comfortable with your existing site. They're used to the way the site looks and changing it radically could confuse them. So how do you keep them interested and coming back for more? You can take an *evolutionary design approach* to updating your site, incrementally changing the design aesthetic and features. This way, your site will still feel familiar to your users, but it will also be new and fresh.

Use CSS to <u>evolve</u> your site's design

The great thing about designing with web standards is that when you want to change up your site's design, all you need to do is edit the CSS. You don't have to worry about your markup at all (which is one of the benefits of designing to web standards—separation of content and style).

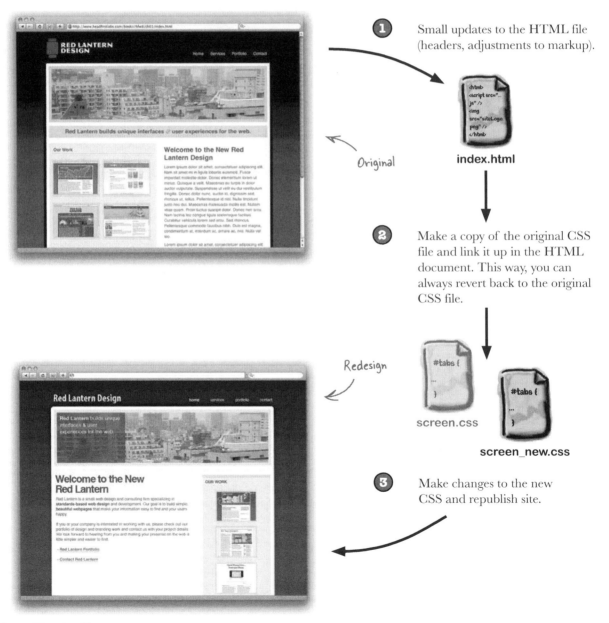

1 Small updates to the HTML file (headers, adjustments to markup).

index.html

Original

2 Make a copy of the original CSS file and link it up in the HTML document. This way, you can always revert back to the original CSS file.

Redesign

screen.css

screen_new.css

3 Make changes to the new CSS and republish site.

LONG EXERCISE

Now that Jane's settled on a new design for the Red Lantern site, it's time to get to work revising and editing the site's CSS and markup.

1 Open up the current Red Lantern site files, copy the main CSS file and rename it to something different. Now you can change the page style without affecting the original design.

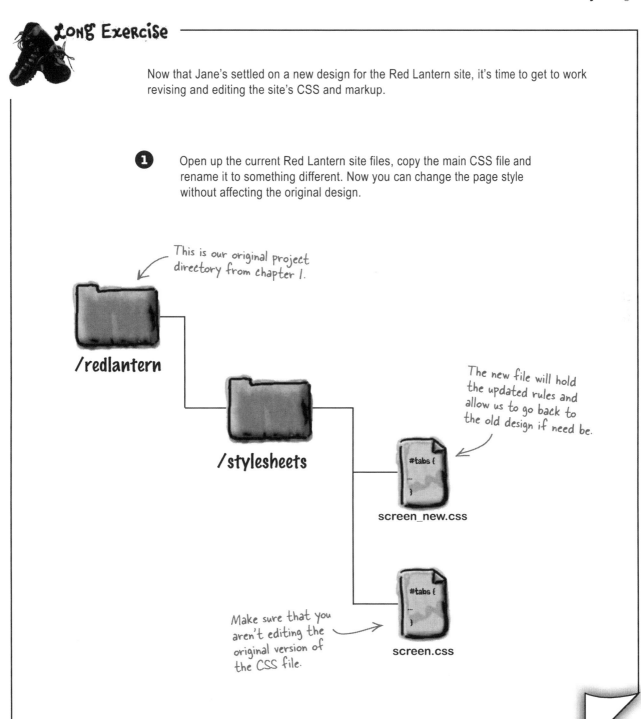

This is our original project directory from chapter 1.

/redlantern

/stylesheets

The new file will hold the updated rules and allow us to go back to the old design if need be.

#tabs {
...
}

screen_new.css

Make sure that you aren't editing the original version of the CSS file.

#tabs {
...
}

screen.css

Continues on the next page.

LONG Exercise

2

The only changes you need to make to the markup are linking the new (copied) stylesheet and removing the header image from the HTML (we'll use CSS to add it back later).

Add the new stylesheet to the XHTML document. Because it's an exact copy of the original, it will look the same but will act as the framework for the new changes.

```
<!DOCTYPE html PUBLIC "-//W3C//DTD XHTML 1.0 Strict//EN"
    "http://www.w3.org/TR/xhtml1/DTD/xhtml1-strict.dtd">
<html xmlns="http://www.w3.org/1999/xhtml" xml:lang="en" lang="en">
<head>
    <title>Red Lantern Design</title>
    <meta http-equiv="Content-Type" content="text/html; charset=utf-8" />
    <link rel="stylesheet" href="/css/screen.css" type="text/css" media="screen" />
    <link rel="stylesheet" href="/css/screen_new.css" type="text/css"
media="screen" />
</head>
<body>
    <div id="masthead">
        <h1><img alt="Red Lantern logo" src="images/rl_logo.png" /></h1>
        <h1><img alt="Red Lantern logo" src="images/rl_logo_updated.png"
/></h1>
        <ul id="nav">
            <li><a class="active" title="Red Lantern home" href="index.
html">Home</a></li>
            <li><a title="Design services" href="services.html">Services</a></
li>
            <li><a title="Our work" href="portfolio.html">Portfolio</a></li>
            <li><a title="Contact Red Lantern" href="contact.html">Contact</a></
li>
        </ul>
    </div>
    <div id="wrap">
        <div id="header">
            <img alt="tokyo buildings" src="images/tokyo.jpg" />
            <h1><strong>Red Lantern</strong> builds unique interfaces
<span class="amp">&amp;</span> user experiences for the web.</h1>
        </div>
```

Update the logo.

Our text wrapped, but this is all one line in the file.

Remove the <img> tag (the header's background image will move to the CSS file). Change up the #header <h1> tag also.

3 Update the new CSS file to reflect the following changes. The code you need to change is on the next page.

Add a subtle rounded corner to the layout and slight drop shadow to separate the main layout from the background.

Update the logotype for Red Lantern.

Move the header tagline from the body to a <div> in the header image.

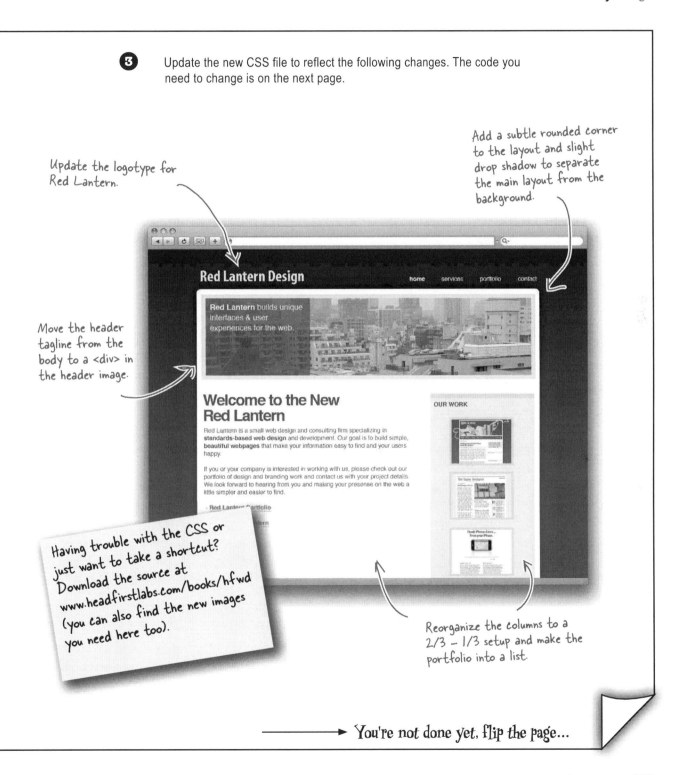

Having trouble with the CSS or just want to take a shortcut? Download the source at www.headfirstlabs.com/books/hfwd (you can also find the new images you need here too).

Reorganize the columns to a 2/3 – 1/3 setup and make the portfolio into a list.

→ You're not done yet, flip the page...

LONG EXERCISE

Add new rules to screen_new.css so the Red Lantern site matches the comps from the graphic designer. (We crossed out the old rules; you just need to add the new ones.)

```
#masthead {
        margin: 0 auto;
        margin-top: 20px;
        width: 800px;
        color: #fff;



}
```

The #masthead rule is where we need to put the rounded corner image.

```
#nav {
        float: right;
        margin: 50px 10px 0 0;



        font-size: 1.4em;
}
```

Because the logo image has changed, you need to adjust the nav list so it's positioned properly.

```
#wrap {
        clear: both;
        margin: 0 auto;
        padding: 10px;
        width: 780px;
        background: #fff;
        border: 10px solid #5c0505;



}
#header img {
        border: 10px solid #ccc;

#header {



}
```

This is where you need to add the main image we removed from the header.

```
#header h1 {
        font-size: 2em;
```

Then the <h1> can be repositioned to match the designer's comp.

```
        margin: 10px 0 0 0;
        padding: 10px;
        text-align: center;
        background: url('../images/tagline_bg.gif') repeat-x;
}
```

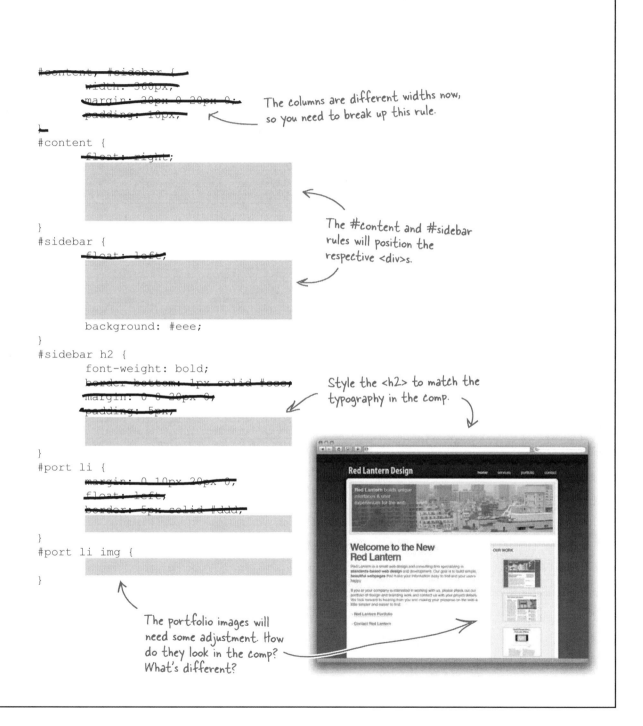

```
#content, #sidebar {
        width: 560px;
        margin: 20px 0 20px 0;
        padding: 10px;
}
```

The columns are different widths now, so you need to break up this rule.

```
#content {
        float: right;




}
#sidebar {
        float: left;




        background: #eee;
}
```

The #content and #sidebar rules will position the respective <div>s.

```
#sidebar h2 {
        font-weight: bold;
        border-bottom: 1px solid #ccc;
        margin: 0 0 20px 0;
        padding: 5px;



}
```

Style the <h2> to match the typography in the comp.

```
#port li {
        margin: 0 10px 20px 0;
        float: left;
        border: 5px solid #ddd;


}
#port li img {


}
```

The portfolio images will need some adjustment. How do they look in the comp? What's different?

LONG EXERCISE SOLUTION

Let's take a look at the changes you made to the Red Lantern CSS file. Remember, rules that were not changed or removed can just be left the same as the old site.

Left side of rounded_header.gif (this is a long image with rounded corners on both ends).

```
#masthead {
        margin: 0 auto;
        margin-top: 20px;
        width: 800px;
        color: #fff;
        height: 70px;
        background: url('../images/rounded_header.gif') no-repeat bottom;
}
#nav {
        float: right;
        margin: 0 10px 0 0;
        padding: 30px 0 0 0;
        font-size: 1.4em;
}
```

Adding a height and background image, we can give the corners a simple rounded look.

```
#wrap {
        clear: both;
        margin: 0 auto;
        padding: 10px;
        width: 780px;
        background: #fff;
        border: 10px solid #5c0505;
        border-top: none;
}
#header {
        height: 180px;
        background: url('../images/tokyo_updated.jpg') no-repeat;
        border: 10px solid #eee;
}
#header h1 {
        font-size: 2em;
        line-height: 1.2em;
        padding: 20px;
        color: #eee;
        width: 200px;
        font-weight: normal;
}
```

Did you get this on? Because #masthead has a background now, you need to remove the top border from the #wrap <div>.

Now that the main image file is no longer hardcoded into the HTML file, you can use a new image as the <h1> background in the CSS file.

This lets you keep the semantics of the <h1> tag but make the text appear as though it's part of the image.

```
#content {
        float: left;
        width: 500px;
        margin: 0 0 10px 0;
        padding: 10px;
}
#sidebar {
        float: right;
        margin: 20px 0 20px 0;
        padding: 10px;
        width: 240px;
        border-top: 5px solid #ddd;
        background: #eee;
}
#sidebar h2 {
        font-weight: bold;
        text-transform: uppercase;
        padding: 0 5px 5px 5px;
}
#port li {
        margin: 10px 35px 0 35px;
}
#port li img {
        border: 5px solid #ddd;
}
```

#content and #sidebar get their own widths, and each are floated to either side of the page. 10px padding gives the content of each column a little breathing room.

These final adjustments make the sidebar align and the overall look of the portfolio match the design comp. Each image now has a 5px border

The final screenshot

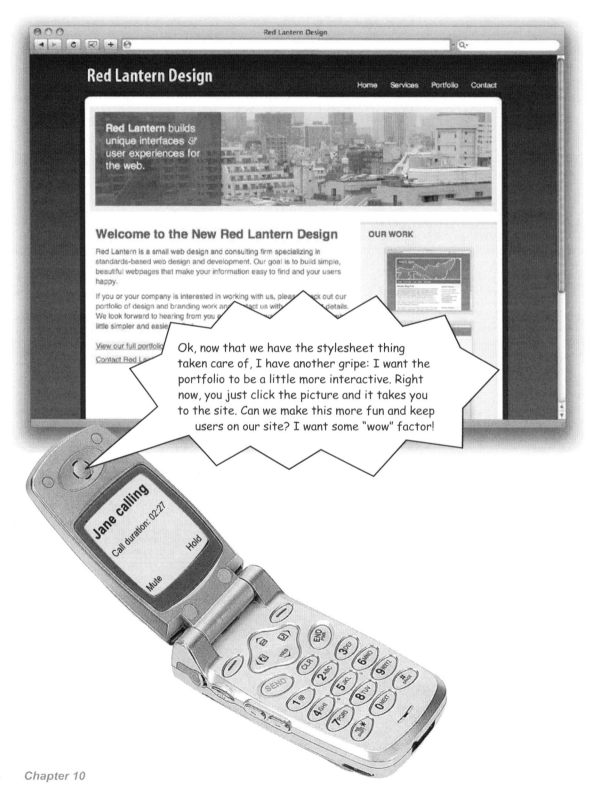

Ok, now that we have the stylesheet thing taken care of, I have another gripe: I want the portfolio to be a little more interactive. Right now, you just click the picture and it takes you to the site. Can we make this more fun and keep users on our site? I want some "wow" factor!

 Sharpen your pencil

Take a look at the following ways to make the sidebar portfolio more interactive. Match the technique with its list of pros and cons.

Flash

Pros: Good mix of interactivity and compatibility.
Cons: Some browsers may have this feature disabled or not fully support it.

JQuery JavaScript library

Pros: All code is standards-compliant and will work in most browsers.
Cons: Low level of interactivity.

XHTML + CSS

Pros: Limitless interactivity and animation.
Cons: Content not available in forms other than visual.

Sharpen your pencil
Solution

Let's see how the different effects options shape up:

Flash

Flash adds interactivity at the expense of hiding all your content in a single SWF file.

Pros: Good mix of interactivity and compatibility.
Cons: Some browsers may have this feature disabled or not fully support it.

JQuery JavaScript library

JavaScript is very flexible, and when it teams up with XHTML and CSS, it can be very powerful.

Pros: All code is standards-compliant and will work in most browsers.
Cons: Low level of interactivity.

XHTML + CSS

Although you can do some neat things with just CSS, it doesn't offer the level of interactivity that the owner needs.

Pros: Limitless interactivity and animation.
Cons: Content not available in forms other than visual.

> JavaScript looks like a great way to add some interactivity to the sidebar portfolio.

Hold on a second—I have to write JavaScript? That's complicated stuff, and I'm not a programmer!

You don't need to be a crack programmer to add interactivity with JavaScript.

JavaScript's a popular part of web design. It's used for all kinds of things from screen effects (like image lightboxes) to UI elements (such as sliders or accordion menus). The problem is, JavaScript can be intimidating for someone who's only had experience writing XHTML and CSS.

The solution is JavaScript libraries. These are pre-written JavaScript functions and controls that you can put in a directory on your server and call from within your markup. The cool thing is that you don't need to know very much JavaScript to take advantage of these libraries. They're also generally very lightweight, cross-browser compatible, and standards-compliant.

There are lots of different JavaScript libraries out there. Some of the best include Dojo (www.dojotoolkit.com), Script.aculo.us (http://script.aculo.us), Moo tools (http://mootools.net), Prototype (www.prototypejs.org/), and JQuery (http://jquery.com/).

Want to really dig into JavaScript? Check out this book; it's pretty awesome.

Use JavaScript lightboxes to add interactivity to your site

Lightbox has come to mean any effect that takes an image or HTML page and displays it in a floating box in the middle of the screen. In some libraries, the background of the site fades out to add emphasis to the floating box. We're going to use a library called Facebox. This particular type of lightbox mimics the look of the pop-ups found on the Facebook social networking site. It's going to look great with the updated Red Lantern design.

> This looks great. Let's get this working on our site as soon as possible.

Libraries like Facebox are a great way to add interactivity and highlight images and galleries on your site.

When you click a thumbnail image, a larger copy of the same image is loaded in the center of the screen...

...with a white background, semi-opaque border (with rounded corners to match our new design), and a close button.

Add Facebox to the Red Lantern home page

1 Download the Facebox code from the Head First site:
www.headfirstlabs.com/books/hfwd
and place the downloaded files in their appropriate directories.

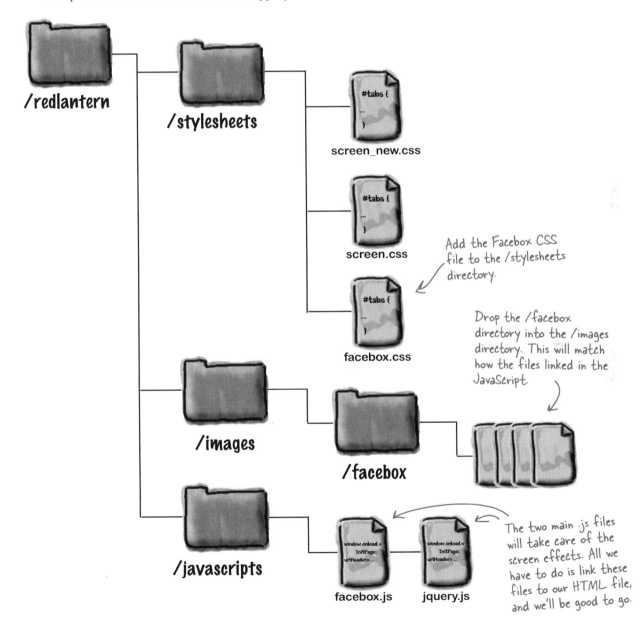

/redlantern

/stylesheets

screen_new.css

screen.css

Add the Facebox CSS file to the /stylesheets directory.

facebox.css

Drop the /facebox directory into the /images directory. This will match how the files linked in the JavaScript.

/images

/facebox

/javascripts

facebox.js   **jquery.js**

The two main .js files will take care of the screen effects. All we have to do is link these files to our HTML file, and we'll be good to go.

Edit your index file

②   Add the CSS file to the header of the `index.html` file.

The Red Lantern index.html file.

```
<!DOCTYPE html PUBLIC "-//W3C//DTD XHTML 1.0 Strict//EN"
        "http://www.w3.org/TR/xhtml1/DTD/xhtml1-strict.dtd">
<html xmlns="http://www.w3.org/1999/xhtml" xml:lang="en" lang="en">
<head>
        <title>Red Lantern Design</title>
        <meta http-equiv="Content-Type" content="text/html; charset=utf-8" />
        <link rel="stylesheet" href="/css/screen_new.css" type="text/css"
media="screen" />
        <link rel="stylesheet" href="/css/facebox.css" type="text/css"
media="screen" />
</head>
<body>
```

The box that appears on the screen has its own stylesheet that controls how the box appears. Add a link to the facebox.css file in the document after the Red Lantern stylesheet.

③   Add the JavaScript links and code to the header of your `index.html` file.

```
<!DOCTYPE html PUBLIC "-//W3C//DTD XHTML 1.0 Strict//EN"
        "http://www.w3.org/TR/xhtml1/DTD/xhtml1-strict.dtd">
<html xmlns="http://www.w3.org/1999/xhtml" xml:lang="en" lang="en">
<head>
        <title>Red Lantern Design</title>
        <meta http-equiv="Content-Type" content="text/html; charset=utf-8" />
        <link rel="stylesheet" href="/css/screen_new.css" type="text/css"
media="screen" />
        <link rel="stylesheet" href="/css/facebox.css" type="text/css"
media="screen" />
        <script src="javascripts/jquery.js" type="text/javascript"></script>
        <script src="javascripts/facebox.js" type="text/javascript"></script>
        <script type="text/javascript">
                jQuery(document).ready(function($) {
                        $('a[rel*=facebox]').facebox()
                })
        </script>
</head>
<body>
```

You need to add links to the new JavaScript files. Put these below the stylesheet links.

Below the links to the JavaScript files is a small bit of code that readies the Facebox JavaScript to act when a link with the proper rel attribute is clicked.

The Facebox code then takes over and uses the linked files and CSS to render the effect on the page.

Exercise **④** Using this example above as a guide, add the Facebox effect to the rest of the list items in the portfolio. Remember to link the thumbnails to their full-size versions and provide the proper rel attribute to the link.

The rel attribute describes the relationship of a link to the current page. Here it's used to tell the Facebox JavaScript when a particular link is clicked.

Add links to the portfolio images that point to a larger version of the same file. This larger image will be displayed in the lightbox.

```
<ul id="port">
     <li><a title="View Detail" href="images/markinjapan_large.jpg" rel="facebox">
<img alt="mark in japan comp" src="images/markinjapan.jpg" /></a></li>
     <li><img alt="audio 2 go comp" src="images/a2g.jpg" /></li>
     <li><img alt="rpm comp" src="images/rpm.jpg" /></li>
</ul>
```

Make sure you fully enclose the existing <img> tags in the <a> tags. Basically, think of the image as if it were text inside the link tag.

Geek Bits

The rel attribute is used to describe the relationship between two resources. In the lightbox case, the link relationship is to the lightbox effect. This is purely a semantic relationship, but other resources (like JavaScript) can use that attribute to treat those links differently then a normal site link.

Exercise Solution

Let's take a look at what our portfolio markup needs to look like for the lightbox effect to work properly:

```
<ul id="port">
        <li><a title="View Detail" href="images/markinjapan_large.jpg" rel="facebox">
<img alt="mark in japan comp" src="images/markinjapan.jpg" /></a></li>
        <li><a title="View Detail" href="images/a2g_large.jpg" rel="facebox">
<img alt="audio 2 go comp" src="images/a2g.jpg" /></a></li>
        <li><a title="View Detail" href="images/rpm_large.jpg" rel="facebox">
<img alt="rpm comp" src="images/rpm.jpg" /></a></li>
</ul>
```

Images aren't the only thing that can appear in the lightbox. Text content within a tag or complete HTML documents can also be displayed through the lightbox.

Each link needs to have the rel="facebox" attribute for the effect to work properly. Without that bit of code, the JavaScript wouldn't know to execute.

TEST DRIVE

Give it a shot. Add all the images and files to your own file structure and load up the page in a browser. How does it look?

Try another browser. Does it work the same way?

there are no
Dumb Questions

Q: You mentioned JavaScript might not be fully compatible with some browsers. What will happen if a user's browser doesn't support it?

A: That's right. Not all browsers support JavaScript. If that happens, since you added a link to the larger image, instead of displaying in the center of the existing page, the browser may still take a shot at displaying the linked image in a new blank page. Users would need to use their browser's back button to get back, but they may still be able to see the larger image.

Q: So if I can put text in a lightbox too, wouldn't users miss out on that if their browser doesn't support JavaScript?

A: It's the same deal. Different browsers handle JavaScript differently, and as you can never be sure what level of support your users' browsers will have, this is another good reason to use JavaScript sparingly. If you're going to use it, make sure the content that it displays isn't crucial to your users' understanding of the site and its content.

Q: Hmm. Would Flash be a better option for adding interactivity?

A: It depends on what you're trying to achieve. If you want rich, animated, multi-media sections, Flash is a good bet, but here we're just showing a larger version of an image. Of course Flash has its own set of limitations (browsers need plugins, not all content is 100% accessible, and so on), so if you've got a site that's mostly content-based, it's best to stick with HTML and CSS for the main presentation and add touches of interactivity here and there with JavaScript or Flash.

Those lightboxes look great, but... I don't know, are they going to keep people coming back to the site regularly? I know our designs are awesome, but I doubt users will be hitting F5 waiting for us to post the next one... Any ideas?

BRAIN POWER

What do you think? How else could we add new content to Red Lantern to keep users coming back over and over?

Hmm. The JavaScript stuff *looks* cool, but it's a one-time thing. How about a blog to keep users coming back?

Keep your content fresh with a blog.

Blogs have become a powerful tool for creating two-way communication with your users. You posting entries, and your users have the opportunity to comment on your posts and each other's comments.

A blog is a relatively easy way to add a constant stream of content to your site—which means that your site will always look fresh and give users a reason to come back.

Blogs also give your site a "voice." Instead of your site being somewhat anonymous, you can speak through your blog posts and reach out to other people.

Watch it!

If you're going to start a blog, make absolutely sure that you've got the time to post regularly.

There's nothing worse than your users coming to your site, only to find that the blog hasn't been updated for 6 months. The only way to attract readers is to give them something new and interesting to read on a fairly regular basis.

Adding blog functionality with WordPress

Jane agrees. She thinks it would be a great idea for the new version of the Red Lantern site to have a blog. That way you guys can write design articles, post news about Red Lantern, and generally have a better avenue of communication with your users.

Jane's done some research and wants to use WordPress (http://wordpress.org). Why? Well, there are a bunch of reasons:

BULLET POINTS

- WordPress is open source–which means there are thousands (perhaps even tens of thousands) of developers around the world contributing their efforts to make it better with every version.

- WordPress only requires PHP and MySQL to run. (Don't worry, we'll talk you through it if those terms sound a little scary.)

- WordPress has an incredibly easy (and legendary) 5 minute install process.

- WordPress features a very simple templating system that lets you change the look of your blog with a click of a button. More importantly, it's really easy to develop your own templates (called "Themes" in WordPress speak). They're all written using CSS... so if you happen to already have a site and want your WordPress blog to look just like it, it's just a matter of adapting the existing CSS.

- Best of all, WordPress is free!

This is default "Kubrick" theme that ships with WordPress and is designed to work with all of the special features of WordPress.

Add a WordPress blog to the Red Lantern site

To get Red Lantern's blog up and running, you need to download WordPress and get it set up on the server. You can download the WordPress files from:
http://wordpress.org/download/

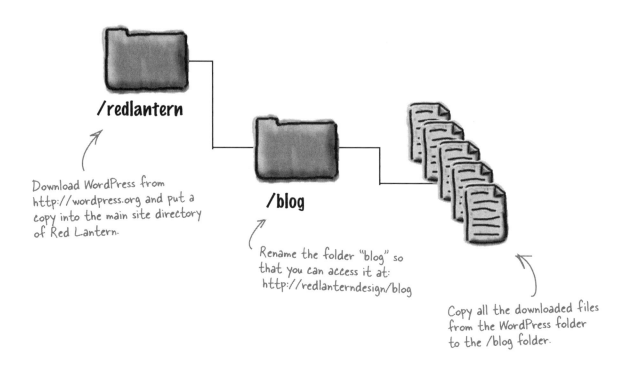

/redlantern

Download WordPress from http://wordpress.org and put a copy into the main site directory of Red Lantern.

/blog

Rename the folder "blog" so that you can access it at:
http://redlanterndesign/blog

Copy all the downloaded files from the WordPress folder to the /blog folder.

 Geek Bits

WordPress requires a server with PHP and MySQL (an open source relational database) to operate properly. If you don't have access to a server or hosting plan (most web hosts fully support WordPress), check out this site and learn how to run WordPress locally on your PC or Mac using XAMPP, an installable set of software that gives you a working web server on your desktop.
http://www.apachefriends.org/en/xampp.html

Exercise

Complete the WordPress installation and get the Red Lantern blog up and running.

You'll have to rename wp-config-sample.php to the following:

1 Edit and rename the **wp-config.php** file so that the parameters match the ones from your own setup.

```
// ** MySQL settings ** //
define('DB_NAME', 'putyourdbnamehere');      // The name of the database
define('DB_USER', 'usernamehere');           // Your MySQL username
define('DB_PASSWORD', 'yourpasswordhere');   // ...and password
define('DB_HOST', 'localhost');              // 99% chance you won't need to change this value

define('DB_CHARSET', 'utf8');
define('DB_COLLATE', '');
```

These four database parameters are needed so that WordPress can build the database tables that will hold the blog data.

2 Following the installer, get the basic blog up and running on your local machine or server. Remember, we want to access WordPress at /blog.

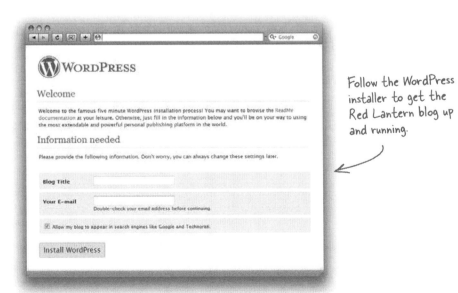

Follow the WordPress installer to get the Red Lantern blog up and running.

Blog Exposed

This week's interview:
Getting to know the Blog

Head First: Welcome, Blog, it's good have you here. To start off, I've got to ask, what's with the name? Blog? Sounds like the sound a dog makes when it's throwing up!

Blog: Really? Is that how this interview is going to go? Ok, I'll bite. The name "Blog" is a shortened version of "weblog," which is a combination of the words "web" and "log." Basically, back in the day when blogs first started out, they were just a log of what people were doing on the Web (cool sites they'd visited, funny photos, yadda, yadda)—hence the name weblog (and then blog).

Head First: Sorry, maybe that wasn't the best way to phrase the first question. You've certainly come a long way from those early days haven't you?

Blog: You bet! Blogs have become a really powerful tool for communicating on the Web. You see blogs everywhere—from personal sites to big corporate sites. Everyone has jumped on the bandwagon!

Head First: Really? That many people have blogs?

Blog: Yeah, we're talking millions, and millions, and... well, you get the idea.

Head First: Wow. That's a lot of people blogging. If there are that many people using blogs out there, it must be super duper easy to set them up?

Blog: Well, yes... and no.

Head First: Yes and no? What kind of answer is that?

Blog: It's complicated.

Head First: Enlighten us, that's what you're for, right?

Blog: The technology behind blogs can be pretty complicated. They are dynamic web applications that store stuff (posts, comments, etc.) in a database on the server and use a server-side language (like PHP) to pull stuff out of that database and put it on the actual site. The good thing is that blogs have become so popular, there are lots of accessible solutions for a wide variety of people with a wide variety of tech savvy.

Head First: Ok, that sounds good–can you talk about some of these solutions?

Blog: Well, blogs generally fall into two categories: hosted and installed. Hosted blog systems are created, administered, and maintained by a third party (usually administered by the user through an easy-to-use online interface). Because the service lives on the host's server, you don't have to deal with installation or server configuration yourself. There are free hosted blog services (like blogger) and paid hosted services (like movable type).

Head First: Ok, I get hosted blogs... what about installed blogs?

Blog: Installed blog systems are basically software that you install on your own web server that run the blog. They can be more complicated than hosted solutions–especially for people who don't have access to a server (or any server experience). The good news is that there are a handful of installed blog systems out there (namely WordPress) that make it about as easy as it can get.

Head First: Wow, I never knew that there was so much to know about blogs. Thanks for stopping by!

Test Drive

Take a look at what the blog looks like after you complete the WordPress installation.

This is what will appear at the /blog/ URL.

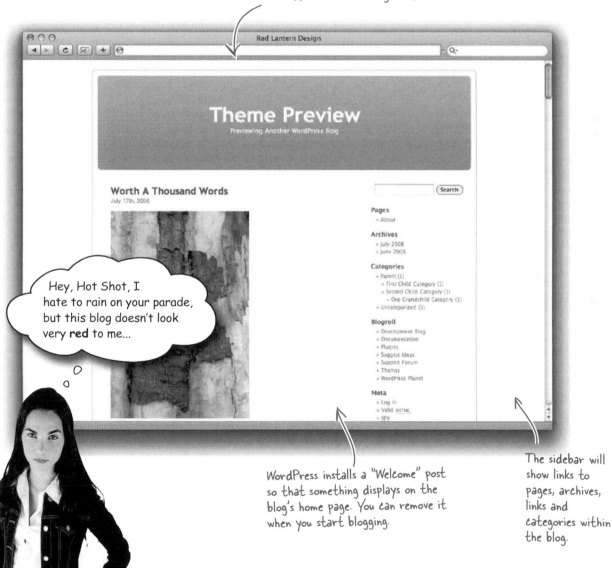

Hey, Hot Shot, I hate to rain on your parade, but this blog doesn't look very **red** to me...

WordPress installs a "Welcome" post so that something displays on the blog's home page. You can remove it when you start blogging.

The sidebar will show links to pages, archives, links and categories within the blog.

Change the look and feel of your blog with themes

Themes for WordPress allow you to change the design of your site by uploading new designs for use in the software. The themes are a collection of files in a directory that hold the PHP code, markup, style and images of the new design. Once uploaded, you can activate a new theme from the WordPress admin panel.

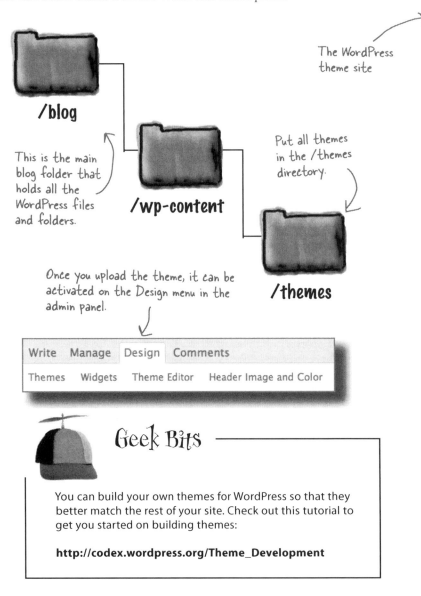

/blog

This is the main blog folder that holds all the WordPress files and folders.

/wp-content

Put all themes in the /themes directory.

/themes

Once you upload the theme, it can be activated on the Design menu in the admin panel.

Write	Manage	Design	Comments
Themes	Widgets	Theme Editor	Header Image and Color

The WordPress theme site

Geek Bits

You can build your own themes for WordPress so that they better match the rest of your site. Check out this tutorial to get you started on building themes:

http://codex.wordpress.org/Theme_Development

A design update and some tweaking of images and CSS.

Wow, this looks great. I think our users will be really pleased with what we've done. I'm looking forward to their blog comments.

The lightbox effect with Facebox

The freshly-installed WordPress blog

Your Web Design Toolbox

You've got Chapter 10 under your belt, and you've added some fresh content to your home page.

BULLET POINTS

- Your personal site is your best PR tool.

- It's important that your site always represents your best and most progressive work.

- Fresh content will send a positive message to your users and keep them coming back.

- A website should evolve (change incrementally) instead of changing radically all the time.

- JQuery is a library of pre-written JavaScript functions and controls that are put in a directory on your server and then called from within your markup.

- A lightbox is a page effect that displays images or other HTML content in a floating frame in the center of your page's layout.

- A blog provides you with a way to keep your content fresh and updated, as well as create a direct line of conversation with your users.

- Hosted blog systems are created, administered, and maintained by a third party (usually administered by the user through an easy to use online interface).

- Installed blogs are made possible by software you install on your web server—they require a database of some sort (like mySQL) and support for a server-side language (like PHP).

11 the business of web design

Mind Your Own Business

I can't even afford a pair of pants since my design got ripped off by a rival web design firm.

Business in a web design book? Are you kidding me?

You've mastered pre-production, information architecture, navigation, color, and even accessibility. What's left in your path to web design mastery? Well, you're going to have to tackle the business issues of web design. You don't need a Harvard MBA, but you better know more than just where you deposit your check... or those checks may stop coming. Let's look at establishing good client relationships and understanding your intellectual property rights. The result? Increased profits and protection for your hard work.

The newest potential client: the Foo Bar

Jane at Red Lantern just got wind of a big potential client: the Foo Bar, a popular restaurant that needs an online presence. After all the work you did for Jane with Red Lantern, she'd like you to take on the work. She's willing to pay you well and give you a stake in her company if you can get the Foo Bar gig.

Seriously... who could pass up a client named the Foo Bar?

The Foo Bar
Steakhouse and Saloon

> I don't like doing work on spec, but I think this job's in the bag... bring us this client, okay?

What Foo Bar wants in a bid:

1 A basic HTML mockup of one page of the site, showing off the site's overall look, feel, and layout.

2 A color scheme for the site, including which design elements would have what color, represented in the HTML mockup.

3 A few succinct ideas for branding and logos that would fit in with the Foo Bar's new online presence.

A quick sketch by the owner

The Foo Bar owner

Here are some colors inspired by the building and bar.

BRAIN BARBELL

Spec work refers to doing a lot of work before getting paid. In this case, the Foo Bar owner wants a site mockup to look at before he commits to your work and Red Lantern design. Why do you think Jane doesn't usually do spec work?

Let's build a quick mockup for the Foo Bar

By now, putting together a mockup should be a piece of cake. Let's
look at some XHTML for a simple version of the Foo Bar:

```html
<!DOCTYPE html PUBLIC "-//W3C//DTD XHTML 1.0 Strict//EN"
        "http://www.w3.org/TR/xhtml1/DTD/xhtml1-strict.dtd">
<html xmlns="http://www.w3.org/1999/xhtml" xml:lang="en" lang="en">
<head>
  <title>The Foo Bar</title>
  <meta http-equiv="Content-Type" content="text/html; charset=utf-8"/>
  <link rel="stylesheet" href="stylesheets/screen.css" type="text/css"
        media="screen" />
</head>
<body>
  <div id="header">
    <img alt="foo bar logo" src="images/foobar_logo.jpg" />
  </div>
  <div id="navigation">
    <ul>
    <li><a class="active" title="Foo Bar home" href="#">Home</a></li>
    <li><a title="Foo Bar menu" href="#">Menu</a></li>
    <li><a title="Foo Bar history" href="#">History</a></li>
    <li><a title="Contact us" href="#">Contact</a></li>
    </ul>
  </div>
  <div id="wrap">
    <h1>Welcome to The Foo Bar. Cold Beer Served Daily.</h1>
    <img alt="foo bar storefront" src="images/foobar_front.jpg" />
    <div id="content">
    <h2>Get to the Foo</h2>
    <p>Lorem ipsum dolor sit amet, consectetuer adipiscing elit. Duis a felis.
       Sed ac mauris eget eros vestibulum luctus.</p>
    <p>Lorem ipsum dolor sit amet, consectetuer adipiscing elit. Duis a felis.
       Sed ac mauris eget eros vestibulum luctus.</p>
    </div>
    <div id="sidebar">
      <h2>Specials</h2>
      <ul id="specials">
        <li>Monday</li>
        <li>Tuesday</li>
        <li>Wednesday</li>
        <li>Thursday</li>
        <li>Friday</li>
      </ul>
    </div>
    <div id="footer">
      <p>Copyright &copy; The Foo Bar, all rights reserved.</p>
    </div>
  </div>
</body>
</html>
```

index.html

Exercise

Create a new stylesheet, screen.css, and add in color and font faces. Use what you've learned so far to give Foo Bar a nice contemporary look. Make sure you create a logical directory structure and link all the files properly in your index.html file, too.

```
body {
        margin: 0;
        padding: 0;
        background: ...................
        border-top: 10px solid ...................
        font-family: Helvetica, sans-serif;
        color: #fff;
}
h2 {
        margin: 0;
        color: ...................
}
#wrap {
        margin: 0 auto;
        width: 800px;
        background: ...................
        border-left: 5px solid ...................
        border-right: 5px solid ...................
}
#wrap h1 {
        margin: 0;
        padding: 10px;
        text-align: center;
        background: ...................
        border-bottom: 1px solid ...................
        color: #fff;
        font-weight: normal;
        font-family: Georgia, serif;
}
```

```
#navigation ul {
        padding: 15px;
}
#navigation ul li a {
        color: ...................
        font-weight: bold;
        font-size: large;
        text-decoration: none;
}
#navigation ul li a.active {
        color: #fff;
}
#sidebar h2 {
        background: ...................
        margin: 0 0 10px 0;
        padding: 5px;
}
#footer p {
        margin: 0;
        padding: 10px;
        background: ...................
        text-align: center;
}
```

Play around with different combinations of the colors the Foo Bar owner gave you and see what works best for the layout.

```
#tabs {
...
}
```
screen.css

Exercise Solution

Here are the parts of the CSS file that needed our color treatment. Let's take a look at the final code and see what the finished site looks like.

We used the lightest brown for the background and a slightly darker color for the top border.

```css
body {
    margin: 0;
    padding: 0;
    background: #efedb4;
    border-top: 10px solid #beba9e;
    font-family: Helvetica, sans-serif;
    color: #fff;
}
h2 {
    margin: 0;
    color: #bd8ead;
}
#wrap {
    margin: 0 auto;
    width: 800px;
    background: #362416;
    border-left: 5px solid #281a0f;
    border-right: 5px solid #efedb4;
}
#wrap h1 {
    margin: 0;
    padding: 10px;
    text-align: center;
    background: #553f2d;
    border-bottom: 1px solid #362416;
    color: #fff;
    font-weight: normal;
    font-family: Georgia, serif;
}
```

```css
#navigation ul {
    padding: 15px;
}
#navigation ul li a {
    color: #bd8ead;
    font-weight: bold;
    font-size: large;
    text-decoration: none;
}
#navigation ul li a.active {
    color: #fff;
}
#sidebar h2 {
    background: #553f2d;
    margin: 0 0 10px 0;
    padding: 5px;
}
#footer p {
    margin: 0;
    padding: 10px;
    background: #281a0f;
    text-align: center;
}
```

#tabs {
...
}

screen.css

The #wrap <div> gets the darkest browns and offers a nice contrast with the white text and light background.

/foobar

You can download all the files for the Foo Bar site from the Head First Labs website.

Test Drive

Create (or download) index.html, screen.css, and the Foo Bar images. Fire up your browser, and show the Foo Bar owner your layout and color scheme.

Sorry, Red Lantern. I just didn't like what you came up with. I'm going with someone else... with a totally different look and feel. Sorry!

Then, three months later...

Exercise

Has our design really been ripped off? Before you tell Jane to call the corporate lawyers, we need to be absolutely sure. It's time to do some comparisons. Take a look at both designs below, and write down all their similarities and differences..

This is the design we submitted to Foo Bar.

Here's the design the Foo Bar went with.

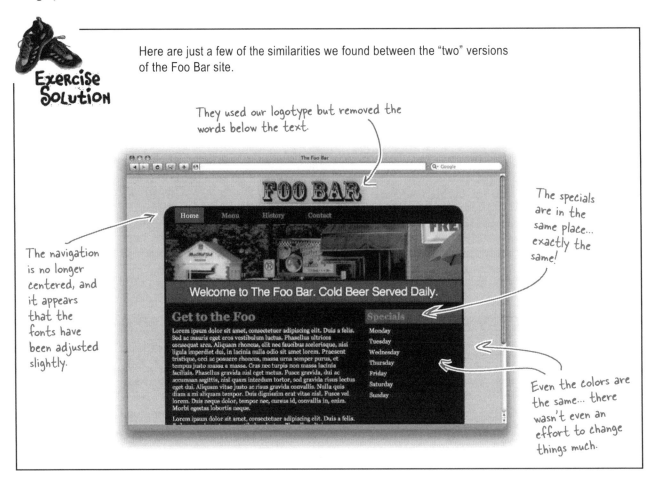

Exercise Solution

Here are just a few of the similarities we found between the "two" versions of the Foo Bar site.

They used our logotype but removed the words below the text.

The navigation is no longer centered, and it appears that the fonts have been adjusted slightly.

The specials are in the same place... exactly the same!

Even the colors are the same... there wasn't even an effort to change things much.

there are no Dumb Questions

Q: There's no way this was an honest mistake, is there?

A: That's a question you've got to ask, but it's usually one that's pretty easy to answer. When two sites look this much alike, it's hard to imagine a situation that doesn't involve stealing designs. Even if you had an exercise to develop a site that looked like the Foo Bar site, you'd probably make more changes than shown above.

Q: But this is the Web. Everyone rips everyone else off, right?

A: Well, it's like Mom said: just because your friends are doing it, doesn't make it right. If everyone else jumped off a cliff... well, you get the idea. When you worked hard on a design, you're entitled to make sure it stays yours.

Q: Okay, they definitely ripped us off. So what do we do?

A: Good question...

Welcome to the world of DESIGN PIRACY

It's been said that imitation is the highest form of flattery. But what happens when you come across a site that's clearly lifted your design? The problem is that the Web makes copying (and stealing!) really, really easy. Source markup is easily viewable (and copyable), images are easily downloaded to a desktop, and CSS is quickly copied.

So what exactly can you do? First, it's important that you know that if you created your site (and your design really is an original work), *you own the copyright*. Second, you don't have to put a copyright notice on the pages in your site for them to be copyrighted. So your design is already copyrighted!

> So we own the copyright. Cool. But what does that mean? What should we actually do if our copyright's being violated?

❶ Send a polite email.
Ask the owner of the offending website to remove your copyrighted material, or take down your copyrighted design. And as angry as you might be, keep it civil. It's far more likely that the offender will respond to your requests if you are polite.

❷ Send a follow-up email and copy Google.
If you don't get a response, or get an ugly reply, send another mail and CC Google at spamreport@google.com. Google is committed to responding to clear violations of copyright. In fact, they're so concerned that their responses to infringement may include removing or disabling access to the site that's infringing on your material.

You'd be surprised what an email can do. Oftentimes the individuals that rip off designs are just hoping you'll never notice. The Web is a big place, you know.

❸ Consult a copyright lawyer.
If nothing else works, gets the lawyers involved. At the very least, a lawyer can deliver a cease and desist notification on your behalf. If you want to, a lawyer can even take your infringement site to court and possibly seek damages on your behalf. Just remember, copyright lawyers aren't cheap!

This should really be considered as a last resort. It has the potential to get expensive fast.

Red Lantern Design <redlantern@gmail.com>

Unauthorized use of copyright

2 messages

Red Lantern Design <redlantern@gmail.com>
Reply-To: redlantern@gmail.com
To: The Foo Bar <contact@thefoobar.com>

Sat, Nov 15, 2008 at 2:17 PM

Be polite, firm, and don't be afraid to mention "legal action" to get your point across.

To whom it may concern,

It has come to our attention that your establishment is using our (Red Lantern Design) copyrighted material without permission. We had recently written a bid for your company and it appears that the design we submitted for consideration has ended up as your homepage. We were not notified that we had won the bid and received no compensation for the use of that design or for our services. We are asking you to please remove the material from your homepage and discontinue any further use of our copyrights or risk legal action taken on our behalf.

Thank you,
Red Lantern Design, LLC

I was expecting this to drag out. I'm glad they are taking the site down.

The Foo Bar <contact@thefoobar.com>
To: redlantern@gmail.com

Red Lantern,

We are terribly sorry for the misunderstanding and it's obvious that the site we have posted definitely looks strikingly similar to the design you submitted. We have removed the copyrighted material and are no longer using any designs or logos associated with Red Lantern. Again, we appologize for the misunderstanding and hope we can avoid any and all legal action. Please let us know if there is anything else we can do.

[quoted text hidden]

Sincerely,
Foo Bar Management

Foo Bar obviously wasn't expecting us to look at their site and seemed eager to avoid legal action. Sometimes just the thought of legal trouble is enough to get people to comply.

Be clear, explicit, polite, and formal in any correspondence with possible design pirates.

Okay, this totally sucks. I have no desire to deal with all this infringement and copyright crap. I just want to design websites!

There's more than one type of web designer.

Some folks just want to design sites. Others have visions of starting companies and pouring over spreadsheets. Of course, most folks fall somewhere in the middle. There are lots of different roles, even just in the web design universe. Are you wondering what parts of web design you need to worry about?

Which of these types of web workers do you think you are?

Information Architects organize content and design navigation.

Front-end Designer

Information Architect

This job is mostly HTML and CSS. Front-end designers are part programmer, part graphic artist, and build much of a site's user interface.

A programmer may be responsible for writing back-end code that controls features of a website. They could also write Javascript and build AJAX functionality.

User Experience Designer

Graphic Designer

User experience designers work with the whole team to develop a consistent, usable interface. They may also be in charge of running and managing usability tests.

A graphic designer may design user interfaces offline, develop artwork, and work closely with the front-end designer to implement an interface.

Programmer

Copywriter

Answer the questions in the Web Worker Job Poll to see what part of the web design universe you fit into. Add your score up at the bottom of the next page and see where you fit.

Exercise

What kind of web worker are you?

Circle the number (1 = Not Interested to 5=Very Interested) that represents your interest in the given task description.

❶ I enjoy writing code that supports the content management of sites and interacts with databases.

1   2   3   4   5

❷ I want to make sure that users can find their way through a site and that the overall design looks great and works properly.

1   2   3   4   5

❸ I like working with content and organizing information on a website.

1   2   3   4   5

❹ I really like design, but I want to be able write some code.

1   2   3   4   5

⑤ I am good at writing HTML and CSS and enjoy taking designs and expressing them in markup and stylesheets.

1   2   3   4   5

⑥ I enjoy making web pages behave like desktop applications with Javascript and AJAX.

1   2   3   4   5

⑦ I like learning about user patterns by observing how others interact with websites.

1   2   3   4   5

⑧ I like to think about navigation and what content is most important to a particular project.

1   2   3   4   5

Use the following key to see where you fit in the web design world:

If you scored 8 or higher on **❶** and **❻** then you might be a **Programmer.**

If you scored 8 or higher on **❷** and **❽** then you might be a **User Experience Designer.**

If you scored 8 or higher on **❸** and **❽** then you might be a **Information Architect.**

If you scored 8 or higher on **❹** and **❺** then you might be a **Front-end Designer.**

So, I'm a front-end designer. I thought so... but what does that have to do with dealing with copyrights and stuff?

Choose your job—and your business—based on knowing who you are in the web universe.

If you're happy being a designer for a web firm, then copyrights probably aren't going to be a problem anytime soon. Then again, with all the good work you're doing for Jane (and your own boss!), you might get asked to join the leadership team of a company one day.

Or if you're really into control and entrepreneurship, you may want to start a company yourself. Knowing who you are helps you choose the right company and the right people to put around you.

And if you are into starting a company, there are lots of different types... just like there was more than one type of web worker:

This is the simplest form of business structure because there isn't actually any structure. All income and liabilities are accrued by the owner on their personal finances.

Sole Proprietor/Partnership

LLC's are a fairly new type of business organization, and their rules vary from state to state. An LLC (or LLP) gives the owner the simplicity of a sole proprietor with the personal finance protection of a corporation.

Limited Liability Companies

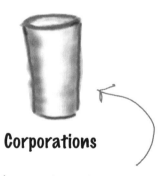

Corporations

A corporation is the most complicated business structure. The company itself becomes its own entity, and strict rules must be followed while running a corporation. Corporations can also be expensive to start, and a good lawyer is a key ingredient.

Exercise

Take a look at the different business descriptions and write in the blank whether you think they are a Sole Proprietorship, an LLC, or a Corporation.

Businesses

Write the business structure you think best fits the description of the company.

Jim and a friend own a small design company together, which they work at full time. Their company supports both of them, and they are thinking about bringing on a third designer to help them with projects.

....

Joe has a full-time job with a large computer company and builds websites in his spare time for small local businesses and friends. He makes some money here and there but not enough to support him full time.

....

Green Giant Design employs 4 full-time people and has a six-figure annual revenue year after year. The owner works as the creative director and likes the fact that her company has remained small and services local companies.

....

Nationalweb is a large design firm with offices in Chicago and New York. Most of their clients are large multi-nationals, and they are even considering opening up a European office in London.

....

Exercise Solution

Let's take a look at how these different companies are structured and organized.

Businesses

Jim and a friend own a small design company together, which they work at full time. Their company supports both of them and they are thinking about bringing on a third designer to help them with projects.

Because this is a partnership, a more formal business structure like an LLC would be best. Plus, this makes finances much easier to deal with.

LLC

Joe has a full-time job with a large computer company and builds websites in his spare time for small local businesses and friends. He makes some money here and there but not enough to support him full time.

Sole Proprietor

Joe doesn't have consistent business, and building websites isn't even his first job. The extra income he makes on the design gigs will just show up on his personal income statements.

Green Giant Design employs 4 full-time people and has six-figure annual revenue year after year. The owner works as the creative director and likes the fact that his company has remained small and services local companies.

LLC

Although Green Giant Design could easily incorporate, an LLC is all they really need right now. There's not a problem with an LLC hiring employees.

Nationalweb is a large design firm with offices in Chicago and New York. Most of their clients are large multi-nationals, and they are even considering opening up a European office in London.

Corporation

Nationalweb does business nationally and possibly internationally. A corporation is the smartest structure for this business.

Jane's musing her structure at Red Lantern Design.

> Red Lantern operates as an LLC. We're really not big enough to incorporate, and LLC's were inexpensive to start. Besides, I'd rather spend my time looking for new business, not dealing with more paperwork. Speaking of new business...

Red Lantern's got a new prospective client

Jane's just received an email from a little San Francisco-based startup called Trilobite Labs, who needs a new site ASAP. Trilobite Labs is building a series of really cool iPhone apps, and they need a site that really reflects their design sensibilities, but don't have the time (or the expertise) to build it themselves. They love Red Lantern's site aesthetic, and Jane needs you to replicate success one more time.

Here's what Trilobite's looking for:

Client Requirements

☐ A static website with a front page, an About page, a contact page, and three separate product pages.

☐ Standards-compliant code. Trilobite's site has to work on all sorts of devices, too.

☐ Some type of screen effect for their product portfolio. Trilobite wants to appear cutting edge to represent their work on iPhone apps.

☐ Several different designs to choose from (paper is fine), and an ability to provide design feedback that will get incorporated into the final site.

☐ Low-key usability testing to make sure there aren't any problems before the site goes live.

One of Trilobite's iPhone apps lets you check lines at the Apple store so you don't have to wait in line for that new 3G iPhone.

Sharpen your pencil

Now that you know what the requirements are for the site, take a few minutes and think about how much a site like this would cost and roughly how much time it would take you to complete. Write down your estimates in the space below.

....
Time (hours)

....
Cost (dollars)

Just guess? There's got to be a better approach. Besides, shouldn't the cost be a result of our hourly rate? How should we come up with reasonable rate?

You need to know your hourly rate before bidding on any contract work.

Whether you're working for yourself, Red Lantern Design, or a huge company, you should have an idea of what your hourly rate of work is. Then, you can figure out the time it will take to complete a project and turn that into a real, fair price.

The worst thing you can do is overbid... or underbid. One will leave you out of work, and the other out of money! Here's a really easy way to come up with a reasonable hourly rate:

Your desired annual salary

Hourly Rate = $60,000 / ((8 x 5 x 50) x .60)

Total hours worked in a year (8 hours a day, 5 days a week, 50 weeks a year). This is pretty conservative if you're trying to start a business, you know...

Only about 60% of your time will actually be billable, so you need to multiply your yearly hours by .60.

$50/hour

Sharpen your pencil

Now think about how much time might go into each part of the web design process and write your estimate in the space provided.

Write your total hour estimate in this column.

Initial Input Time

This is the time spent initially meeting with clients and getting to know what their needs are and what they expect from you.

....

Conceptual Time/Pre-production

Pre-production is where you will look at site content, design an information architecture, and come up with storyboards.

....

Drafts and Design Revisions

This is where you will go through the draft and design revision phase, honing in on a final concept for the client's site. Be sure and include time for client feedback!

....

Production Time

This is where you start writing code. HTML, CSS and Javascript could all make an appearance at this stage. Final designs are delivered.

....

Other Costs

These costs could include travel, supplies, and other time or material that should be billed to the client.

....

there are no Dumb Questions

Q: Woah, I have no clue how long any of this stuff will take!

A: That's okay... just take your best guess. Think about similar projects where you've worked on the various stages, and try and remember how much time you spent working. It's okay to just estimate.

Q: And I only estimate actual time that I'm working, not breaks or anything, right?

A: Actually, your estimates should include the entire project time: that means including breaks, trips to get supplies, and anything else related to working on this particular project.

Q: What if I've got other people on my team?

A: Good question. In those cases, two people working for an hour each is two hours of work time. So you're estimating the total "person hours" a project will take, not the number of hours in a day or week.

Sharpen your pencil
Solution

What really goes into designing a website?

Initial Input Time

This is the time spent initially meeting with clients and getting to know what their needs are and what they expect from you.

20 hours

This includes about 5 hours of meeting time, 13 hours of research, and a few for travel.

Conceptual Time/Pre-production

Pre-production is where you will look at site content, design an information architecture, and come up with storyboards.

30 hours

IA diagrams and storyboards could take the better part of two weeks to complete.

Drafts and Design Revisions

This is where you will go through the draft and design revision phase, honing in on a final concept for the client's site. Be sure and include time for client feedback!

40 hours

Time in this stage can vary depending on how your client reacts to the drafts you provided.

Production Time

This is where you start writing code. HTML, CSS and Javascript could all make an appearance at this stage. Final designs are delivered.

40 hours

This time is all production: markup, style and design. Code, code, code.

Other Costs

These costs could include travel, supplies, and other time or material that should be billed to the client.

10 hours

Extra travel time, subcontractor fees, and expenses can all up the time in this category.

Figure out a total bid...

The hourly rate we calculated a few pages back.

Hourly Rate = $60,000 / ((8 x 5 x 50) x .60) = $50/hr

(140 hours) x ($50.00/hr) = $7000.00

This price represents the cost of a small-to medium-sized website done by an individual charging $50/hour.

AIGA's Pricing and Ethical Guidelines book.

there are no Dumb Questions

Q: Do you need all the people in the web design universe to successfully complete a site?

A: No, not really. If you're a freelance web developer, you may wear many hats and be able to work with your clients throughout the design process. If you need to, you can bring in a contractor to complete work that you can't do yourself (like back-end programming).

Q: What's the difference between an LLC and LLP?

A: The two types of structures are essentially the same thing. LLP stands for Limited Liability Partnership and is just an LLC with more than one shareholder or owner. Most of the time, you will see professional services like accounting and law firms organize as LLPs.

Q: Is $50/hour the average? What's the range of hourly rates you can expect to find at design firms?

A: $50/hour is actually on the low end. Professional hourly rates range anywhere from $50-$75/hour all the way up to above $200/hour. These rates vary depending on location, experience, and size of company.

Q: What happens if I underestimate the time it takes to complete a project?

A: This is common. Most projects are quoted on a job estimate and the final price can vary up or down from the original quote. The most important thing you can do is communicate with your client and let them know where you are in your process and how close the final price will be to what you originally quoted.

Q: Is there a resource for finding out what other people are charging and what services cost in other design-related fields?

A: Occasionally the American Institute of Graphic Artists (AIGA) publishes their Pricing and Ethical Guidelines for design professionals. This includes web design and has information on salaries, hourly rates, and industry standards for the field.

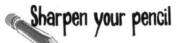

Sharpen your pencil

Now that you have a better idea of the time and costs of a typical web project, let's use the Red Lantern estimate worksheet to generate a quote for the Trilobite Labs project. Check off the client requirements as they are covered in the estimate.

Client Requirements

☐ A static website with a front page, an About page, a contact page, and three separate product pages.

☐ Standards-compliant code. Trilobite's site has to work on all sorts of devices, too.

☐ Some type of screen effect for their product portfolio. Trilobite wants to appear cutting edge to represent their work on iPhone apps.

☐ Several different designs to choose from (paper is fine), and an ability to provide design feedback that will get incorporated into the final site.

☐ Low-key usability testing to make sure there aren't any problems before the site goes live.

Red Lantern Project Estimation Worksheet (RLPEW)

Job Description:

Client Name: ....
Project Description: ....
....
....
....

Initial Input Time:

	Hours		Rate		Total
Client Meetings:	4	x	$75/hr	=	$300.00
Background Research:	....	x	....	=	....
Travel:	....	x	....	=	....

Pre-production Time:

	Hours	Rate	Total
In-house Meetings:	 x	.... =	....
Information Architecture:	 x	.... =	....
Wireframes:	 x	.... =	....
Theme Concepts:	 x	.... =	....

Drafts and Design Revisions:

Client Meetings:	 x	....
Storyboards:	 x	....
Storyboard Revisions:	 x	....

> **Copy this sheet!**
>
> We know you won't have any good ideas of all these costs. The idea here is to see what a real bid sheet might look like.
>
> In fact, you may want to copy this sheet for your own bids. The next page has some sample entries for what a real web design job might cost, too.

Production Time:

XHTML and CSS:	 x	.... =	....
Back-end Programming:	 x	.... =	....
Graphics and Artwork:	 x	.... =	....
Copywriting:	 x	.... =	....
Validation and Debugging:	 x	.... =	....

Miscellaneous Expenses:

Fonts and Graphics:	 x	.... =	....
Software:	 x	.... =	....
General Supplies	 x	.... =	....

Totals

....	....
Total Project Hours	Total Cost

Sharpen your pencil
Solution

Now that you have a better idea of the time and costs of a typical web project, let's use the Red Lantern estimate worksheet to generate a quote for the Trilobite Labs project. Check off the client requirements as they are covered in the estimate.

Client Requirements

 A static website with a front page, an About page, a contact page, and three separate product pages.

 Standards-compliant code. Trilobite's site has to work on all sorts of devices, too.

 Some type of screen effect for their product portfolio. Trilobite wants to appear cutting edge to represent their work on iPhone apps.

 Several different designs to choose from (paper is fine), and an ability to provide design feedback that will get incorporated into the final site.

 Low-key usability testing to make sure there aren't any problems before the site goes live.

Red Lantern Project Estimation Worksheet (RLPEW)

Job Description:

Client Name: Trilobite Labs

Project Description: A website with less than 10 pages that will be used to promote a product (software). Client would like to see multiple design ideas before deciding on a final version. All code must validate.

The job description briefly outlines what the project entails. It's also a nice refresher if you work on lots of projects.

Initial Input Time:

	Hours		Rate		Total
Client Meetings:	4	x	$75/hr	=	$300.00
Background Research:	20	x	$75/hr	=	$1500.00
Travel:	1	x	$75/hr	=	$75.00

20 hours should get us through the initial phase of the project. This is mostly research looking at what other companies in your clients field are doing. This is sometimes called competitive analysis.

Pre-production Time:

	Hours		Rate		Total
In-house Meetings:	2	x	$75/hr	=	$150.00
Information Architecture:	18	x	$75/hr	=	$1350.00
Wireframes:	10	x	$75/hr	=	$750.00
Theme Concepts:	6	x	$75/hr	=	$450.00

Pre-production is important and can save you lots of time and headaches down the line if done properly.

Drafts and Design Revisions:

Client Meetings:	2	x	$75/hr	=	$150.00
Storyboards:	15	x	$75/hr	=	$1125.00
Storyboard Revisions:	5	x	$75/hr	=	$375.00

Drafts and Production is where your design really starts to shine. This is where the client will first see where all that time has gone.

Production Time:

XHTML and CSS:	30	x	$75/hr	=	$2250.00
Back-end Programming:	0	x	$75/hr	=	$0.00
Graphics and Artwork:	10	x	$75/hr	=	$750.00
Copywriting:	2	x	$75/hr	=	$150.00
Validation and Debugging:	4	x	$75/hr	=	$300.00

These expenses are not billed hourly. Typically they are billed at cost plus some percentage of markup.

Miscellaneous Expenses:

Fonts and Graphics:	–	x	–	=	$200.00
Software:	–	x	–	=	$55.00
General Supplies	–	x	–	=	$100.00

Totals

Building great websites takes time and money.

129 hours	$10,030.00
Total Project Hours	Total Cost

> The guys from Trilobite Labs think your estimate's a bit high. We can't lose another bid... got any ideas?

Talking back is highly recommended.

It's pretty much a foregone conclusion that you're going to have potential clients who'll look at your estimates and immediately start to argue that the price tag is too high. If you're experienced, confident in your design skills, and have done a good job estimating project costs, it's part of your job to explain to a potential client why the cost estimate is what it is.

It isn't "against the rules" to respond to a client with a justification for your bid. Unless you have a really solid reason, you shouldn't let a client bully you into lowering your price. This not only devalues your skills as a designer, but might put you in a position where you're putting more work into a project than you're actually getting paid for–which is a good way to *ruin* a business, rather than *run* one.

Use a proposal letter to deliver a detailed quote to a client

A proposal letter details all your costs to a client. But it can also make it clear exactly how you came up with your bid. Sometimes outlining individual costs is all a client needs to understand the value you could bring to their project.

Exercise

Using the template below, outline the project for Trilobite Labs in a proposal letter so they can see what we're doing and where their money is going.

We need to know who this is for and when we quoted it.

To: ....

....

Date: ....

Service: ....

....

A breakdown of the services and costs will help the client understand what we are doing.

Cost: ....

....

....

....

A tentative schedule so that the client knows how long the project is expected to take.

Schedule: ....

....

....

Terms ....

These are the payment and contract terms.

....

....

Exercise Solution

Let's look at a completed proposal letter for Trilobite Labs:

To: Trilobite Labs

1234 Michigan Ave

Date: November 24, 2008

Make sure you get the address right. That's pretty important.

Service: A 6-8 page website using valid code which includes all information design, graphic design and XHTML page templates.

Outline the service and cost so the customer knows exactly what they are getting into.

Cost:

Planning and Pre-production	$4575.
Design Drafts	$1650.
Production	$3450.
Expenses	$355.
TOTAL	$10,030.

Schedule:

4 weeks: Deliver IA and wireframes

8 weeks: Design drafts and revisions

16 weeks: Final delivery

A schedule will help keep you on task and give your client an idea of when they can expect a final finished product.

Terms 25% is required to start project, the remainder of which will be paid upon delivery. This quote is good for 60 days.

Set terms so you get paid on time, and make sure that the client signs the letter to make it official.

The Trilobite podcast: a(nother) new challenge

In the midst of waiting for a decision from Trilobite Labs about your bid, you get a call for their CEO. Over lunch a couple of days ago, the guys at Trilobite came up with another idea that they want to throw into the mix: podcasting. Trilobite really wants to start an official company podcast that covers all of the intricacies of developing for the iPhone and iPod Touch. It's up to you to work out how podcasting fits into the bid you've already put together.

But there's a wrinkle: Trilobite's really worried about protecting their podcast. They want people to be able to download the podcast for free (and share it with anyone they want). What they don't want, though, is for some other website to take their podcast and re-sell it. It's up to you to handle this problem, along with the rest of their web-related design issues.

Trilobite wants to upload the company podcasts to the Apple iTunes Store.

Use <u>Creative</u> <u>Commons</u> to license your work

Copyright law is complicated. (Remember our issues with the Foo Bar stealing our design?) So where does this leave the average artist, producer, writer, developer, or musician who wants to communicate how they want their work used by others, but doesn't want to swim in the shark-infested waters of traditional copyright? It leaves us with the Creative Commons.

The Creative Commons (http://creativecommons.org/) is a non profit organization dedicated to expanding the range of creative works available for others to build upon legally and to share. They've developed a series of simple copyright licenses that protect the "base rights" of the creator. These Creative Commons Licenses have become an enormous force in the modern world of media production.

Creative Commons was founded in 2002 by researchers from MIT, Harvard and Stanford.

 BRAIN POWER

Copyright issues arise more than you might think. Can you come up with three things you've done in the last 12 months you might want to copyright and protect?

Creative Commons Licenses

This page would not be possible without Creative Commons (http:// creativecommons.org/about/license/).

Attribution (by)

This license lets others distribute, remix, tweak, and build upon your work, even commercially, as long as they credit you for the original creation. This is the most accommodating of licenses offered, in terms of what others can do with your works licensed under Attribution.

Attribution Share Alike (by-sa)

This license lets others remix, tweak, and build upon your work even for commercial reasons, as long as they credit you and license their new creations under the identical terms. This license is often compared to open source software licenses. All new works based on yours will carry the same license, so any derivatives will also allow commercial use.

Attribution No Derivatives (by-nd)

This license allows for redistribution, commercial and non-commercial, as long as it is passed along unchanged and in whole, with credit to you.

Attribution Non-commercial (by-nc)

This license lets others remix, tweak, and build upon your work non-commercially, and although their new works must also acknowledge you and be non-commercial, they don't have to license their derivative works on the same terms.

Attribution Non-commercial Share Alike (by-nc-sa)

This license lets others remix, tweak, and build upon your work non-commercially, as long as they credit you and license their new creations under the identical terms. Others can download and redistribute your work just like the by-nc-nd license, but they can also translate, make remixes, and produce new stories based on your work. All new work based on yours will carry the same license, so any derivatives will also be non-commercial in nature.

Attribution Non-commercial No Derivatives (by-nc-nd)

This license is the most restrictive of our six main licenses, allowing redistribution. This license is often called the "free advertising" license because it allows others to download your works and share them with others as long as they mention you and link back to you, but they can't change them in any way or use them commercially.

Based on the requirements below, choose the Creative Commons license that best meets the needs of the Trilobite podcast.

1 Trilobite wants anyone to be able to download, copy, distribute, and broadcast their podcasts.

2 Trilobite wants to make sure that they always get credit for the podcast when it is copied, distributed, or broadcasted, in any format.

3 Trilobite wants to make sure that the podcast isn't altered, edited, or mashed-up in any way, and when it's distributed or broadcasted, it's done so verbatim. No chopping up, please!

4 Trilobite wants to make sure that if the podcast is distributed or broadcasted, it isn't for commercial reasons (for example, no third party can make money by reselling the podcast).

Exercise Solution

What license did you choose? Did it meet all four criteria listed below?

1   Trilobite wants anyone to be able to download, copy, distribute, and broadcast their podcasts.

Creative Commons is perfect, especially when distributing online with a well–thought–out plan.

2   Trilobite wants to make sure that they always get credit for the podcast when it is copied, distributed, or broadcasted, in any format.

3   Trilobite wants to make sure that the podcast isn't altered, edited, or mashed-up in any way, and when it's distributed or broadcasted, it's done so verbatim. No chopping up, please!

4   Trilobite wants to make sure that if the podcast is distributed or broadcasted, it isn't for commercial reasons (for example, no third party can make money by reselling the podcast).

by–nc almost worked, but it allows you to modify the original work, something Trilobite did not want happening.

The Attribution Non–commercial No Derivatives license will work perfectly for the podcast.

Just got word that we won the bid for the Trilobite project. They liked what they saw, and once they looked at the breakdown of costs, they realized that they were getting real value. They also really appreciated you figuring out the licensing. Nice work!

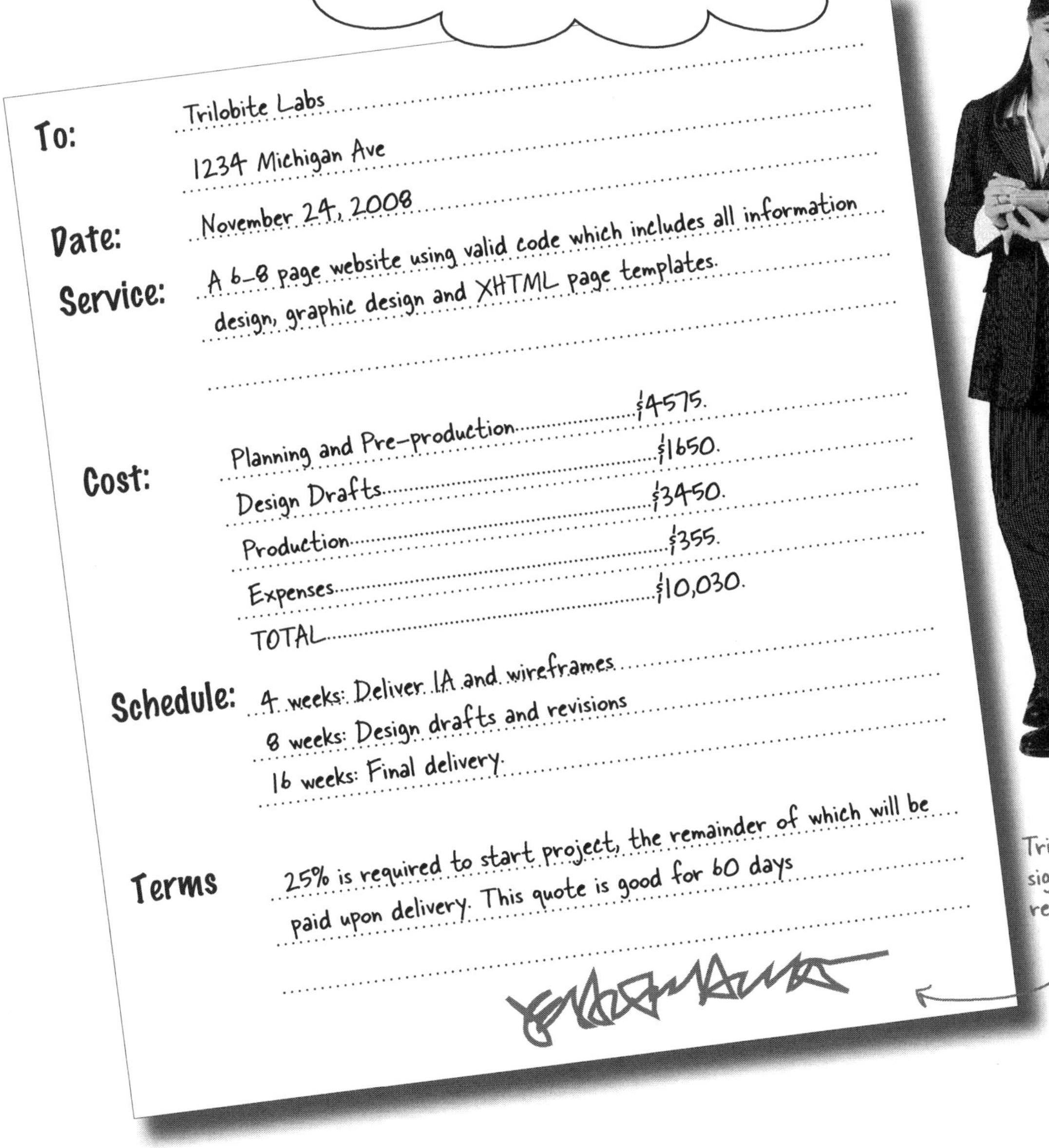

To: Trilobite Labs

1234 Michigan Ave

Date: November 24, 2008

Service: A 6-8 page website using valid code which includes all information design, graphic design and XHTML page templates.

Cost:

Planning and Pre-production	$4575.
Design Drafts	$1650.
Production	$3450.
Expenses	$355.
TOTAL	$10,030.

Schedule:
4 weeks: Deliver IA and wireframes
8 weeks: Design drafts and revisions
16 weeks: Final delivery.

Terms 25% is required to start project, the remainder of which will be paid upon delivery. This quote is good for 60 days

Trilobite has signed and is ready to go.

CHAPTER 11

Your Web Design Toolbox

At this point, it's time to take things out into the world. Stop reading. Well, read the bullets below, and then stop reading. Or maybe after you read the appendix...

...in any case, you're a web designer! Put this book down and go design. Go make beautiful, accessible, usable websites. The Web could use a lot more of 'em.

BULLET POINTS

- Any original work (design, code, etc.) is copyrighted–regardless of whether you put a copyright statement on it or not.

- A polite email asking that copyrighted material be taken down is an effective strategy for protecting your copyrighted work.

- Developing and presenting a professional identity and capitalizing on that identity is extremely important to being a successful web worker.

- It's important to understand all the different roles in the development of a website and where you fit in within that structure.

- Sole Proprietors, LLCs, and Corporations are business structures that allow varying degrees of liability protection and act as framework for how you run your business.

- Do your homework when bidding on new work. Make sure you are charging appropriate rates and not shortchanging yourself because of low-ball estimates.

- The hourly rate of a web designer can be anywhere from $50/hr in small markets to over $200/hr for large projects at larger firms.

- Use a Proposal Letter to outline the terms of a project for a client to make sure they understand what they are paying for and what they are getting.

- Making sure that both you and your client are clear about what is expected of one another will save you a lot of trouble in the long run.

- A Creative Commons License is a way to communicate how you want your creative works used by others.

appendix i: leftovers
The Top Ten Things (we didn't cover)

We've really covered a lot of ground in this book. The thing is, there are some important topics and tidbits that didn't quite fit into any of the previous chapters. We feel pretty strongly about these and think that if we didn't at least cover them in passing, we'd be doing you a disservice. That is where this chapter comes into the picture. Well, it's not really a chapter; it's more like an appendix (ok, it *is* an appendix). But it's an awesome appendix of the top ten best bits that we couldn't let you go without.

#1: Cross-cultural & international design

The Web is a truly global place—and that means your websites have to be too. People from every corner of the globe are checking out *your* sites. The thing is, everyone has a different cultural, linguistic, and ethnic background—all of which might impact how they interpret your site's design. There are some things you should keep in mind when you are designing a site for an international audience (or an audience whose culture is different from your own).

Icons have different cultural meanings

Icons are cool and can convey a lot of information in a little bit of space. But what an icon means to you might be completely different from what that icons means to someone in another country or culture:

In the U.S., the shopping cart is synonymous with shopping, and is, therefore, a great icon for "checking out" on a website.

In many other parts of the world, shoppers bring their own shopping bags to the store. So a shopping <u>bag</u>, and not a shopping <u>cart</u>, might be a more appropriate metaphor for "checking out."

Different languages have different lengths

If you translate the content of your site into a variety of different languages—a process called **localization**—you'll find that phrases may take up a lot more space than they originally did. Take a look:

English

"Click here for current site news."

German

"Klicken Sie hier für gegenwärtige Aufstellungsortnachrichten."

Cyrillic (Macedonian, Russian, Serbian and Ukrainian, etc.)

Щелкните здесь для в настоящее время весточки места

If you originally design your site in English and then go to translate it to German, you're going to find that the phrases take up more space—throwing your carefully planned design into chaos. So what can you do? You either need to design your site so that an increased number of characters doesn't really have an impact on your layout, or you'll need to reformat your site after you translate the content into the target language. Either way, you can't ignore language lengths if your site is going to be translated.

Is that the month or the year?

Even something as simple as how date and time are displayed can differ from country to country. If your site has the date or time formatted incorrectly for that national or cultural context, your users might get confused, or even miss an important event or deadline. Here are just a few date and time formats you'll want to think about:

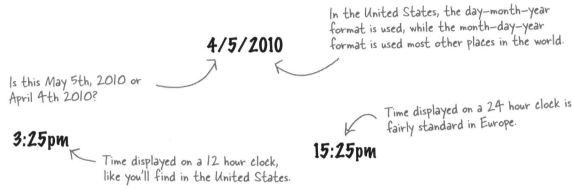

In the United States, the day–month–year format is used, while the month–day–year format is used most other places in the world.

4/5/2010

Is this May 5th, 2010 or April 4th 2010?

Time displayed on a 24 hour clock is fairly standard in Europe.

3:25pm

15:25pm

Time displayed on a 12 hour clock, like you'll find in the United States.

Is that <u>really</u> the flag you want to use?

It's fairly common to see flag icons used to indicate language choice. English might be represented by the Union Jack, and French represented by the flag of France. The problem with this is that nationality (and flags) *don't represent language*. There are lots of people who don't live in France who speak French. So some users might feel frustrated or even alienated that your site equates their native language with some other country. Instead of using flag icons to indicate language choice, simply spell the language out in the actual language—English, Francais, Deutsche, etc.

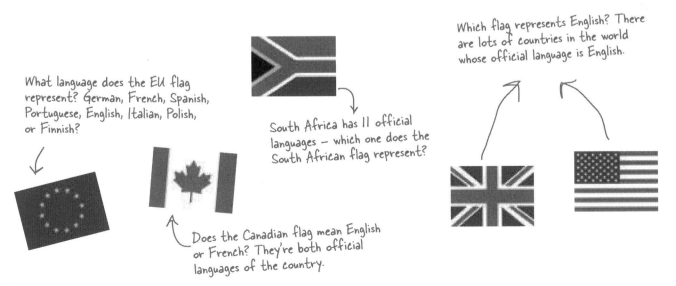

What language does the EU flag represent? German, French, Spanish, Portuguese, English, Italian, Polish, or Finnish?

South Africa has 11 official languages — which one does the South African flag represent?

Which flag represents English? There are lots of countries in the world whose official language is English.

Does the Canadian flag mean English or French? They're both official languages of the country.

#2: The future of web markup

The web is constantly evolving. New markup and style specifications are being proposed, developed, and implemented by the **World Wide Web Consortium** (W3C)—all of which will have an impact on how web designers do their thing. Most notable are HTML 5 and XHTML 2.

HTML 5 vs. XHTML 2

Both HTML5 and XHTML2 are specifications currently being developed by the W3C. This often causes confusion, as many people believe that XHTML 1.x was the successor to HTML 4.01 (and that HTML is effectively dead). So what's the difference between XHTML 2 and HTML 5? XHTML 2 is pretty much the successor of XHTML 1.x—it's designed to be the Web's general-purpose markup language, with a minimum of default features that are easy to extend using CSS and other technologies. The most important goal for the XHTML 2 working group is to further separate document content and structure from document presentation. To these ends, the XHTML 2 working group has completely removed elements such as `basefont`, `big`, `font`, `s`, `strike`, `tt`, `u`, `small`, `b`, `i`, and `hr`. The XHTML 2 group has also been less concerned with backward compatibility, which has led them to drop some of the syntactic baggage present in earlier incarnations of HTML. The result is a cleaner, more concise language... but one that won't work with old HTML (and some XHTML) web pages.

HTML 5 has taken a radically different approach. Instead of being a markup language for the web (as its ancestor HTML 4 was), HTML 5 is all about moving away from document markup and creating a language specifically for web applications. So a lot of the HTML 5 specification focuses on creating a more robust, full-featured client-side environment for web application development by providing a variety of APIs (and elements that work specifically with those APIs). Examples include the 2D drawing API, which can be used with the new `canvas` element, and an API for playing `video` and `audio`, which can be used with the new video and audio elements.

Among many of the cool things you can expect in both HTML 5 and XHTML 2 are navigation lists. In XHTML 2, navigation lists look something like this:

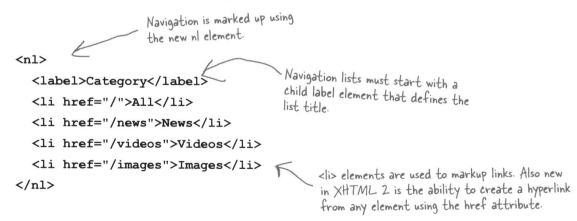

Navigation is marked up using the new nl element.

```
<nl>
    <label>Category</label>
    <li href="/">All</li>
    <li href="/news">News</li>
    <li href="/videos">Videos</li>
    <li href="/images">Images</li>
</nl>
```

Navigation lists must start with a child label element that defines the list title.

<li> elements are used to markup links. Also new in XHTML 2 is the ability to create a hyperlink from any element using the href attribute.

In HTML 5, navigation lists look a little something like this:

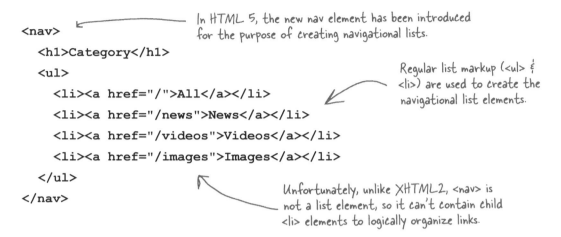

```
<nav>
    <h1>Category</h1>
    <ul>
        <li><a href="/">All</a></li>
        <li><a href="/news">News</a></li>
        <li><a href="/videos">Videos</a></li>
        <li><a href="/images">Images</a></li>
    </ul>
</nav>
```

In HTML 5, the new nav element has been introduced for the purpose of creating navigational lists.

Regular list markup (<ul> & <li>) are used to create the navigational list elements.

Unfortunately, unlike XHTML2, <nav> is not a list element, so it can't contain child <li> elements to logically organize links.

The whole point of navigational lists (especially in XHTML2) is to create simple, lightweight navigation markup that can then be styled using CSS.

When are they coming?

Neither XHTML 2 nor HTML 5 have been officially released by the W3C (though draft specifications and recommendations for both have been released). So when will you see official releases? Honestly, there's no good way to know. Because of the open and collaborative nature of developing these sorts of specifications, discussion and deliberation by the members of the individual working groups will go on until the job is done and everyone gets a chance to contribute. In the grand scheme of things, the release of the final specifications are not the issue. What is important is when (and how fast) browser developers completely adopt the new standards.

For a full rundown on the HTML5 specification, check out http://www.w3.org/html/wg/html5/.

To explore the XHTML2 specification, visit http://www.w3.org/TR/xhtml2/

HTML 5 is really geared towards web applications. Red Lantern isn't interested in that, so I think we should focus on XHTML 2 in the future.

One of our clients, the Red Lantern CEO

#3: The future of CSS

Just like HTML and XHTML, CSS is marching forward. While XHTML 2 and HTML 5 are cool from the perspective of web design, CSS 3 (the next version of CSS) is really the icing on the cake. One of the most interesting things about CSS 3 is that it will be released as a series of modules—instead of one big single release. This means that CSS can be updated faster, as modules can come out individually. Modules can be changed and updated independent of other modules, too, which means that you don't have to wait for the next "big" revision of CSS to get a particular update of your favorite module.

While there are lots of cool modules out there, one of the coolest is the multi-column module. It offers new CSS properties that let designers specify the number of columns an element should have. This not only allows designers to create documents that look more print-like, but it changes the process of creating multi-column layouts entirely.

The multi-column module includes the following new CSS properties:

- `column-count` determines the number of columns into which the content of the element will flow.

- `column-width` describes the width of each column.

- `column-gap` sets the padding between columns.

- `column-rule` defines a border between columns.

For a full ru down on all the CSS 3 modules, check out http://www.w3.org/TR/

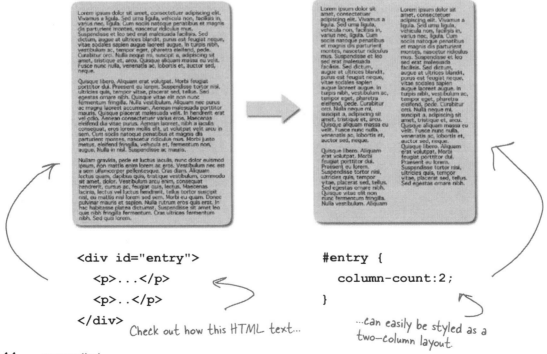

```
<div id="entry">
    <p>...</p>
    <p>..</p>
</div>
```
Check out how this HTML text...

```
#entry {
    column-count:2;
}
```
...can easily be styled as a two-column layout.

#4: Designing for mobile devices

Over the past couple of years, design for mobile devices has become a really big deal. Not only are new mobile network infrastructures coming online that allow for faster data transfer, but new and far more powerful devices are hitting the market and becoming widely available and adopted.

Devices such as Google's Andorid-based phones or the Apple iPhone are changing the face of the mobile Web.

If you are designing for mobile devices, there are some things you should think about:

- Even though many mobile devices now have a zoom and browse feature, you still need to remember that you are designing for a device with a screen that is far smaller than you are probably used to. While there is variation, the screen real estate of a mobile device usually comes in around 320 x 240. As a result, you are going to have to be incredibly frugal when designing your layout... there's just not a lot of screen real estate to work with.

- Many carriers still charge customers for the amount of data that's pushed to their phone. This means you need to create pages that have a very light footprint. Besides, mobile connectivity is still quite a bit slower than what you're used to on desktops or laptops. The smaller the file size of the page, the faster it will download.

- Above all else, test your design on as many mobile devices as possible (or the target device—which you can identify using audience research).

Create a stylesheet specifically for mobile devices using the CSS "handheld" media type. That way, you can format your page according to the limitations of the device.

#5: Developing web applications

The web has developed to the point where you can not only create web pages, but you can also create **web applications**—websites that act (in one way or another) like a desktop application. These web applications don't just display information, they actually **do** something.

To create a web app, you'll need to work in a server-side scripting or programming language. Options include PHP, Ruby on Rails, Perl, or ASP.NET. Each language has its own strengths and weaknesses, and with a little research, you'll find the one that fits your needs. The language you choose is determined by the server on which you'll be hosting your web app. Remember that some servers will support one web language but not another.

Remember, though, just because you may be coding a web app, you've still got to use good design principles. Here are a few books that can get you started with web apps:

#6: Rhythm in your layout

Rhythm—the *repetition of design elements*—is a term often used in print design. But don't think rhythm is *just* about print design... it's just as important on the Web. Repetition allows you to create consistency, which contributes to the layout's visual logic. Repeat a common element or theme, and your site feels intuitive, more usable, and logical to users.

Let's take a look at how repetition can be used:

All the text has silhouettes, even in the smaller content headers. That creates a sense of flow: design rhythm.

Background pattern in the header repeats at a regular interval.

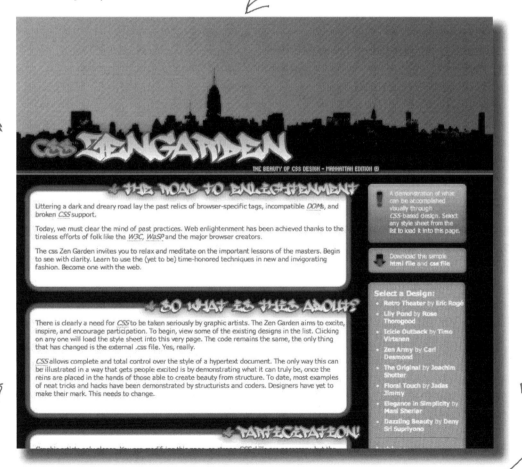

Each piece of content is in the same sort of structure, creating repetition down the length of the page.

The sidebar elements are different colors, but they're the same shape as well. More rhythm.

#7: Text contrast

Back in Chapter 7, we talked a lot about how to make content more scannable. But *scannable* text isn't necessarily *legible* text. Legible text is text that's easy to read because of the colors and contrast, not because it's easy (or hard) to understand.

There are a lot of things you can do to make your text more legible. Most importantlyt, make sure that you have a high contrast between the color of your text and the color of your background. If there isn't much contrast between your text color and your background color, users are going to find your text hard to read the text.

> However, the potential of the web to deliver full scale applications didn't hit the mainstream till Google introduced Gmail, quickly followed by Google Maps, web based applications with rich user interfaces and PC-equivalent interactivity. The collection of technologies used by Google was christened AJAX, in a seminal essay by Jesse James Garrett of web design firm Adaptive Path.

White text on a black background (called negative text) is very legible because there is a high contrast between text color and background color.

Black text on a white background (called positive text) is very legible because there is a high contrast between text color and background color.

> The bursting of the dot-com bubble in the fall of 2001 marked a turning point for the web. Many people concluded that the web was overhyped, when, in fact, bubbles and consequent shakeouts appear to be a common feature of all technological revolutions. Shakeouts typically mark the point at which an ascendant technology is ready to take its place at center stage.

> The first of those principles was "The web as platform." Yet that was also a rallying cry of Web 1.0 darling, Netscape, which went down in flames after a heated battle with Microsoft. What's more, two of our initial Web 1.0 exemplars, DoubleClick and Akamai, were both pioneers in treating the web as a platform. People don't often think of it as "web services," but in fact, ad serving was the first widely deployed web service, and the first widely deployed "mashup" (to use another term that has gained currency of late).

When there isn't much contrast between the color of the text and the background color, the text is very hard to read.

#8: Match link names with their destination page

As we talked about back in Chapter 6, signposting is one of the guiding principles of usable and intuitive navigation design. However, there are many other ways to give users a clear indication of where they are, where they can go, and a confirmation that they've arrived at the right place. One simple technique is to make sure you match the name of a link with the destination page's title. That way, users will immediately know they've arrived where they expected to be when they clicked on the link.

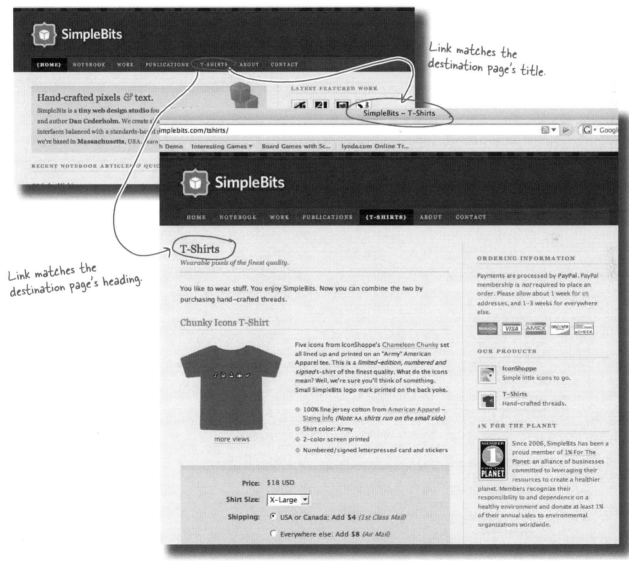

Link matches the destination page's title.

Link matches the destination page's heading.

#9: Contrast is a fundamental layout device

Contrast applies to more than just text and background color. **Contrast**, more broadly, is the juxtapositioning of dissimilar graphic elements. Sounds fancy, but it's not that difficult.

Contrast is commonly used to create emphasis in a layout. The idea is simple: the greater the difference between a design element and its surroundings, the more that particular element will stand. In the context of layout, there are generally two things that create contrast: color and containers. When you put elements on your page in a container (callout, column, window, etc.), they stand out from the elements closeby. So when you apply contrasting colors to an element and its surroundings, that element will stand out.

You can use contrast to obviously identify different parts of your layout or focus the user's eye towards a particularly important aspect of your layout.

Both a container and color are used to emphasize the site's identity.

Both color and a container are used to focus the user's eye towards the site's important introductory information.

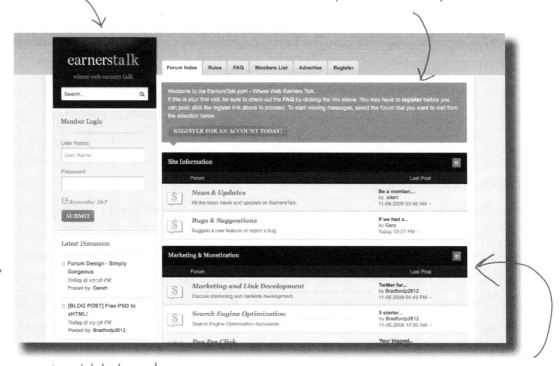

The contrast between the site's background color and the background color of the main content area focuses the user's eye towards what's important in the site.

A contrasting color is used to focus the user's eye on important headers.

#10: More tools for design

There are lots of great online and offline tools that will help you envision, create, and implement your design. We're not talking about visual markup editors like Dreamweaver here. Instead, we're talking about tools that actually help with the process of design. We've already talked about Kuler (a great little online app for creating color schemes), but there are so many more. Here are a couple of the good ones:

Pencil is an incredibly powerful little open source app that is designed specifically to create storyboards, interface prototypes and design diagrams. It comes in two flavors: a Firefox add-on and a desktop app (only Windows and Linux—sorry, no Mac version yet). Honestly, Pencil is pretty much an image editing application with features (such as built-in GUI stencils) geared specifically towards interface design and prototyping. Best of all, it's completely free. **http://www.evolus.vn/Pencil**

WriteMaps is a web application for building robust information architecture diagrams. On top of this, it allows you to share and collaboratively edit your IA diagrams with others. Like Pencil, WriteMaps is also free. **http://writemaps.com**

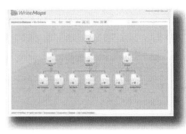

Web Developer is a Firefox add-on that puts a host of web development and testing tools at your fingertips. With it, you can directly edit the CSS of a currently displayed web page, display all of a site's style sheets by media type, outline all block-level elements in a page, automatically resize the browser window, and directly edit the markup of a currently displayed web page. **http://chrispederick.com/work/web-developer/**

CSSTidy is an open source desktop application (available for Windows, Linux, and Mac) which parses and optimizes CSS. It can easily reduce the size of your CSS by 25%—which is especially good if you are obsessed with optimization or are designing for a platform where small file size matters (like a mobile device). **http://csstidy.sourceforge.net**

Firebug is an open source (and free) Firefox extension, much like Web Developer, that puts a wealth of web design, development, and testing tools at your fingertips. With it, you can inspect and edit markup and CSS, view a page's various CSS containers (box model), view a page's response time (download time) broken down by file type, debug and execute JavaScript on the fly, and inspect JavaScript performance (among many other things). **http://getfirebug.com/**

Index

Symbols

960 (CSS framework) 143

A

\<a\> tag
    rel attribute 391
    tabindex attribute 291–293
        more than just 308–311
accessibility 275–318
    about 296
    background images 307
    color
        alternatives for communicating information 302–305
        without depending on color 306–308
    color blindness 295, 302–305
    defined 277
    hearing disabilities 295
    law 296
    screen readers 278
        alt attribute (\<img\> tag) 282–284
        longdesc attribute (\<img\> tag) 285–287
        markup 280
        titles, headings, and descriptions 280
    tabbing through website 289–293
    tabindex attribute (\<a\> tag)
        more than just 308–311
    WCAG (see WCAG)
AIGA's Pricing and Ethical Guidelines 425
alt attribute (\<img\> tag) 282–284
ambiguous navigation 75
analytics tools 364
asymmetrical balance 137
Attribution (by) (Creative Commons License) 434

Attribution No Derivatives (by-nd) (Creative Commons License) 434
Attribution Non-commercial (by-nc) (Creative Commons License) 434
Attribution Non-commercial No Derivatives (by-nc-nd) (Creative Commons License) 434
Attribution Non-commercial Share Alike (by-nc-sa) (Creative Commons License) 434
Attribution Share Alike (by-sa) (Creative Commons License) 434
audience 110
    informed decisions 129
    (see also usability)
Audio-2-Go project 276–318
    alt attribute (\<img\> tag) 283–284
    background images 307
    color blindness 304–305
    color without depending on color 306–308
    longdesc attribute (\<img\> tag) 286–287
    site message 280
    tabbing through website 289–293
    tabindex attribute (\<a\> tag) 291–293
        more than just 308–311
    Test Drive
        alt attribute (\<img\> tag) 284
        beyond tabindexes 311
        color, without depending on color 307
        longdesc attribute (\<img\> tag) 287
        overall accessibility 316
        tabindexes 293
    WCAG checkpoints 313–316
    WCAG Priority 1 300

B

background images and accessibility 307
base color 170

Behind the Scenes, usability testing 349

bidding on contract work 422–429

block hover navs 157

block navigation elements 212–213
    floating 213

Blog Exposed 398

blogs 394–399
    hosted blog systems 402
    installed 402
    warning 394
    WordPress 395–399
        themes 400

Blueprint 140–144
    content and navigation markup 151
    CSS rules 144

brainstorming 45

breadcrumb trails 225

Browsershots 343

browser template 21

browser testing 343

Bullet Points
    blogs 402
    breadcrumb trails 225
    business structures 438
    card sorting 107
    color schemes 191
    color wheel 191
    communicating information 107
    copyrighted material 438
    Creative Commons License 438
    CSS Grid-based framework 157
    design process 36
    fresh content 402
    golden ratio 157
    grids 157
    headings 273
    horizontal navigation 225
    hosted blog systems 402
    IA diagrams 36, 107

IA (Information Architecture) 36, 225
icons as navigational elements 225
installed blogs 402
inverted pyramid 273
JQuery 402
Kuler 191
lightboxes 402
lists 273
moderator scripts 367
naming your navigational elements 225
open-ended questions 367
personas 157
pre-production 67
primary navigation 225
proposal letter 438
rule of thirds 157
sans-serif fonts 273
scannability 36
screen real estate 157
screen resolution 157
secondary navigation 225
serif fonts 273
site statistics 367
storyboards 36, 67
surveys 157, 367
tetradic color scheme 191
top level navigation 36
triadic color scheme 191
usability testing 367
user-centered design 36
vertical navigation 225
visual metaphor 67
WordPress 395
writing for the web 36

business of web design 403–438
    AIGA's Pricing and Ethical Guidelines 425
    bidding on contract work 422–429
    corporations 418–420
    Creative Commons 433–436
    Creative Commons License 434
    delivering detailed quote to client 431–432
    design piracy 413–414

Foo Bar project 404–413
    CSS stylesheets 407–408
    design piracy 412–414
    mockup 406
    what Foo Bar wants in a bid 405
  LLC (Limited Liability Companies) 418–420
  proposal letter 431–432
  Red Lantern Design, bidding on contract work
    422–429
  Sole Proprietor/Partnership 418–420
  Trilobite Labs project 421–438
    requirements 421
  web designers, types of 415–420
business structures 438

C

card sorting 80–95, 107
  Mark in Japan 82–85
  orphaned cards 90
  related stacks 86–89
  running successful card sort 80
  site hierarchy 93–94
  stack names 87
Card Sorts Exposed 81
categories of information 74–76
category names 77
clear top navigation categories 76
College of New Media project 194–226
  floating block navigation 213
  IA diagrams 197–198
  screen.css 219
  secondary navigation 222–223
  Test Drive 199, 203, 220
    secondary navigation 224
  updating XHTML to use textural links 218
  using icons for navigation 215–217
color
  alternatives for communicating information 302–305
  without depending on color 306–308
color blindness 295, 302–305

color, designing with 159–192
  base color 170
  color wheel 167–172
    color schemes 170–172
  contrasting colors 185
  digital color wheel 175–178
  emotion 163–166
  emphasized colors 185
  Kuler 175–179
  principles 185
  saturation 180–181
  tetradic color scheme 182–184
  triadic color schemes 171
color mockups 52–55
color palettes 46
color schemes 170–172, 184, 191
  base color 170
  double complementary scheme 182
  saturation 180–181
  tetradic 182–184
  triadic 171
color wheel 167–172, 191
  base color 170
  color schemes 170–172
  digital color 175–178
column-count property 444
column-gap property 444
column-rule property 444
column-width property 444
communicating information 72, 107
compressing copy 247
content
  fresh, keeping website (see evolutionary design)
  page elements 49–50
  removing unnecessary 247
content versus style 146–147
contrast 450
contrasting colors 185
copyrighted material 438

copyright infringment 412–414

copywriter 415

corporations 418–420

Creative Commons 433–436

Creative Commons License 434, 438

cross-cultural design 440–441
    dates and time 441
    flag icons 441
    icons 440
    localization 440

CSS
    column-count property 444
    column-gap property 444
    column-rule property 444
    column-width property 444
    evolutionary design 385–386
    future of 444
    :hover pseudo-property 344–346
    joining XHTML and CSS
        Mark in Japan 58–59
    .page declaration 223
    secondary navigation
        College of New Media project 223
    using to evolve site design 376–383

CSS frameworks 140, 143

CSS Grid-based framework 157

CSS stylesheets
    block navigation 213
    College of New Media project 219
        secondary navigation 223
    Foo Bar project 407–408
    horizontal tabs 204
    Mark in Japan project 57, 103–104
    RPM Records project 154–155
        Blueprint CSS rules 144
        cleaning up layout 149
        layout and typographic details 154–155
        optimized for 1024x768 128
    SampleRate project 174
        updates 186
    vertical navigation 206

CSSTidy 451

D

dates and time 441

debugging tools 451

design elements, repetition of 447

design piracy 412–414
    steps to follow 413–414

design process 6, 36

design sketches (see sketches)

design tools 451

Deutanopia 304

developing web application 446

digg.com 254

digital color wheel 175–178

disabilities 277, 295

<div> tags, "wrap" 102

double complementary scheme 182

E

editing text down 249

emphasized colors 185

evolutionary design 369–402
    blogs 394–400
        WordPress 395–399
        WordPress themes 400
    Flash 385–386
    JavaScript 387–393
    JQuery JavaScript library 385–386
    lightboxes 388–393
    radically changing site 375
    using CSS to evolve site design 376–383
    XHTML and CSS 385–386

F

FaceBox 388–393

Firebug 451

Fireside Chats
  content versus style 146–147
  serif versus sans-serif fonts 270–271
  storyboards 23

flag icons 441

Flash 385–386, 393

floating block navigation 213

flowcharting programs 96

focus groups 322–327
  cost 325

fonts 46, 268
  serif versus sans-serif fonts 270–271

Foo Bar project 404–413
  CSS stylesheets 407–408
  design piracy 412–414
  mockup 406
  Test Drive 409
  what Foo Bar wants in a bid 405

footer 49, 51, 102

framework 143

fresh, keeping website (see evolutionary design)

front-end designer 415

functionality 17

future of
  CSS 444
  web markup 442–443

G

Geek Bits
  flowcharting programs 96
  rel attribute <a> tag 391
  serif and sans-serif fonts 268

WordPress 396
  themes 400

generic browser stats 343

golden ratio 133–138, 157
  RPM Records 135–138

Google Analytics 364

graphic designer 415

grid-based sites 132–143
  asymmetrical balance 137
  CSS framework 143
  golden ratio 133–138
  rule of thirds 134
  symmetrical balance 137

grids 157

H

headings 259–263, 264–266, 273
  fonts 268
  level of importance 269
  naming 198
  navigation 198
  navigation headings 77
  screen readers 280

hearing disabilities 295

Hipster Intelligencer Online 233–274
  project specifications 234
  Ready Bake Code 237
  Test Drive 239, 250
    headings and lists 267
    lists and inverted pyramids 258

horizontal buttons menu type 15

horizontally-tabbed navigation 204–205, 225

horizontal tabs menu type 15

hosted blog systems 402

:hover pseudo-property 344–346

HTML5 versus XHTML2 442–443

I

IA diagrams 7, 11, 36, 95–100, 107
    College of New Media project 197–198
    flowcharting programs 96
    Mark in Japan 97–98
IA (Information Architecture) 7–12, 36, 79
    card sorting (see card sorting)
    navigation 197–198, 225
    themes 99
icons 46, 440
    as navigational elements 215–217, 225
<img> tags
    alt attribute 282–284
    longdesc attribute 285–287
inconsistent navigation 208
information architect 415
Information Architecture (see IA)
informed decisions 129
installed blogs 402
international design 440–441
    dates and time 441
    flag icons 441
    icons 440
    localization 440
inverted pyramid 241–246, 249, 252–254, 273

J

JavaScript 387–393
    lightboxes 388–393
JAWS 278, 287
JQuery 402
JQuery JavaScript library 385–386

K

knowing your audience (see usability)
Kuler 175–179, 191
    warning 176
Kuler Up Close 176

L

language flag icons 441
layout and design 109–158
    audience 110
    grid-based sites (see grid-based sites)
    informed decisions 129
    personas 114–120
    requirements 139
    resolution 122–129
    vertical ratios 152
    XHTML and CSS optimized for 1024x768 128
layouts 35
    Mark in Japan 52–55
lightboxes 388–393, 402
link names, matching with destination pages 449
links, textural 216–218
listening to your users (see usability)
lists 251, 255–258, 263, 273
    ordered 257
    unordered 102, 257
    XHTML 257
LLC (Limited Liability Companies) 418–420
LLP (Limited Liability Partnership) 425
localization 440
longdesc attribute (<img> tag) 285–287

M

Mark in Japan project
  card sorting 82–85
  clear top navigation categories 76
  color mockups 52–55
  CSS stylesheet 57
  IA diagrams 97–98
  index.html 102
  joining XHTML and CSS 58–59
  layouts 52–55
  organizing your site 70–108
    categories of information 74–76
    communicating information 72
  pre-production 38–68
    visual metaphor 40–55
  screen.css 103–104
  site structure 101
  storyboards 64–66
  themes, developing 46–48
  visual metaphor, developing 46–48
  XHTML mockup 56
markup
  future of web markup 442–443
  screen readers 280
menu types 15
Mint 364
mobile devices, designing for 445
mockups, Mark in Japan 52–55
    XHTML mockup 56
moderator scripts 351–357, 367
  contruction 355–357
Moderator Scripts dissected 352–353
mouse, tabbing through website without 289–293

N

naming headings 198
naming your navigational elements 225
navigation 35, 193–226
  ambiguous 75
  block elements 212–213
    floating 213
  categories 74–76, 99
  clear top navigation categories 76
  headings 77, 198
  horizontally-tabbed 204–205
  IA (Information Architecture) 197–198
  icons 215–217
  inconsistent 208
  page elements 49–50
  primary 221, 225
  secondary 221–224
  top level 13–14
  vertical 206–207
newsvine.com 254
No Dumb Questions
  bidding on contract work 423, 425
  browser testing 343
  category names 77
  color blindness 295
  color schemes 184
  copyright infringment 412
  CSS framework 143
  disabilities 295
  editing text down 249
  Flash 393
  generic browser stats 343
  headings 263
  hearing disabilities 295
  IA and themes 99
  IA diagrams 11, 99
  inverted pyramid 249
  JavaScript 393
  Kuler 179
  lightboxes 393
  lists 263
  LLC versus LLP 425
  longdesc attribute (<img> tag) 287
  naming navigational elements 198
  navigation categories 99
  personas 117

No Dumb Questions (*continued*)

    reading online 239

    screen real estate 127

    screen resolutions 127

    Section 508 301

    semantics 200

    storyboards 66

    surveys

        jargon 331

        limits to open-ended questions 339

        open-ended questions 328

        tabindexes 295

    themes 51

    usability testing, number of participants 359

    vertical navigation 207

    visual indicators 306

    visual metaphor 51

    WCAG Priority 1 301

O

OmniGraffle 96

open-ended questions 328

    limits 339

ordered lists 257

organizing your site 69–108

    card sorting (see card sorting)

    categories of information 74–76

    clear top navigation categories 76

    communicating information 72

    IA diagrams (see IA diagrams)

    moving from pre-production to production 100

    navigation headings 77

orphaned cards (card sorting) 90

P

.page declaration (CSS) 223

page elements

    content 49–50

    footer 49, 51

    navigation 49–50

    shaping visual metaphor 49–51

    sidebars 49, 51

    whitespace 49–50

Pencil 451

personas 114–120, 139, 157

Photoshop

    storyboards 66

podcasts 433

pre-production 35, 37–68

    defined 40

    mockups 52–55

    moving from pre-production to production 100

        complete process 106

    storyboards 61, 67

        Mark in Japan 64–66

    themes 41–55

        developing 46–48

    visual metaphor 40–55, 67

        developing 46–48

        page elements shaping 49–51

primary navigation 221, 225

programmer 415

proposal letter 431–432, 438

Protanopia 305

prototypes 24–25

R

radically changing site 375

reading online 239

Ready Bake Code

    Hipster Intelligencer Online 237

    Red Lantern Design prototype 25

Red Lantern Design 2–36

    bidding on contract work 422–429

    evolutionary design 372–402

        adding FaceBox 389

        lightboxes 388–393

        using CSS to evolve site design 376–383

        WordPress blog 395–399

IA (Information Architecture) 7–12
   prototype 24–25
   sketches 16–19
      functionality 17
   storyboards 21–23
   Test Drive 26
      lightboxes 392
      scannability 34
      WordPress 399
   top level navigation 13–14
   Trilobite Labs project 421–438
      estimate worksheet 428–429
      podcast 433
      requirements 421
   writing for the web 28–33
      scannability checklist 31–32
rel attribute <a> tag 391
removing unnecessary content 247
repetition of design elements 447
requirements 139
resolution 122–129, 157
   640x480 123
   800x600 123
   1024x768 122
   1280x800 122
   managing 126
   screen real estate 124
rhythm in layout 447
RPM Records project 113–158
   Blueprint 140–144
      CSS rules 144
   content and navigation markup 151
   final user survey 338–339
   Golden Ratio 135–138
   :hover pseudo-property 344–346
   layout and typographic details with CSS 154–155
   personas 114–120
   requirements 139
   surveys, results 340–341
   Test Drive 149–150, 156
      simple test page 129
      usability fixes 362

   usability 320–368
   usability testing, results 360–362
   XHTML and CSS optimized for 1024x768 128
rule of thirds 134, 157

S

Safari, tabbing through website 289
SampleRate project 160–192
   CSS basic page layout 174
   CSS updates 186
   XHTML 173
sans-serif fonts 268, 273
   serif versus sans-serif fonts 270–271
saturation 180–181
scannability 28–33, 36, 263
   checklist 31–32
   Red Lantern Design Test Drive 34
   what makes text scannable? 29
scenarios 323–324
screen readers 278
   alt attribute (<img> tag) 282–284
   longdesc attribute (<img> tag) 285–287
   markup 280
   titles, headings, and descriptions 280
screen real estate 121, 124, 127, 157
screen resolution 122–129, 157
   640x480 123
   800x600 123
   1024x768 122
   1280x800 122
   managing 126
   screen real estate 124
secondary navigation 221–224
Section 508 of the U.S. Federal Rehabilitation Act 296
semantics 200
serif fonts 268, 273
   serif versus sans-serif fonts 270–271
sidebars 49, 51

site hierarchy and card sorting 93–94

site message 280

site statistics 363–366, 367
    website analytics tools 364

sketches 16–19
    functionality 17

slashdot.org 254

Sole Proprietor/Partnership 418–420

stacks (card sorting) 86–89
    stack names 87

storyboards 21–23, 36, 61, 67
    Mark in Japan 64–66
    Photoshop 66

Strict XHTML 102

surveys 157, 322–342, 367
    asking the right questions 328–341
    cost 325
    jargon 331
    open-ended questions 328, 367
        limits 339
    RPM Records
        final user survey 338–339
        results 340–341

Surveys Exposed 327

symmetrical balance 137

T

tabbing through website 289–293
    Safari 289

tabindex attribute (<a> tag) 291–293
    more than just 308–311

tech.originalsignal.com 254

testing tools 451

tetradic color scheme 182–184, 191

text, scannability 28–33
    checklist 31–32
    what makes text scannable? 29

text contrast 448

textural links 216–218

themes 41–55
    defined 42
    developing 46–48
    IA and 99

tools for design 451

top level navigation 13–14, 36
    clear top navigation categories 76

triadic color scheme 171, 191

Trilobite Labs project 421–438
    podcast 433
    Red Lantern Design
        estimate worksheet 428–429
    requirements 421

Tritanopia 305

U

unordered lists 102, 257

usability 319–368
    browser testing 343
    focus groups 322–327
        cost 325
    generic browser stats 343
    :hover pseudo-property 344–346
    site statistics 363–366
        website analytics tools 364
    surveys 322–342
        asking the right questions 328–341
        cost 325
        jargon 331
        open-ended questions 328
        RPM Records final user survey 338–339

usability testing 347–362, 367
    Behind the Scenes 349
    friends and family 359
    moderator scripts 351–357
        contruction 355–357
    number of participants 359
    on a budget 351

user-centered design 35, 36

user experience 146–147

user experience designer 415

users 110
  informed decisions 129
  (see also usability)
U.S. Federal Rehabilitation Act 296

V

vertical menu type 15

vertical navigation 206–207, 225

vertical ratios 152

vertical tabs menu type 15

Visio 96

visual indicators 306

visual metaphor 40–55, 67
  brainstorming 45
  page elements shaping 49–51

VoiceOver 278

W

Watch it!
  blogs 394
  Kuler 176
  WCAG checkpoints 308

WCAG checkpoints 308
  Audio-2-Go project 313–316

WCAG (Web Content Accessibility Guidelines) 298
  Priority 1 298–301, 308–311

web applications 446

web designers, types of 415–420

Web Developer (Firefox add-in) 451

web markup, future of 442–443

web-safe colors 303

website analytics tools 364

whitespace 49–50

WordPress 395–399
  Geek Bits 396
  themes 400

workflow 6

"wrap" <div> 102

WriteMaps 451

writing for the web 28–33, 35, 36, 227–274
  editing text down 249
  headings 259–263, 264–266
    fonts 268
    level of importance 269
  inverted pyramid 241–246, 249, 252–254
  lists 251, 255–258
  reading online 239
  removing unnecessary content 247
  serif versus sans-serif fonts 270–271
  what makes text scannable? 29

X

XAMPP 396

XHTML
  College of New Media project
    secondary navigation 222
    updating XHTML to use textural links 218
  evolutionary design 385–386
  Foo Bar project 406
  horizontal tabs 204
  lists 257
  Mark in Japan project 56
    index.html 102
    joining XHTML and CSS 58–59
  RPM Records project
    content and navigation markup 151
    optimized for 1024x768 128
  SampleRate project 173
  Strict XHTML 102
  vertical navigation 206

XHTML2 versus HTML5 442–443

Y

Yahoo UI (YUI) Grid CSS 143

2313113R10265

Made in the USA
San Bernardino, CA
06 April 2013